# BATTLE ANGEL ALITA

## MARS CHRONICLE

PRESENTED BY YUKITO KISHIRO

**2**

D1096673

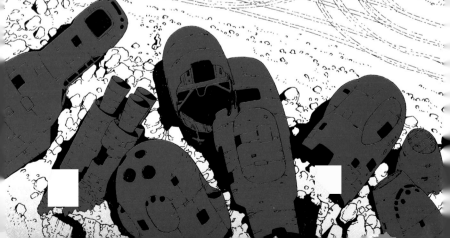

# BATTLE ANGEL ALITA MARS CHRONICLE

PRESENTED by YUKITO KISHIRO

## CONTENTS

**ADDITIONAL STAFF:**
TSUTOMU KISHIRO / EMIYA KINARI

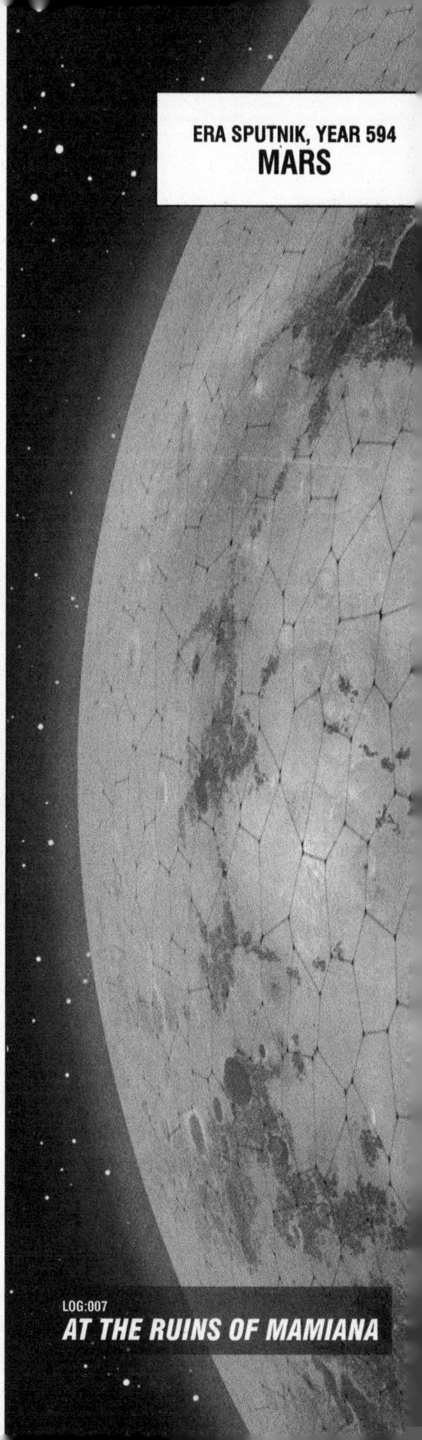
ERA SPUTNIK, YEAR 594
MARS
LOG:007
AT THE RUINS OF MAMIANA

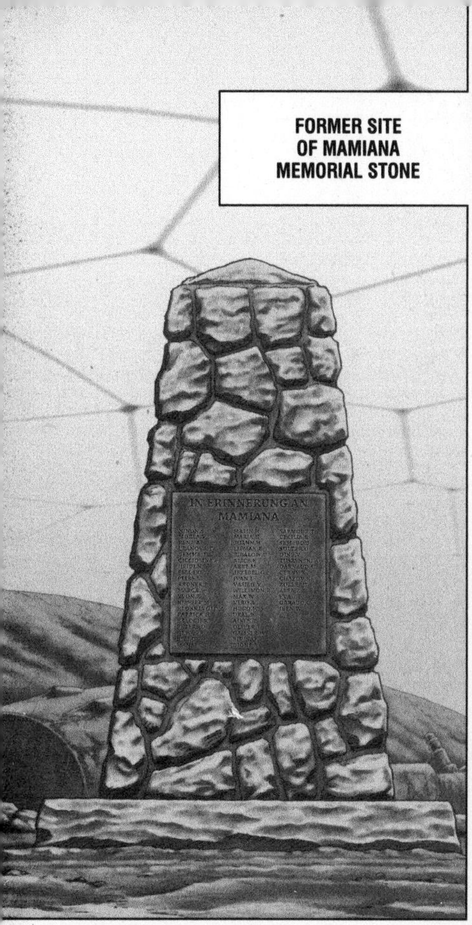
FORMER SITE OF MAMIANA MEMORIAL STONE
IN ERINNERUNG AN MAMIANA

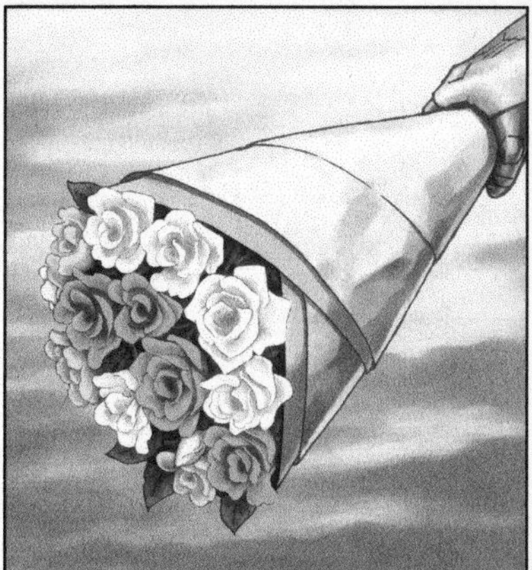

## LOG:007

# AT THE RUINS OF MAMIANA

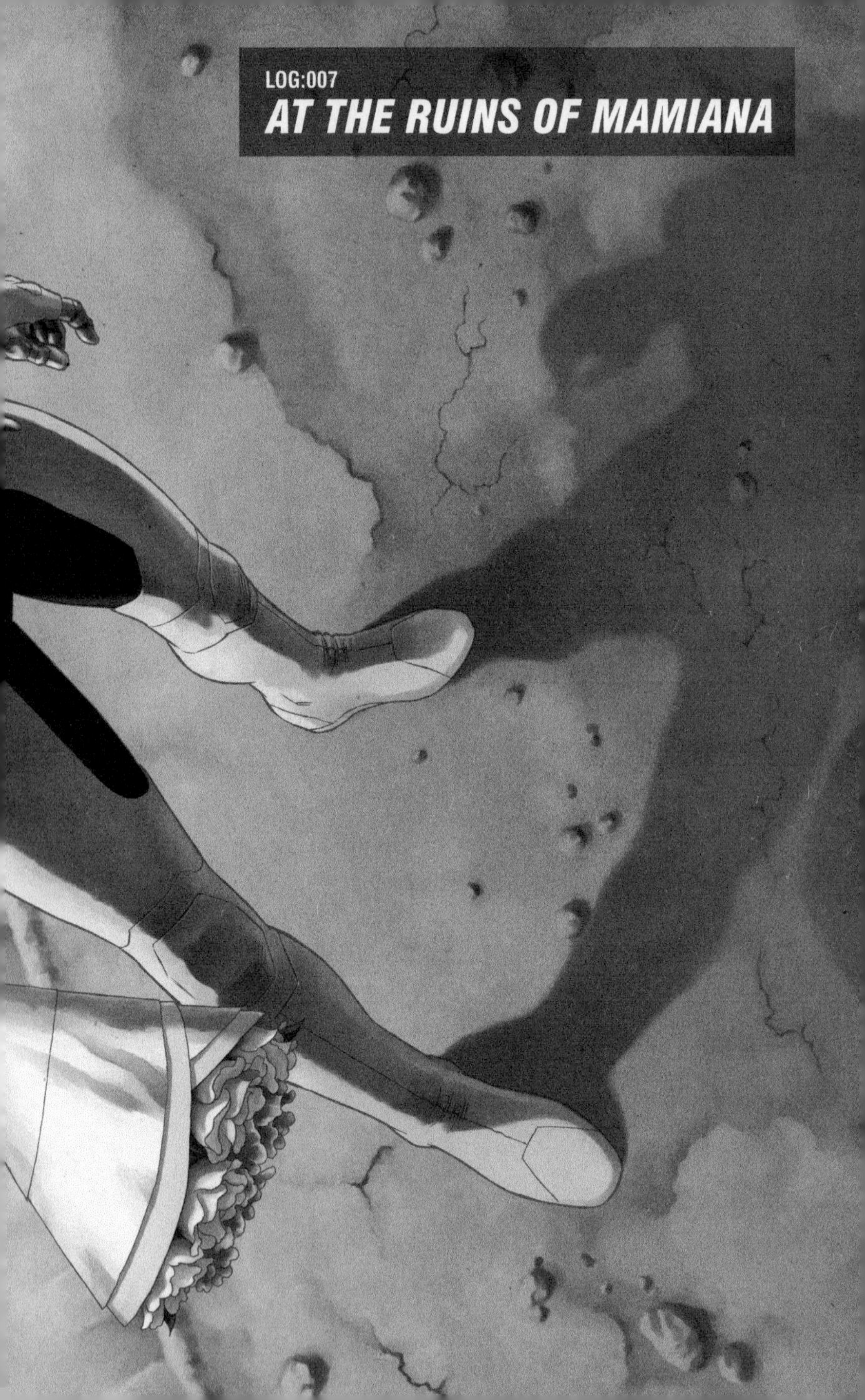

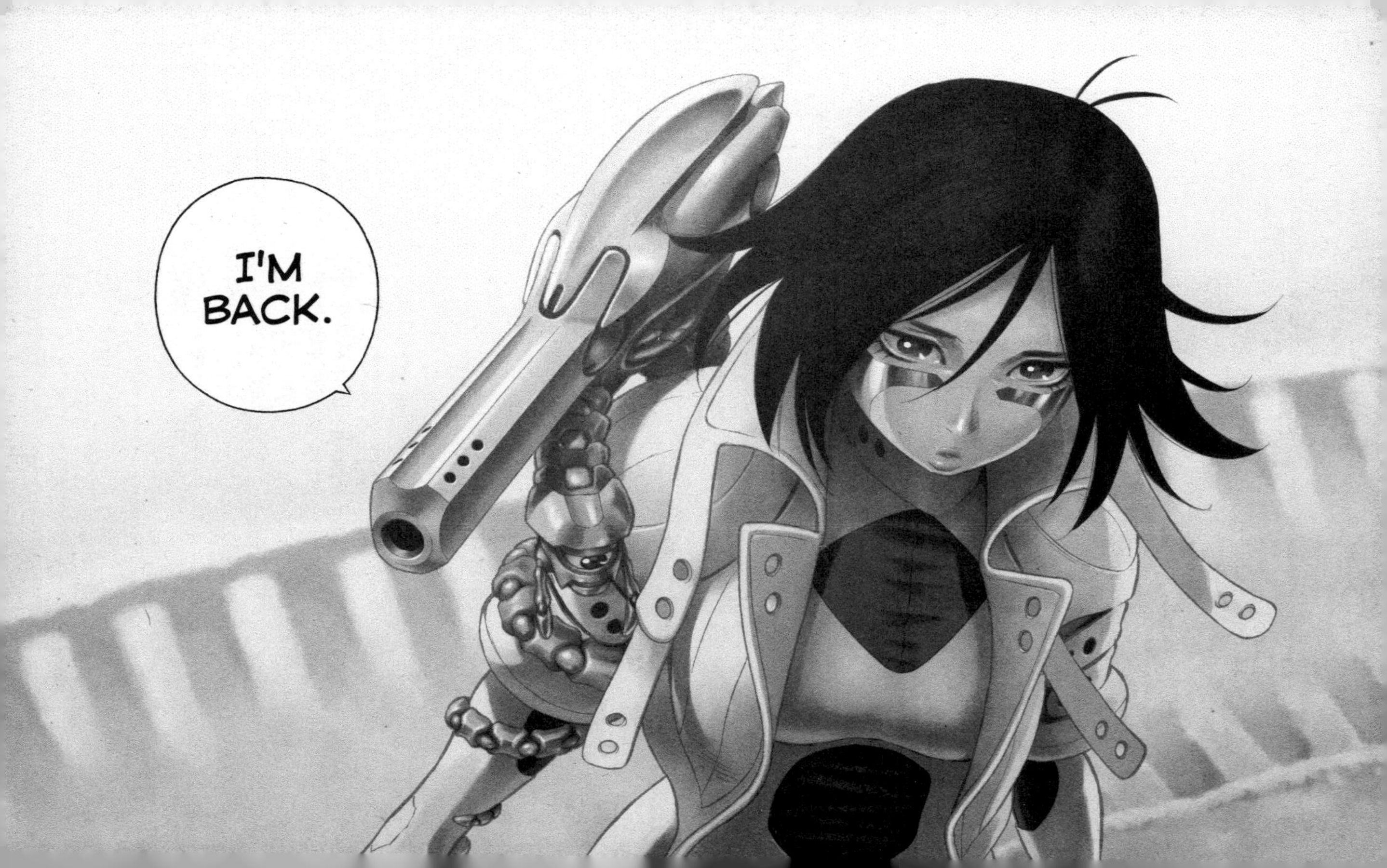
I'M BACK.

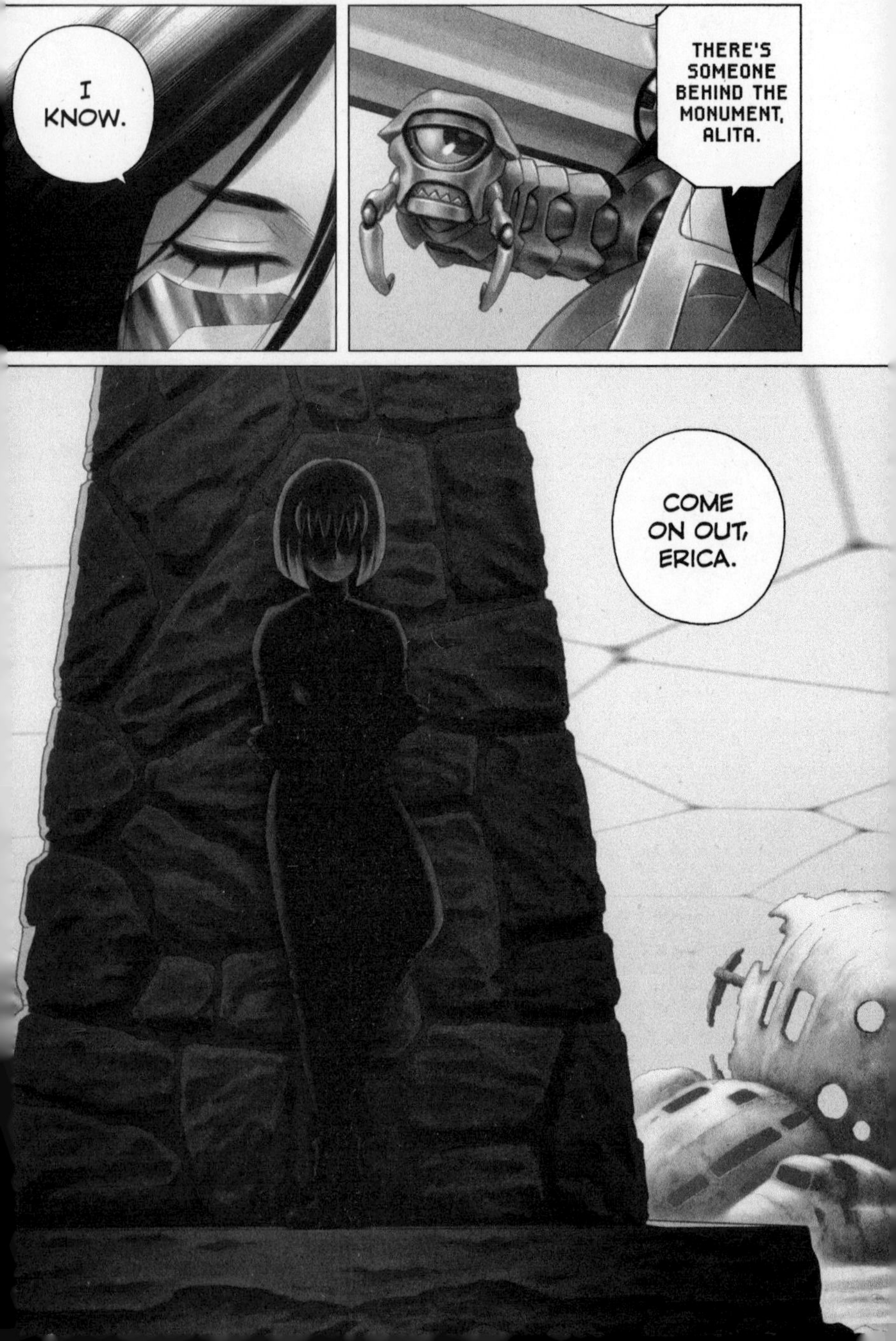
THERE'S SOMEONE BEHIND THE MONUMENT, ALITA.
I KNOW.
COME ON OUT, ERICA.

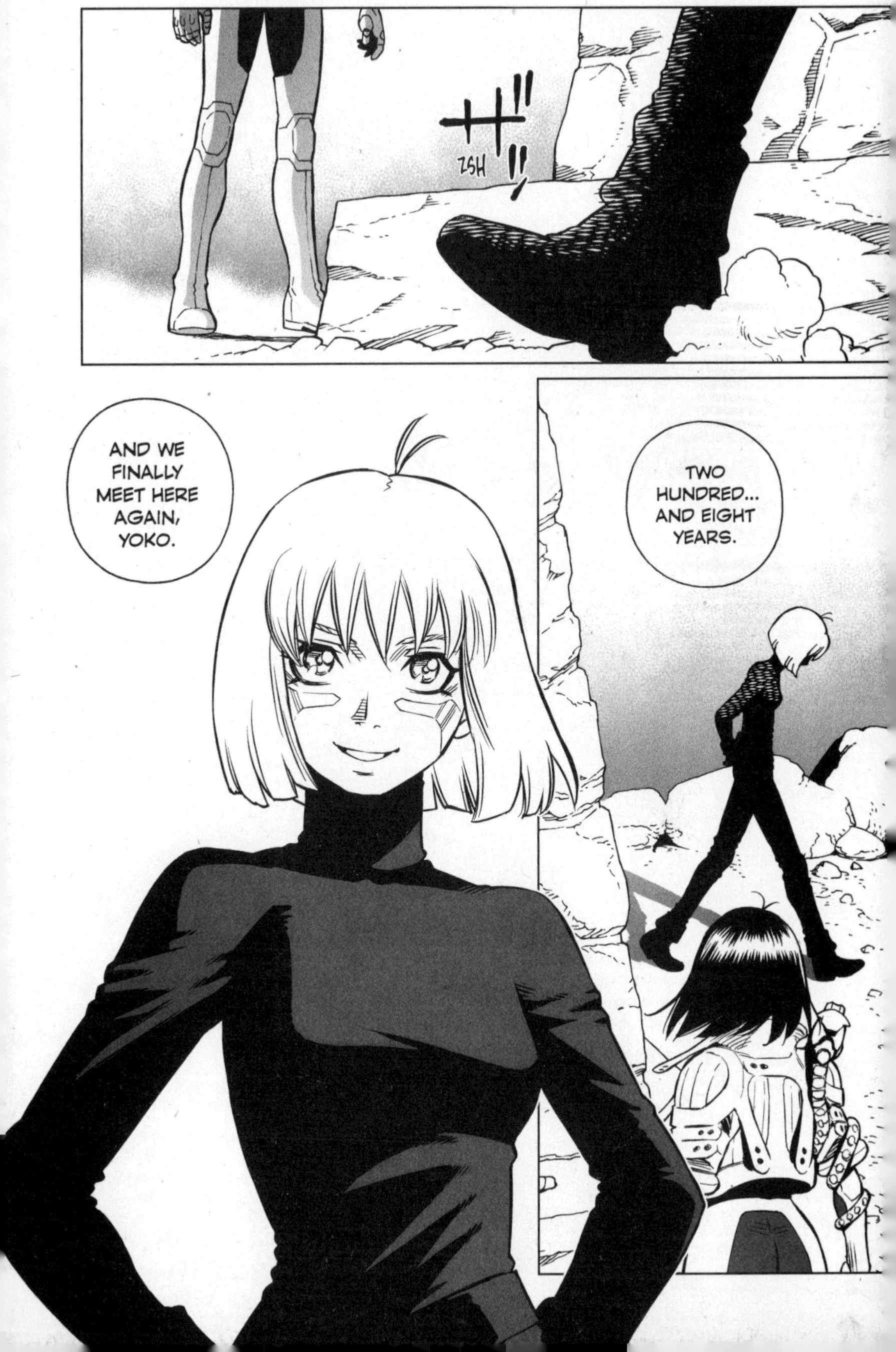
ZSH
TWO HUNDRED... AND EIGHT YEARS.
AND WE FINALLY MEET HERE AGAIN, YOKO.

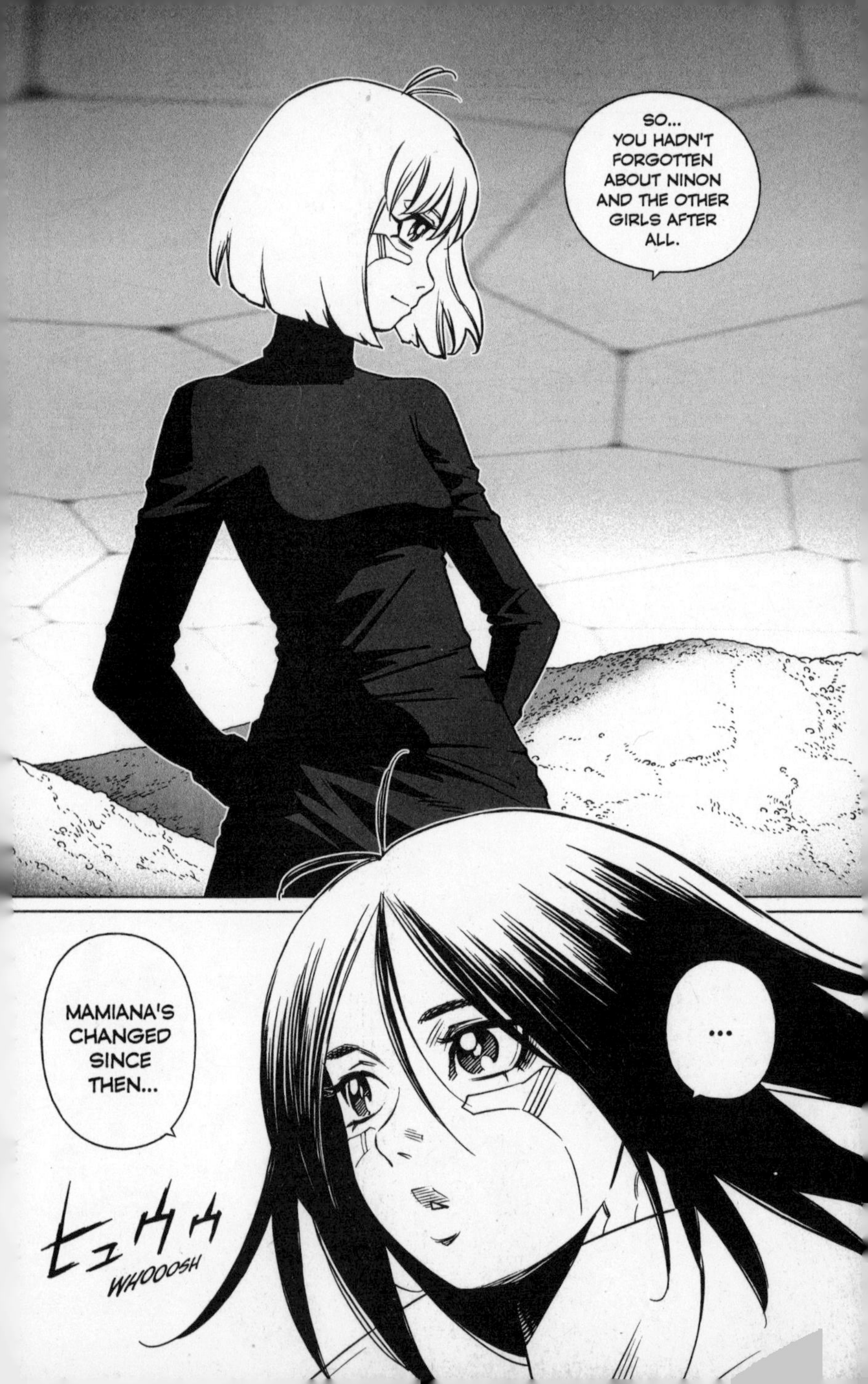
SO... YOU HADN'T FORGOTTEN ABOUT NINON AND THE OTHER GIRLS AFTER ALL.
...
MAMIANA'S CHANGED SINCE THEN...
ヒュウゥ
WHOOOSH

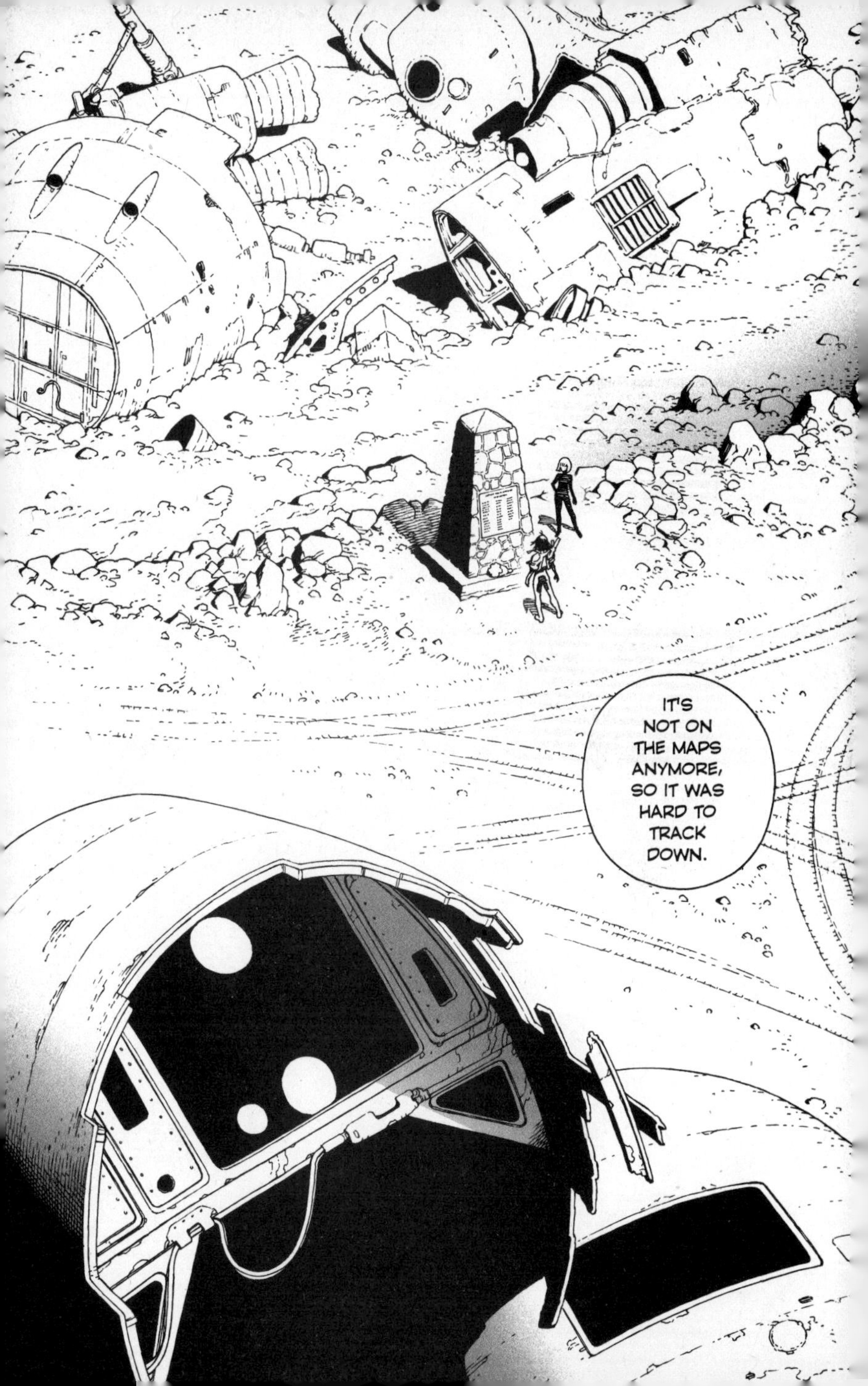
IT'S NOT ON THE MAPS ANYMORE, SO IT WAS HARD TO TRACK DOWN.

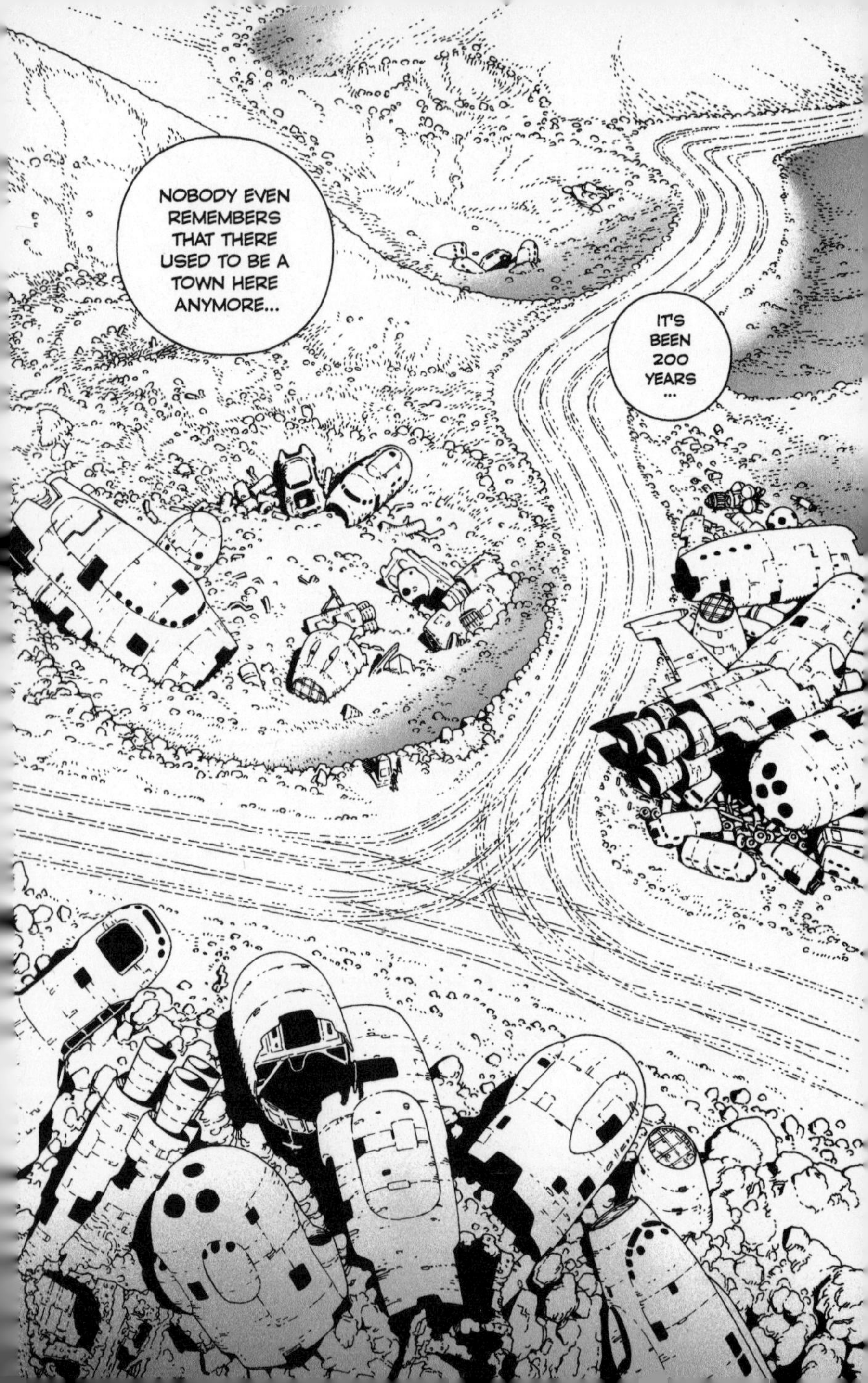
IT'S BEEN 200 YEARS ...
NOBODY EVEN REMEMBERS THAT THERE USED TO BE A TOWN HERE ANYMORE...

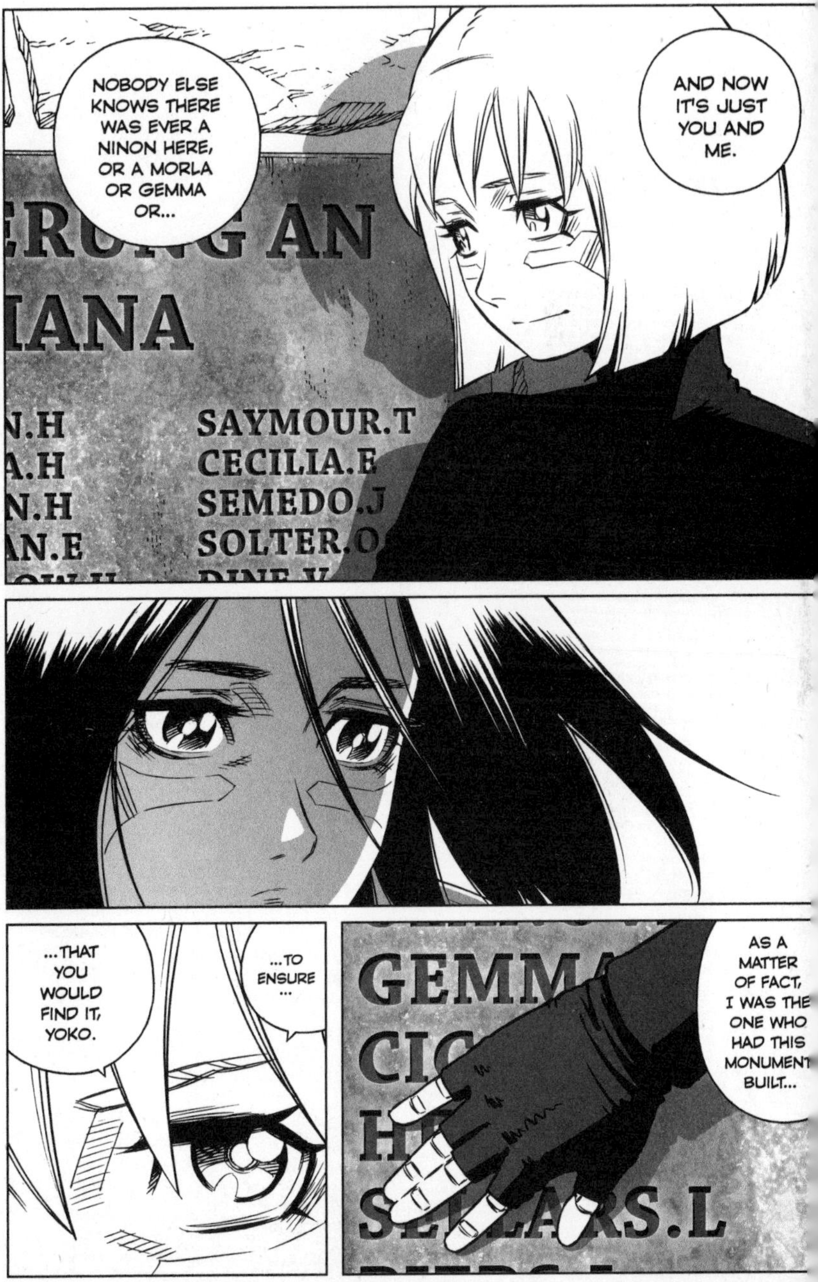
AND NOW IT'S JUST YOU AND ME.
NOBODY ELSE KNOWS THERE WAS EVER A NINON HERE, OR A MORLA OR GEMMA OR...
SAYMOUR.T
CECILIA.E
AS A MATTER OF FACT, I WAS THE ONE WHO HAD THIS MONUMENT BUILT...
...TO ENSURE ...
...THAT YOU WOULD FIND IT, YOKO.

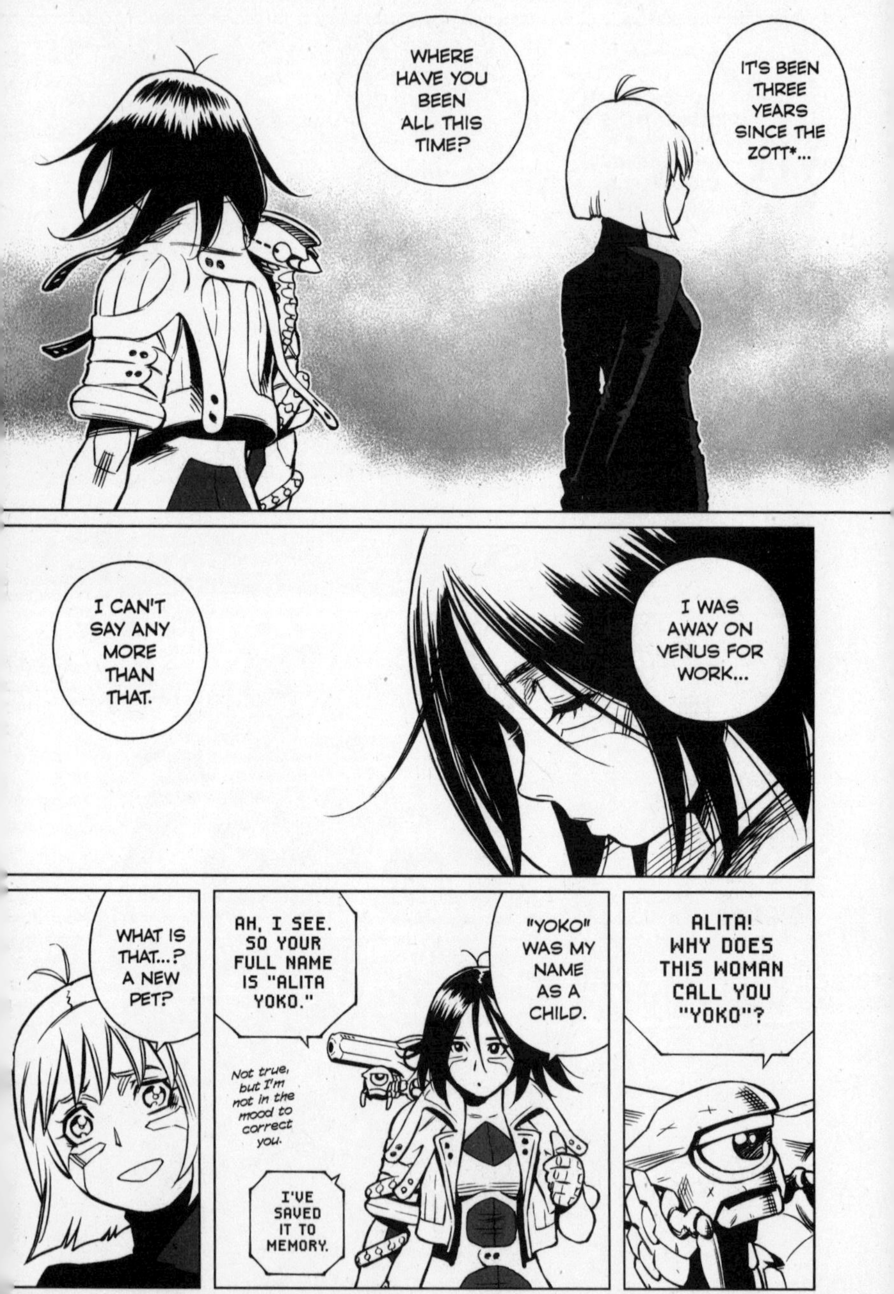
IT'S BEEN THREE YEARS SINCE THE ZOTT*...
WHERE HAVE YOU BEEN ALL THIS TIME?
I WAS AWAY ON VENUS FOR WORK...
I CAN'T SAY ANY MORE THAN THAT.
ALITA! WHY DOES THIS WOMAN CALL YOU "YOKO"?
"YOKO" WAS MY NAME AS A CHILD.
AH, I SEE. SO YOUR FULL NAME IS "ALITA YOKO."
Not true, but I'm not in the mood to correct you.
I'VE SAVED IT TO MEMORY.
WHAT IS THAT...? A NEW PET?

**OTT:** Zenith of Things Tournament. See Chapters 25-106 of *Last Order.*

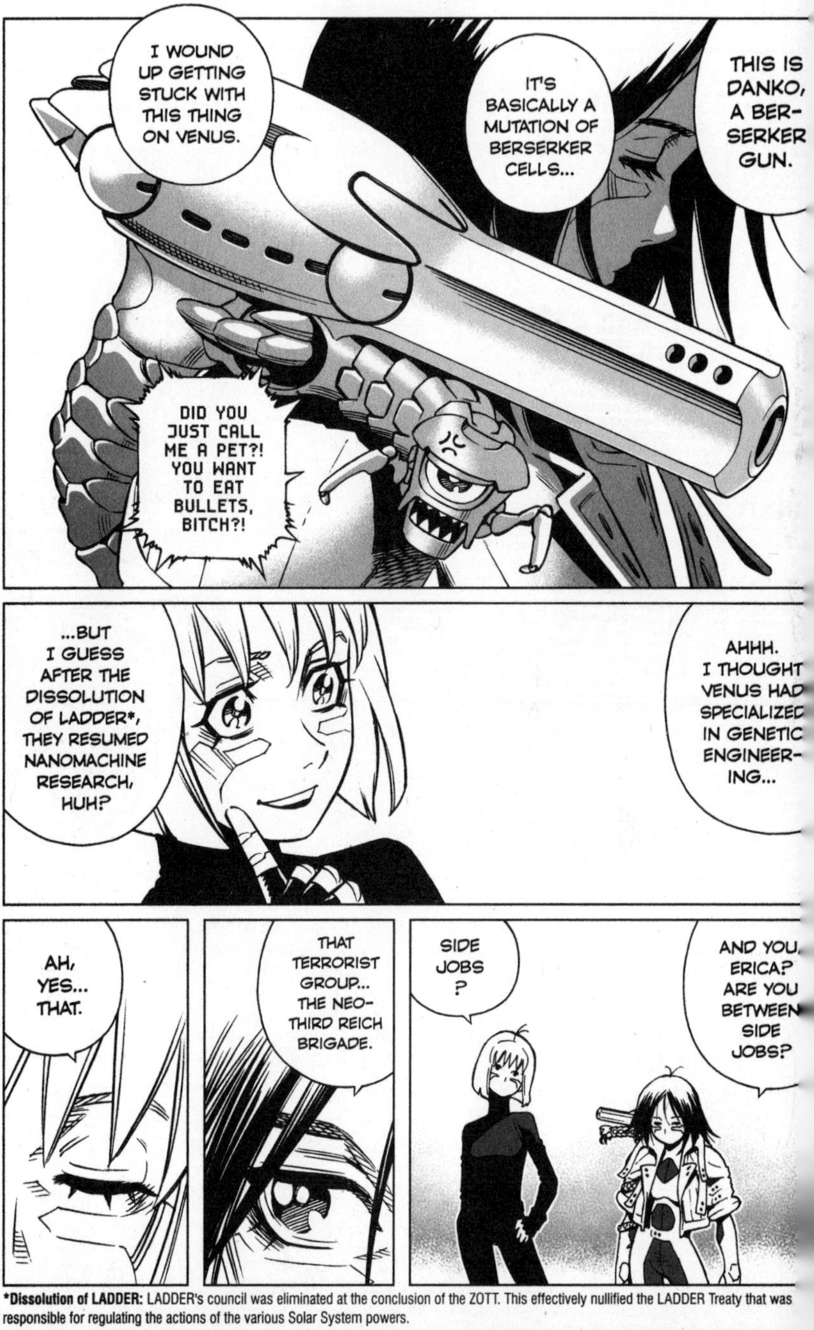
THIS IS DANKO, A BERSERKER GUN.
IT'S BASICALLY A MUTATION OF BERSERKER CELLS...
I WOUND UP GETTING STUCK WITH THIS THING ON VENUS.
DID YOU JUST CALL ME A PET?! YOU WANT TO EAT BULLETS, BITCH?!
AHHH. I THOUGHT VENUS HAD SPECIALIZED IN GENETIC ENGINEERING...
...BUT I GUESS AFTER THE DISSOLUTION OF LADDER*, THEY RESUMED NANOMACHINE RESEARCH, HUH?
AND YOU, ERICA? ARE YOU BETWEEN SIDE JOBS?
SIDE JOBS?
THAT TERRORIST GROUP... THE NEO-THIRD REICH BRIGADE.
AH, YES... THAT.

***Dissolution of LADDER:** LADDER's council was eliminated at the conclusion of the ZOTT. This effectively nullified the LADDER Treaty that was responsible for regulating the actions of the various Solar System powers.

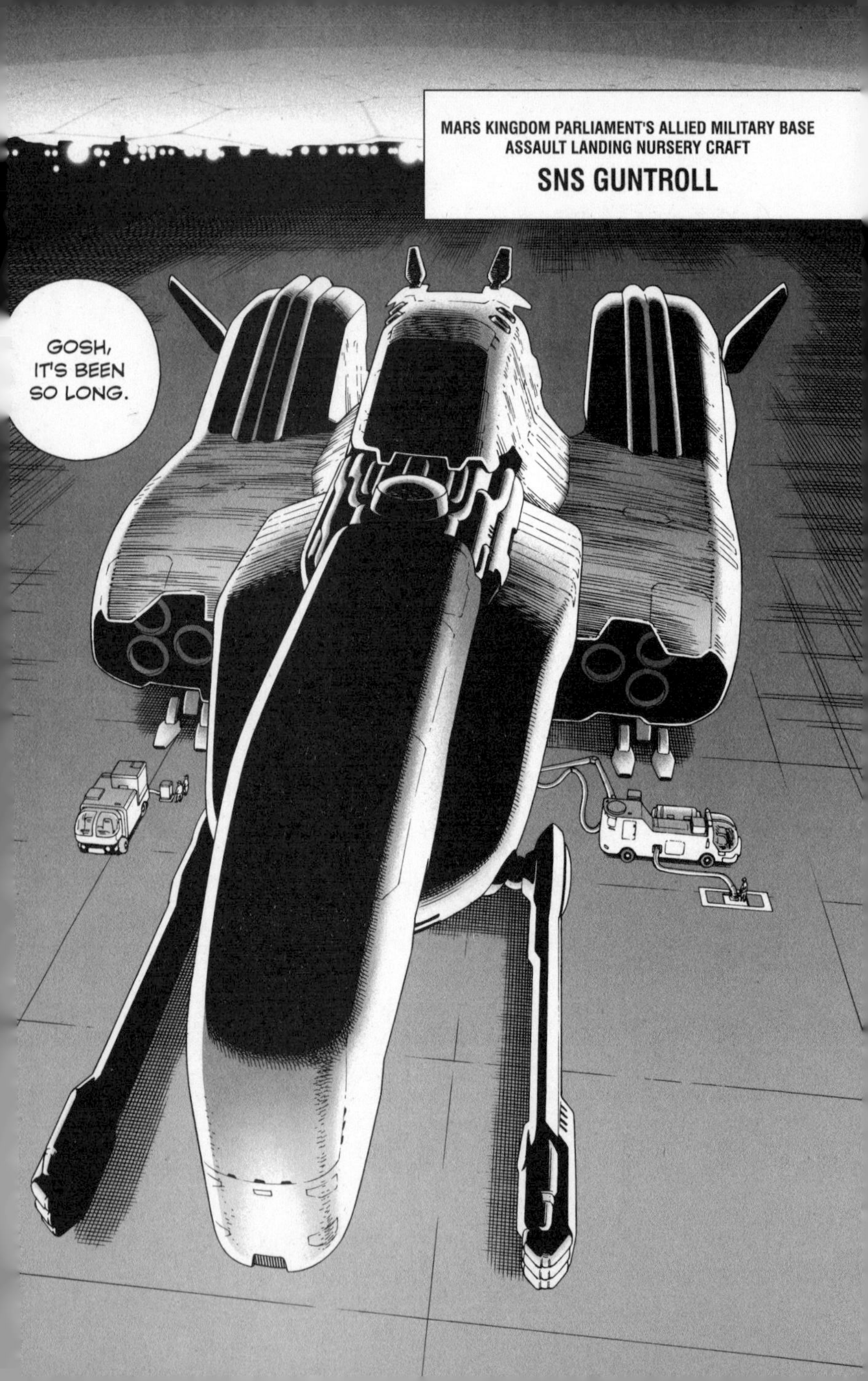
MARS KINGDOM PARLIAMENT'S ALLIED MILITARY BASE
ASSAULT LANDING NURSERY CRAFT
SNS GUNTROLL
GOSH, IT'S BEEN SO LONG.

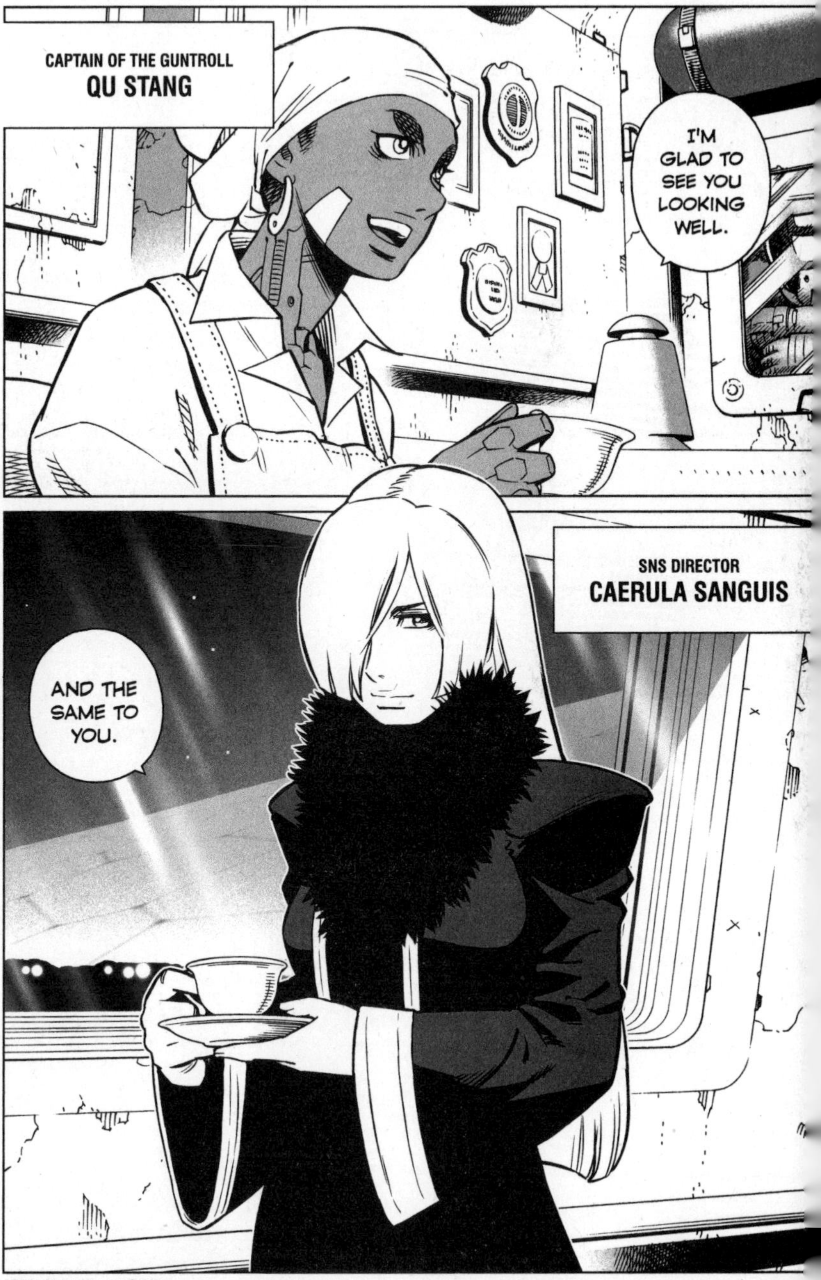
CAPTAIN OF THE GUNTROLL
QU STANG
I'M GLAD TO SEE YOU LOOKING WELL.
SNS DIRECTOR
CAERULA SANGUIS
AND THE SAME TO YOU.

*SNS: Stellar Nursery Society.

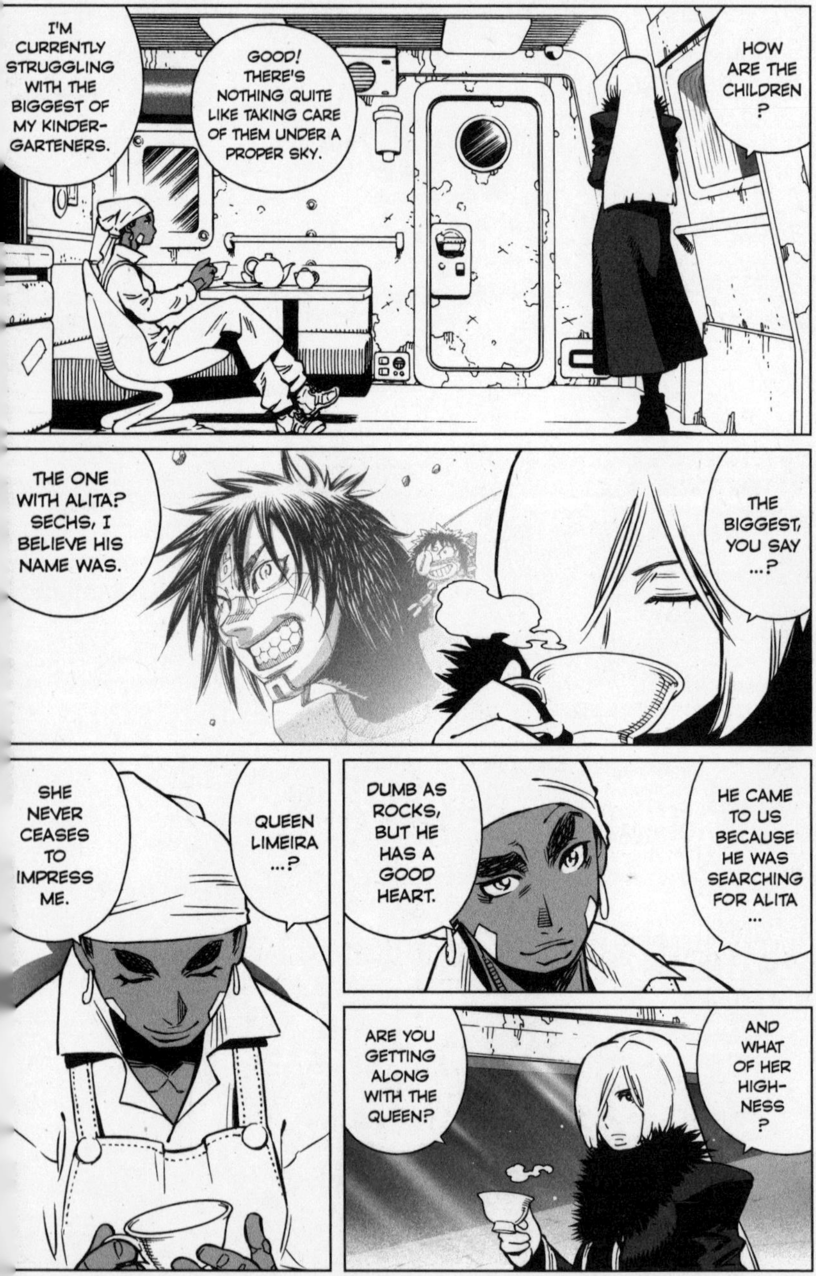
HOW ARE THE CHILDREN ?
GOOD! THERE'S NOTHING QUITE LIKE TAKING CARE OF THEM UNDER A PROPER SKY.
I'M CURRENTLY STRUGGLING WITH THE BIGGEST OF MY KINDER-GARTENERS.
THE BIGGEST, YOU SAY ...?
THE ONE WITH ALITA? SECHS, I BELIEVE HIS NAME WAS.
HE CAME TO US BECAUSE HE WAS SEARCHING FOR ALITA ...
DUMB AS ROCKS, BUT HE HAS A GOOD HEART.
AND WHAT OF HER HIGH-NESS ?
ARE YOU GETTING ALONG WITH THE QUEEN?
QUEEN LIMEIRA ...?
SHE NEVER CEASES TO IMPRESS ME.

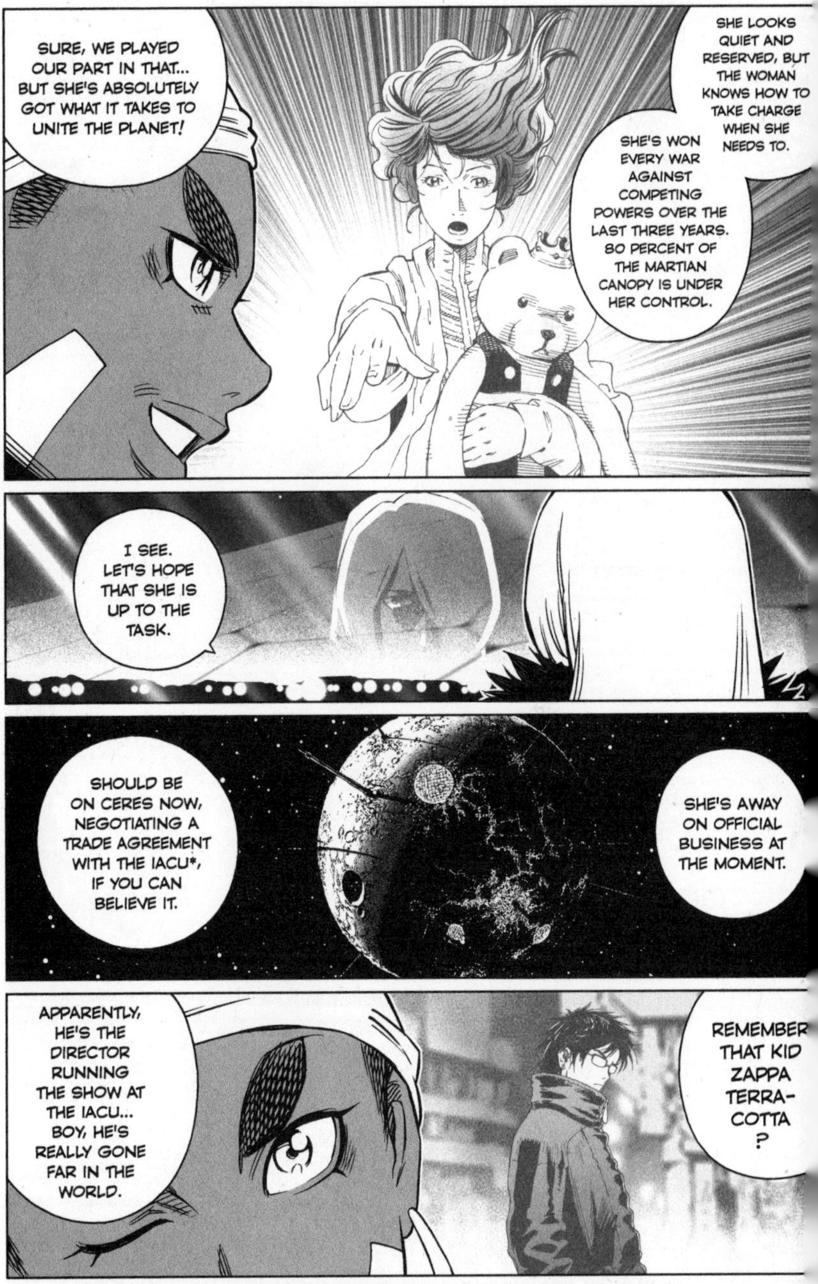
SHE LOOKS QUIET AND RESERVED, BUT THE WOMAN KNOWS HOW TO TAKE CHARGE WHEN SHE NEEDS TO.
SHE'S WON EVERY WAR AGAINST COMPETING POWERS OVER THE LAST THREE YEARS. 80 PERCENT OF THE MARTIAN CANOPY IS UNDER HER CONTROL.
SURE, WE PLAYED OUR PART IN THAT... BUT SHE'S ABSOLUTELY GOT WHAT IT TAKES TO UNITE THE PLANET!
I SEE. LET'S HOPE THAT SHE IS UP TO THE TASK.
SHE'S AWAY ON OFFICIAL BUSINESS AT THE MOMENT.
SHOULD BE ON CERES NOW, NEGOTIATING A TRADE AGREEMENT WITH THE IACU*, IF YOU CAN BELIEVE IT.
REMEMBER THAT KID ZAPPA TERRA-COTTA ?
APPARENTLY, HE'S THE DIRECTOR RUNNING THE SHOW AT THE IACU... BOY, HE'S REALLY GONE FAR IN THE WORLD.

***IACU:** Inter-Asteroid Commerce Union. A group of colonies on the four largest asteroids: Ceres, Pallas, Vesta, and Hygiea.

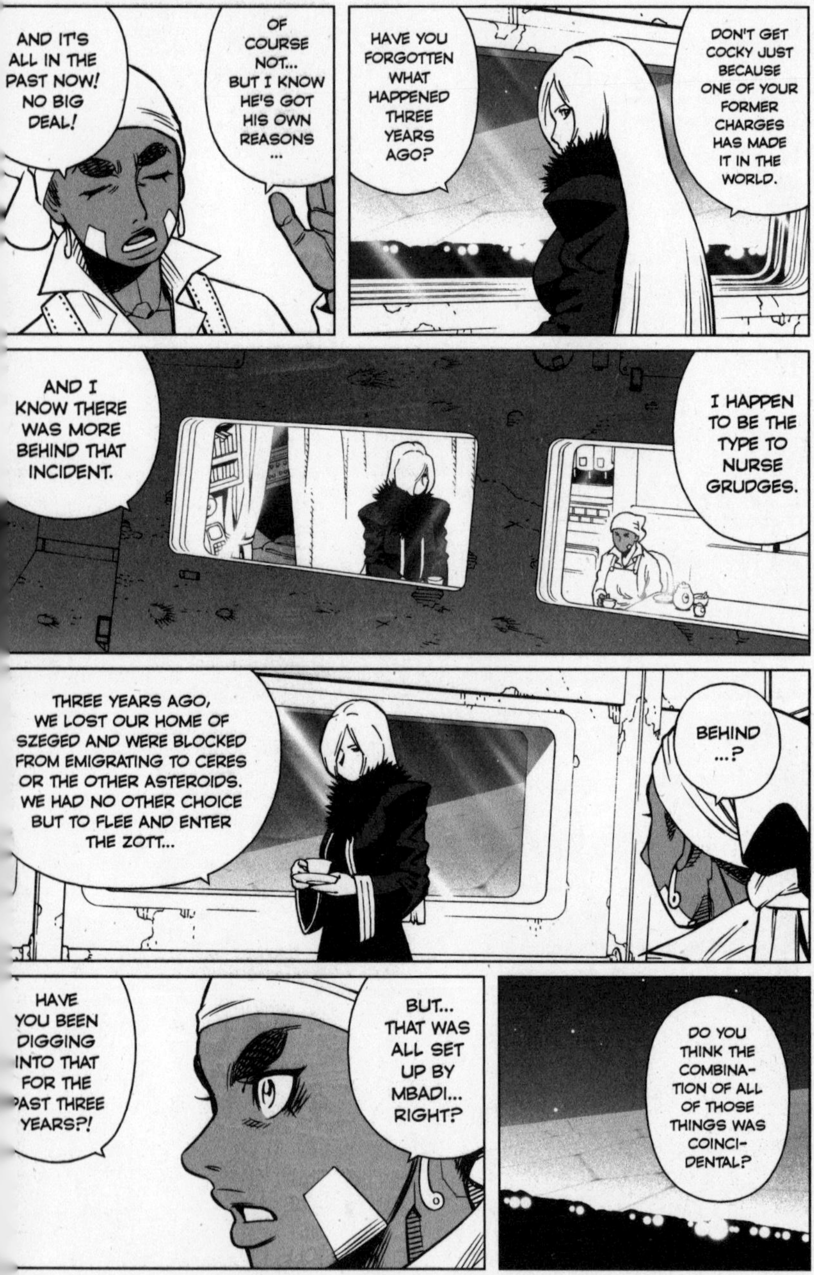
DON'T GET COCKY JUST BECAUSE ONE OF YOUR FORMER CHARGES HAS MADE IT IN THE WORLD.
HAVE YOU FORGOTTEN WHAT HAPPENED THREE YEARS AGO?
OF COURSE NOT... BUT I KNOW HE'S GOT HIS OWN REASONS ...
AND IT'S ALL IN THE PAST NOW! NO BIG DEAL!
I HAPPEN TO BE THE TYPE TO NURSE GRUDGES.
AND I KNOW THERE WAS MORE BEHIND THAT INCIDENT.
BEHIND ...?
THREE YEARS AGO, WE LOST OUR HOME OF SZEGED AND WERE BLOCKED FROM EMIGRATING TO CERES OR THE OTHER ASTEROIDS. WE HAD NO OTHER CHOICE BUT TO FLEE AND ENTER THE ZOTT...
DO YOU THINK THE COMBINATION OF ALL OF THOSE THINGS WAS COINCIDENTAL?
BUT... THAT WAS ALL SET UP BY MBADI... RIGHT?
HAVE YOU BEEN DIGGING INTO THAT FOR THE PAST THREE YEARS?!

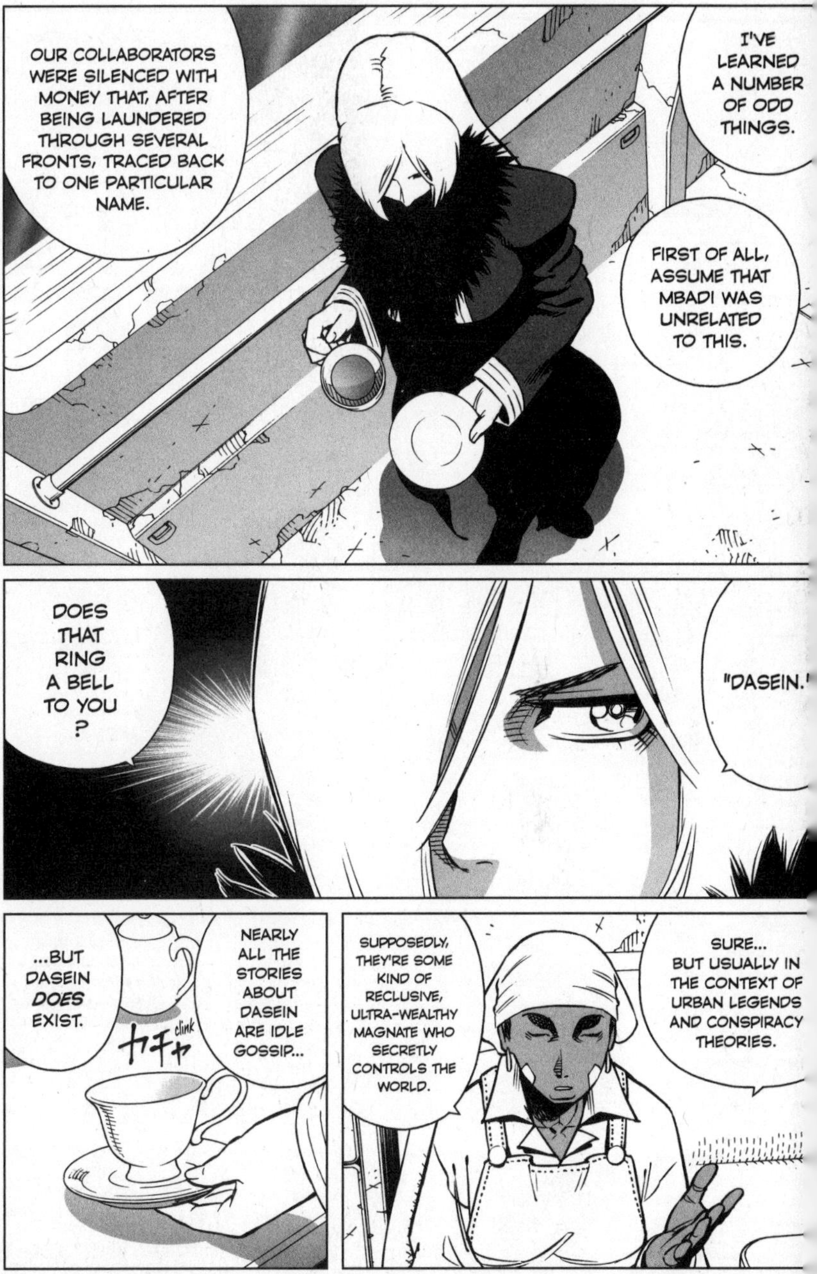
I'VE LEARNED A NUMBER OF ODD THINGS.
FIRST OF ALL, ASSUME THAT MBADI WAS UNRELATED TO THIS.
OUR COLLABORATORS WERE SILENCED WITH MONEY THAT, AFTER BEING LAUNDERED THROUGH SEVERAL FRONTS, TRACED BACK TO ONE PARTICULAR NAME.
"DASEIN."
DOES THAT RING A BELL TO YOU?
SURE... BUT USUALLY IN THE CONTEXT OF URBAN LEGENDS AND CONSPIRACY THEORIES.
SUPPOSEDLY, THEY'RE SOME KIND OF RECLUSIVE, ULTRA-WEALTHY MAGNATE WHO SECRETLY CONTROLS THE WORLD.
NEARLY ALL THE STORIES ABOUT DASEIN ARE IDLE GOSSIP...
カチャ clink
...BUT DASEIN *DOES* EXIST.

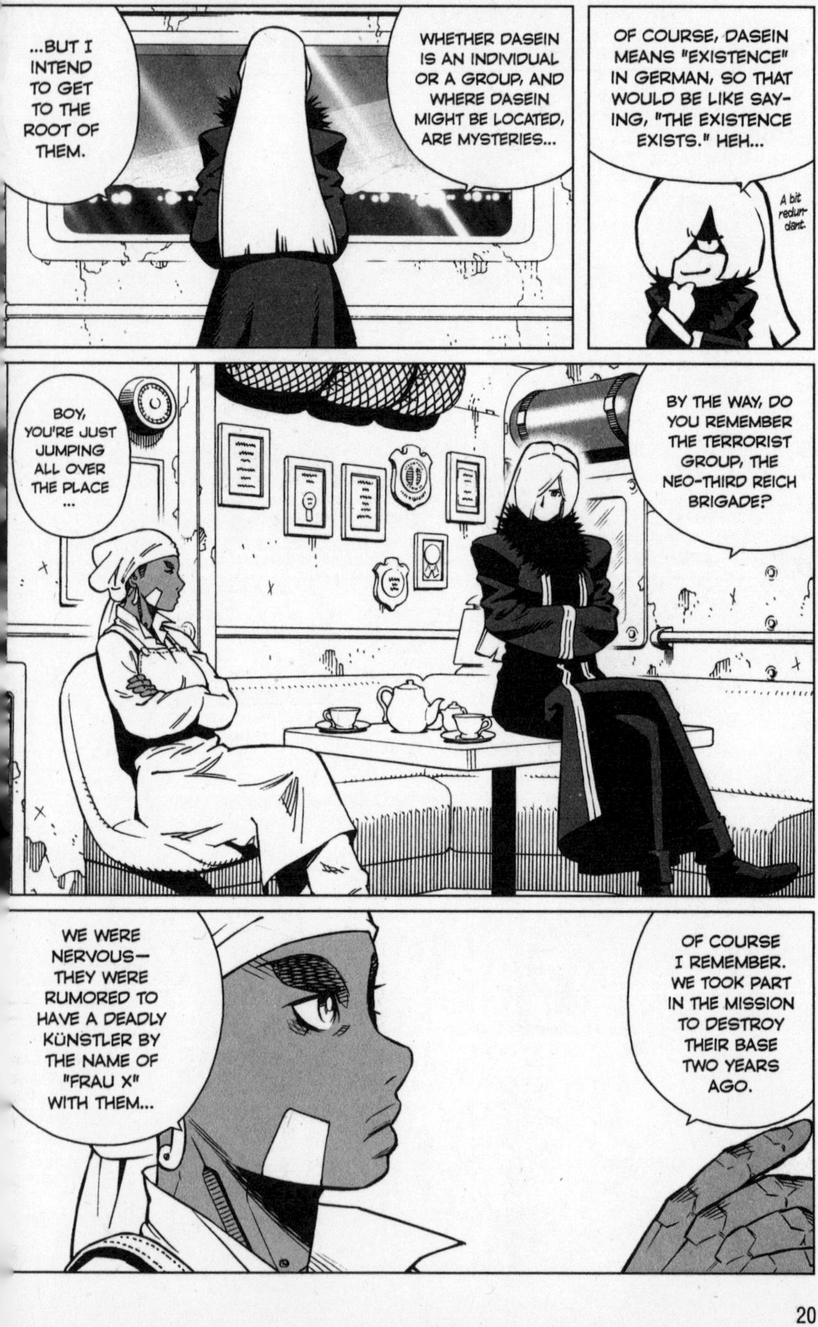
OF COURSE, DASEIN MEANS "EXISTENCE" IN GERMAN, SO THAT WOULD BE LIKE SAY-ING, "THE EXISTENCE EXISTS." HEH...
A bit redun-dant.
WHETHER DASEIN IS AN INDIVIDUAL OR A GROUP, AND WHERE DASEIN MIGHT BE LOCATED, ARE MYSTERIES...
...BUT I INTEND TO GET TO THE ROOT OF THEM.
BY THE WAY, DO YOU REMEMBER THE TERRORIST GROUP, THE NEO-THIRD REICH BRIGADE?
BOY, YOU'RE JUST JUMPING ALL OVER THE PLACE ...
OF COURSE I REMEMBER. WE TOOK PART IN THE MISSION TO DESTROY THEIR BASE TWO YEARS AGO.
WE WERE NERVOUS— THEY WERE RUMORED TO HAVE A DEADLY KüNSTLER BY THE NAME OF "FRAU X" WITH THEM...

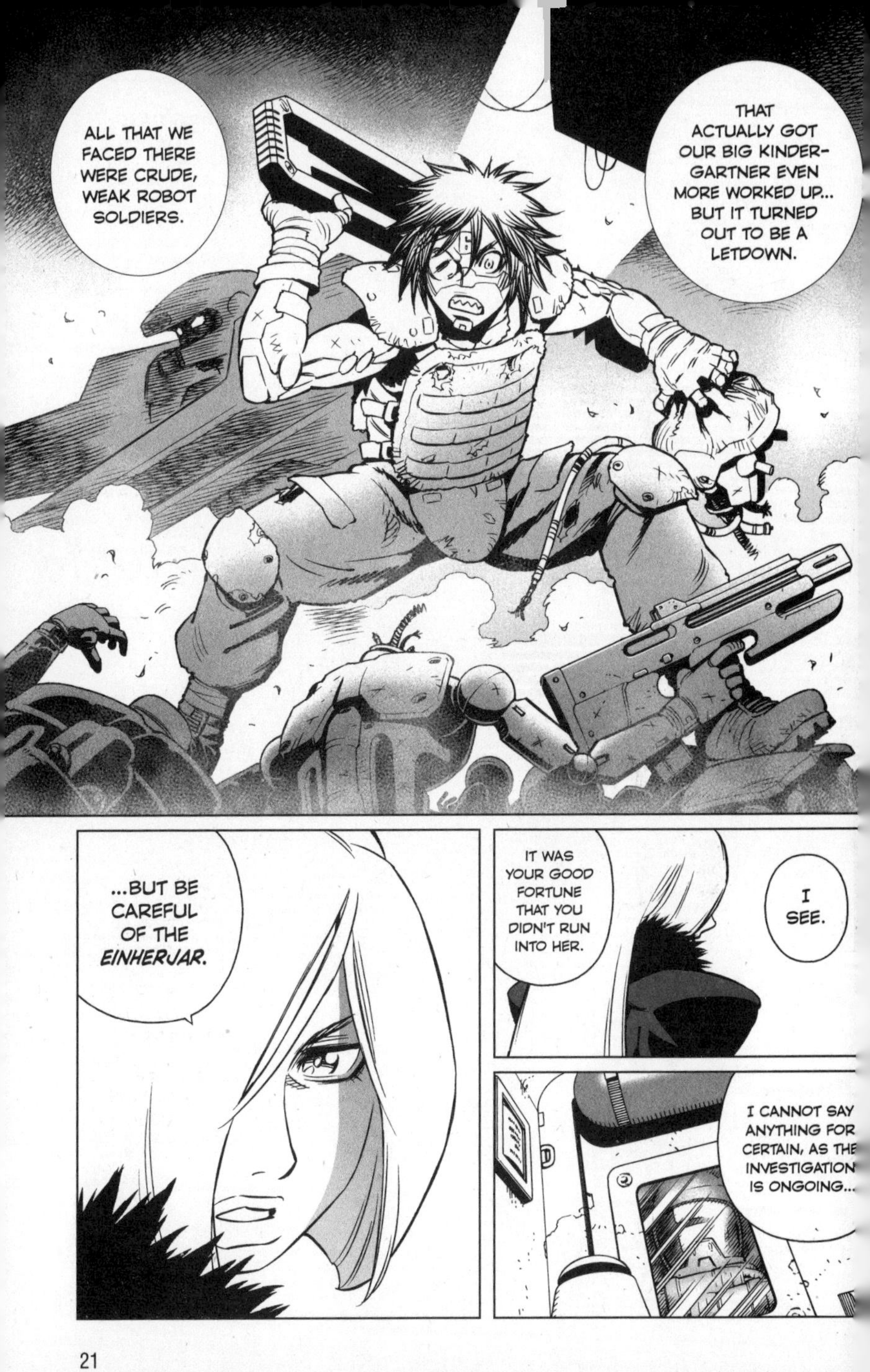
THAT ACTUALLY GOT OUR BIG KINDER-GARTNER EVEN MORE WORKED UP... BUT IT TURNED OUT TO BE A LETDOWN.
ALL THAT WE FACED THERE WERE CRUDE, WEAK ROBOT SOLDIERS.
IT WAS YOUR GOOD FORTUNE THAT YOU DIDN'T RUN INTO HER.
I SEE.
I CANNOT SAY ANYTHING FOR CERTAIN, AS THE INVESTIGATION IS ONGOING...
...BUT BE CAREFUL OF THE *EINHERJAR*.

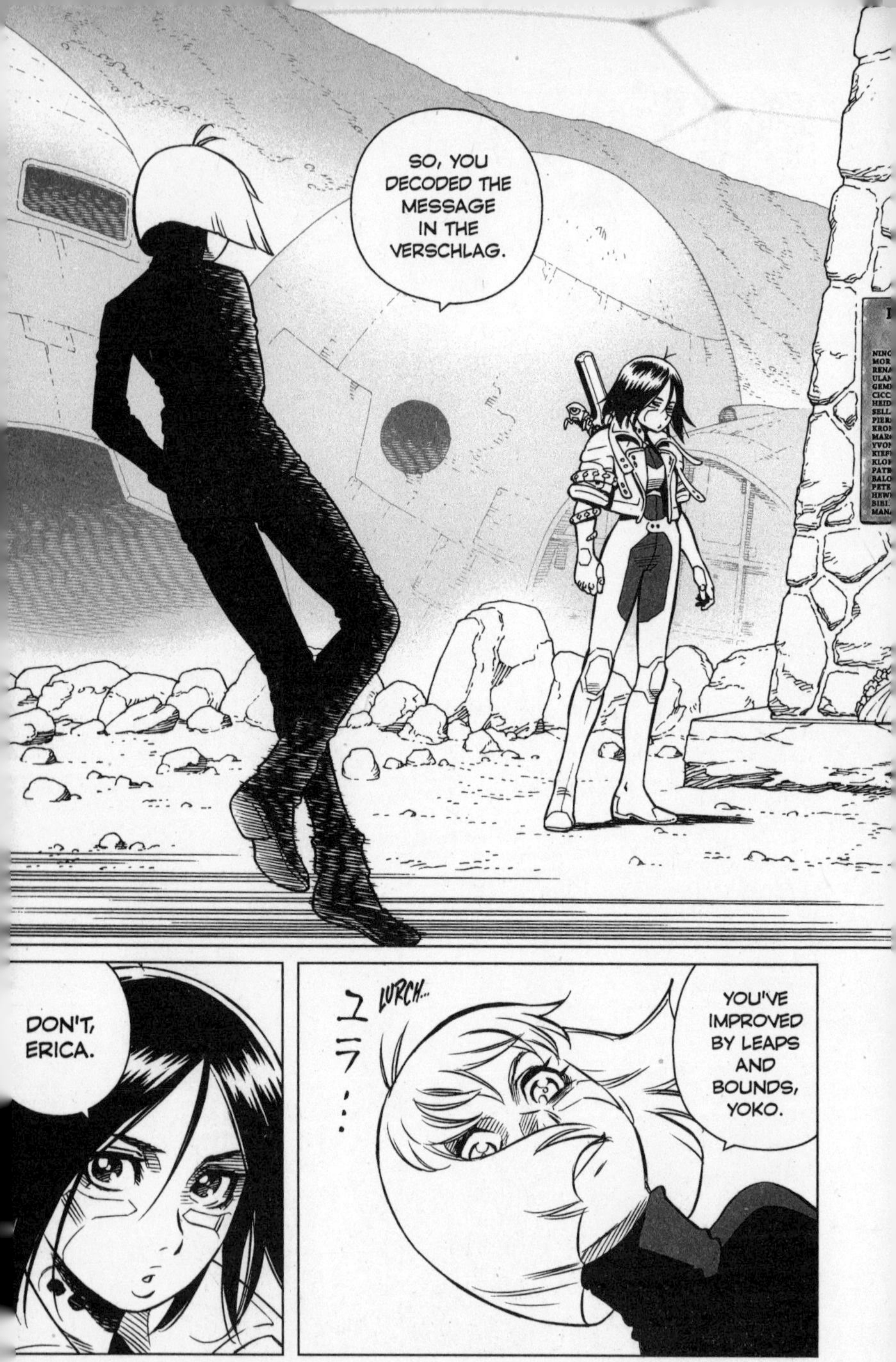
SO, YOU DECODED THE MESSAGE IN THE VERSCHLAG.
LURCH...
ユラ…
YOU'VE IMPROVED BY LEAPS AND BOUNDS, YOKO.
DON'T, ERICA.

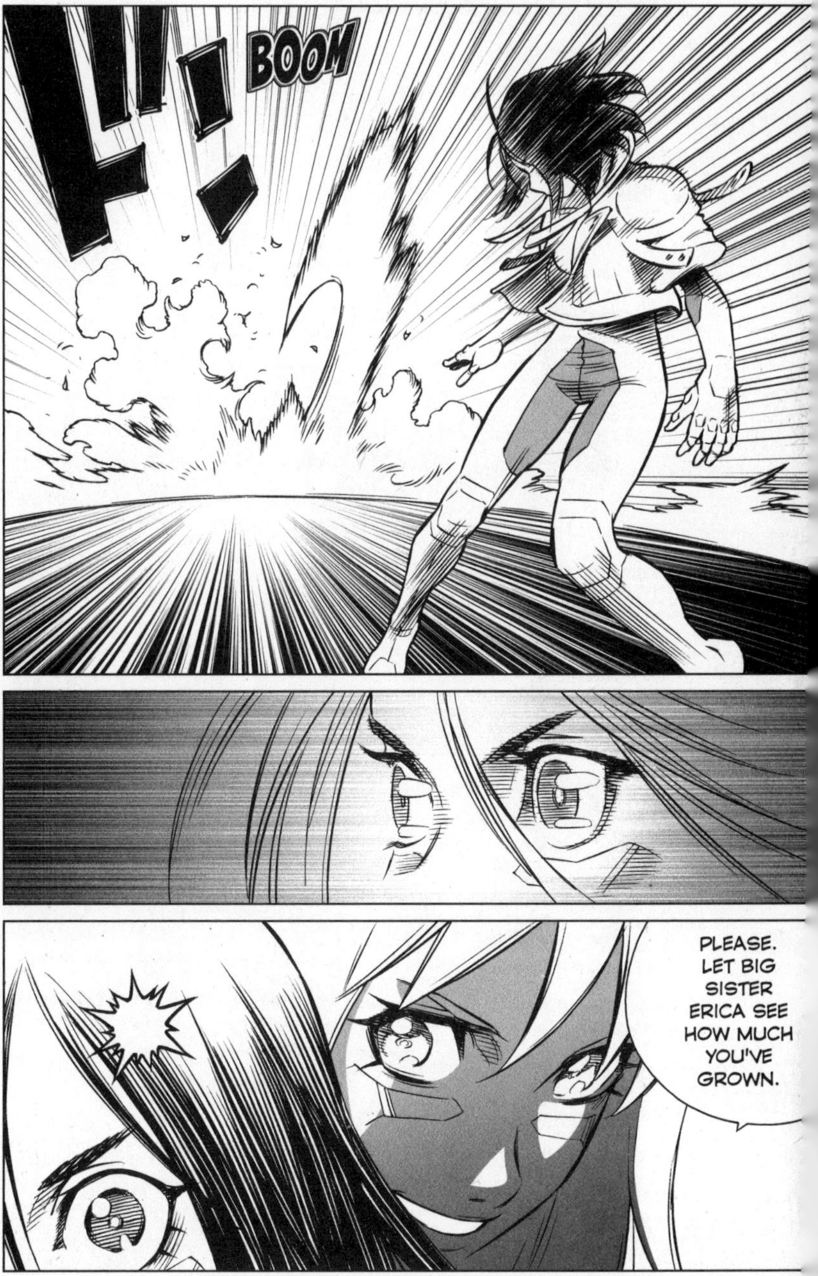
BOOM
PLEASE. LET BIG SISTER ERICA SEE HOW MUCH YOU'VE GROWN.

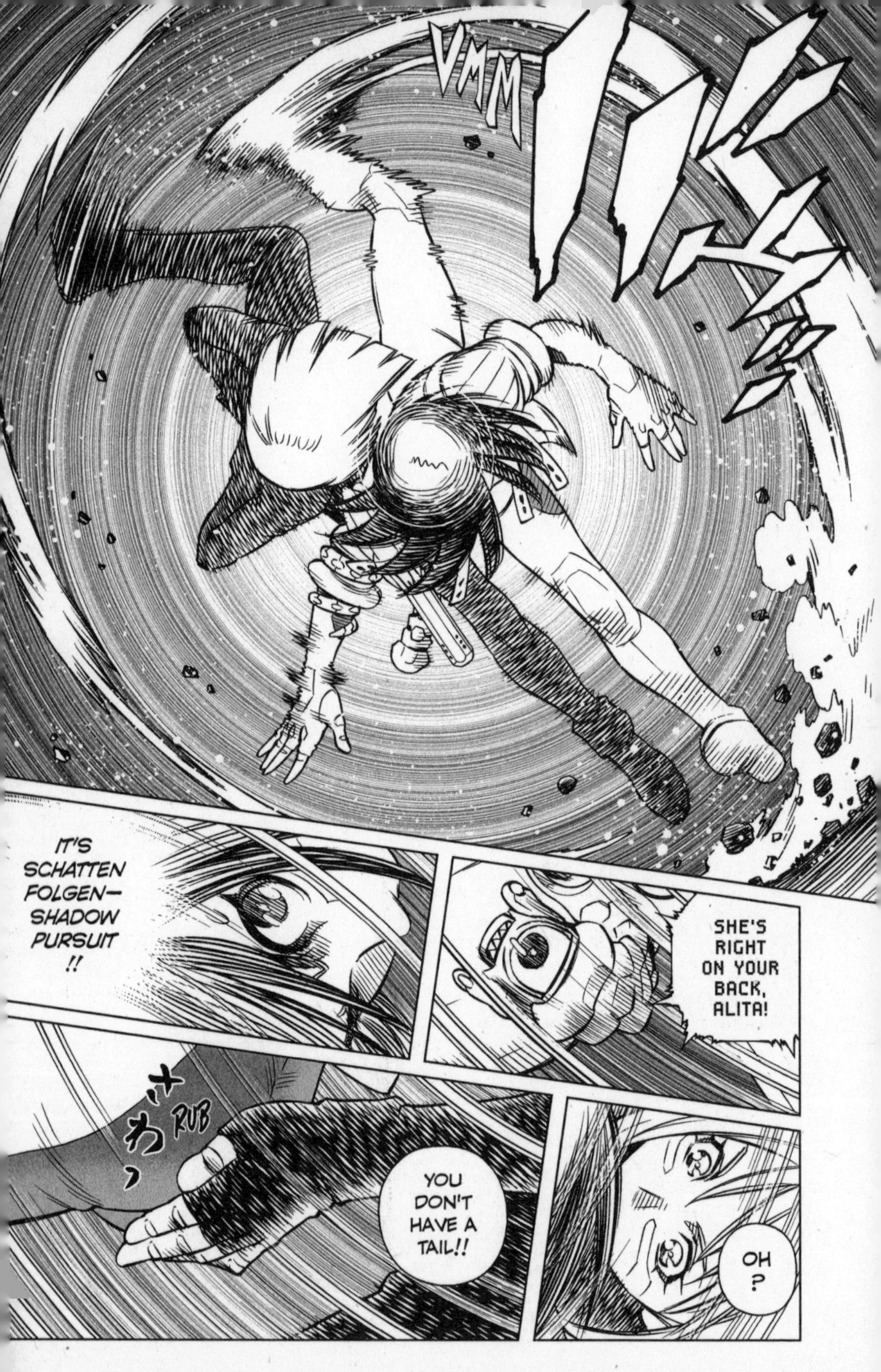
VMM
SHE'S RIGHT ON YOUR BACK, ALITA!
IT'S SCHATTEN FOLGEN—SHADOW PURSUIT!!
OH ?
YOU DON'T HAVE A TAIL!!
RUB

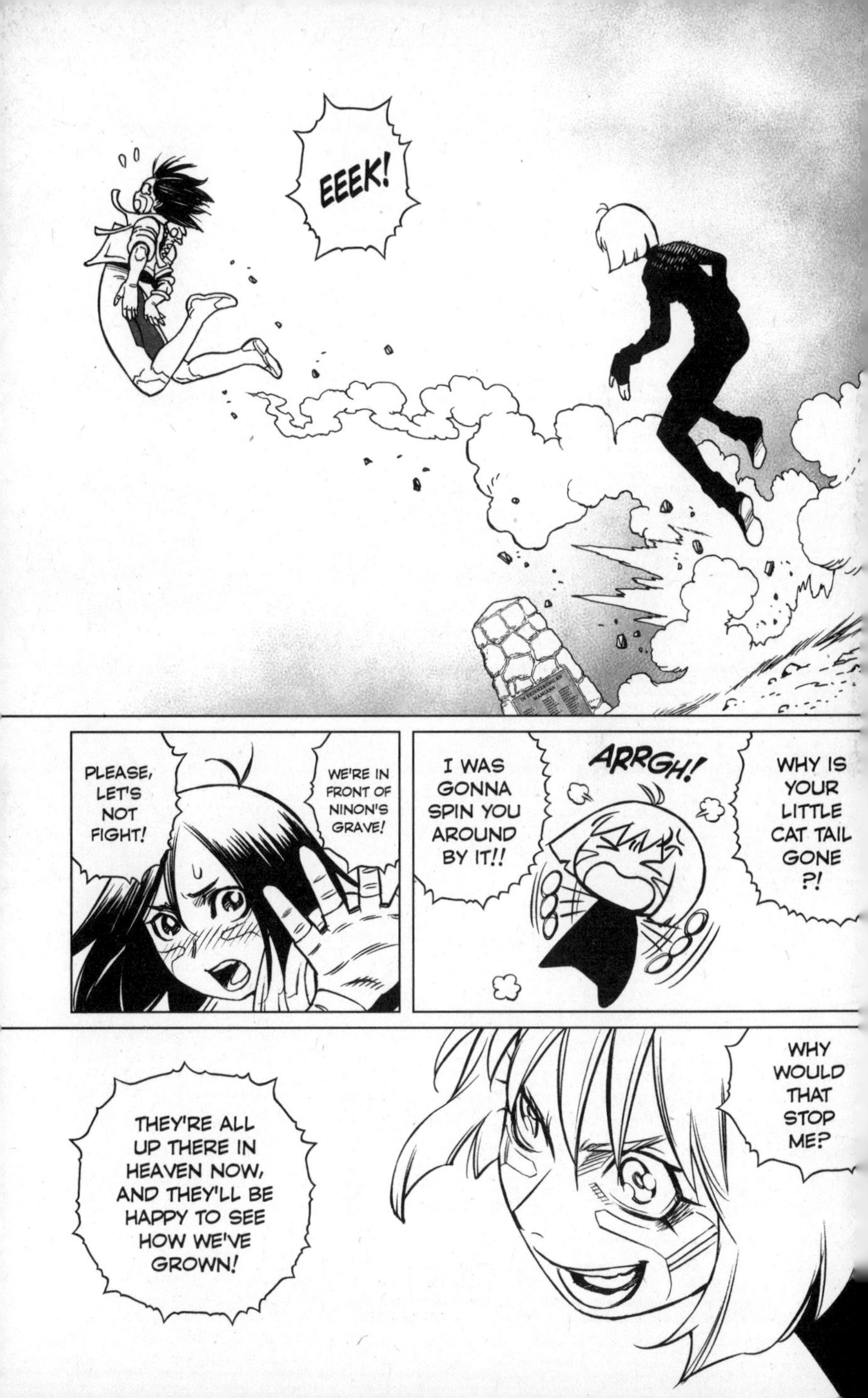
EEEK!
WHY IS YOUR LITTLE CAT TAIL GONE?!
ARRGH!
I WAS GONNA SPIN YOU AROUND BY IT!!
WE'RE IN FRONT OF NINON'S GRAVE!
PLEASE, LET'S NOT FIGHT!
WHY WOULD THAT STOP ME?
THEY'RE ALL UP THERE IN HEAVEN NOW, AND THEY'LL BE HAPPY TO SEE HOW WE'VE GROWN!

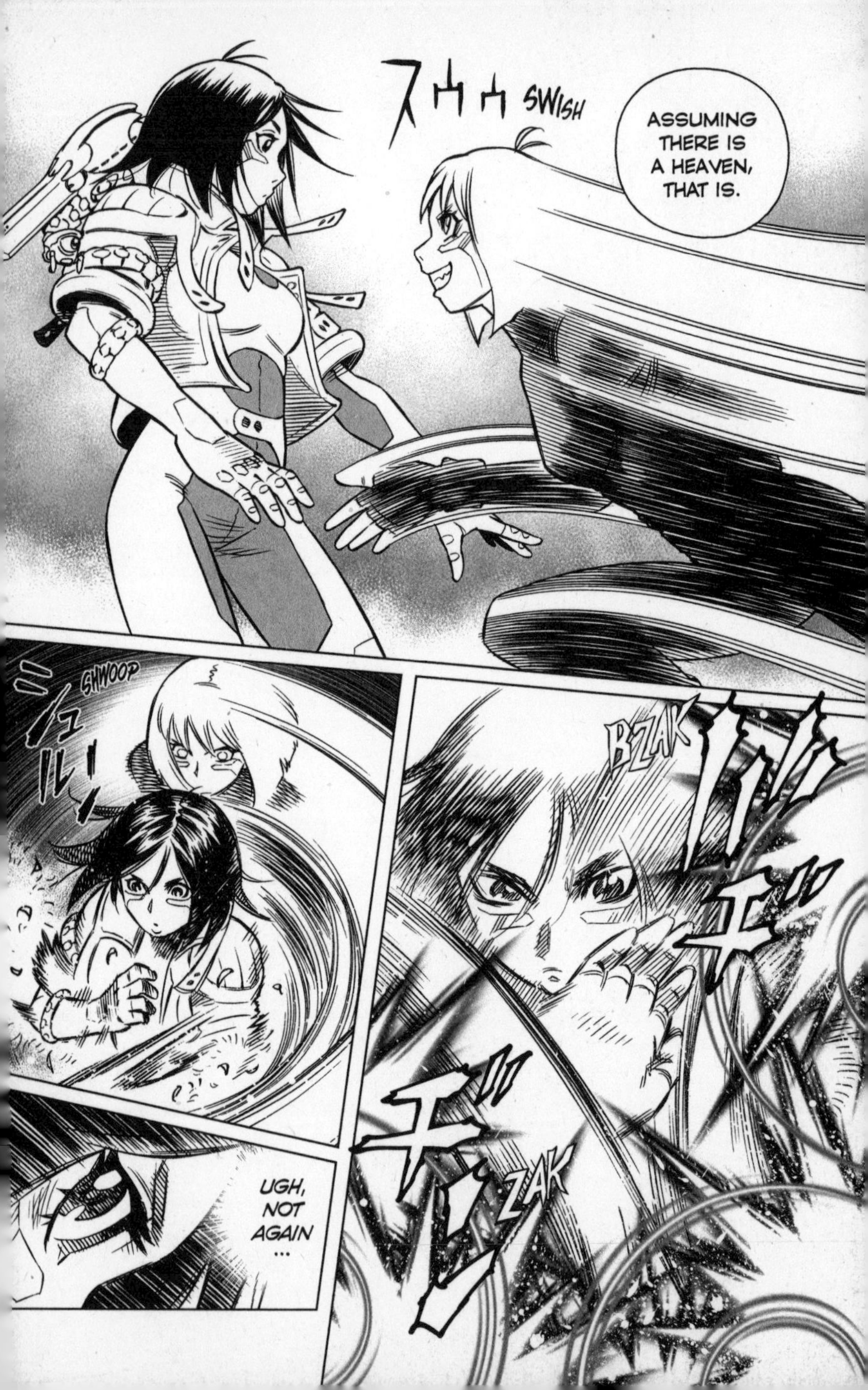
SWISH
ASSUMING THERE IS A HEAVEN, THAT IS.
BZAK
ZAK
SHWOOP
UGH, NOT AGAIN ...

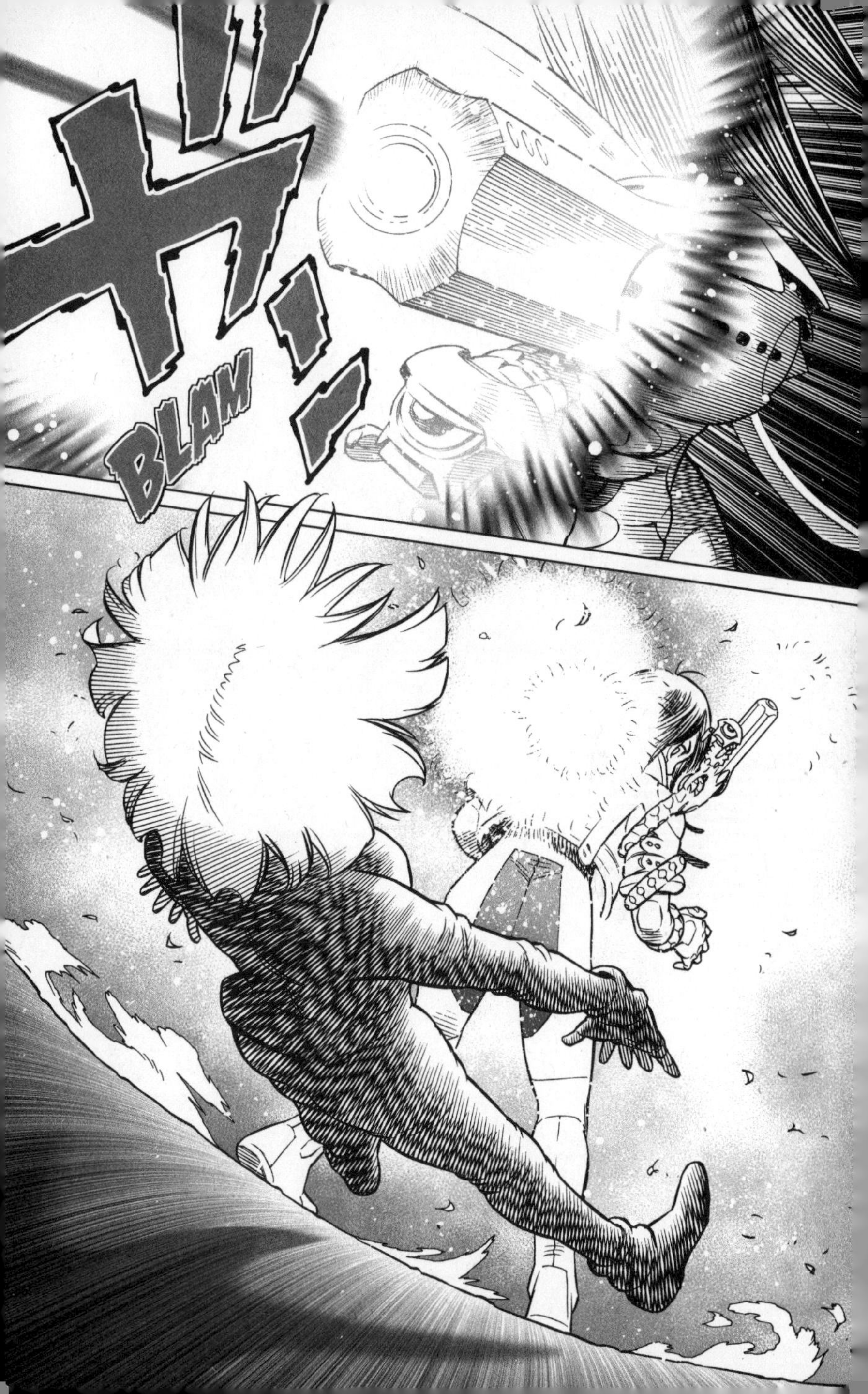
BLAM

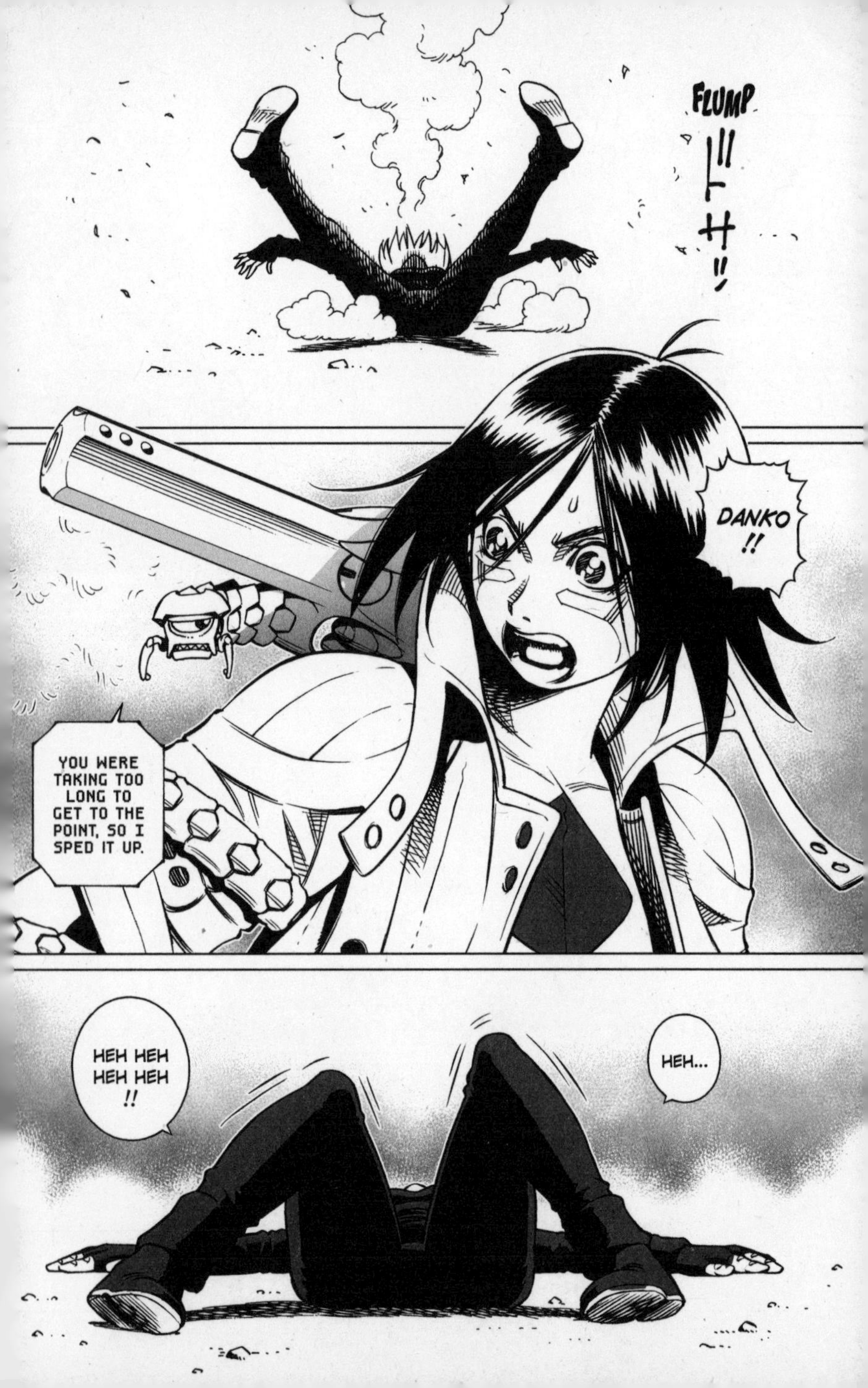
FLUMP
ドサッ
DANKO !!
YOU WERE TAKING TOO LONG TO GET TO THE POINT, SO I SPED IT UP.
HEH...
HEH HEH HEH HEH !!

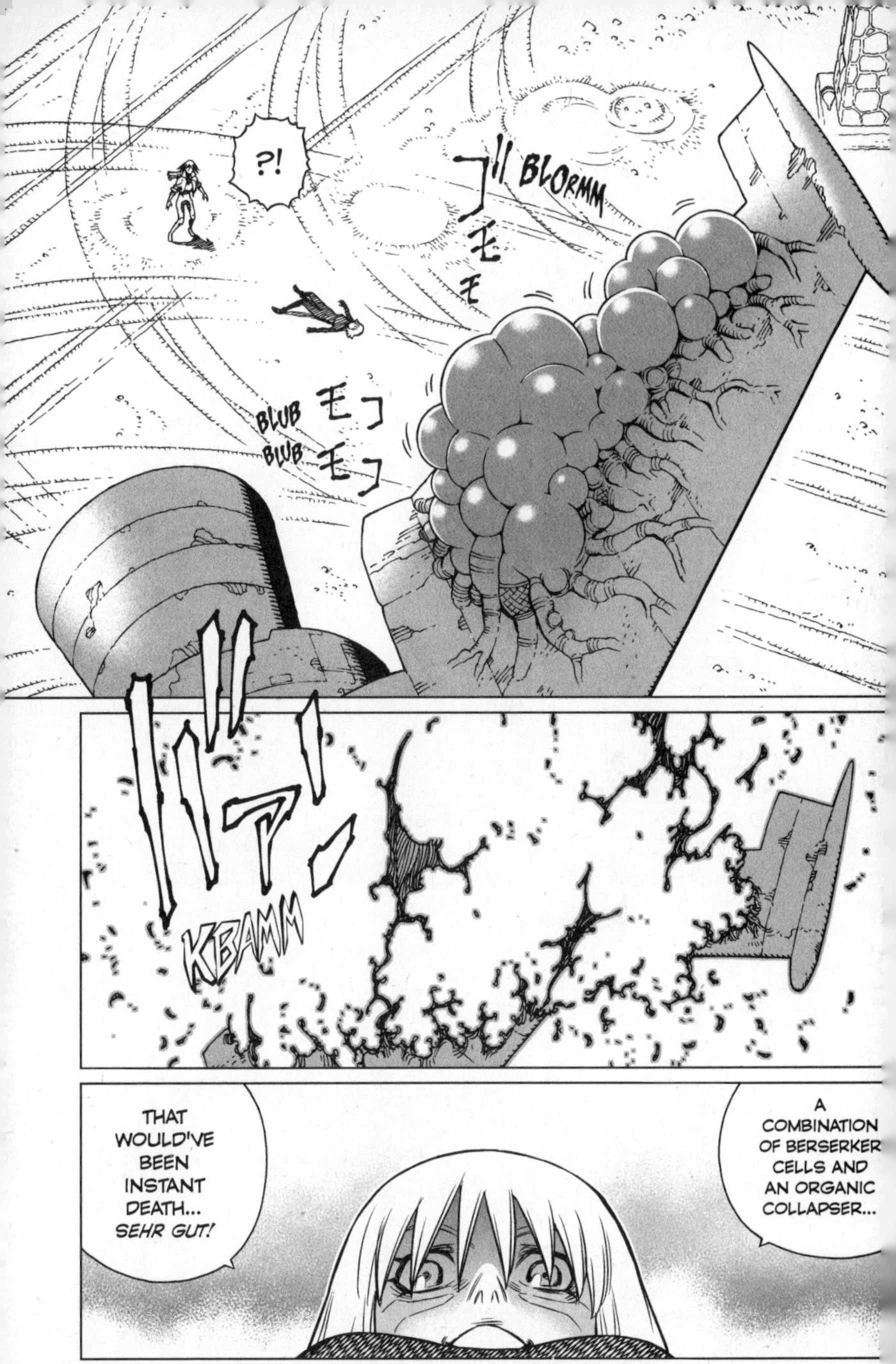
BLORMM
?!
BLUB
BLUB
KBAMM
A COMBINATION OF BERSERKER CELLS AND AN ORGANIC COLLAPSER...
THAT WOULD'VE BEEN INSTANT DEATH... SEHR GUT!

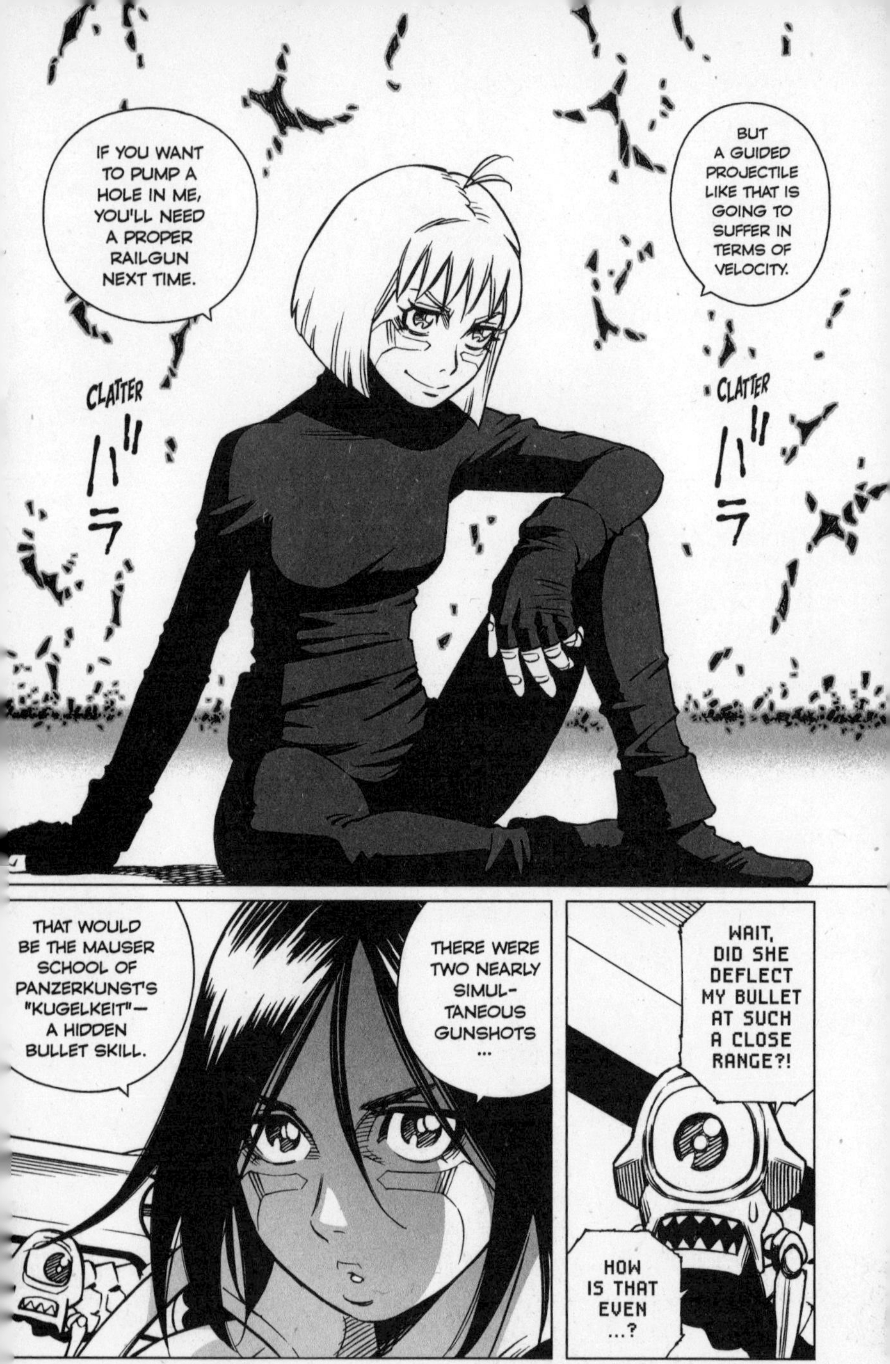
BUT A GUIDED PROJECTILE LIKE THAT IS GOING TO SUFFER IN TERMS OF VELOCITY.
IF YOU WANT TO PUMP A HOLE IN ME, YOU'LL NEED A PROPER RAILGUN NEXT TIME.
CLATTER
バラ
CLATTER
バラ
WAIT, DID SHE DEFLECT MY BULLET AT SUCH A CLOSE RANGE?!
HOW IS THAT EVEN ...?
THERE WERE TWO NEARLY SIMUL-TANEOUS GUNSHOTS ...
THAT WOULD BE THE MAUSER SCHOOL OF PANZERKUNST'S "KUGELKEIT"— A HIDDEN BULLET SKILL.

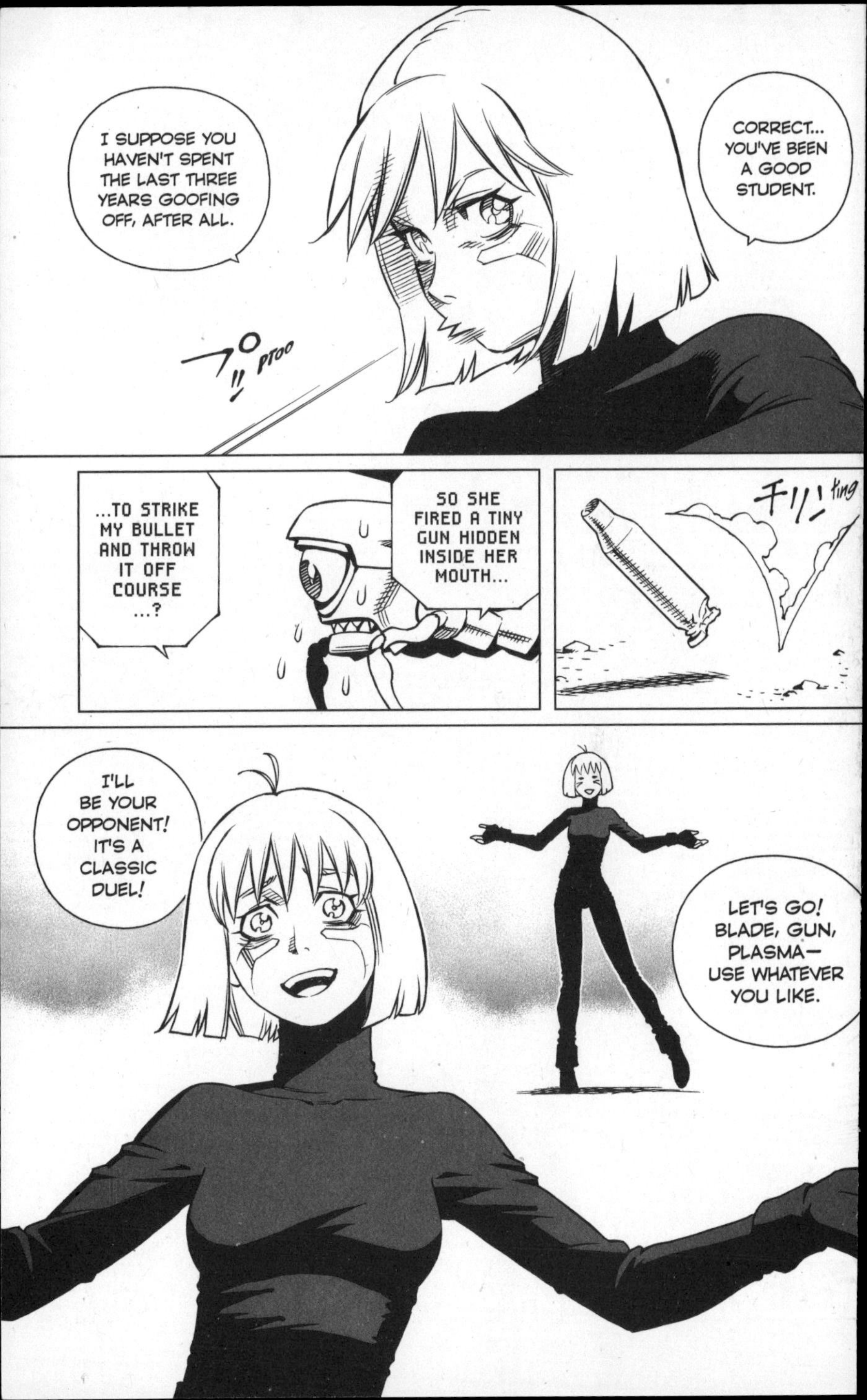
CORRECT... YOU'VE BEEN A GOOD STUDENT.
I SUPPOSE YOU HAVEN'T SPENT THE LAST THREE YEARS GOOFING OFF, AFTER ALL.
PTOO
ting
SO SHE FIRED A TINY GUN HIDDEN INSIDE HER MOUTH...
...TO STRIKE MY BULLET AND THROW IT OFF COURSE ...?
I'LL BE YOUR OPPONENT! IT'S A CLASSIC DUEL!
LET'S GO! BLADE, GUN, PLASMA— USE WHATEVER YOU LIKE.

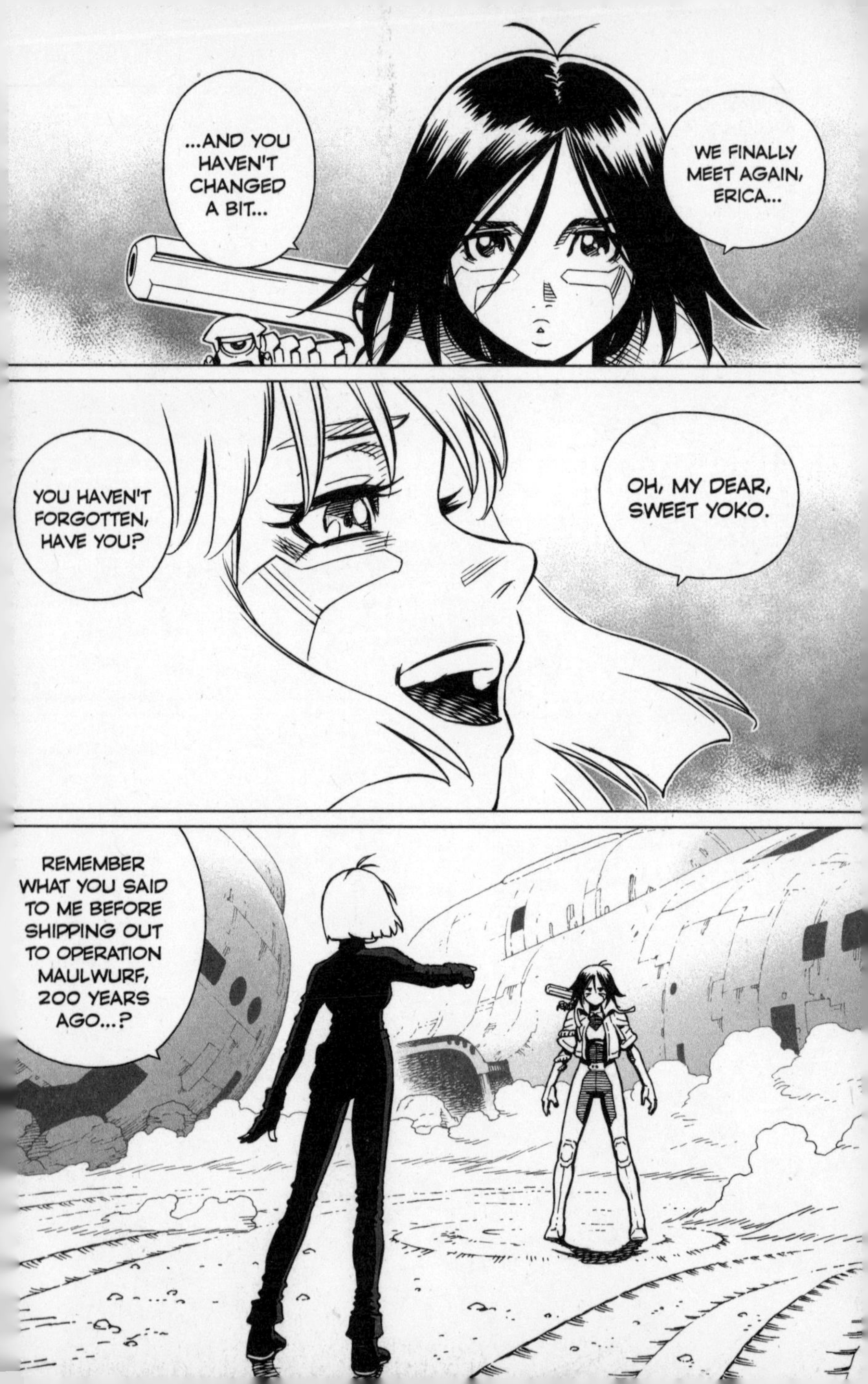
WE FINALLY MEET AGAIN, ERICA...
...AND YOU HAVEN'T CHANGED A BIT...
OH, MY DEAR, SWEET YOKO.
YOU HAVEN'T FORGOTTEN, HAVE YOU?
REMEMBER WHAT YOU SAID TO ME BEFORE SHIPPING OUT TO OPERATION MAULWURF, 200 YEARS AGO...?

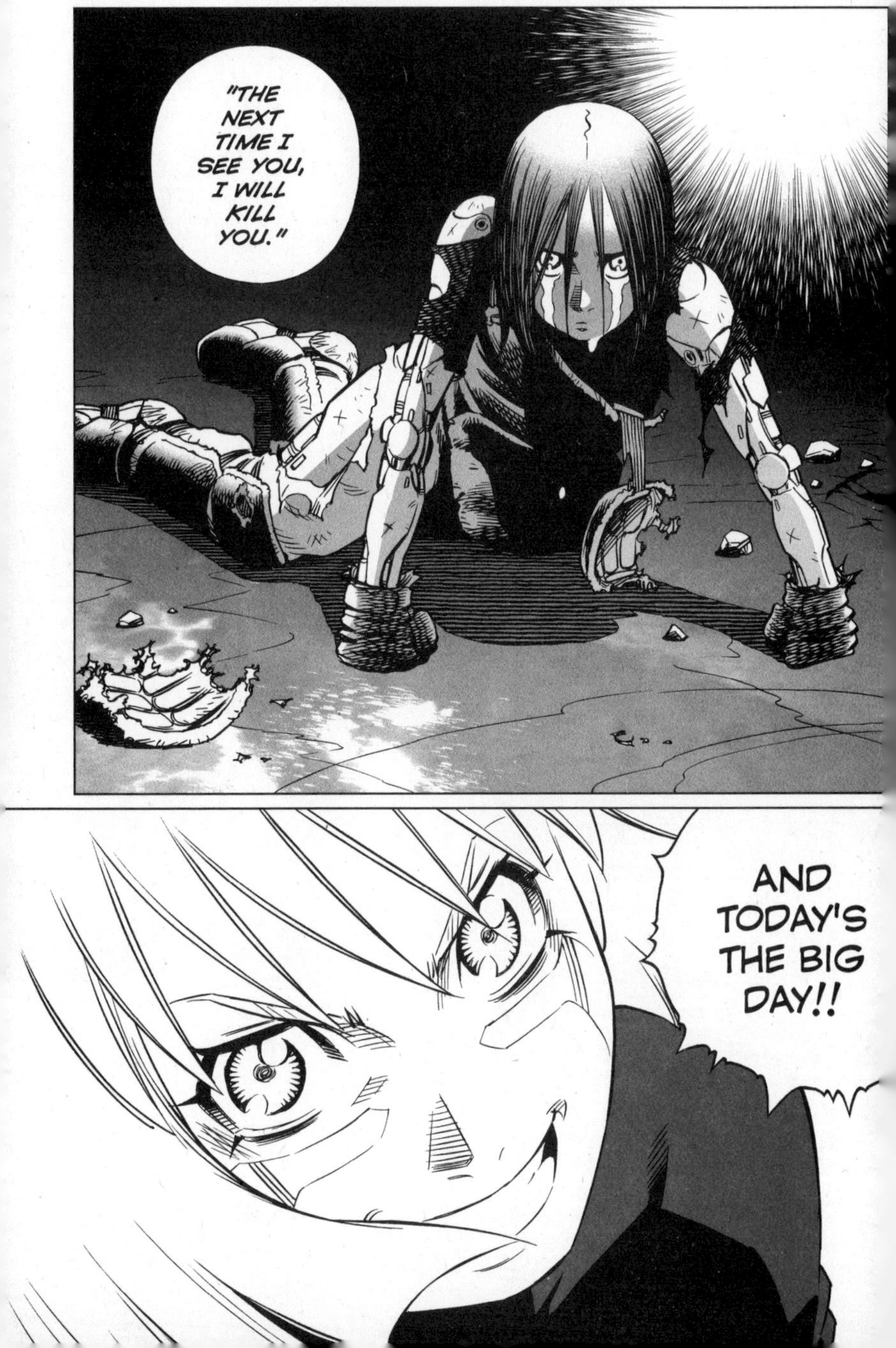
"THE NEXT TIME I SEE YOU, I WILL KILL YOU."
AND TODAY'S THE BIG DAY!!

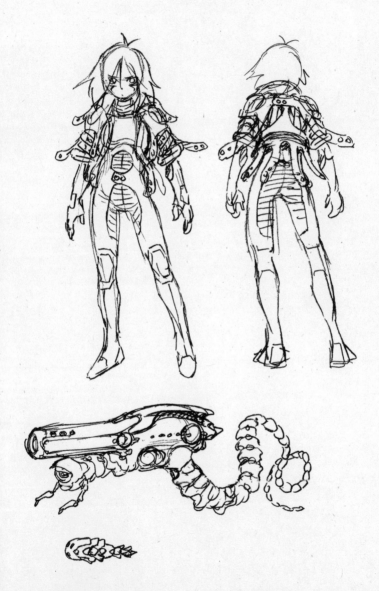

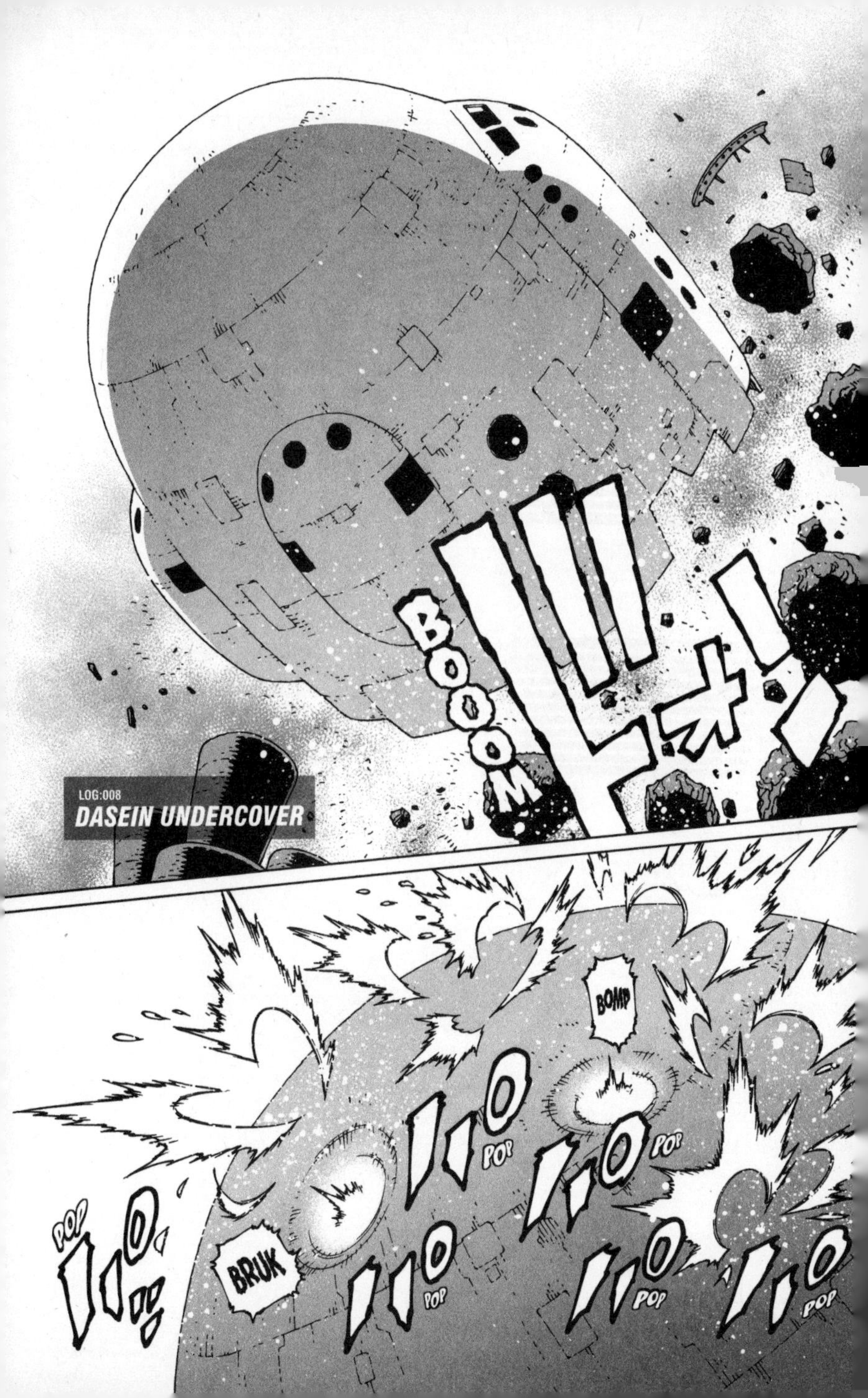
LOG:008
DASEIN UNDERCOVER
BOOOOM
BOMP
POP
POP
POP
POP
POP
BRUK
POP

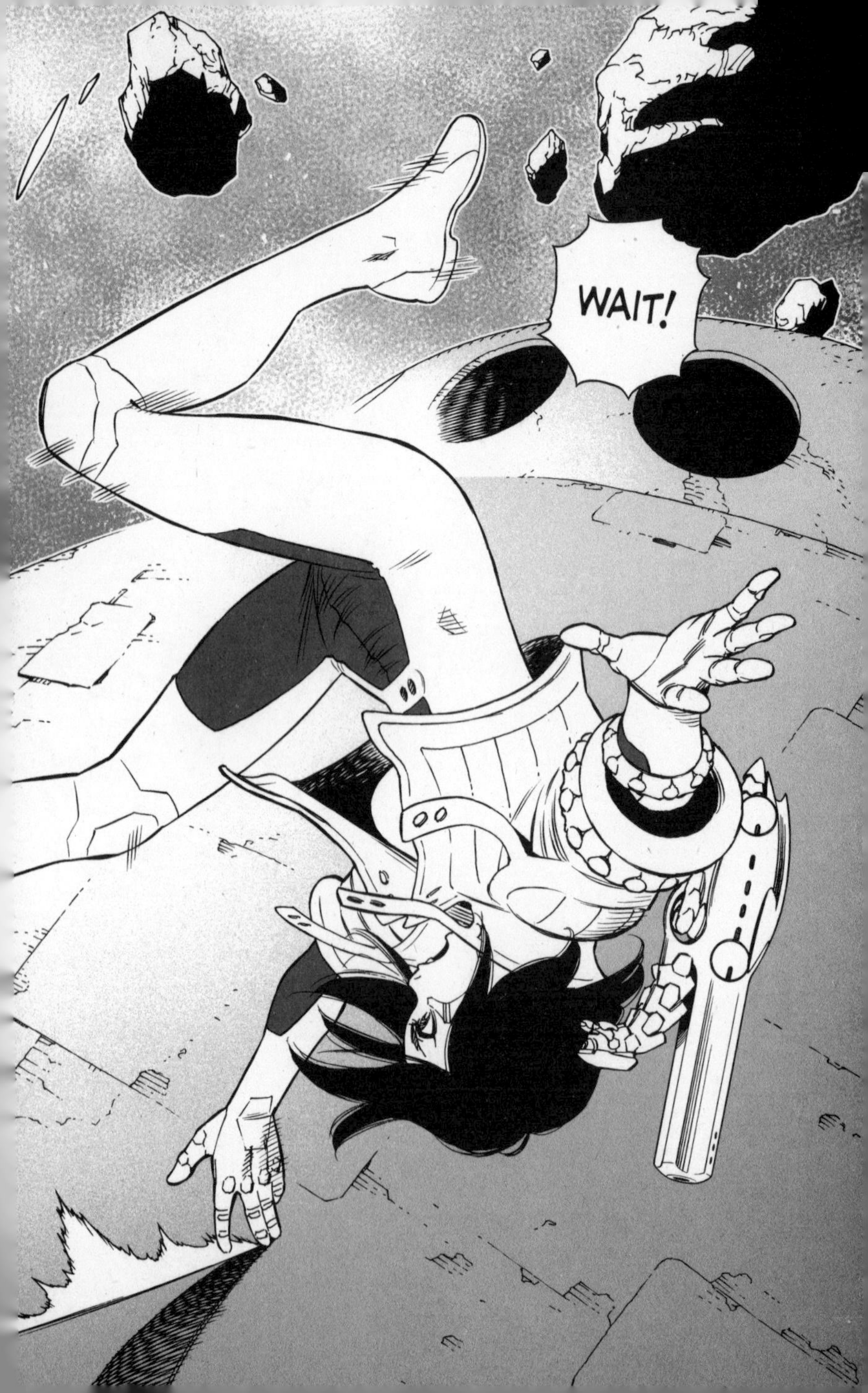
WAIT!

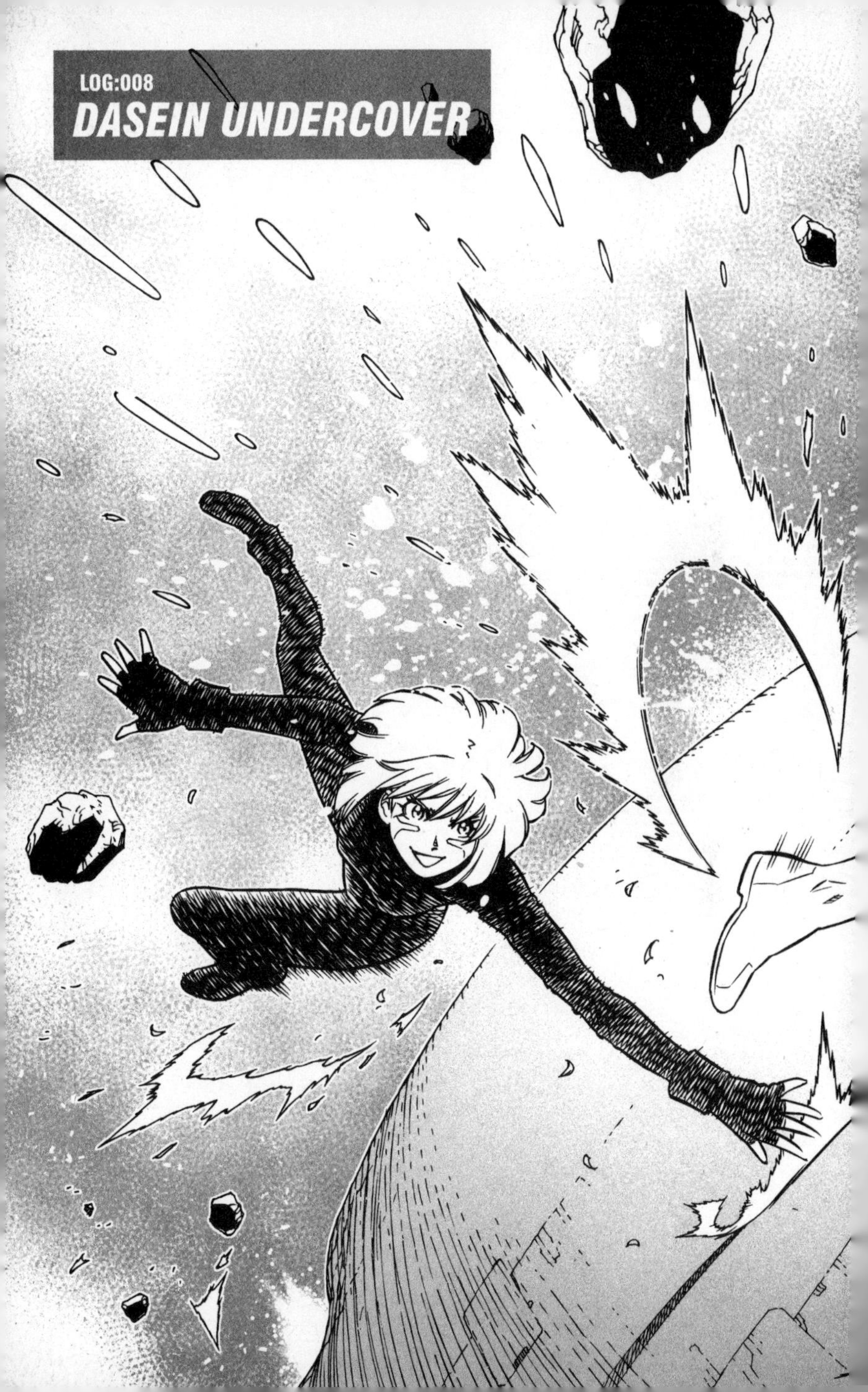
LOG:008
DASEIN UNDERCOVER

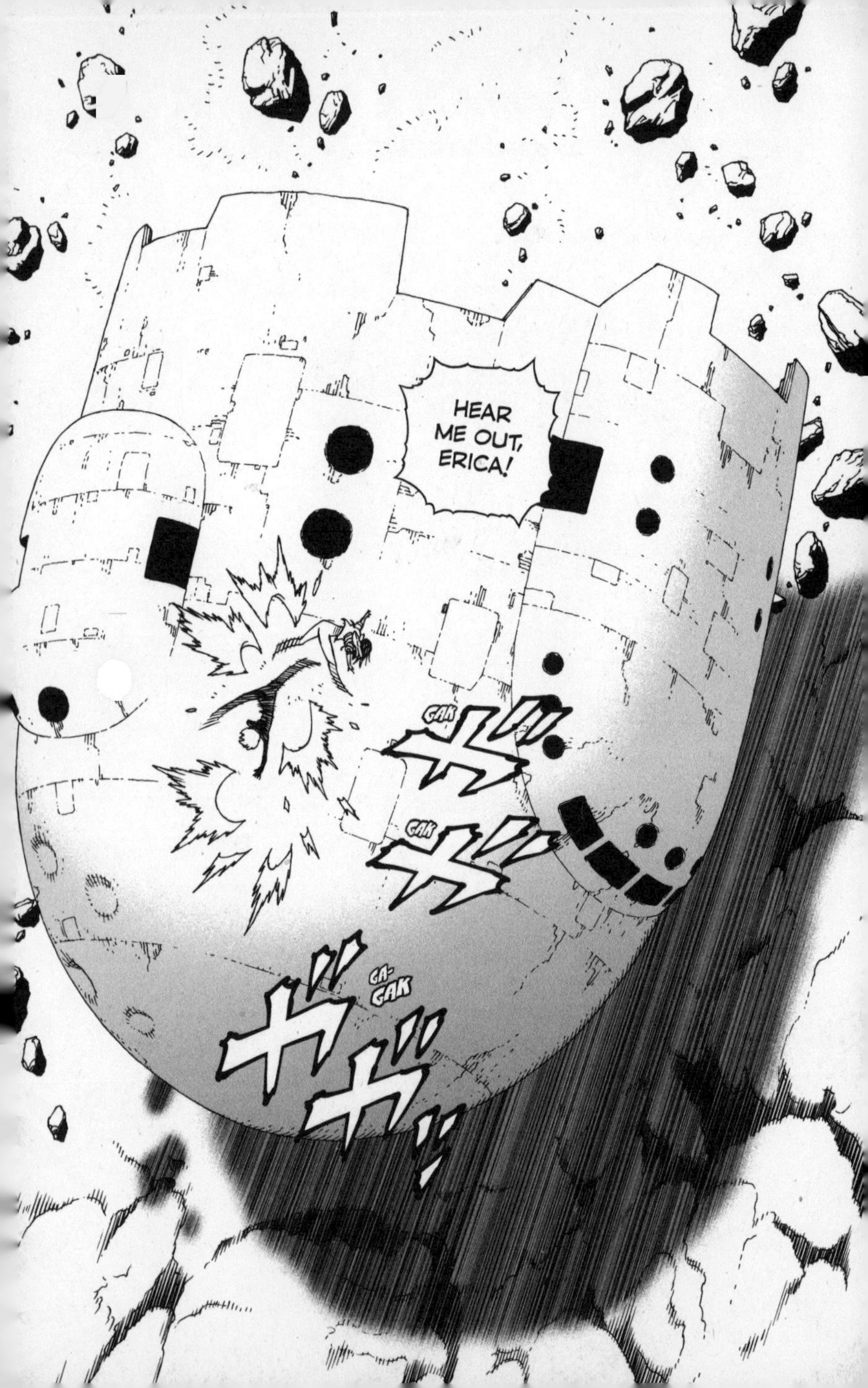
HEAR ME OUT, ERICA!
GAK
GAK
GA-GAK

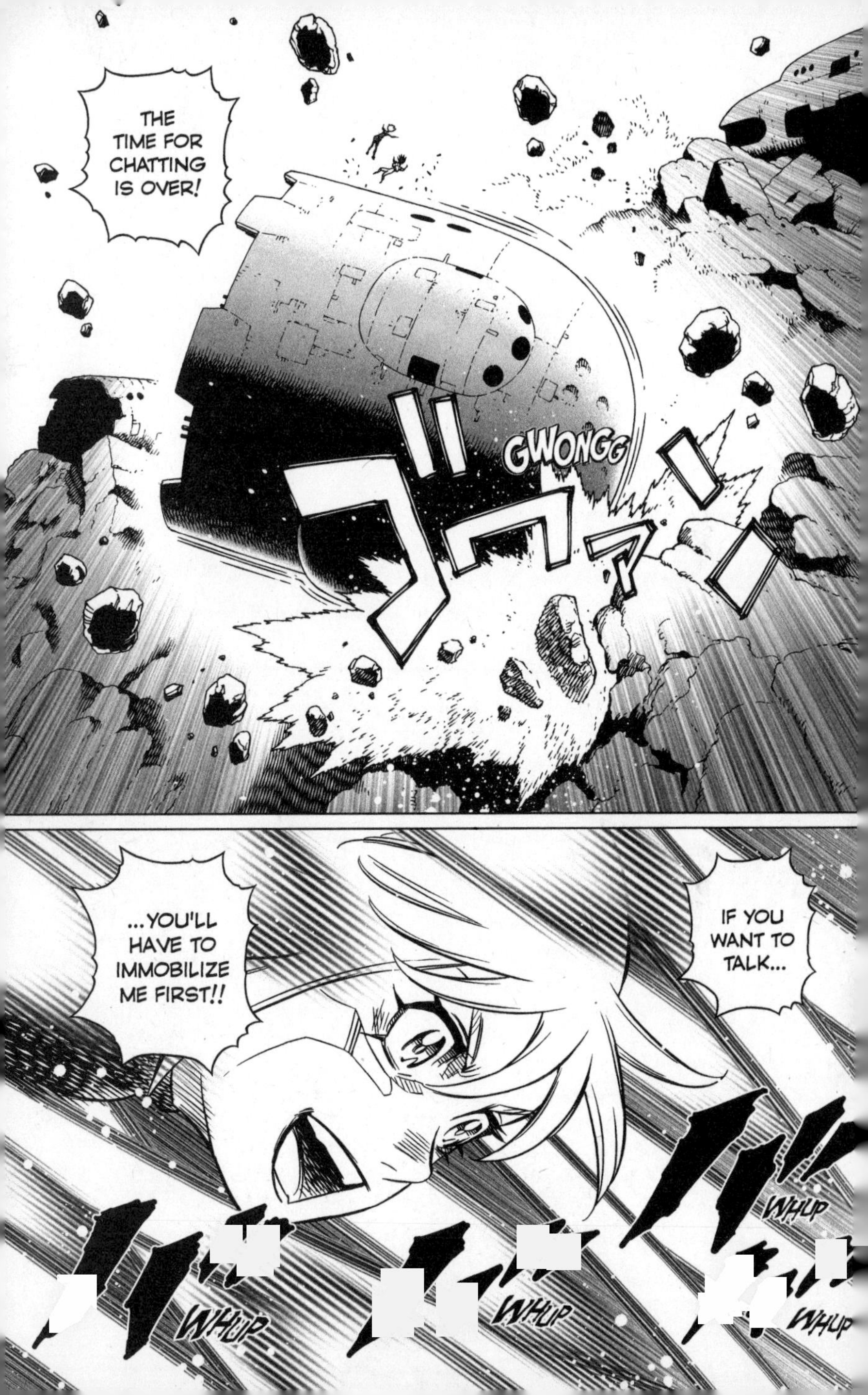
THE TIME FOR CHATTING IS OVER!
GWONGG
IF YOU WANT TO TALK...
...YOU'LL HAVE TO IMMOBILIZE ME FIRST!!
WHUP
WHUP
WHUP

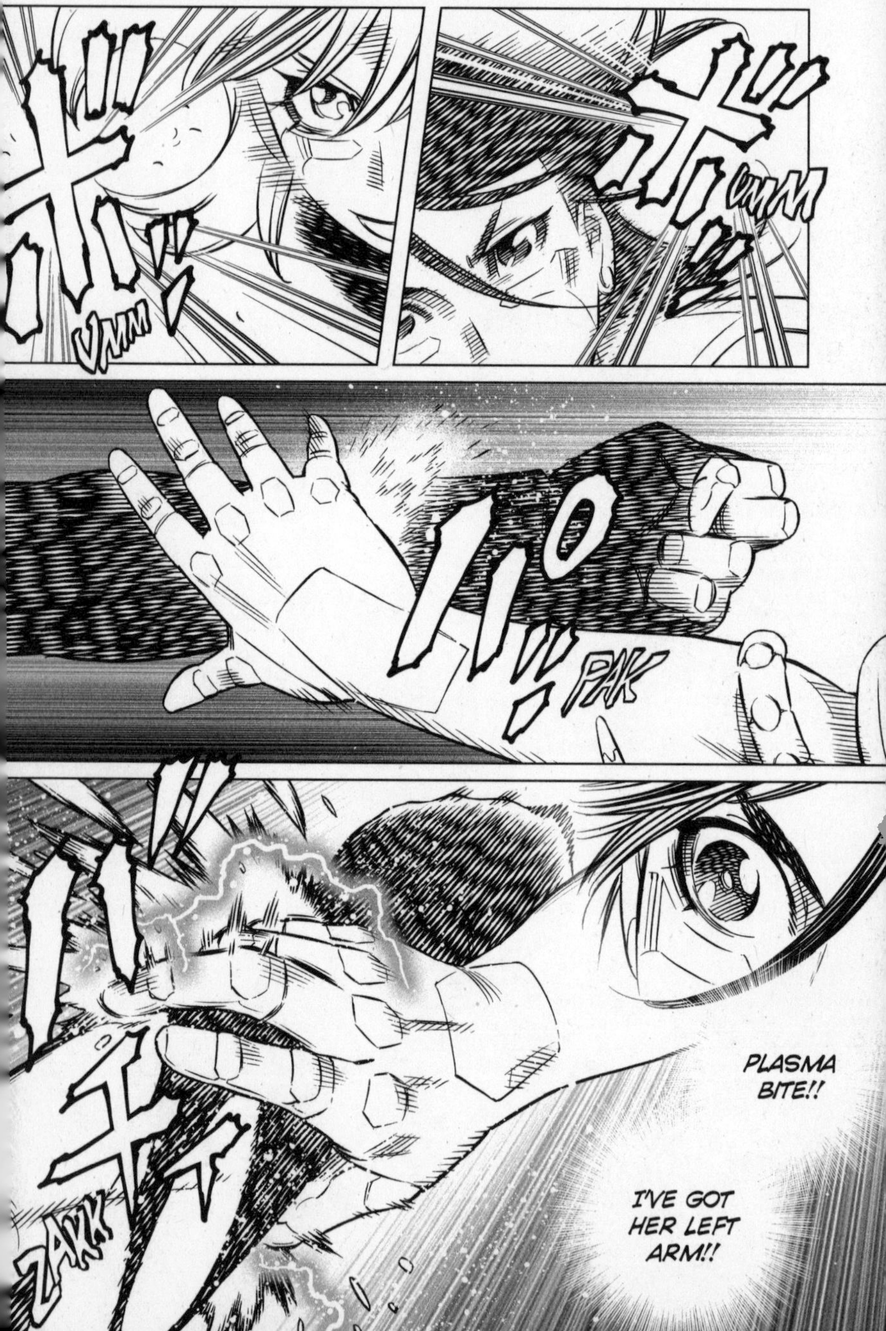
VMM
VMM
PAK
PLASMA BITE!!
I'VE GOT HER LEFT ARM!!
ZAKK

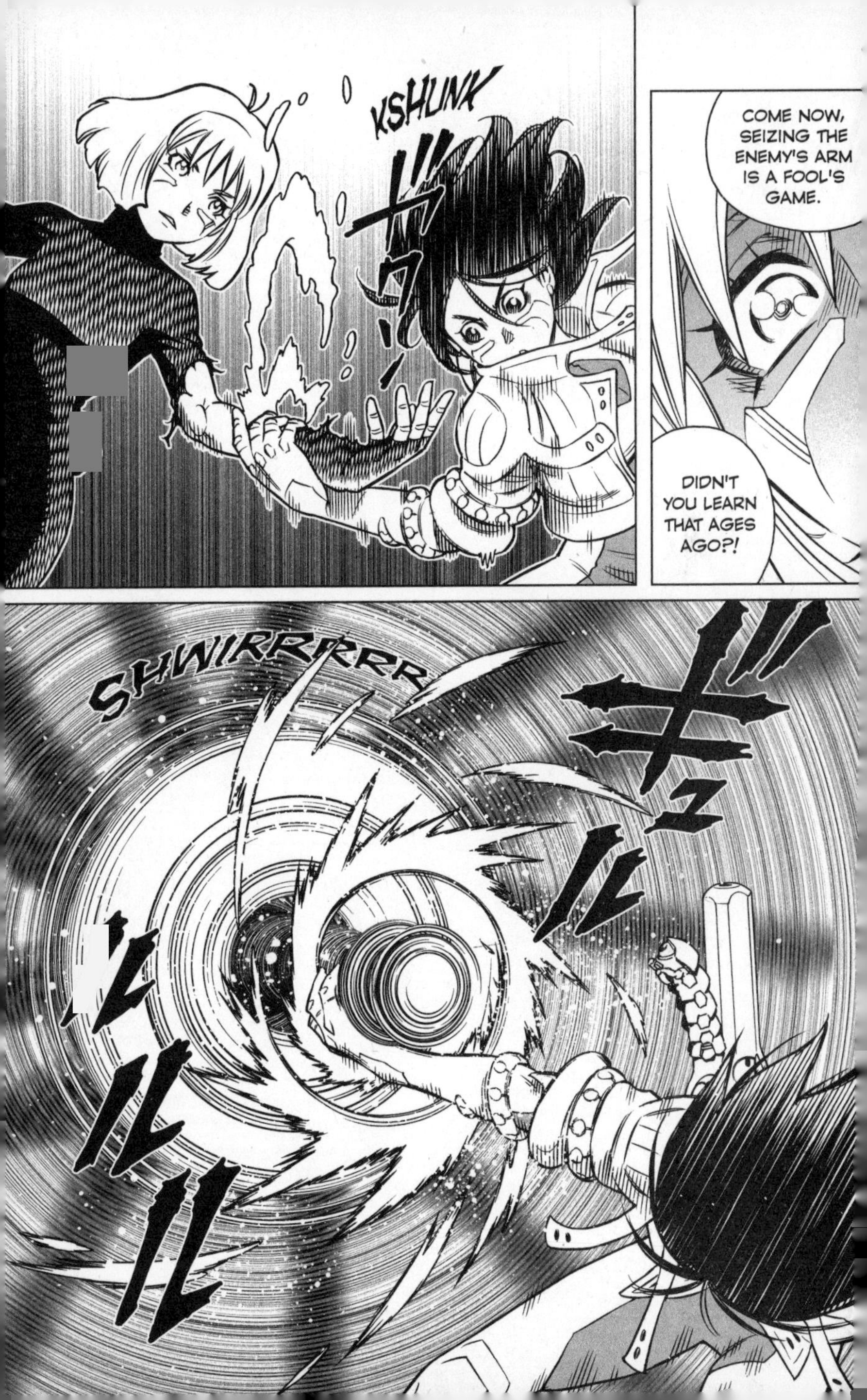
COME NOW, SEIZING THE ENEMY'S ARM IS A FOOL'S GAME.
DIDN'T YOU LEARN THAT AGES AGO?!
KSHUNK
SHWIRRRRRR

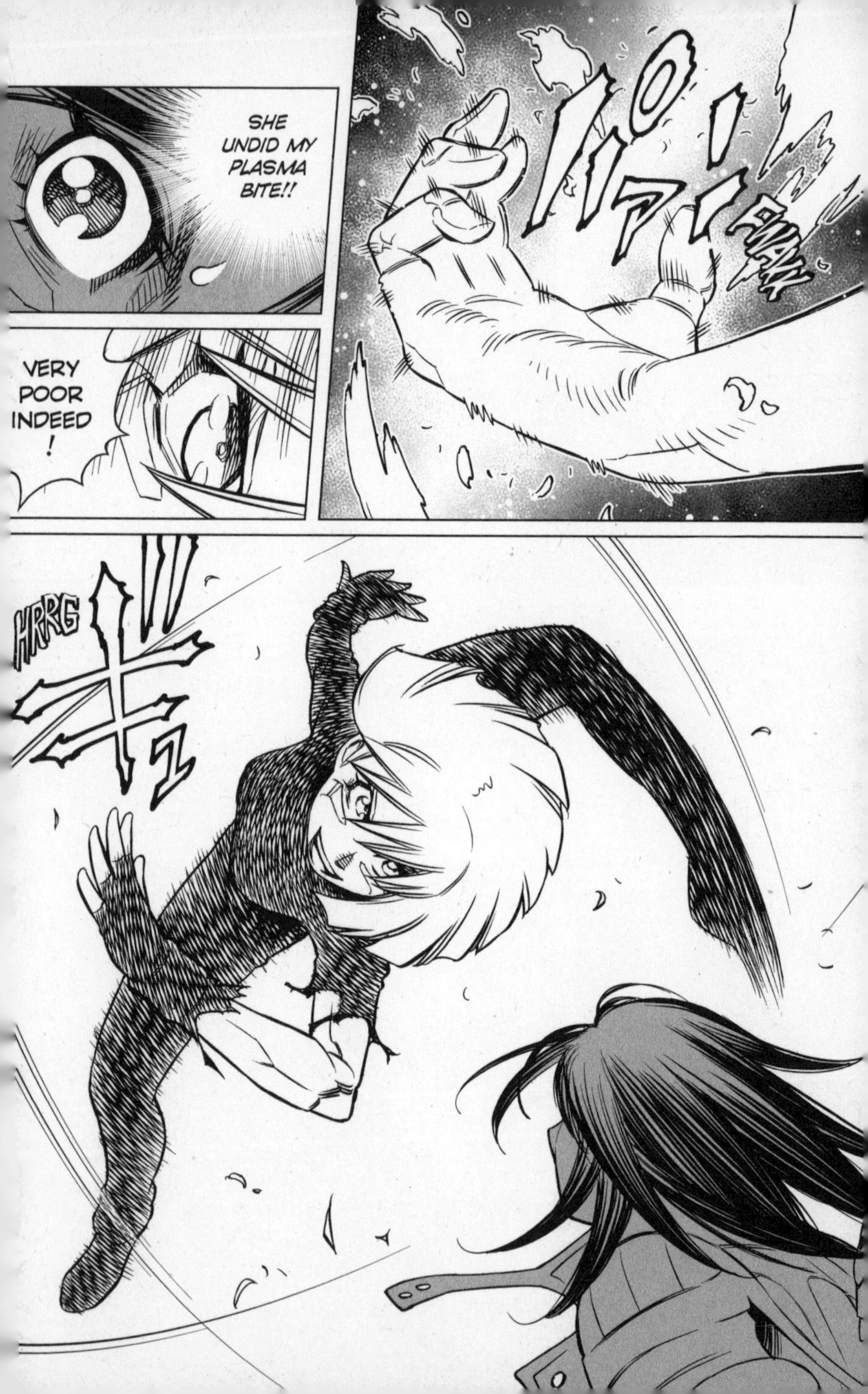
PWAK
SHE UNDID MY PLASMA BITE!!
VERY POOR INDEED!
HRRG

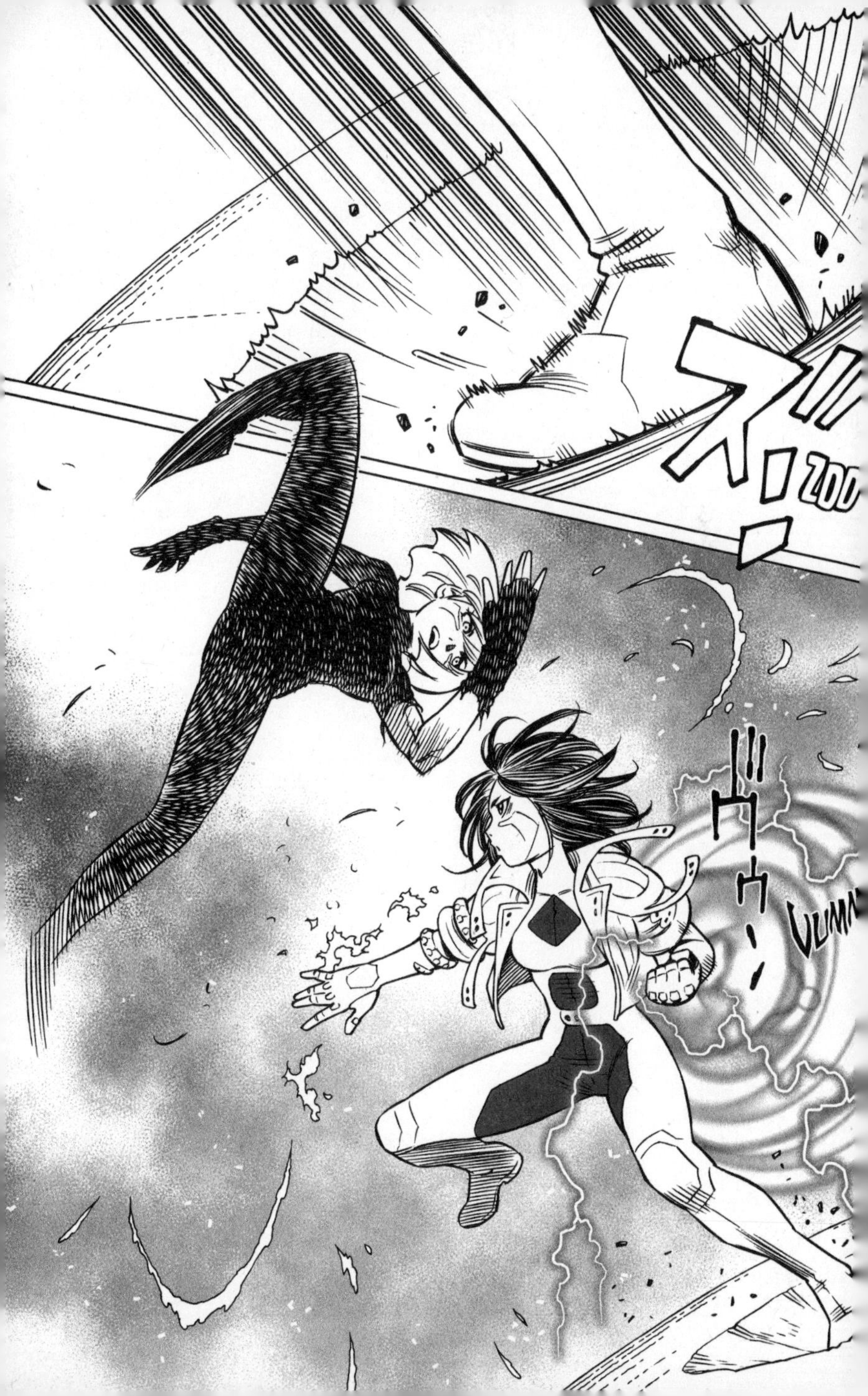
ズ!
ZOO
ヴゥー
VUMM

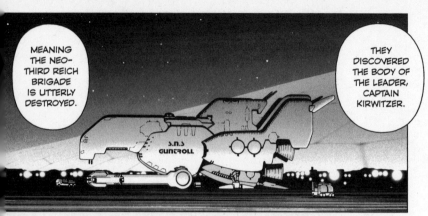

THEY DISCOVERED THE BODY OF THE LEADER, CAPTAIN KIRWITZER.
S.N.S GUNTROLL
MEANING THE NEO-THIRD REICH BRIGADE IS UTTERLY DESTROYED.
WHAT YOU'RE HOLDING IS THE AUTOPSY REPORT FROM THE DEIMOS COMPANY, WHICH RECOVERED THE BODY.
male
e : Klaus Kirwitzer
IT HAS NOT BEEN MADE PUBLIC.
WH... WHAT IS THIS ?!

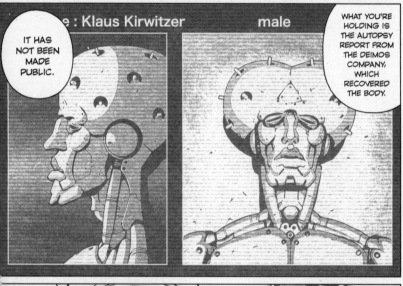

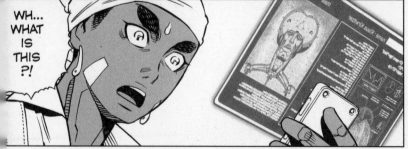

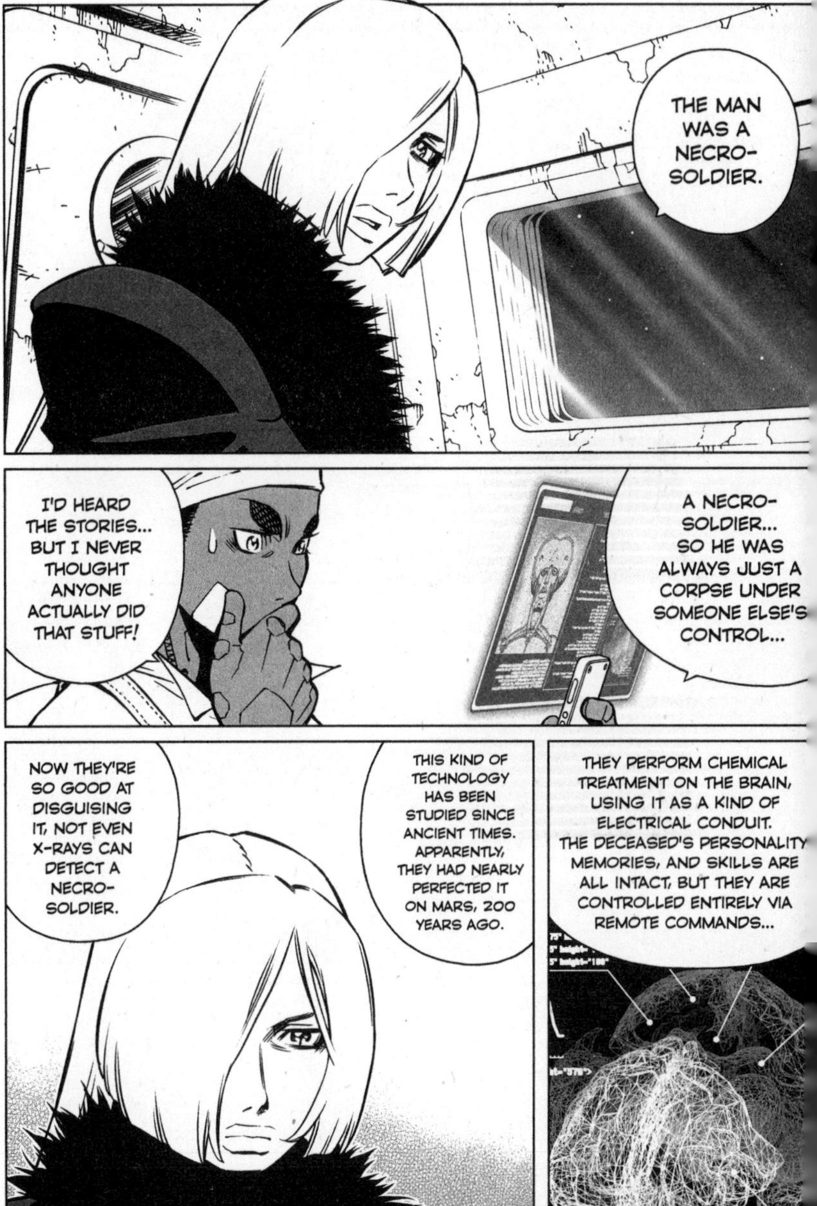
THE MAN WAS A NECRO-SOLDIER.
A NECRO-SOLDIER... SO HE WAS ALWAYS JUST A CORPSE UNDER SOMEONE ELSE'S CONTROL...
I'D HEARD THE STORIES... BUT I NEVER THOUGHT ANYONE ACTUALLY DID THAT STUFF!
THEY PERFORM CHEMICAL TREATMENT ON THE BRAIN, USING IT AS A KIND OF ELECTRICAL CONDUIT. THE DECEASED'S PERSONALITY, MEMORIES, AND SKILLS ARE ALL INTACT, BUT THEY ARE CONTROLLED ENTIRELY VIA REMOTE COMMANDS...
THIS KIND OF TECHNOLOGY HAS BEEN STUDIED SINCE ANCIENT TIMES. APPARENTLY, THEY HAD NEARLY PERFECTED IT ON MARS, 200 YEARS AGO.
NOW THEY'RE SO GOOD AT DISGUISING IT, NOT EVEN X-RAYS CAN DETECT A NECRO-SOLDIER.

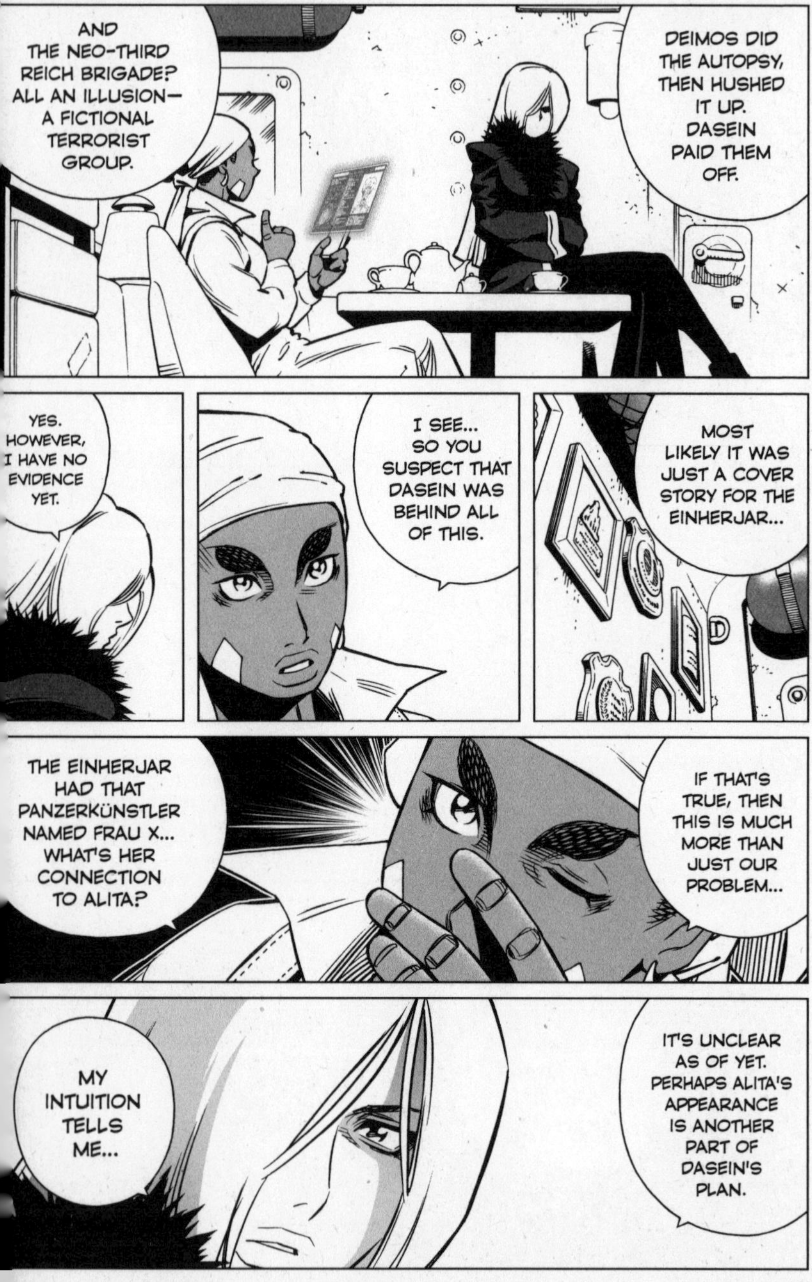
DEIMOS DID THE AUTOPSY, THEN HUSHED IT UP. DASEIN PAID THEM OFF.
AND THE NEO-THIRD REICH BRIGADE? ALL AN ILLUSION— A FICTIONAL TERRORIST GROUP.
MOST LIKELY IT WAS JUST A COVER STORY FOR THE EINHERJAR...
I SEE... SO YOU SUSPECT THAT DASEIN WAS BEHIND ALL OF THIS.
YES. HOWEVER, I HAVE NO EVIDENCE YET.
IF THAT'S TRUE, THEN THIS IS MUCH MORE THAN JUST OUR PROBLEM...
THE EINHERJAR HAD THAT PANZERKÜNSTLER NAMED FRAU X... WHAT'S HER CONNECTION TO ALITA?
IT'S UNCLEAR AS OF YET. PERHAPS ALITA'S APPEARANCE IS ANOTHER PART OF DASEIN'S PLAN.
MY INTUITION TELLS ME...

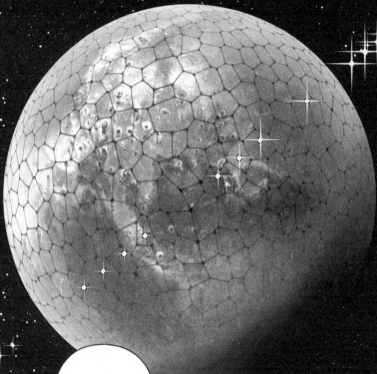

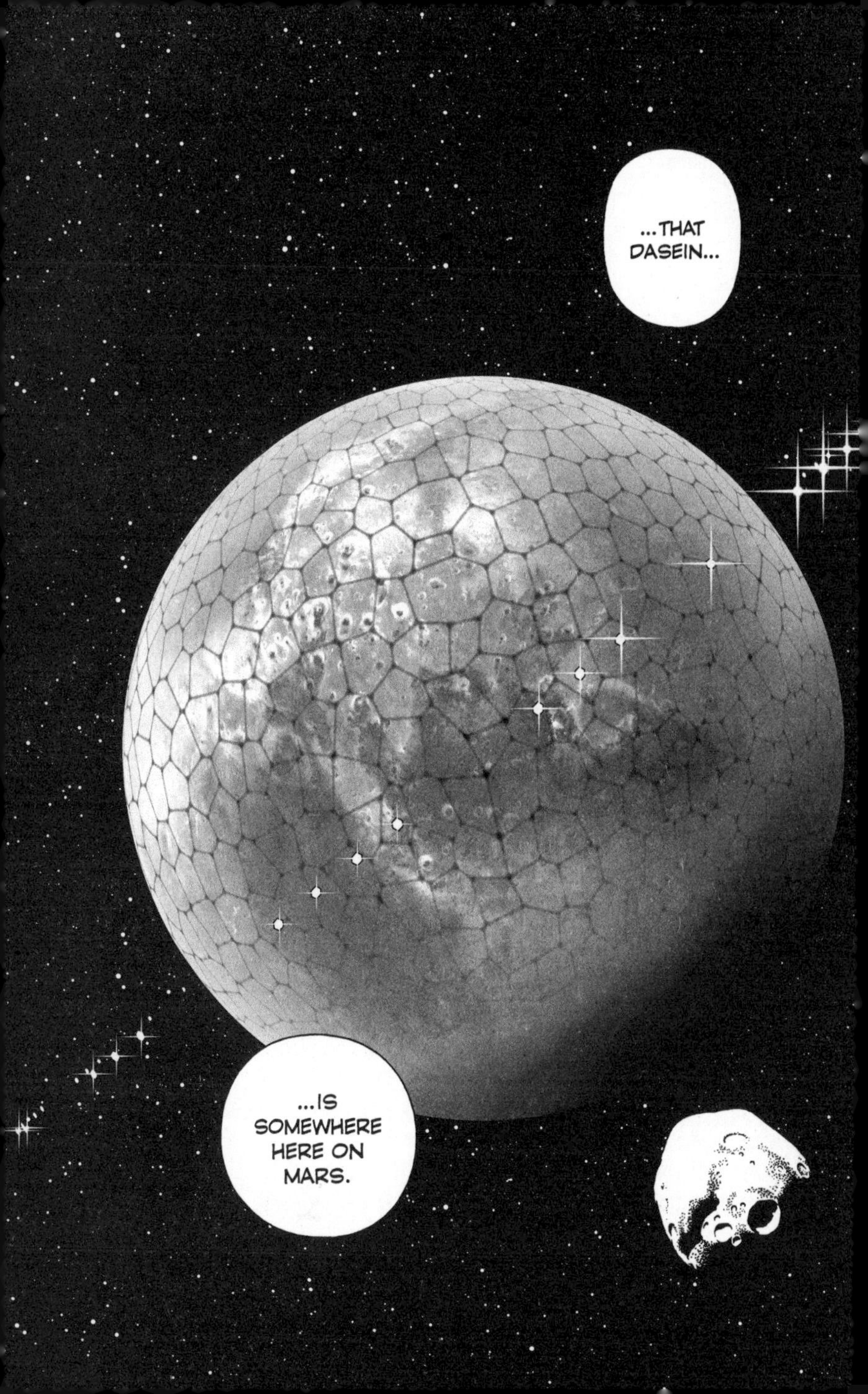

...THAT DASEIN...

...IS SOMEWHERE HERE ON MARS.

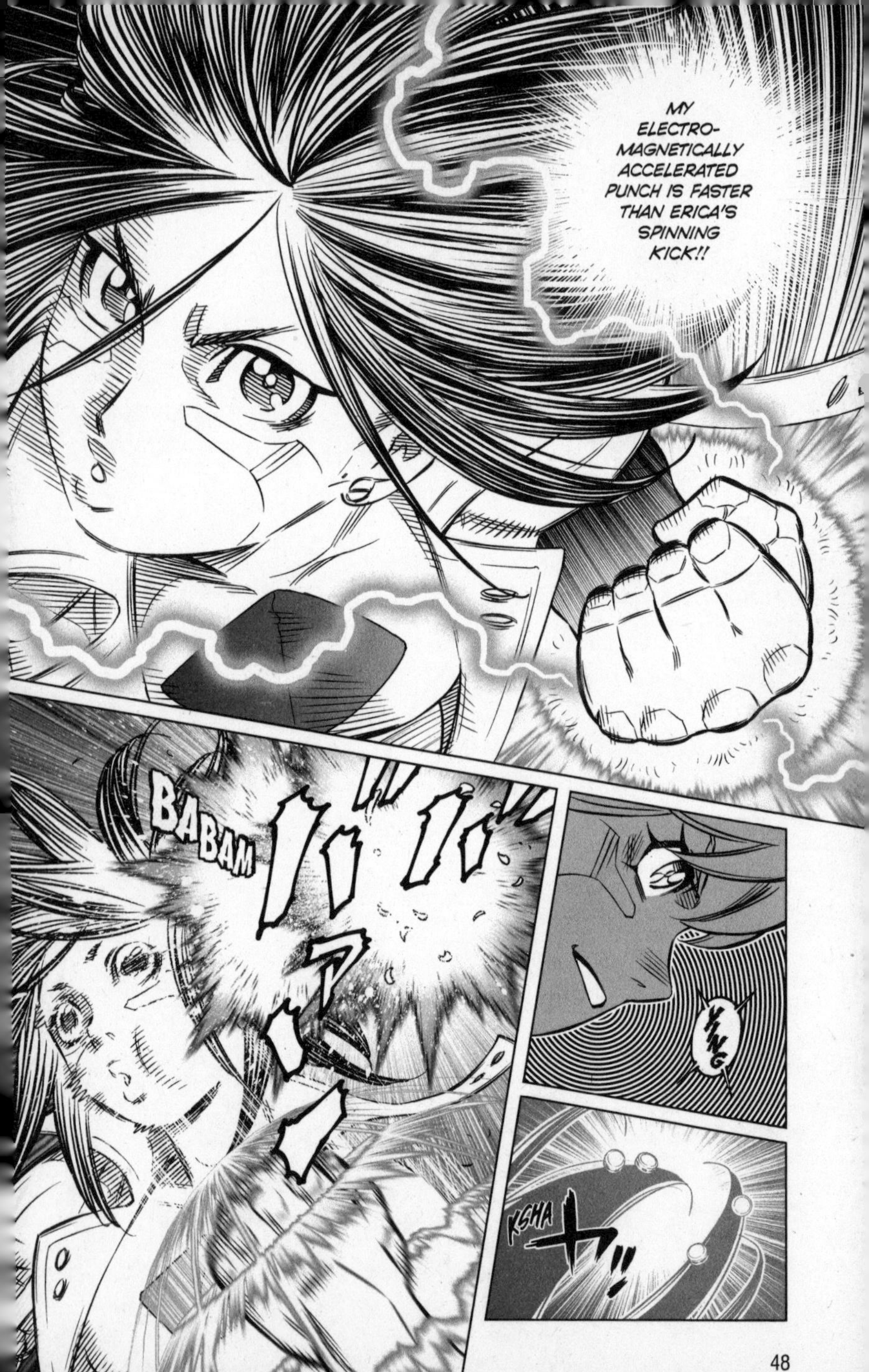
MY ELECTRO-MAGNETICALLY ACCELERATED PUNCH IS FASTER THAN ERICA'S SPINNING KICK!!
VWING
KSHA
BABAM

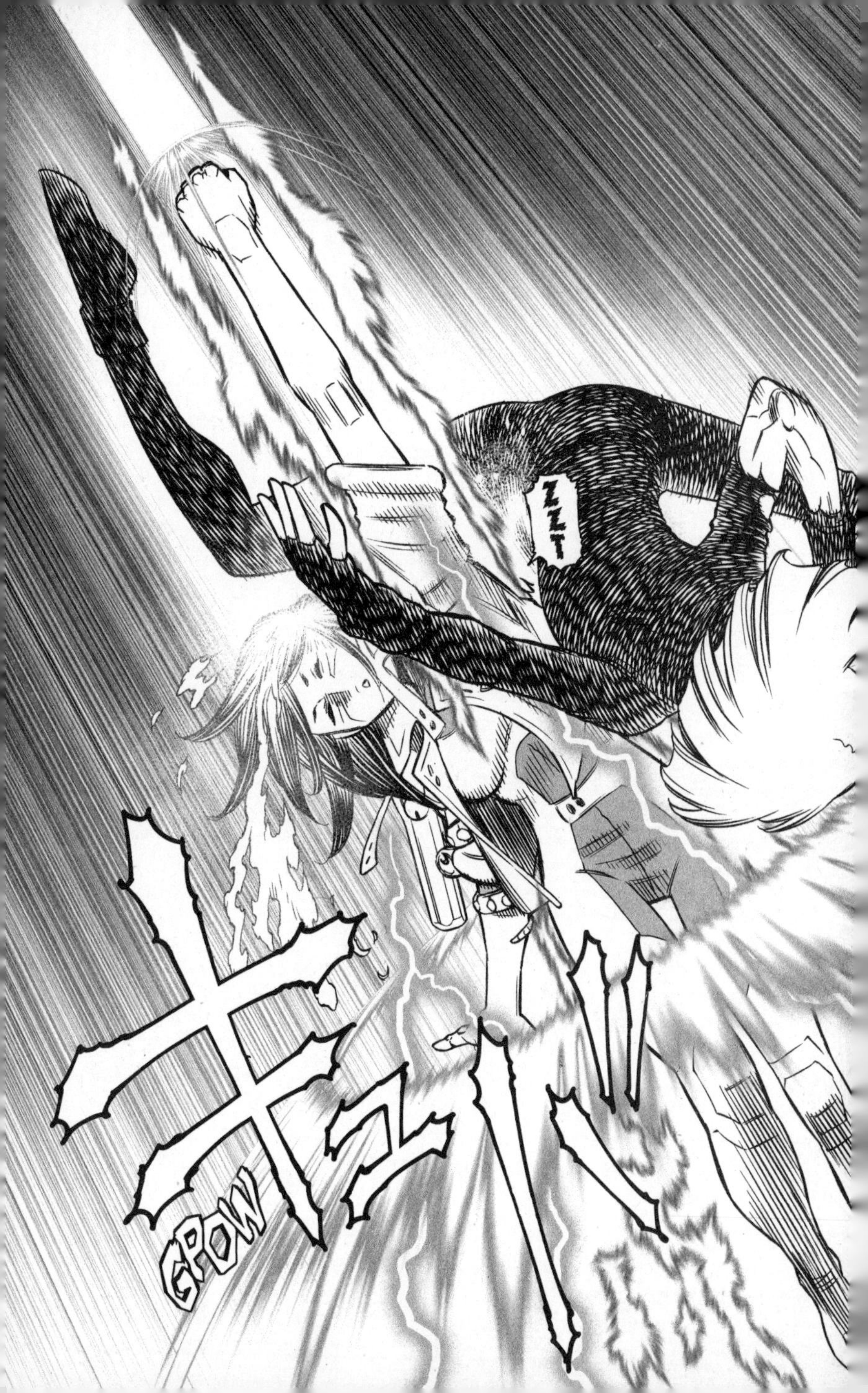
ZZZT
GPOW

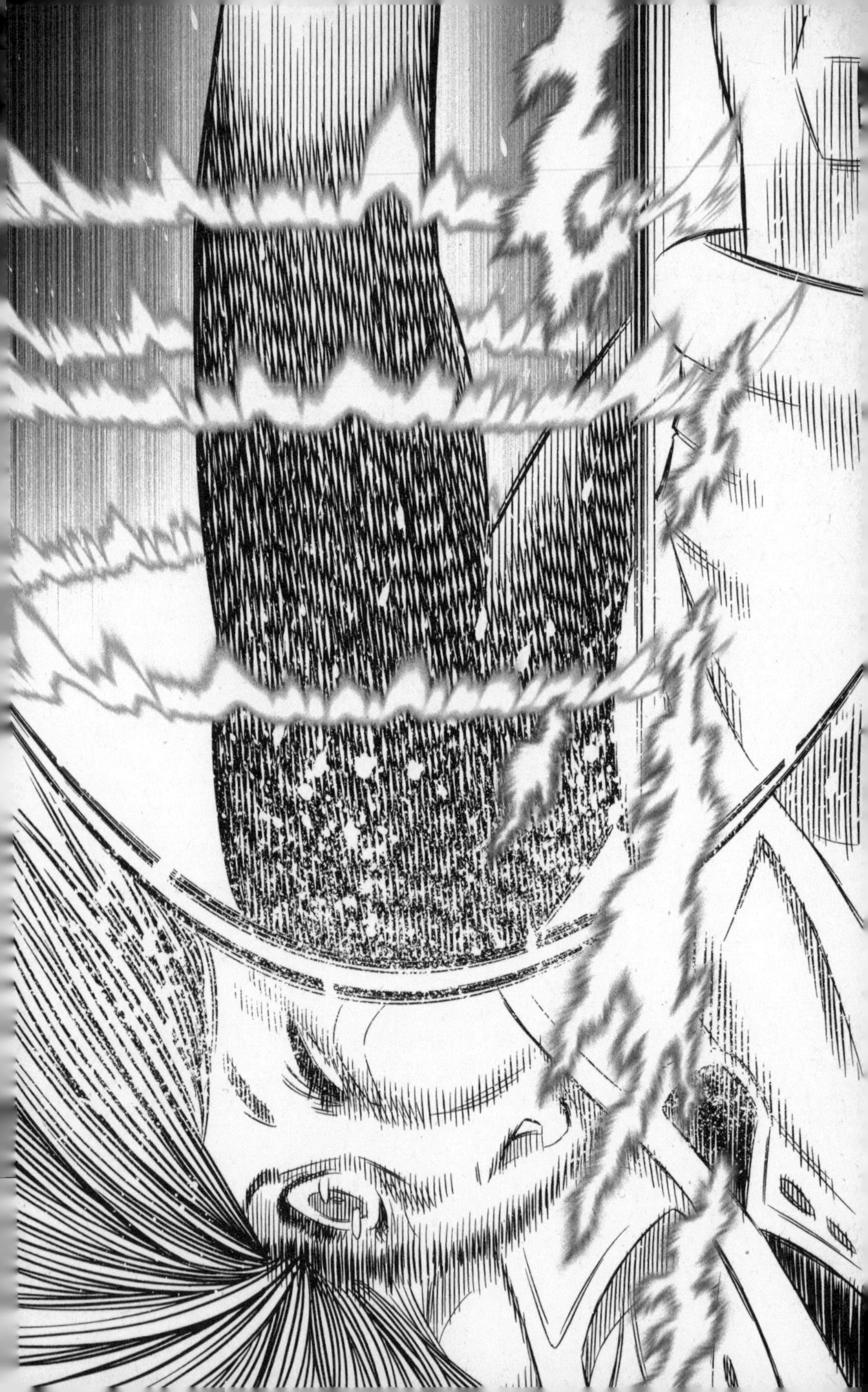

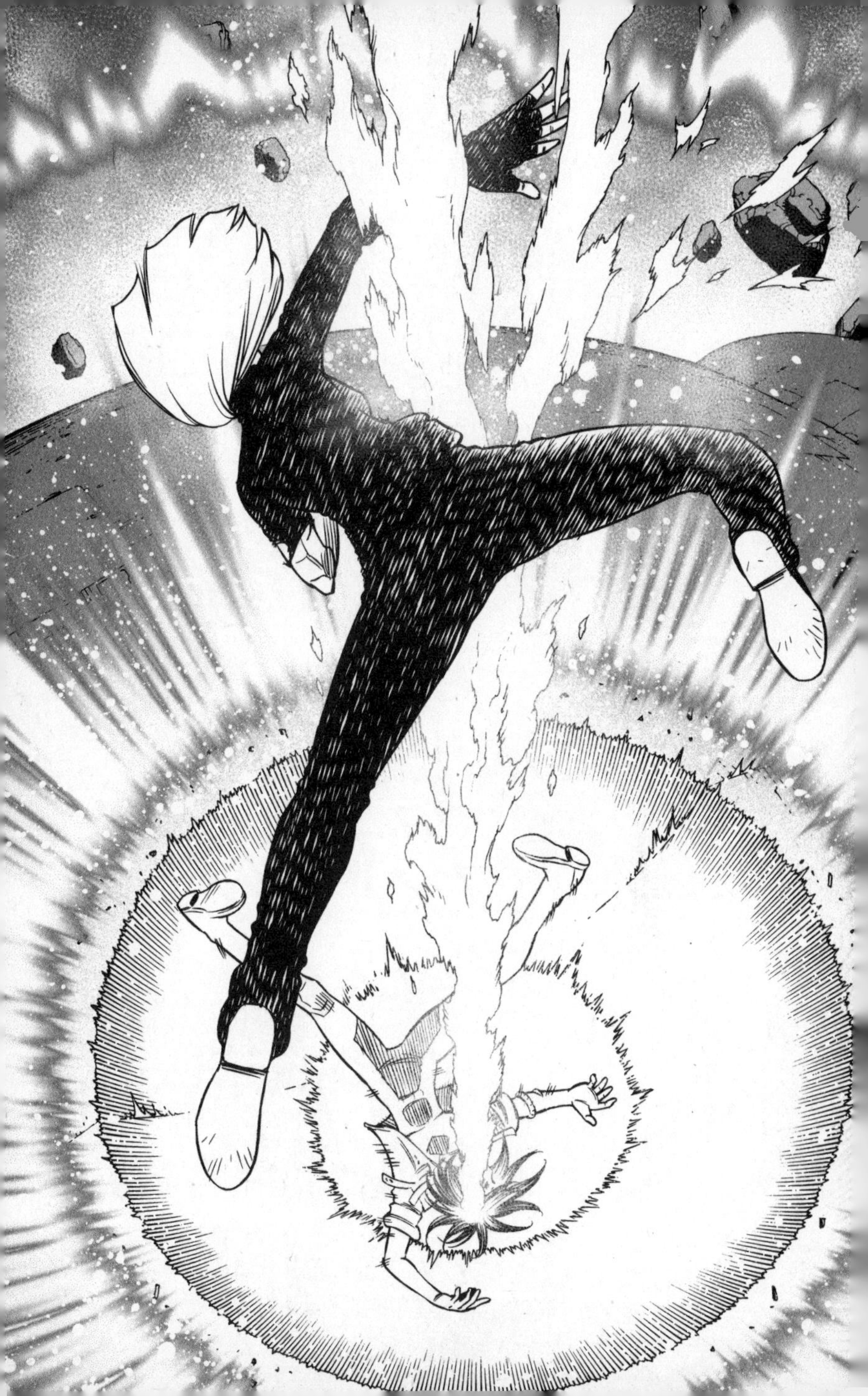

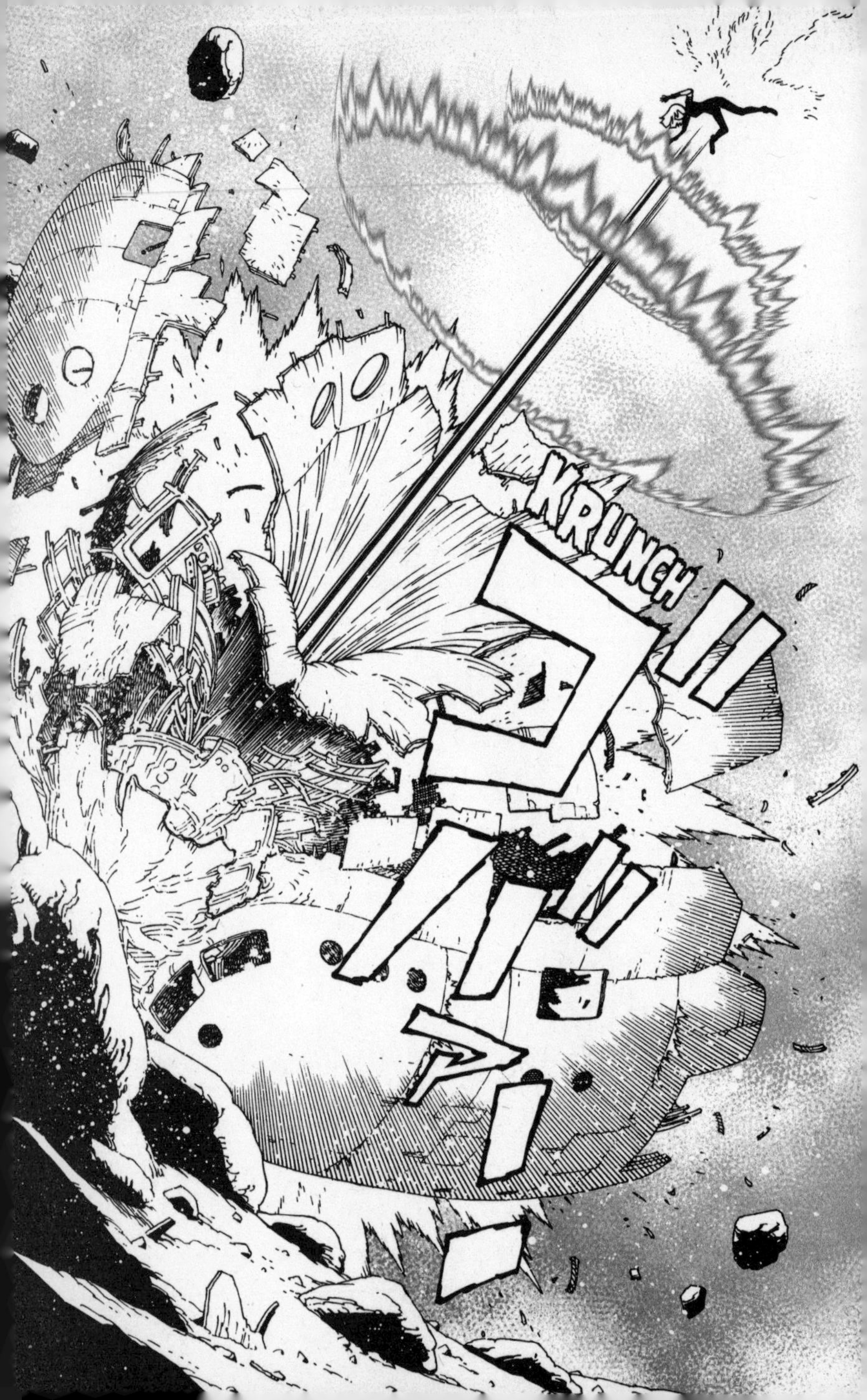
KRUNCH
ゴシャア

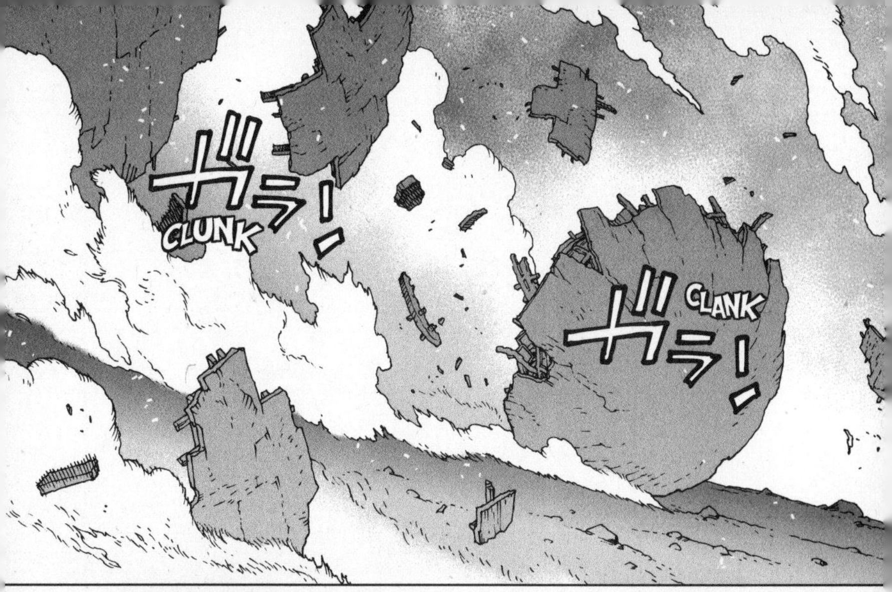
CLANK
ガラ!
ガラ!
CLUNK

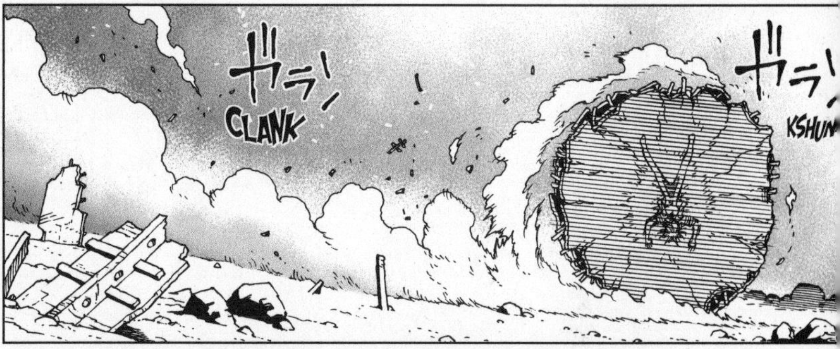
ガラ!
KSHUN
ガラ!
CLANK

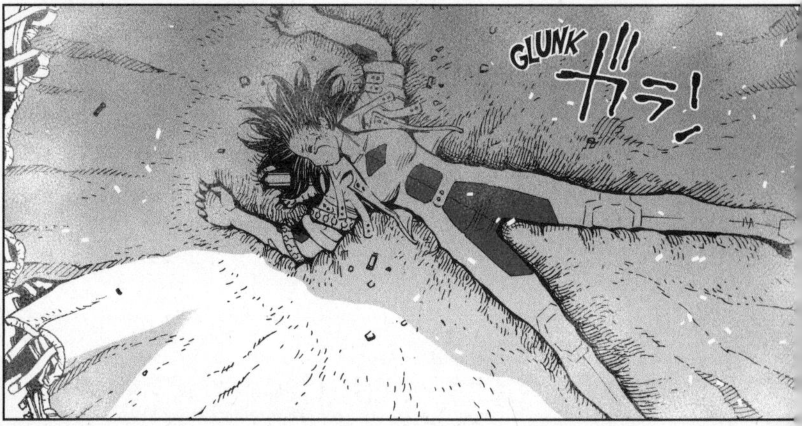
GLUNK
ガラ!

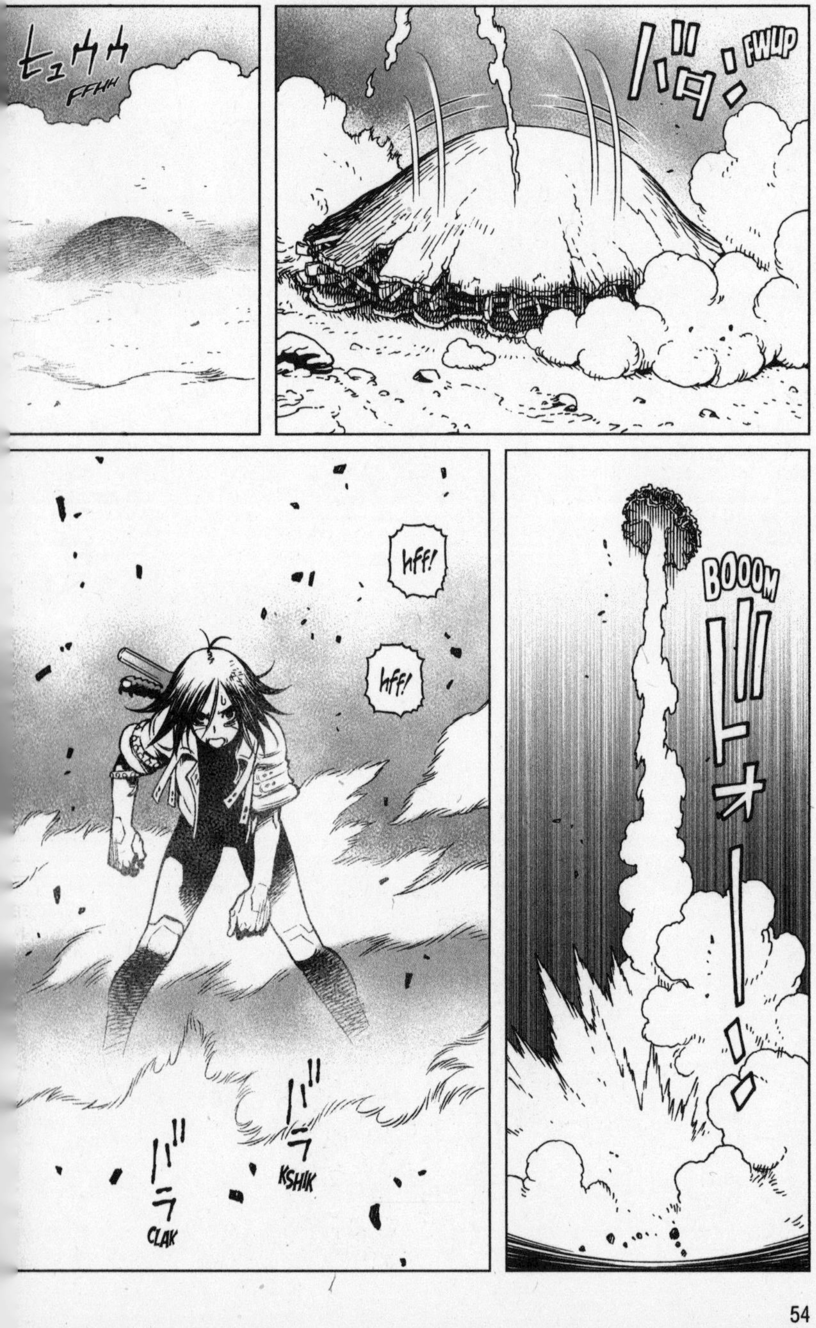
バダン
FWUP
ヒュウウ
FFHW
BOOOM
ドオー!
hff!
hff!
バラ
KSHIK
バラ
CLAK

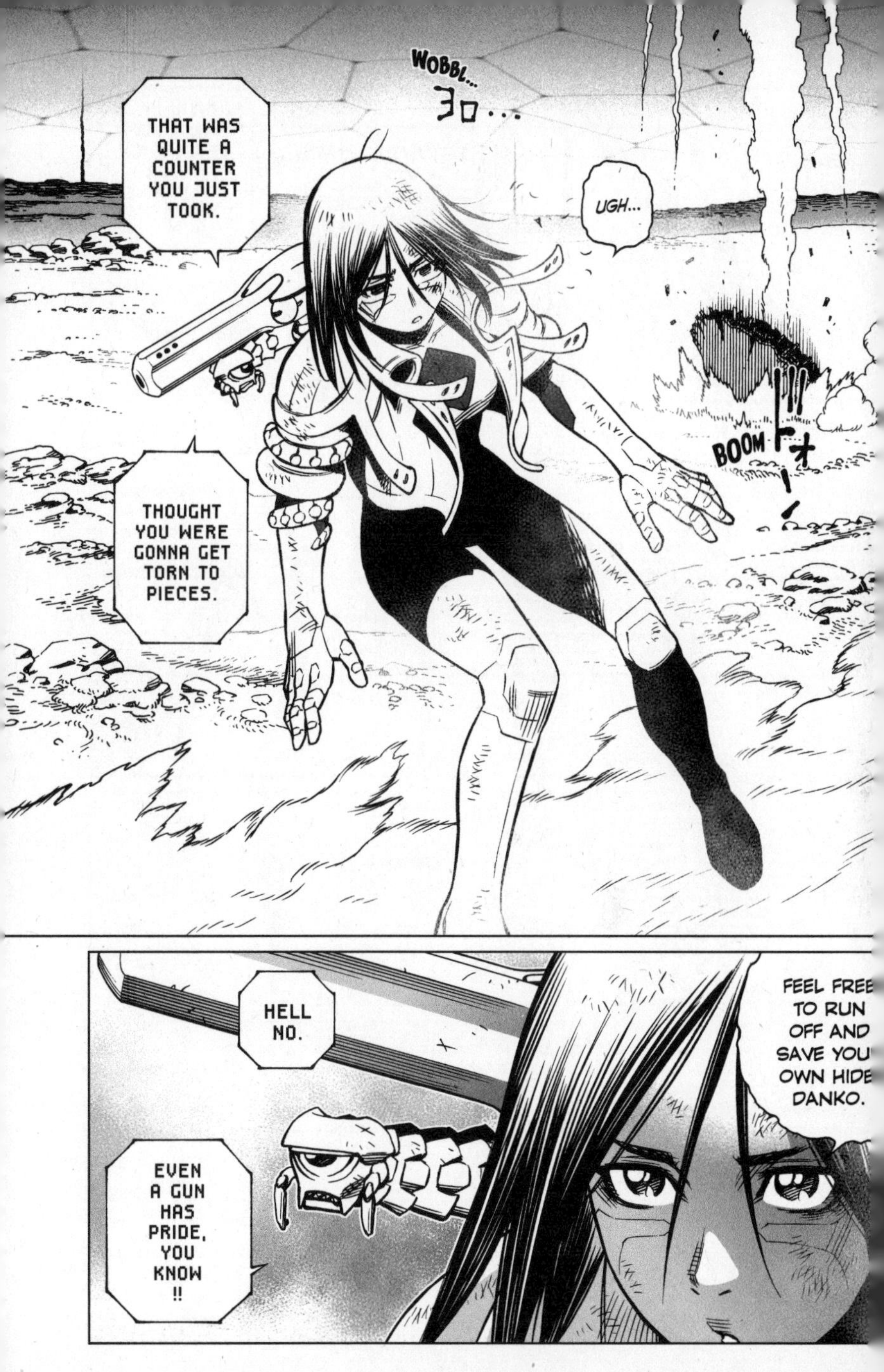
WOBBL... ヨロ...
UGH...
BOOM ドォ
THAT WAS QUITE A COUNTER YOU JUST TOOK.
THOUGHT YOU WERE GONNA GET TORN TO PIECES.
FEEL FREE TO RUN OFF AND SAVE YOU OWN HIDE DANKO.
HELL NO.
EVEN A GUN HAS PRIDE, YOU KNOW!!

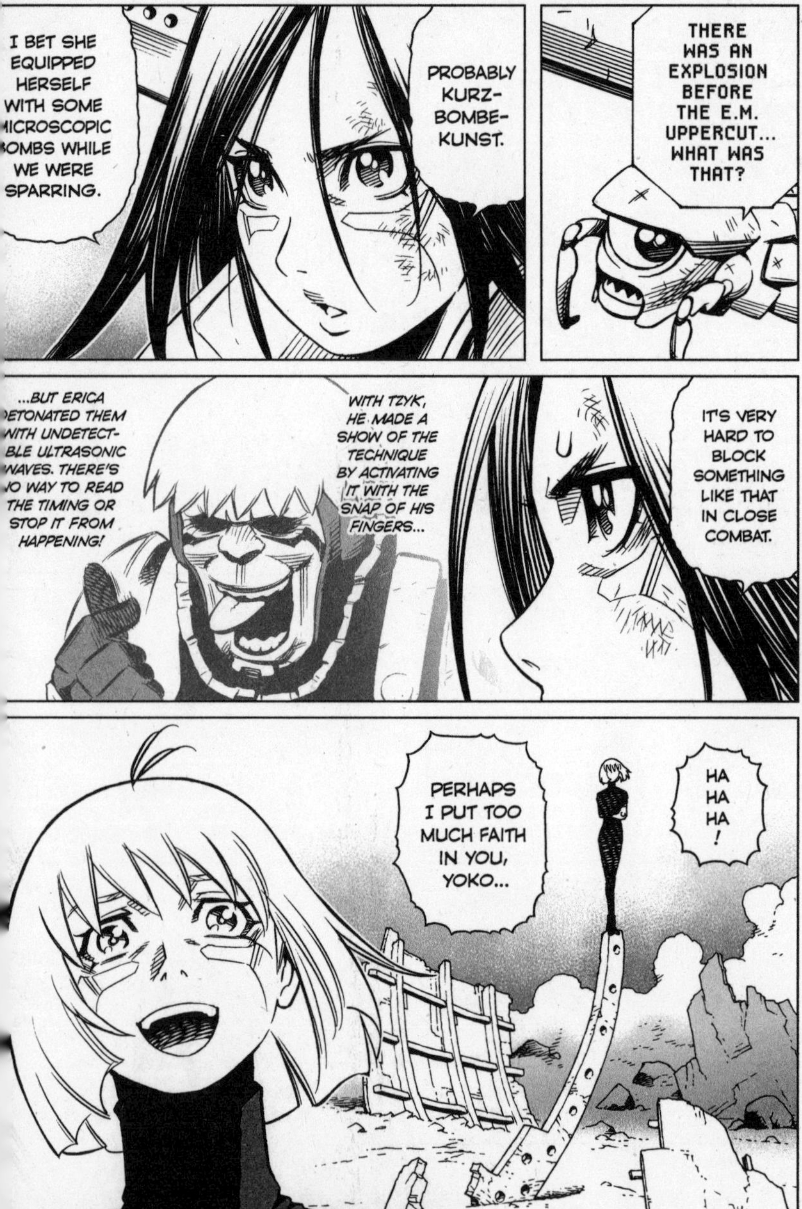
THERE WAS AN EXPLOSION BEFORE THE E.M. UPPERCUT... WHAT WAS THAT?
PROBABLY KURZ-BOMBE-KUNST.
I BET SHE EQUIPPED HERSELF WITH SOME ICROSCOPIC OMBS WHILE WE WERE SPARRING.
IT'S VERY HARD TO BLOCK SOMETHING LIKE THAT IN CLOSE COMBAT.
WITH TZYK, HE MADE A SHOW OF THE TECHNIQUE BY ACTIVATING IT WITH THE SNAP OF HIS FINGERS...
...BUT ERICA ETONATED THEM ITH UNDETECT-BLE ULTRASONIC AVES. THERE'S O WAY TO READ THE TIMING OR STOP IT FROM HAPPENING!
HA HA HA!
PERHAPS I PUT TOO MUCH FAITH IN YOU, YOKO...

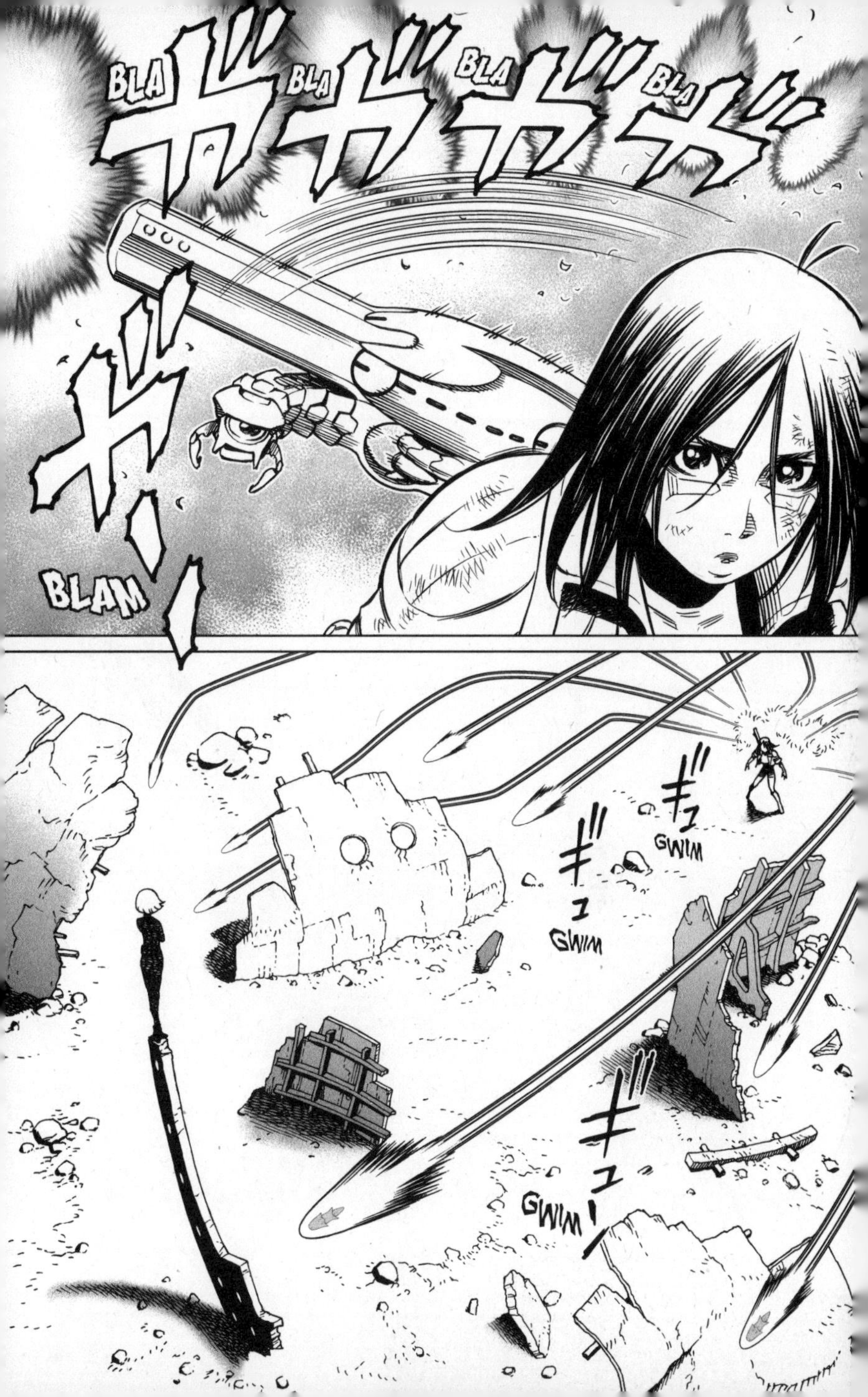
BLA BLA BLA BLA
BLAM
GWIM
GWIM
GWIM!

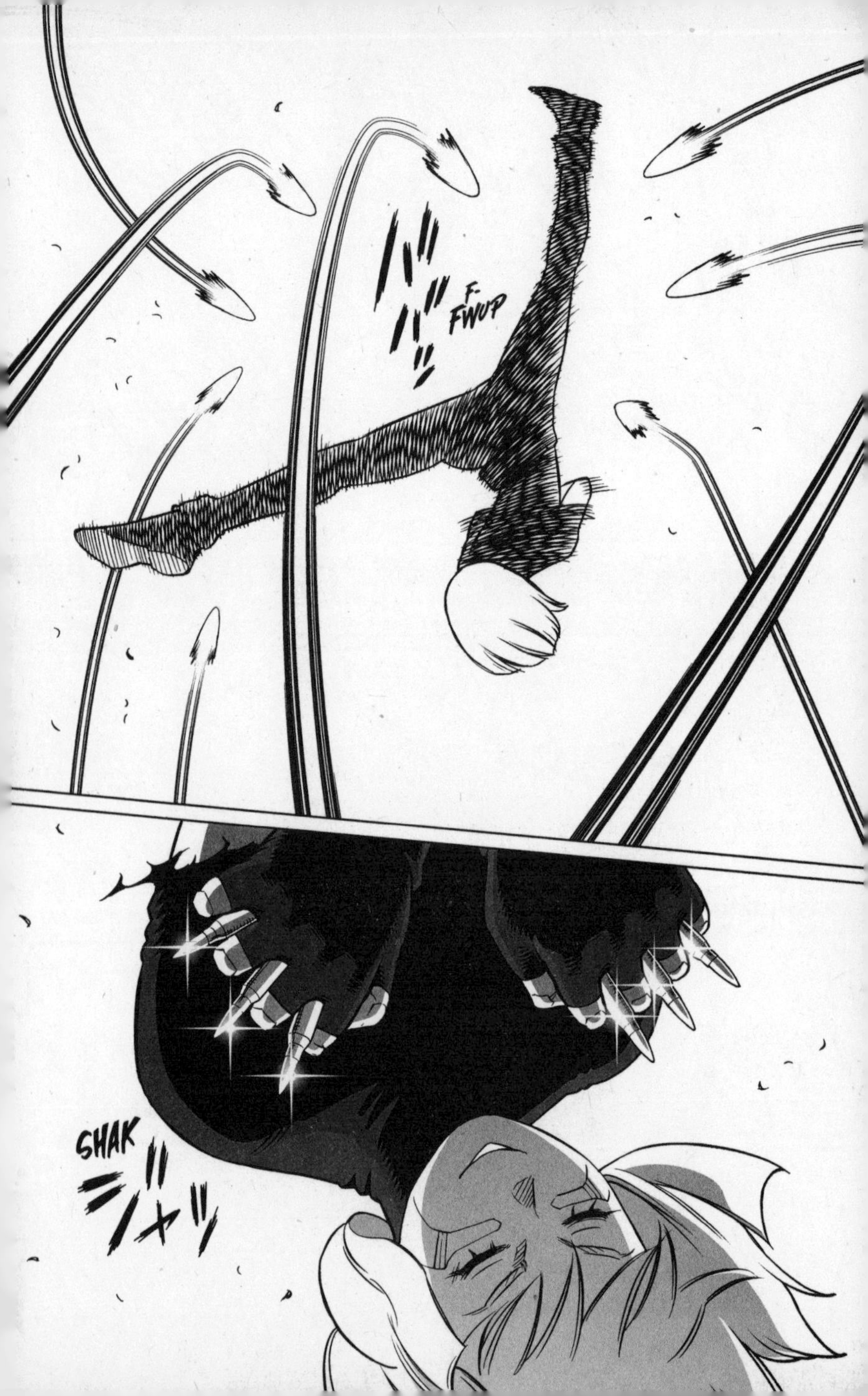
F-FWUP
SHAK

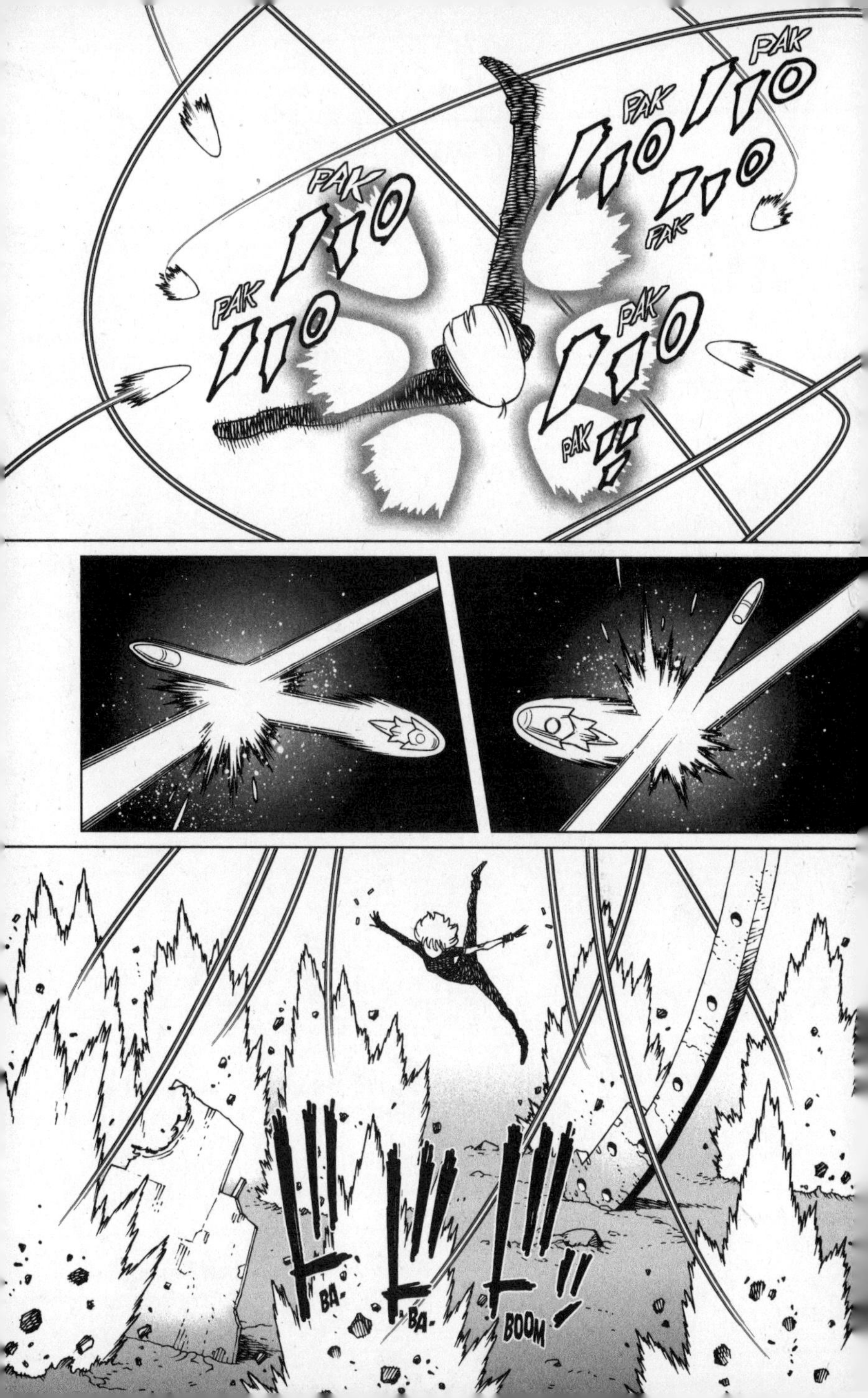
PAK
PAK
PAK
PAK
PAK
PAK
PAK
BA-
BA-
BOOM!!

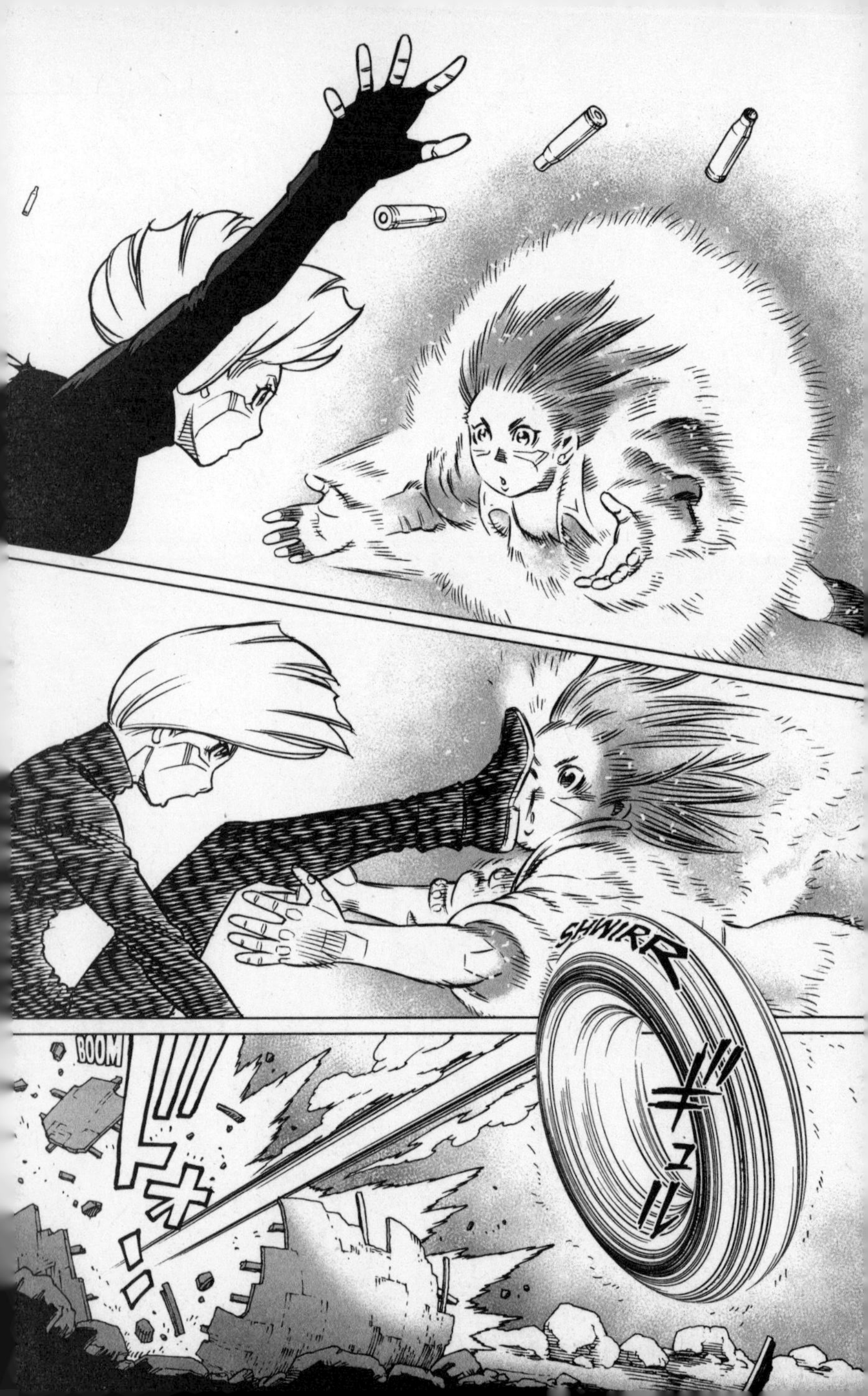
SHWIRR
BOOM

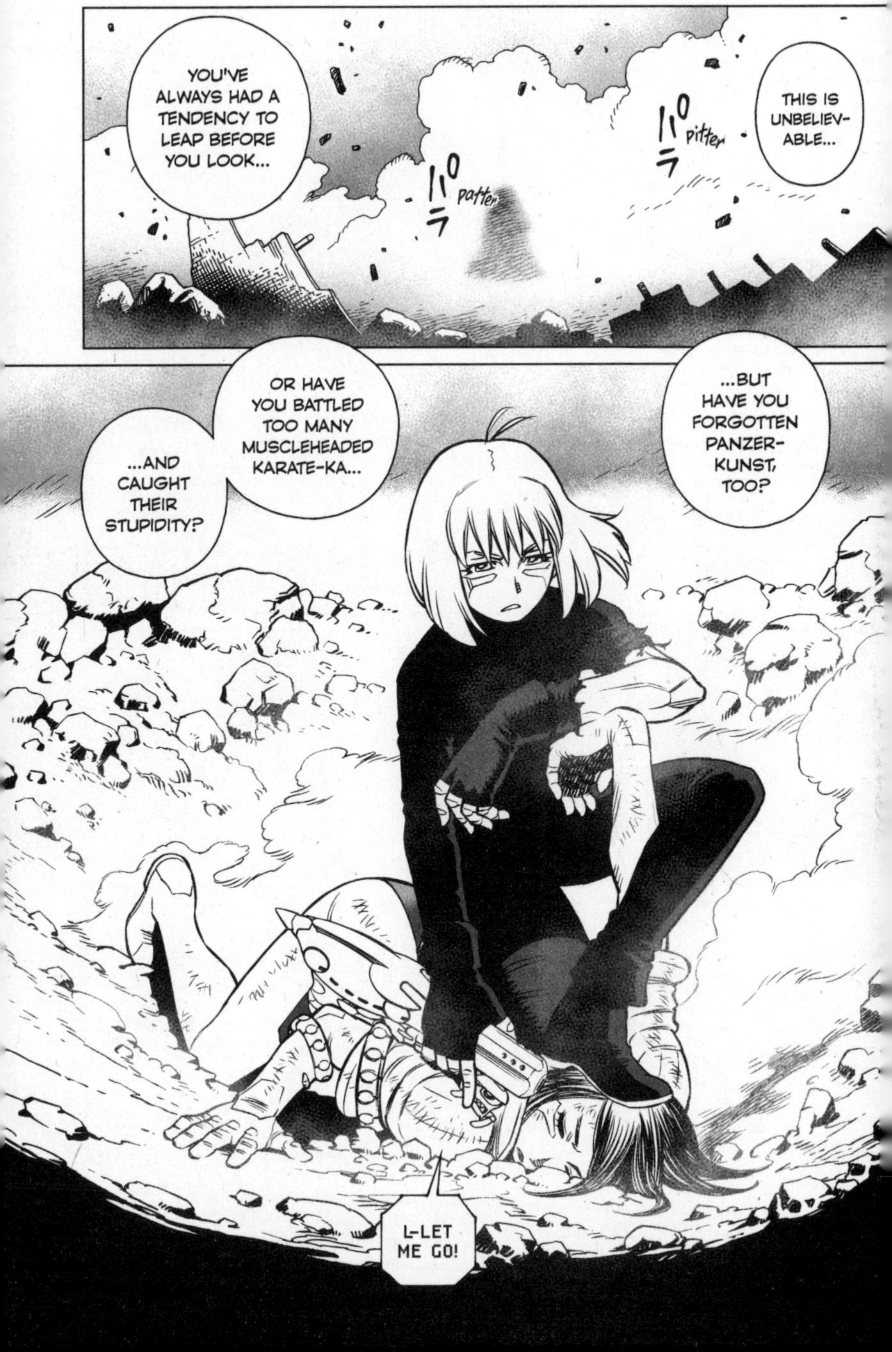
THIS IS UNBELIEV-ABLE...
pitter
patter
YOU'VE ALWAYS HAD A TENDENCY TO LEAP BEFORE YOU LOOK...
...BUT HAVE YOU FORGOTTEN PANZER-KUNST, TOO?
OR HAVE YOU BATTLED TOO MANY MUSCLEHEADED KARATE-KA...
...AND CAUGHT THEIR STUPIDITY?
L-LET ME GO!

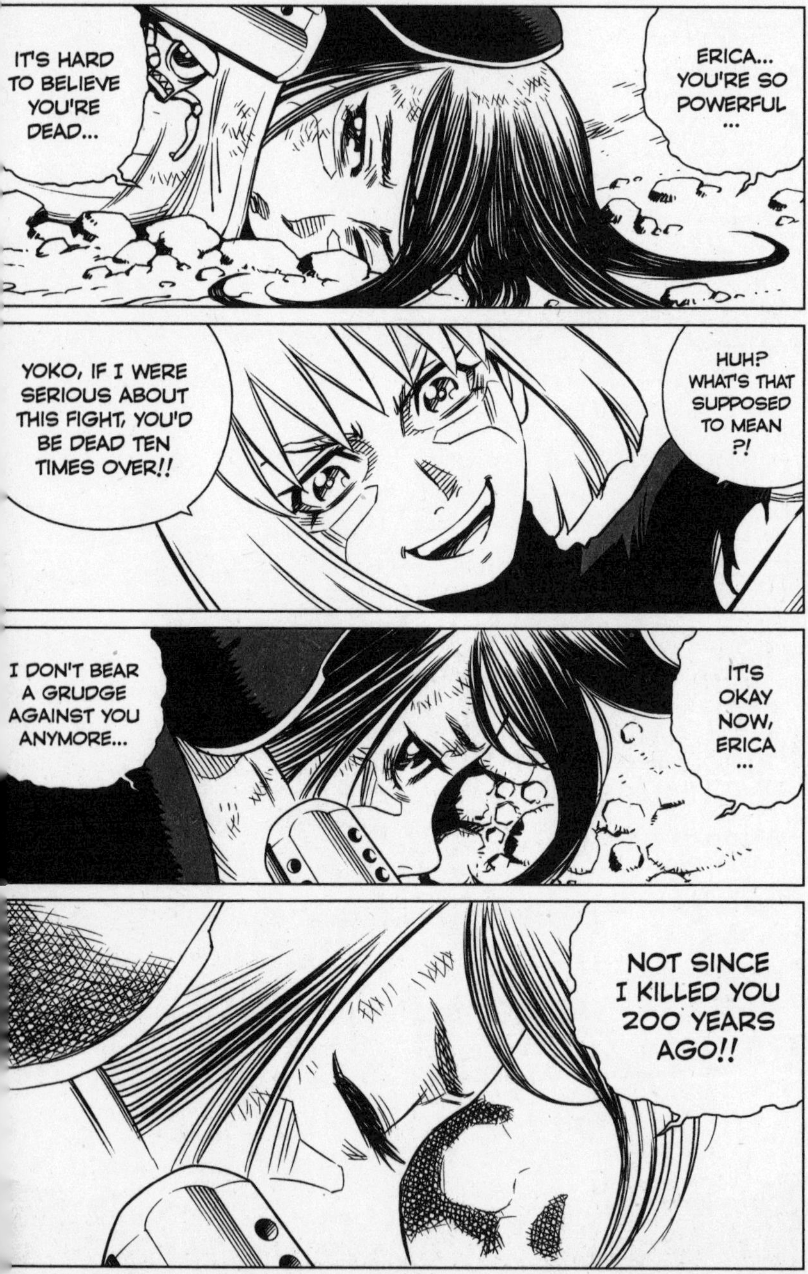
ERICA... YOU'RE SO POWERFUL ...
IT'S HARD TO BELIEVE YOU'RE DEAD...
HUH? WHAT'S THAT SUPPOSED TO MEAN ?!
YOKO, IF I WERE SERIOUS ABOUT THIS FIGHT, YOU'D BE DEAD TEN TIMES OVER!!
IT'S OKAY NOW, ERICA ...
I DON'T BEAR A GRUDGE AGAINST YOU ANYMORE...
NOT SINCE I KILLED YOU 200 YEARS AGO!!

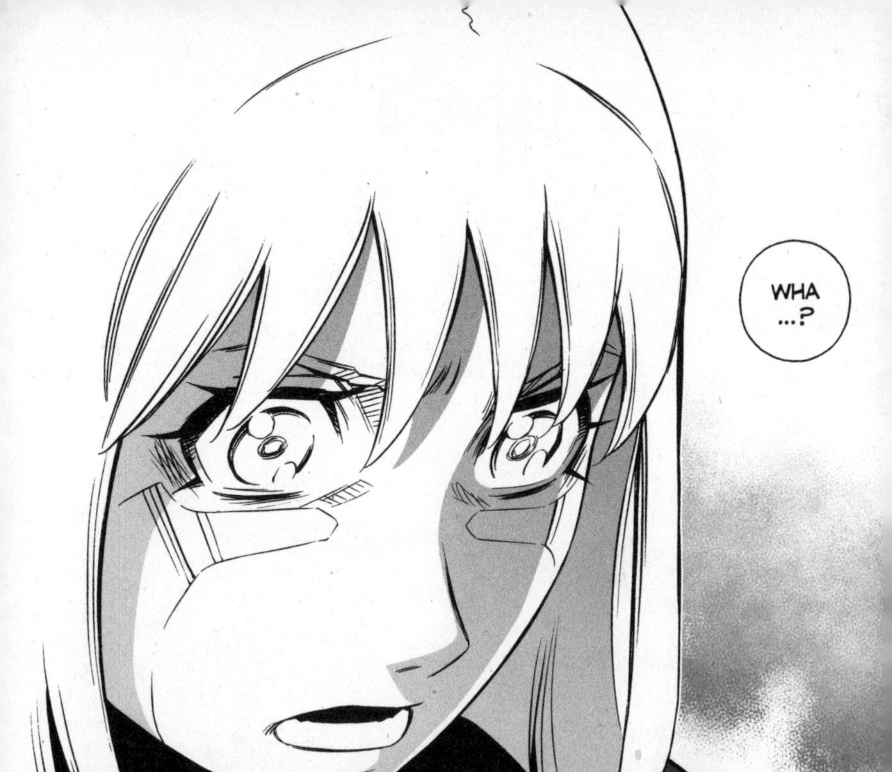
WHA
...?
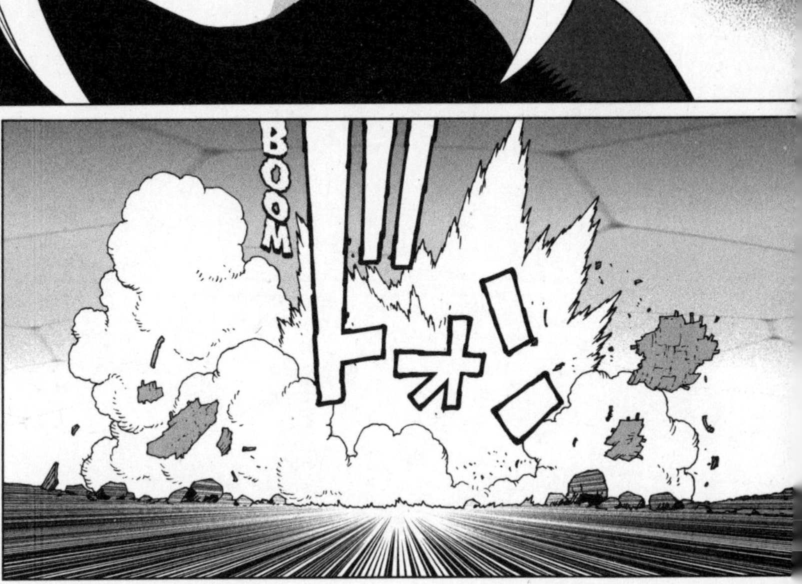
BOOM
ドオーン

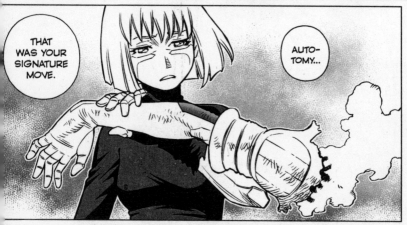

THAT WAS YOUR SIGNATURE MOVE.

AUTO-TOMY...

IF THAT'S A JOKE, IT'S NOT A FUNNY ONE...

YOU "KILLED" ME...?

THEN WHAT WOULD THAT MAKE ME? A GHOST?!

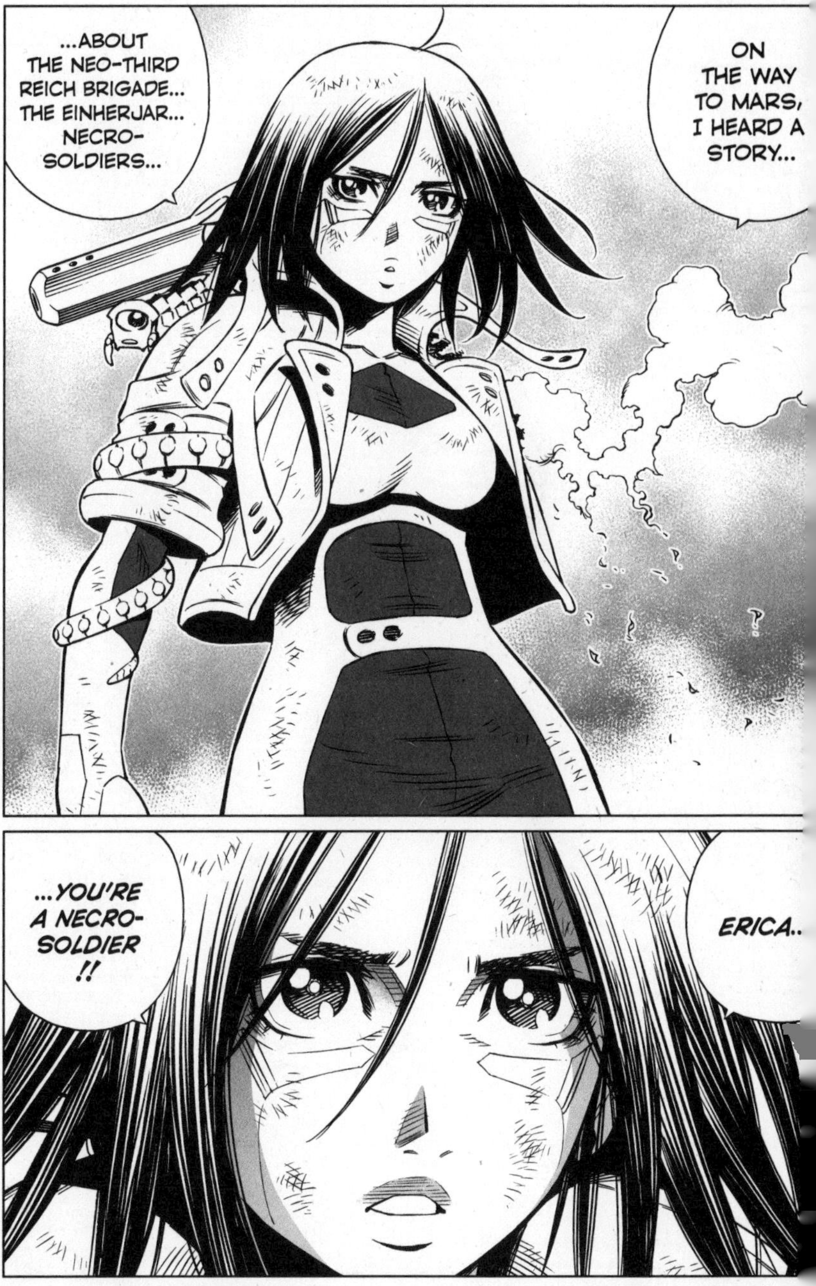
ON THE WAY TO MARS, I HEARD A STORY...
...ABOUT THE NEO-THIRD REICH BRIGADE... THE EINHERJAR... NECRO-SOLDIERS...
ERICA..
...YOU'RE A NECRO-SOLDIER !!

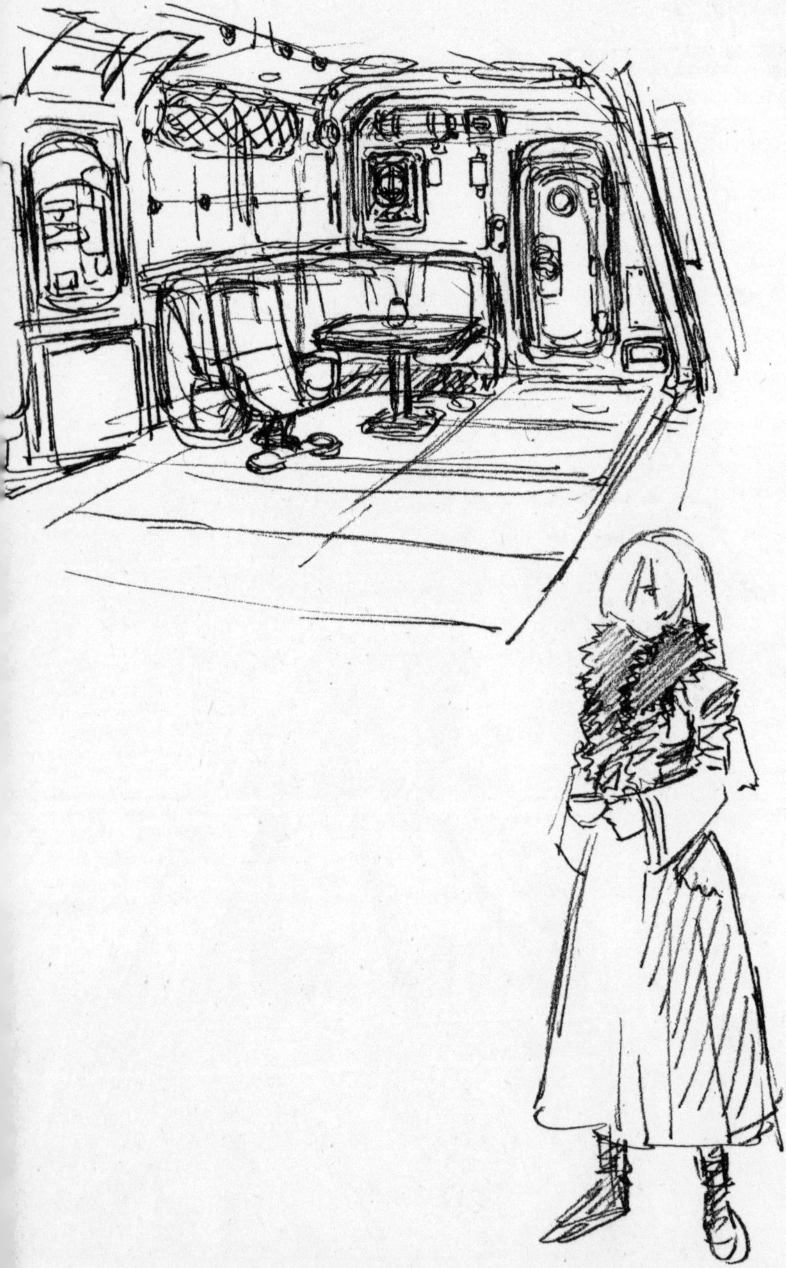

LOG:009

# EINHERJAR

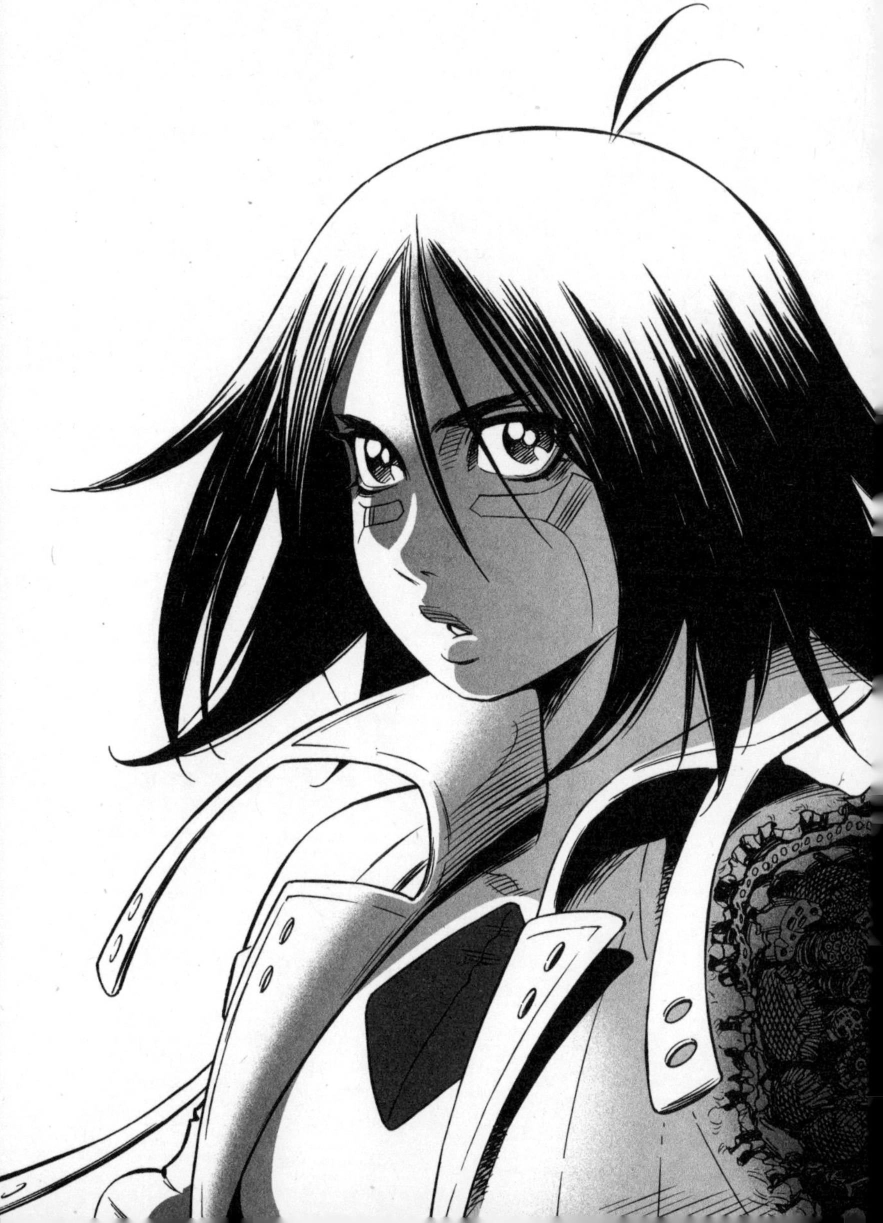

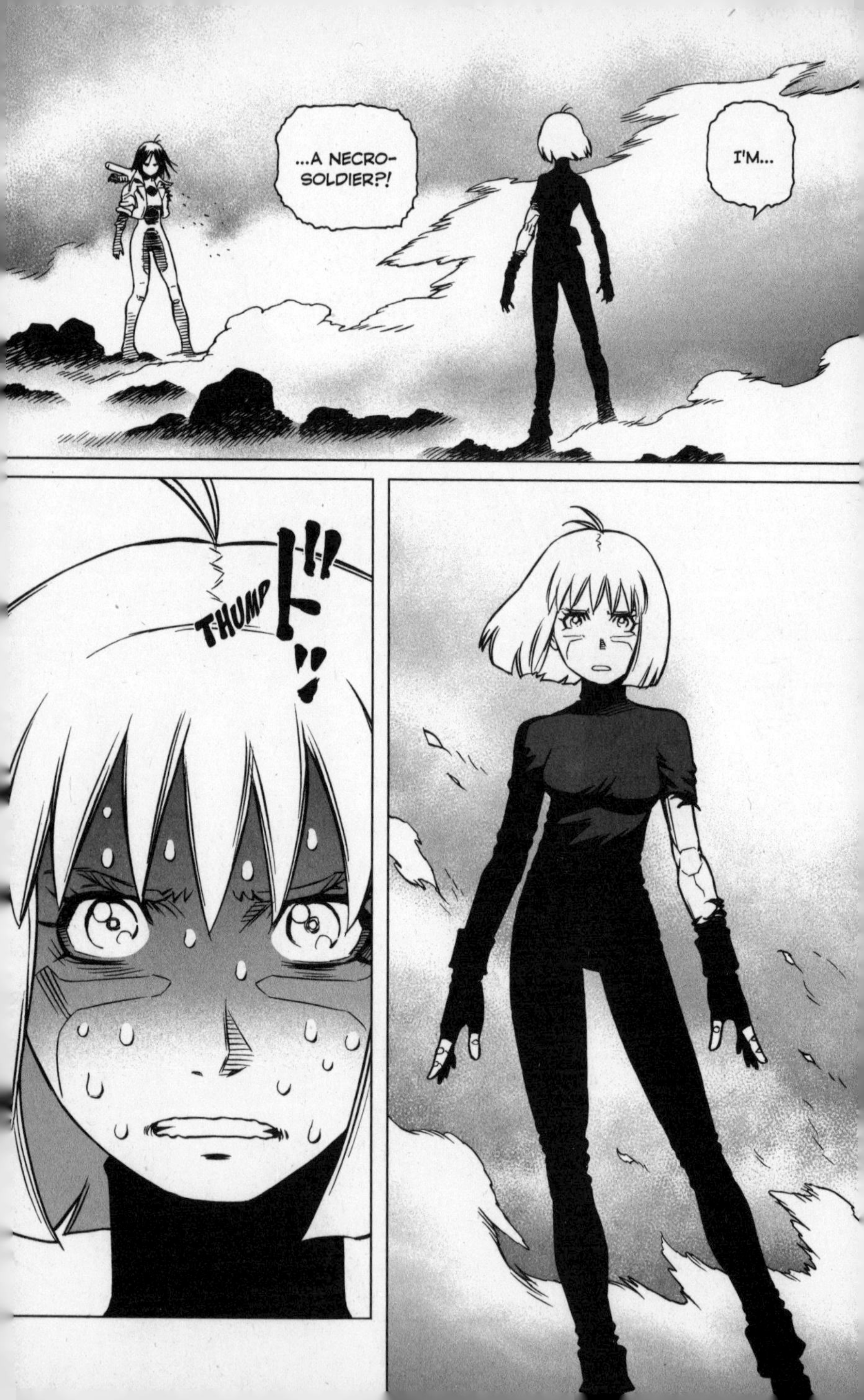
I'M...
...A NECRO-SOLDIER?!
THUMP

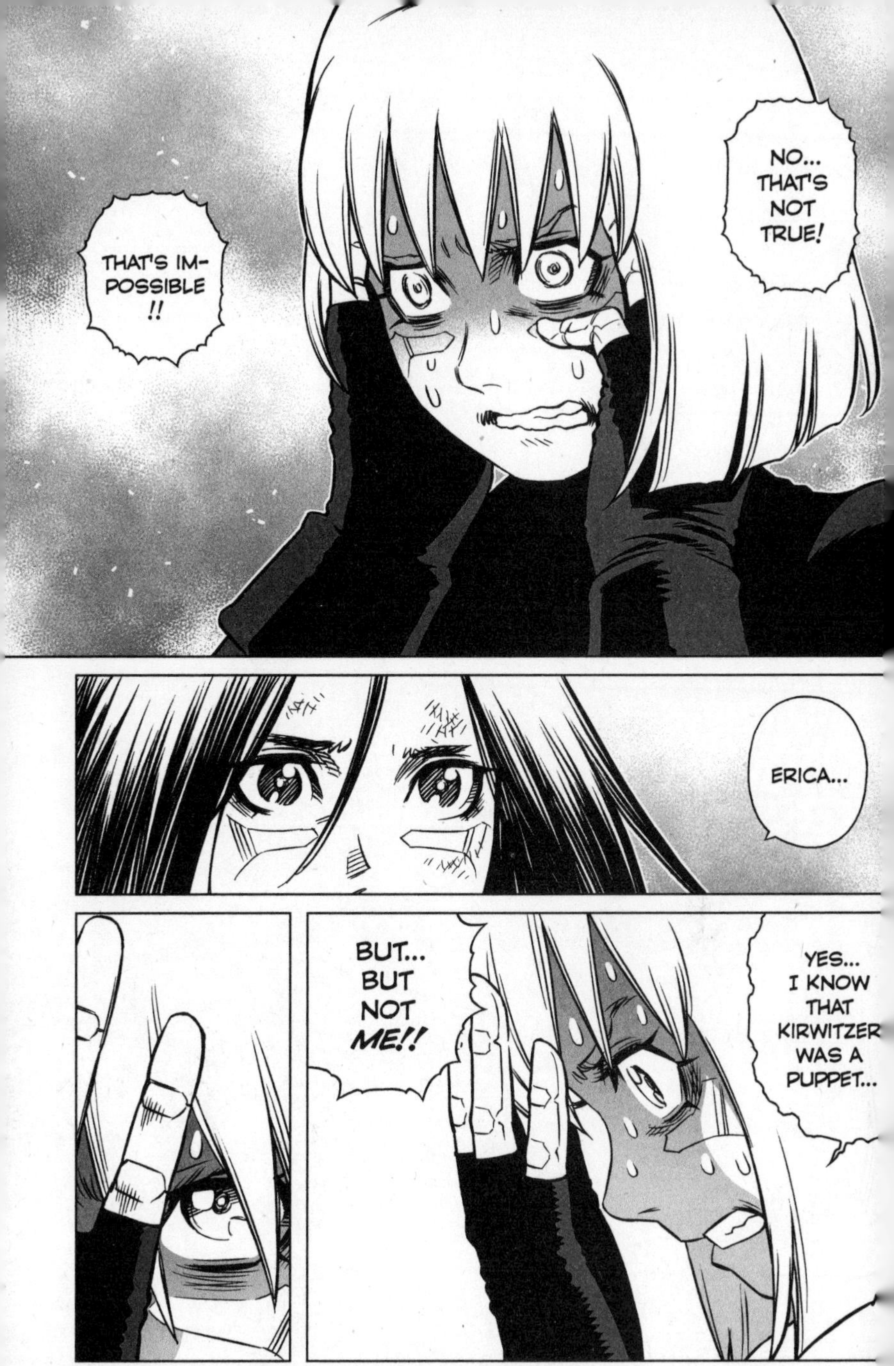
NO... THAT'S NOT TRUE!
THAT'S IM-POSSIBLE !!
ERICA...
YES... I KNOW THAT KIRWITZER WAS A PUPPET...
BUT... BUT NOT ME!!

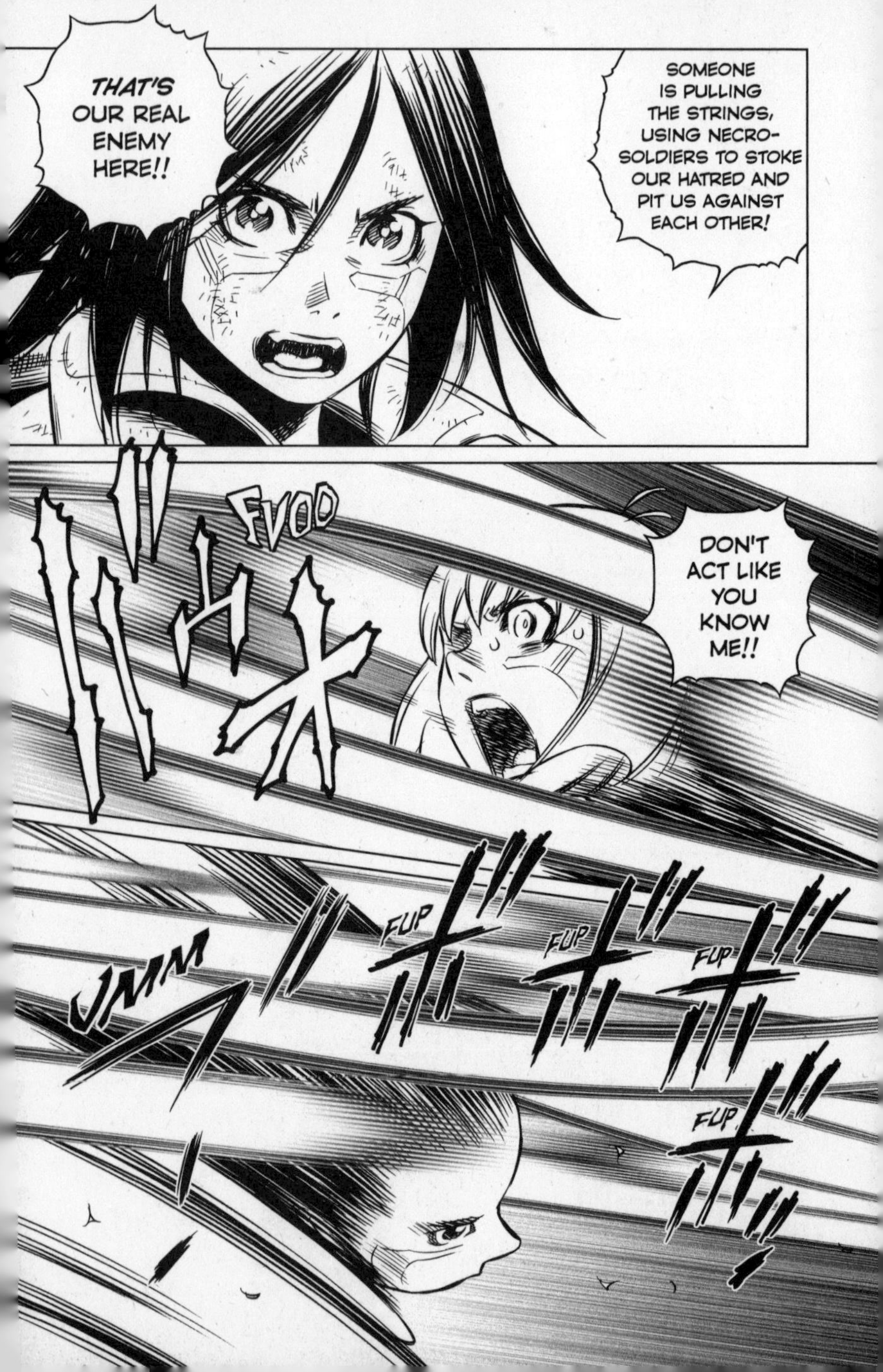
SOMEONE IS PULLING THE STRINGS, USING NECRO-SOLDIERS TO STOKE OUR HATRED AND PIT US AGAINST EACH OTHER!
*THAT'S* OUR REAL ENEMY HERE!!
DON'T ACT LIKE YOU KNOW ME!!
FVOO
FUP
FUP
FUP
FUP
JMM

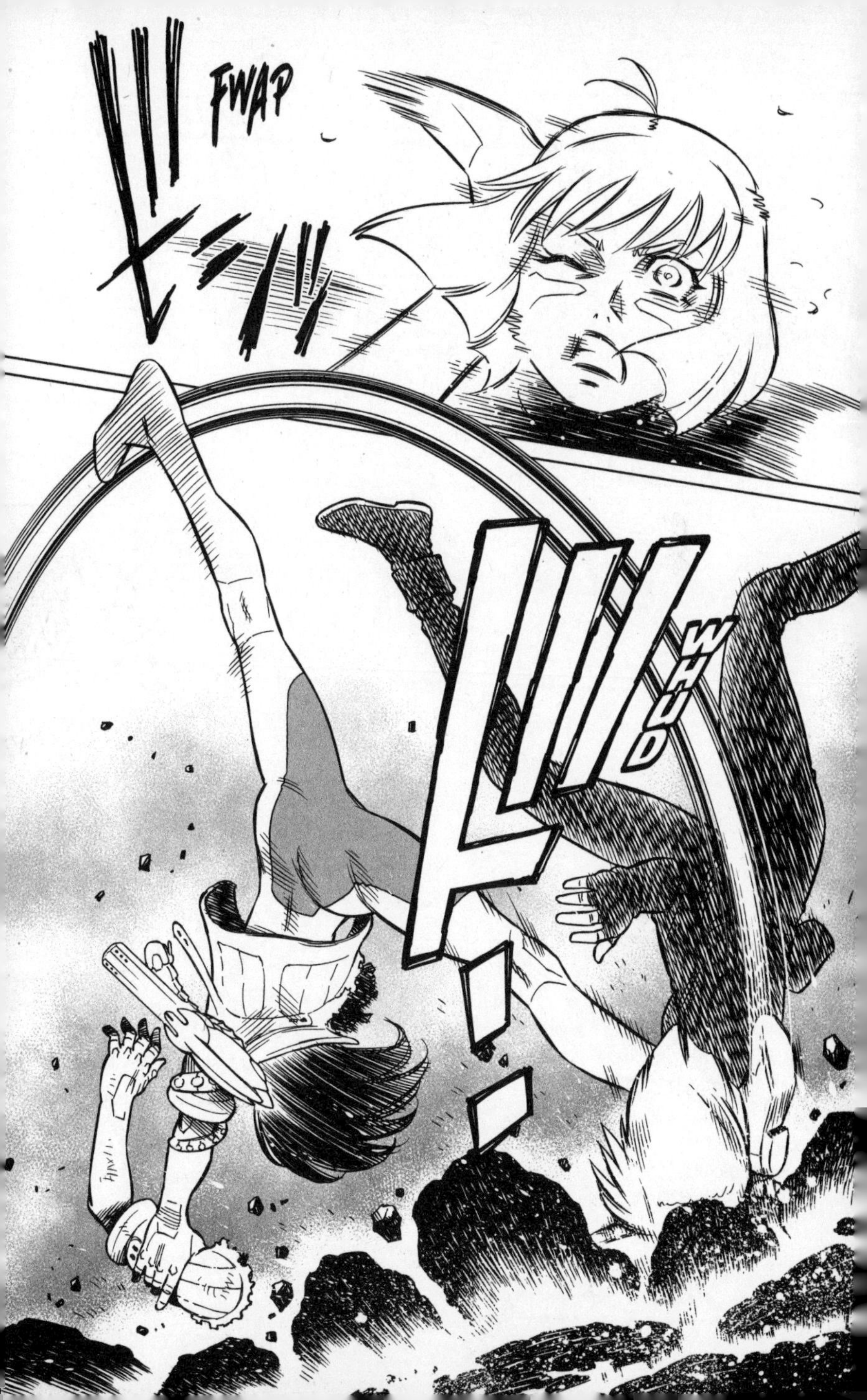
FWAP
WHUD

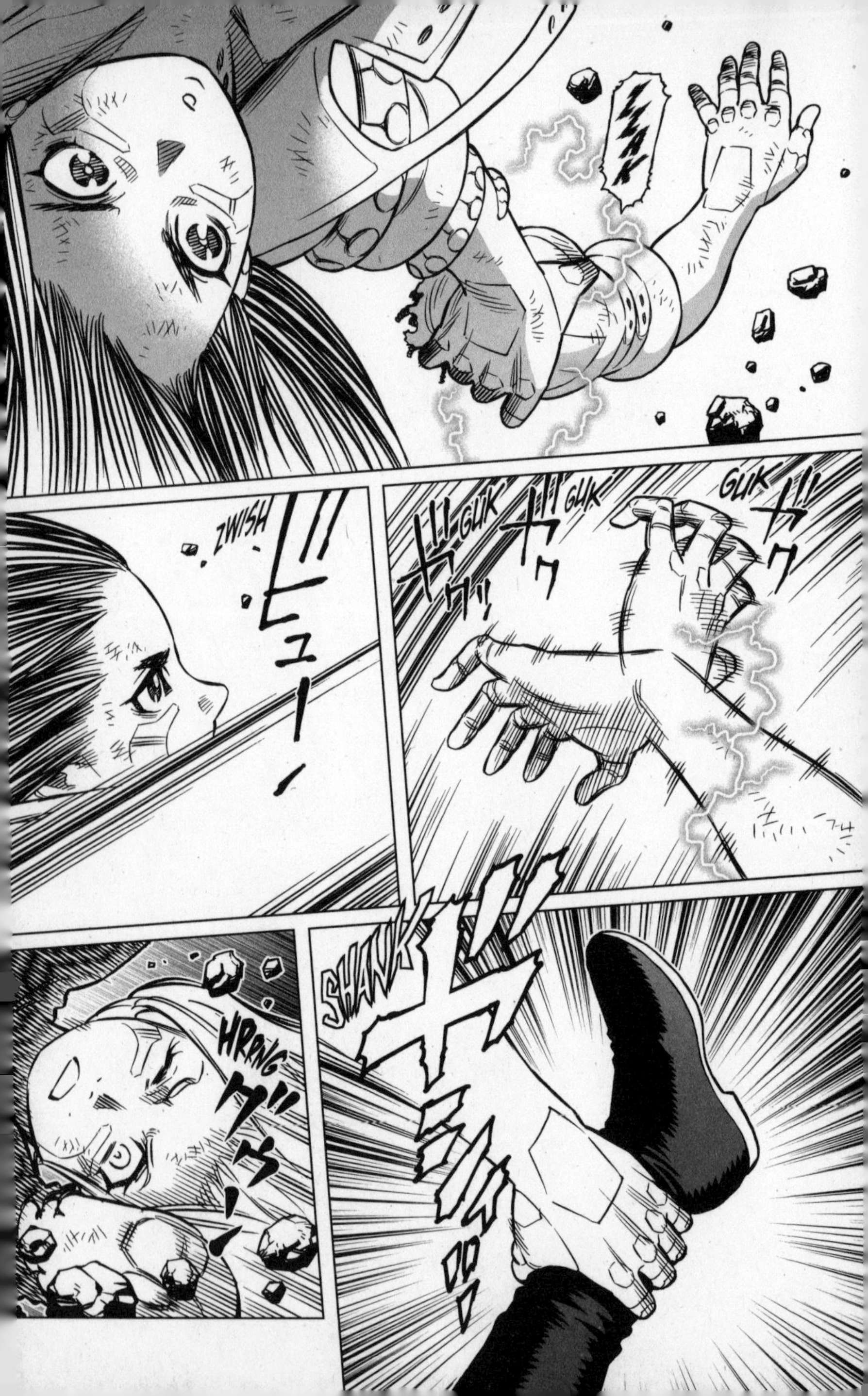

ZZAK
GUK
GUK
GUK
ZWISH
SHANK
HRRNG

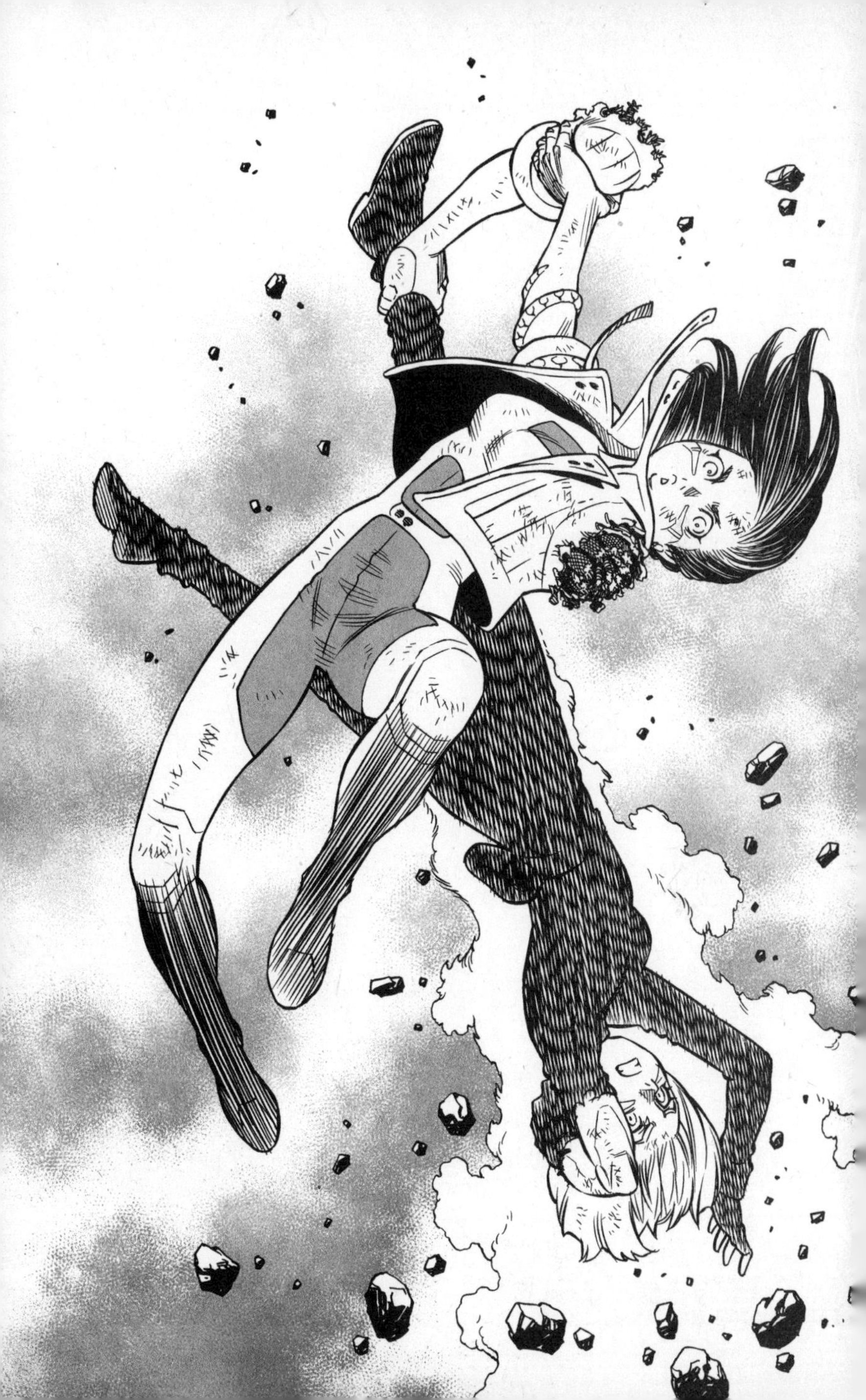

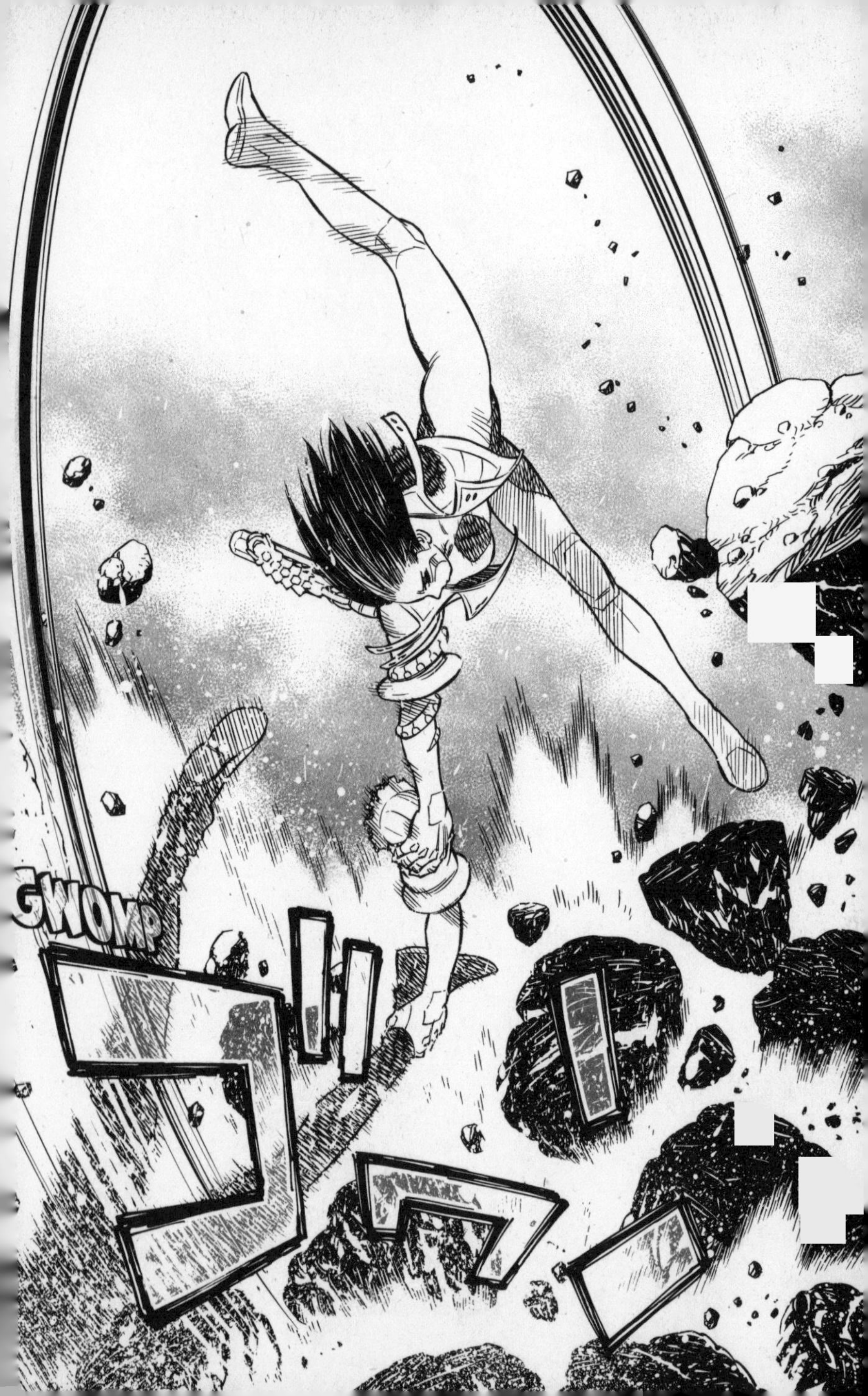
GWOMP

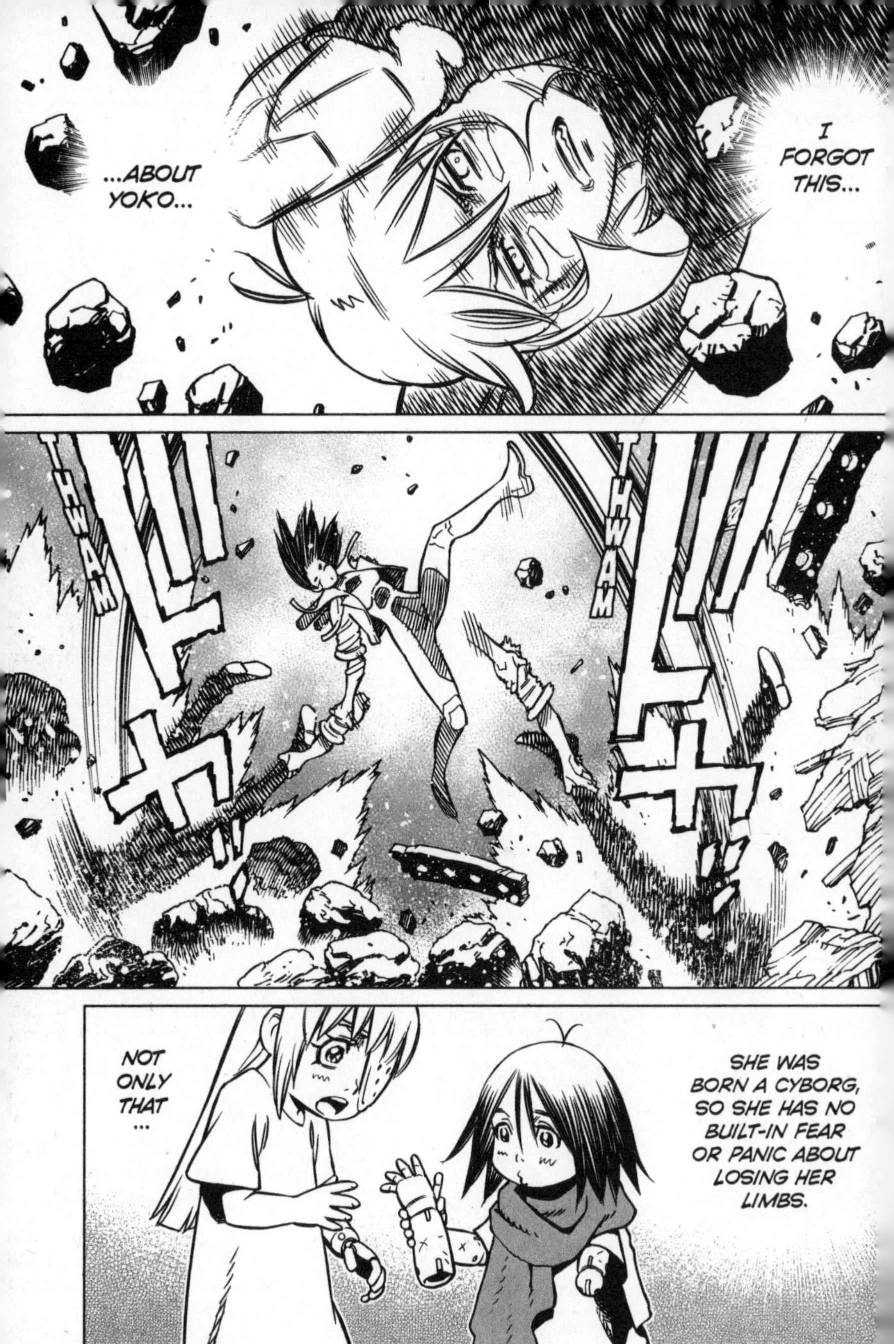
I FORGOT THIS...
...ABOUT YOKO...
THWAM
THWAM
SHE WAS BORN A CYBORG, SO SHE HAS NO BUILT-IN FEAR OR PANIC ABOUT LOSING HER LIMBS.
NOT ONLY THAT...

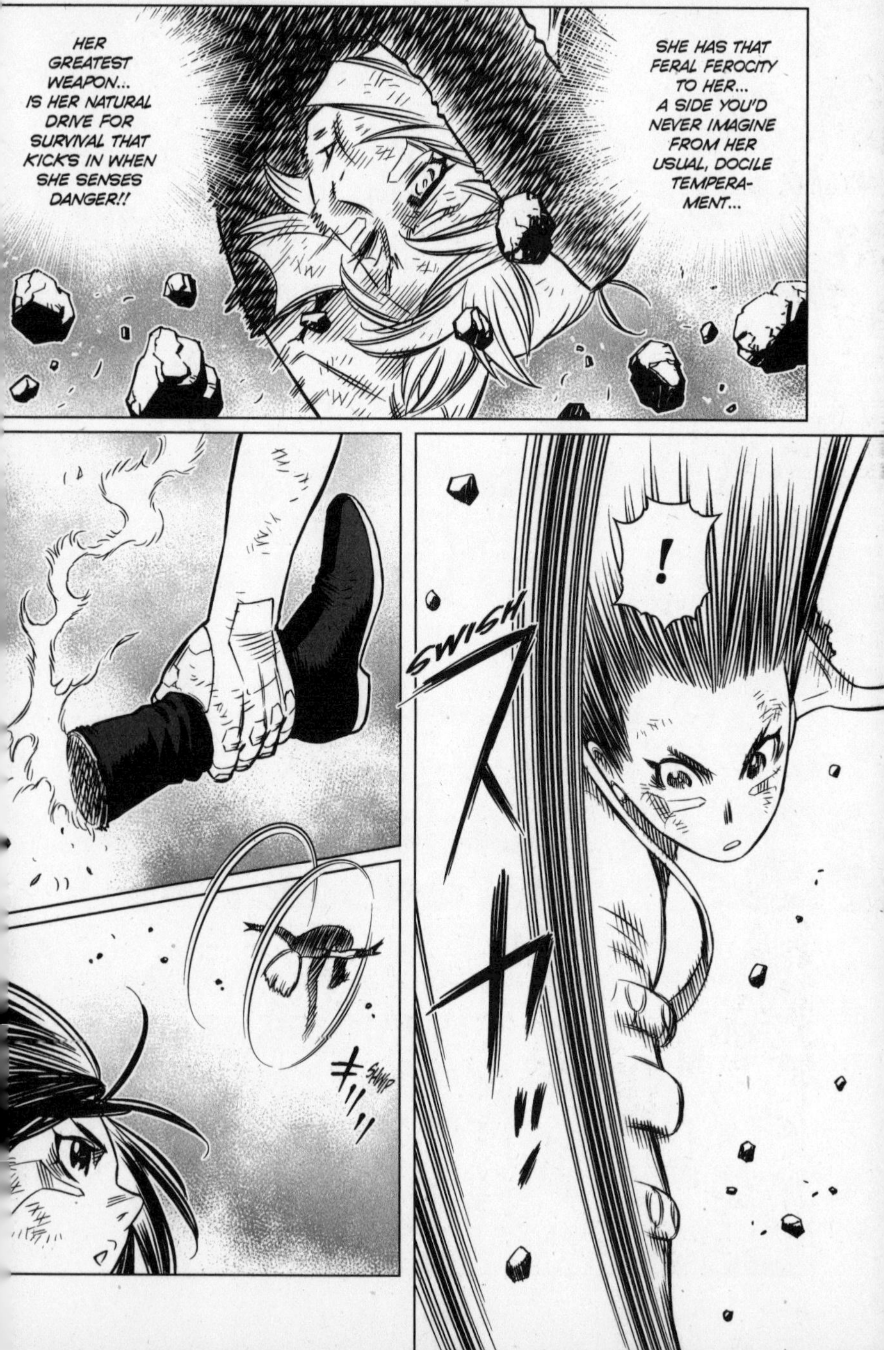
SHE HAS THAT FERAL FEROCITY TO HER... A SIDE YOU'D NEVER IMAGINE FROM HER USUAL, DOCILE TEMPERA-MENT...
HER GREATEST WEAPON... IS HER NATURAL DRIVE FOR SURVIVAL THAT KICKS IN WHEN SHE SENSES DANGER!!
!
SWISH

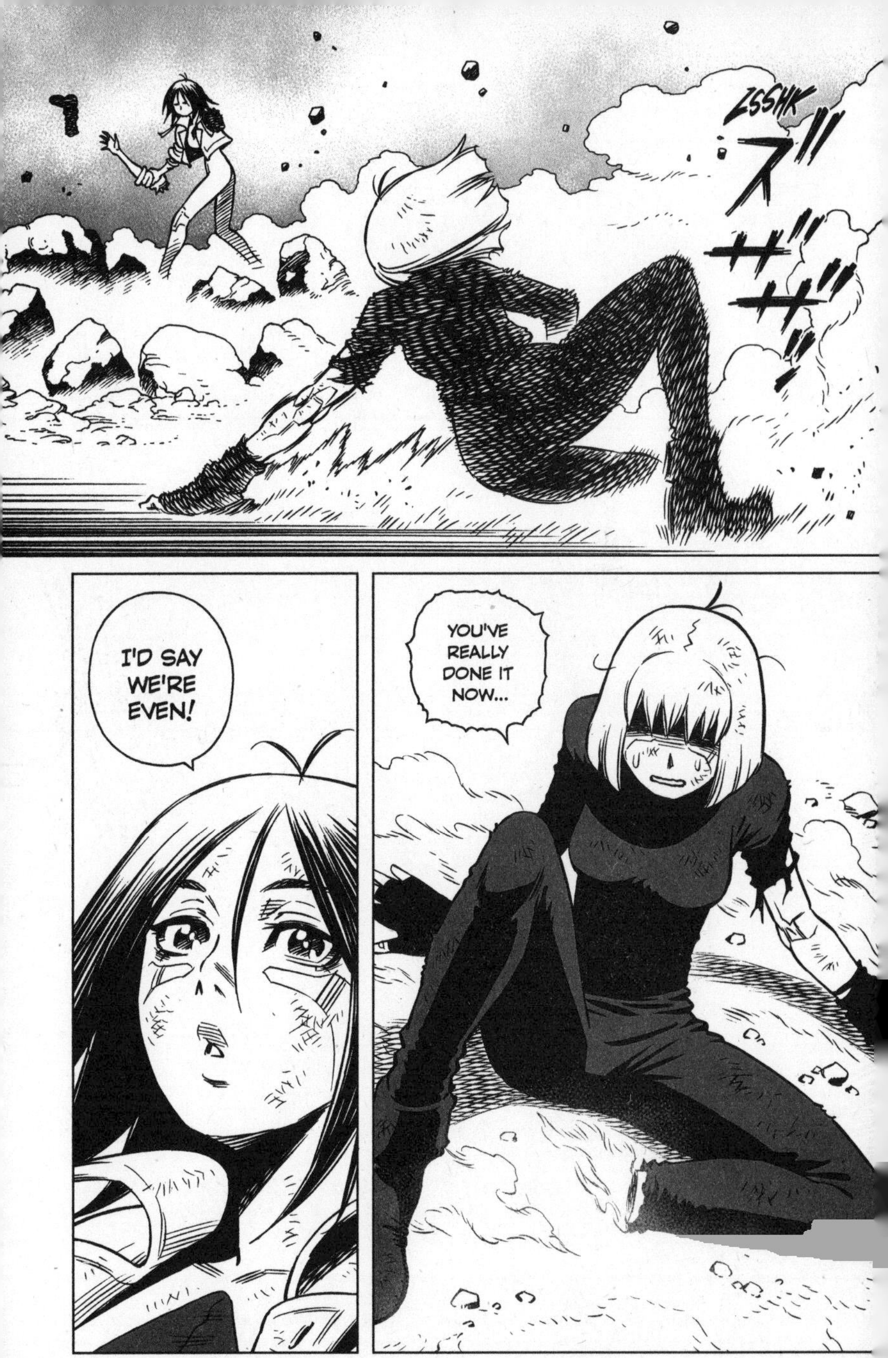
ZSSHK
ズザザ
YOU'VE REALLY DONE IT NOW...
I'D SAY WE'RE EVEN!

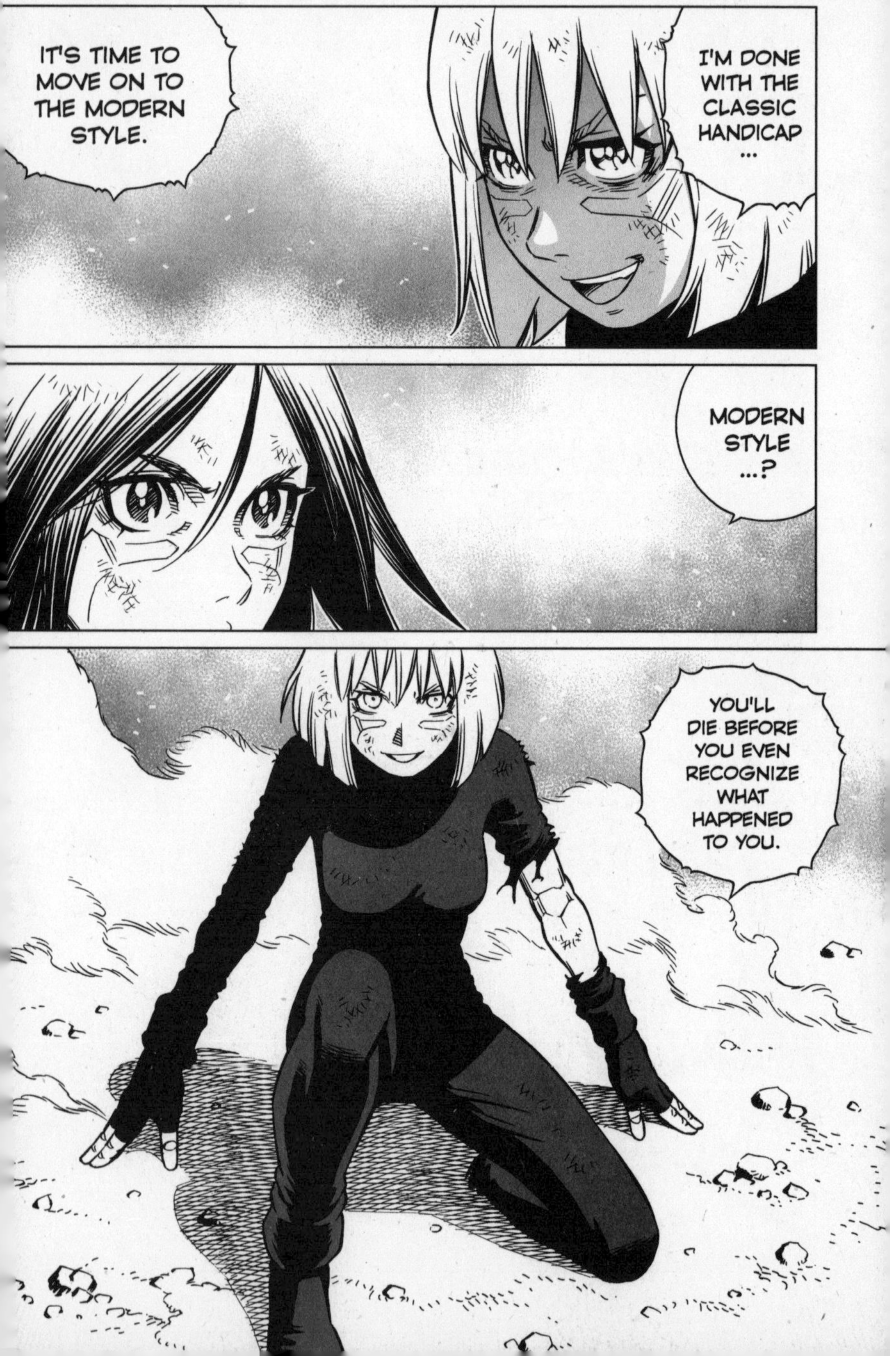
I'M DONE WITH THE CLASSIC HANDICAP ...
IT'S TIME TO MOVE ON TO THE MODERN STYLE.
MODERN STYLE ...?
YOU'LL DIE BEFORE YOU EVEN RECOGNIZE WHAT HAPPENED TO YOU.

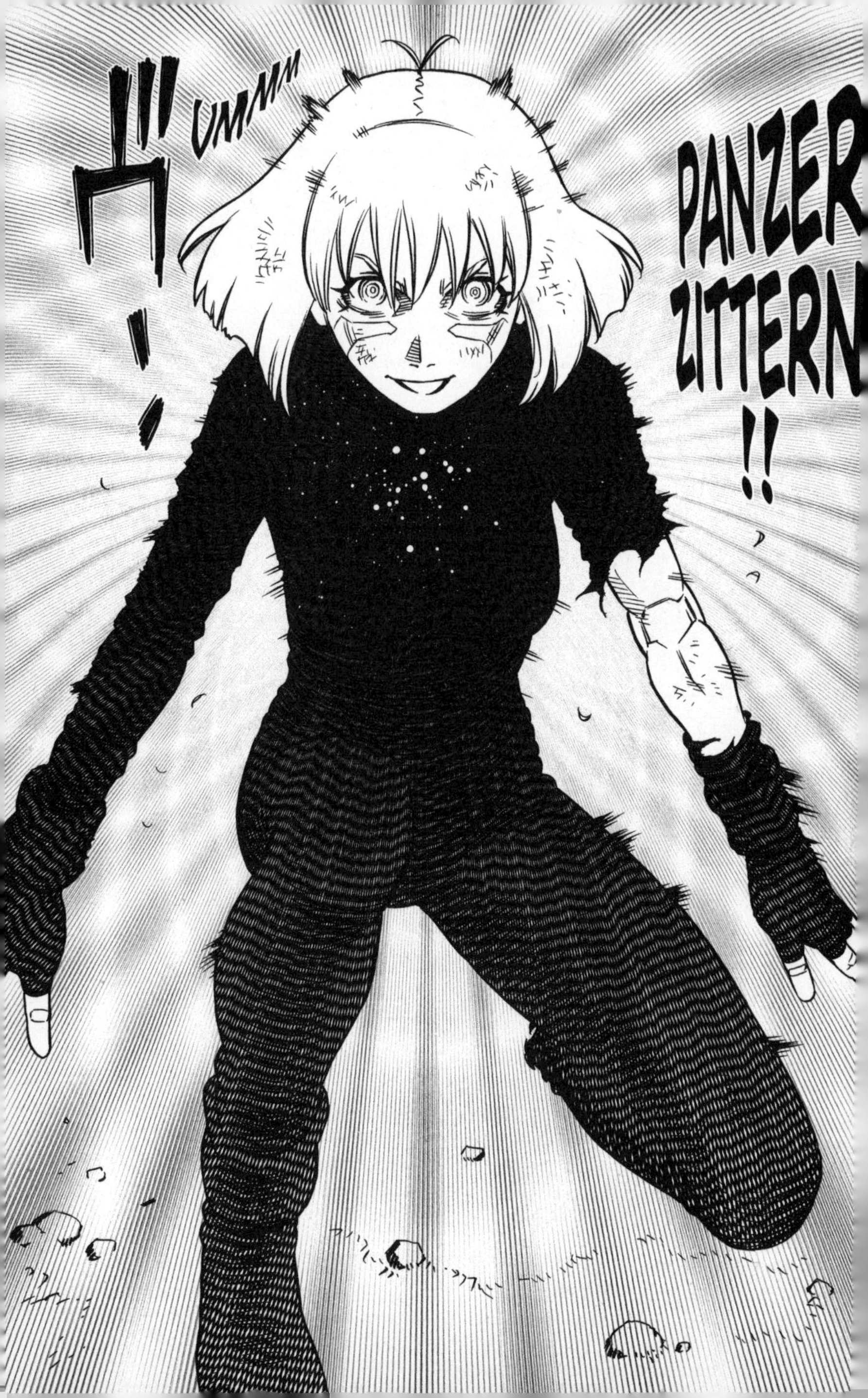
PANZER ZITTERN!!
UMMM

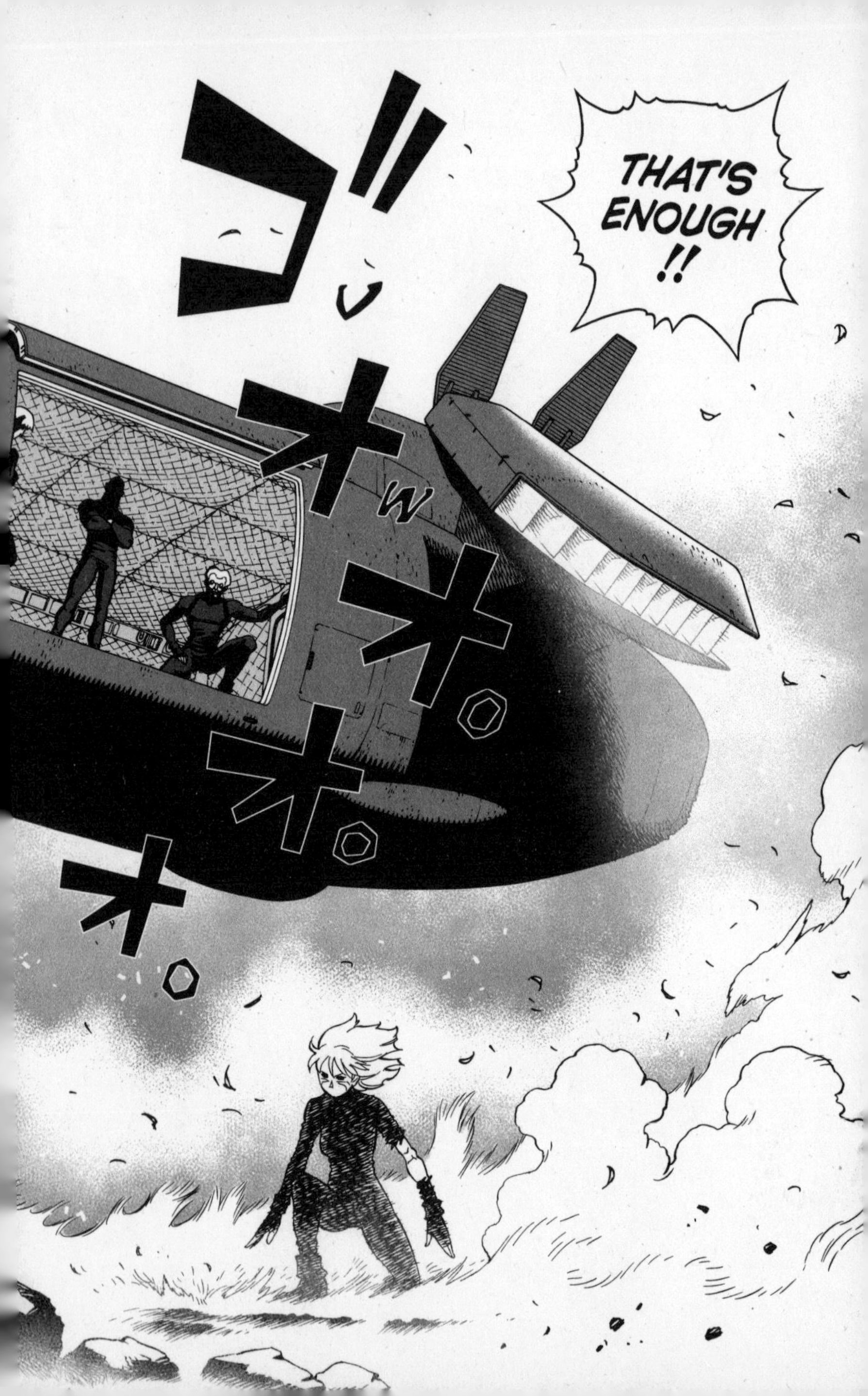
THAT'S ENOUGH !!
ゴゴォォォォ

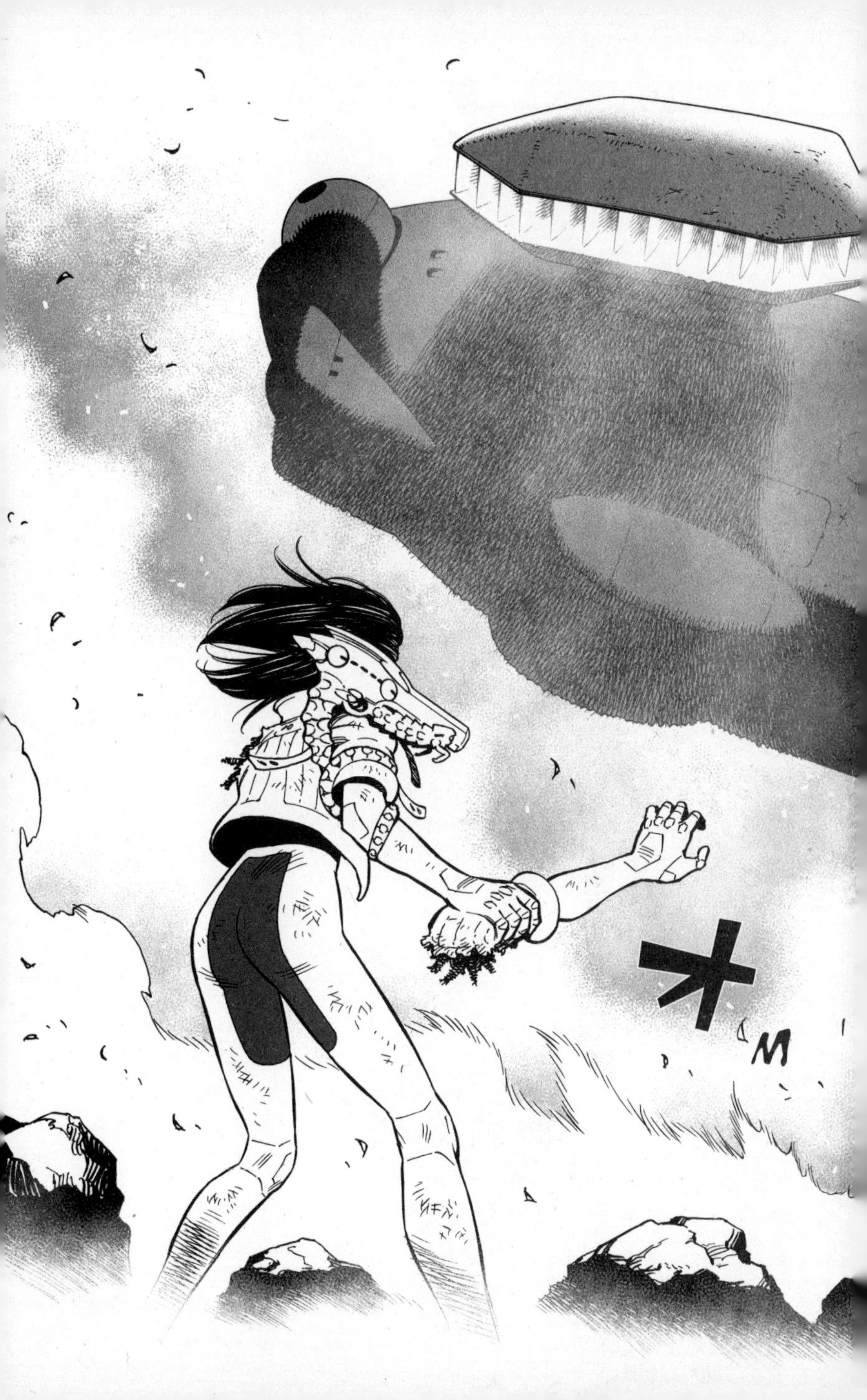
オ

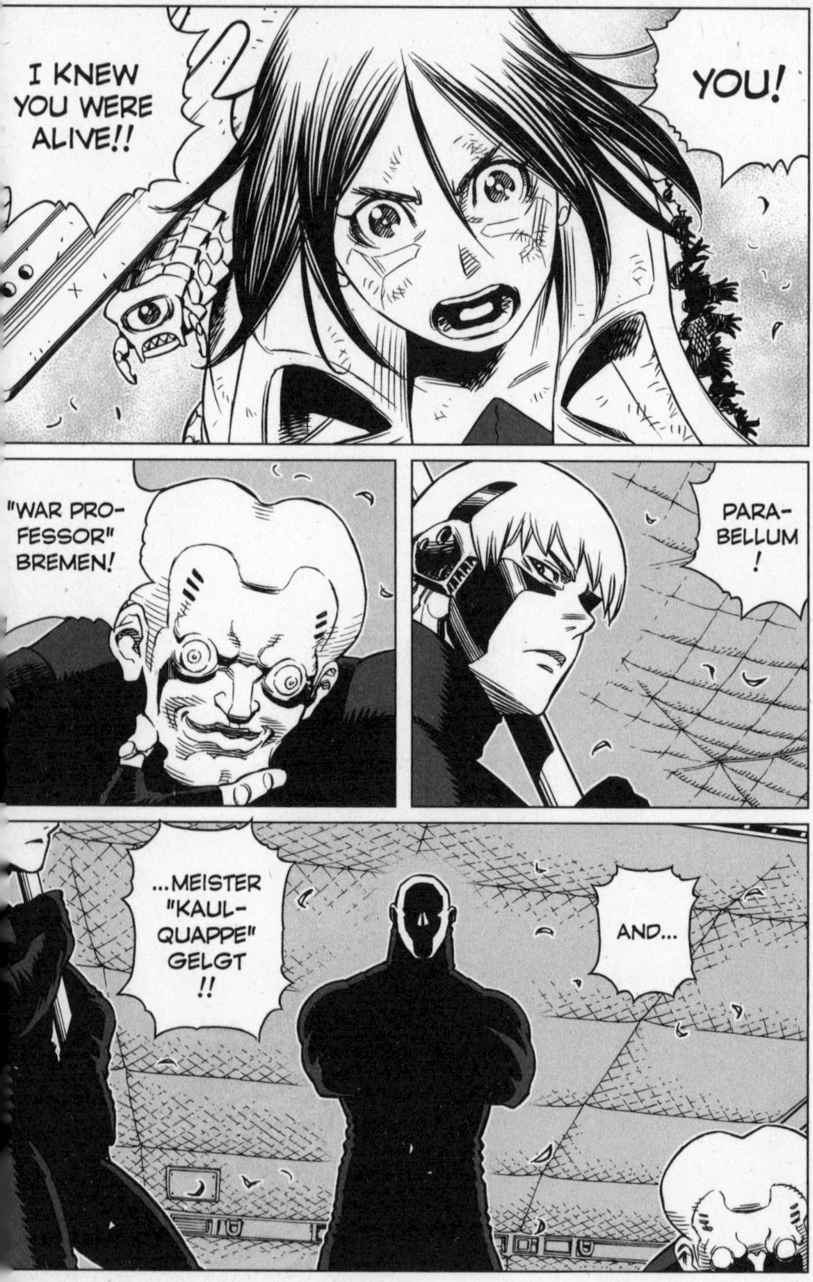
YOU!
I KNEW YOU WERE ALIVE!!
PARA-BELLUM !
"WAR PRO-FESSOR" BREMEN!
AND...
...MEISTER "KAUL-QUAPPE" GELGT !!

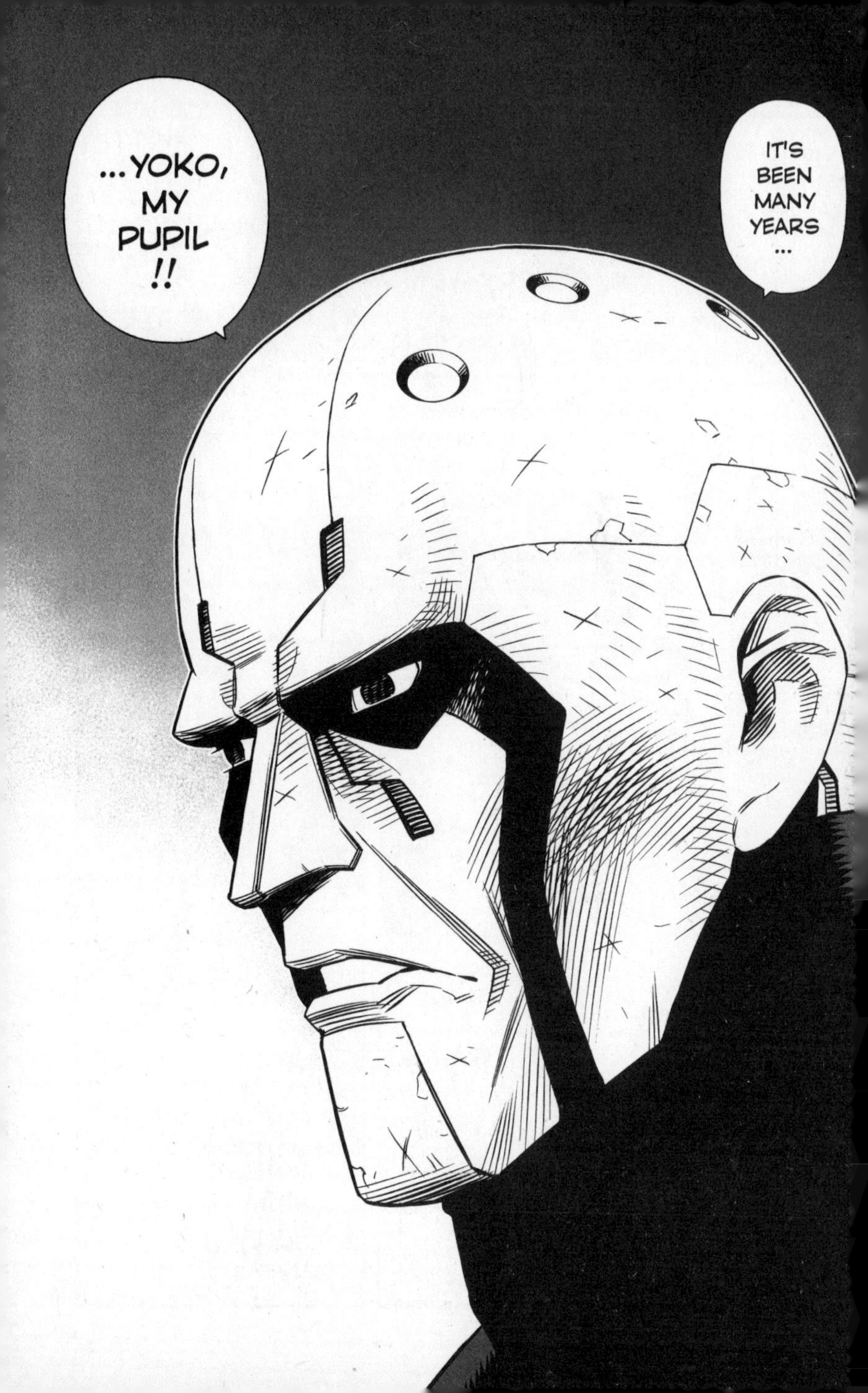
IT'S BEEN MANY YEARS ...
...YOKO, MY PUPIL !!

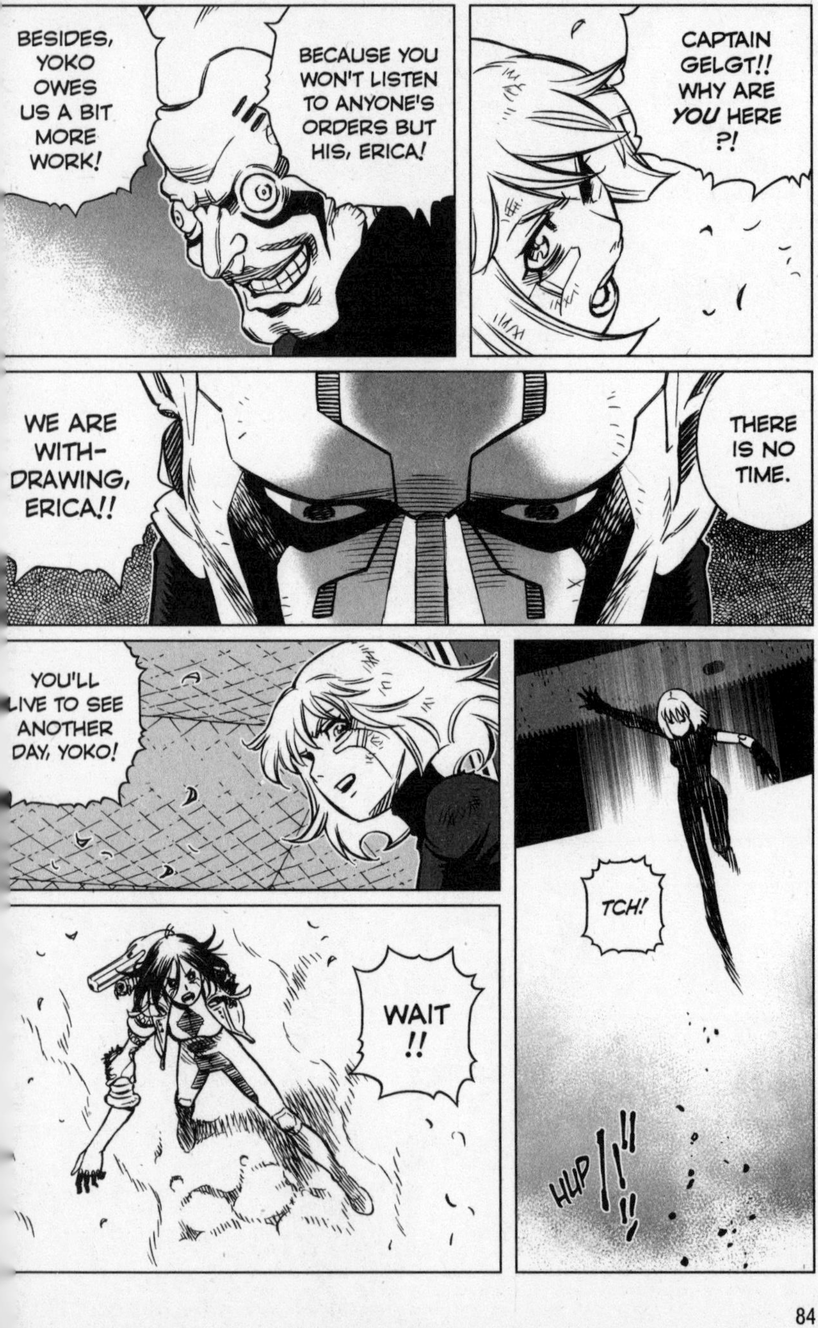
CAPTAIN GELGT!! WHY ARE *YOU* HERE ?!
BECAUSE YOU WON'T LISTEN TO ANYONE'S ORDERS BUT HIS, ERICA!
BESIDES, YOKO OWES US A BIT MORE WORK!
THERE IS NO TIME.
WE ARE WITH-DRAWING, ERICA!!
TCH!
HUP!!!
YOU'LL LIVE TO SEE ANOTHER DAY, YOKO!
WAIT!!

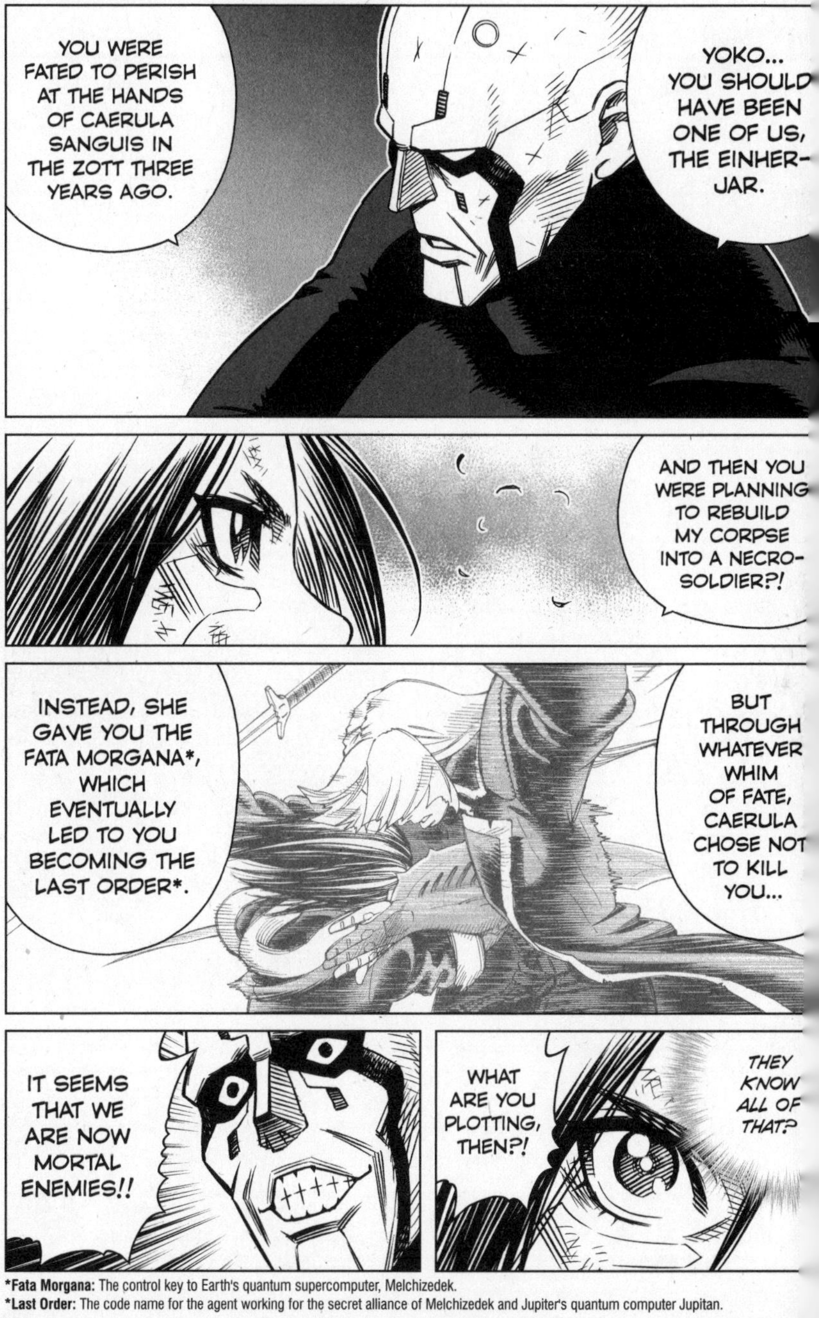
YOKO... YOU SHOULD HAVE BEEN ONE OF US, THE EINHER-JAR.
YOU WERE FATED TO PERISH AT THE HANDS OF CAERULA SANGUIS IN THE ZOTT THREE YEARS AGO.
AND THEN YOU WERE PLANNING TO REBUILD MY CORPSE INTO A NECRO-SOLDIER?!
BUT THROUGH WHATEVER WHIM OF FATE, CAERULA CHOSE NOT TO KILL YOU...
INSTEAD, SHE GAVE YOU THE FATA MORGANA*, WHICH EVENTUALLY LED TO YOU BECOMING THE LAST ORDER*.
THEY KNOW ALL OF THAT?
WHAT ARE YOU PLOTTING, THEN?!
IT SEEMS THAT WE ARE NOW MORTAL ENEMIES!!

***Fata Morgana:** The control key to Earth's quantum supercomputer, Melchizedek.

***Last Order:** The code name for the agent working for the secret alliance of Melchizedek and Jupiter's quantum computer Jupitan.

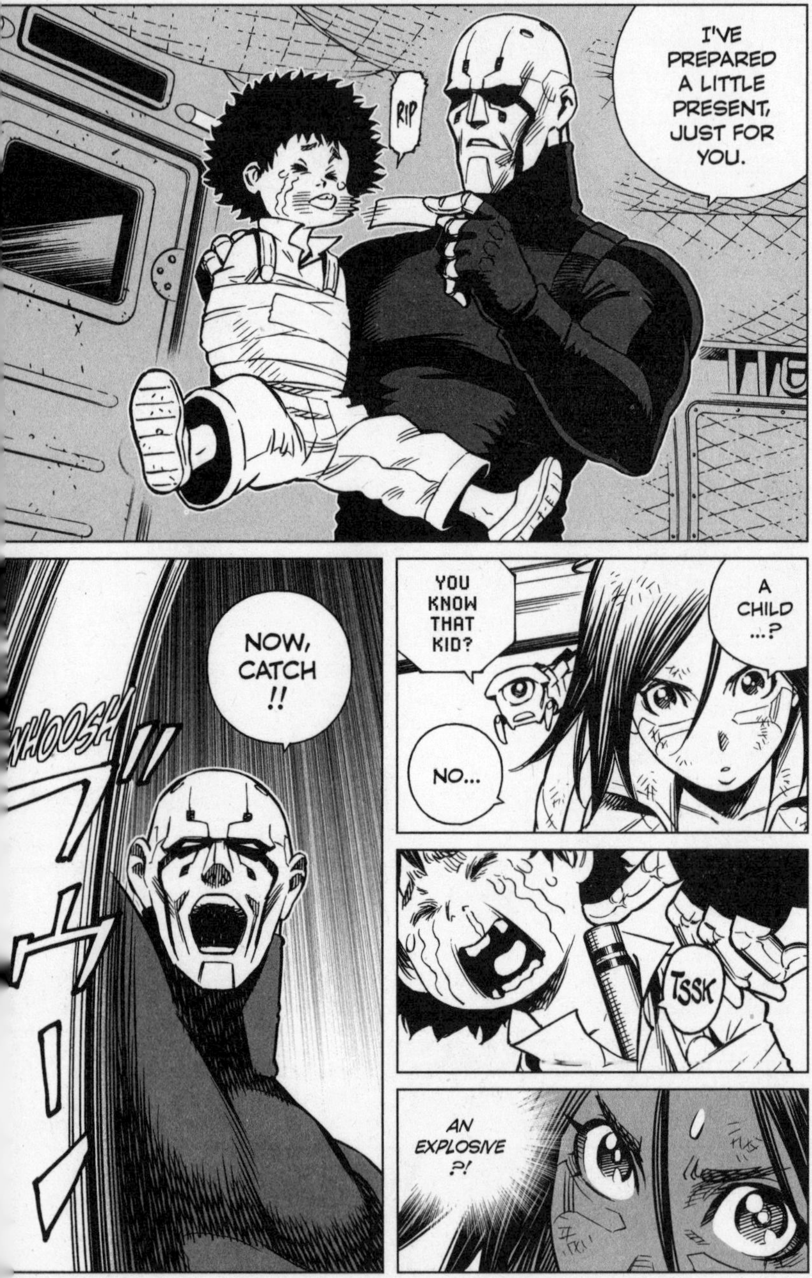
I'VE PREPARED A LITTLE PRESENT, JUST FOR YOU.
RIP
A CHILD ...?
YOU KNOW THAT KID?
NO...
TSSK
AN EXPLOSIVE ?!
NOW, CATCH !!
WHOOSH

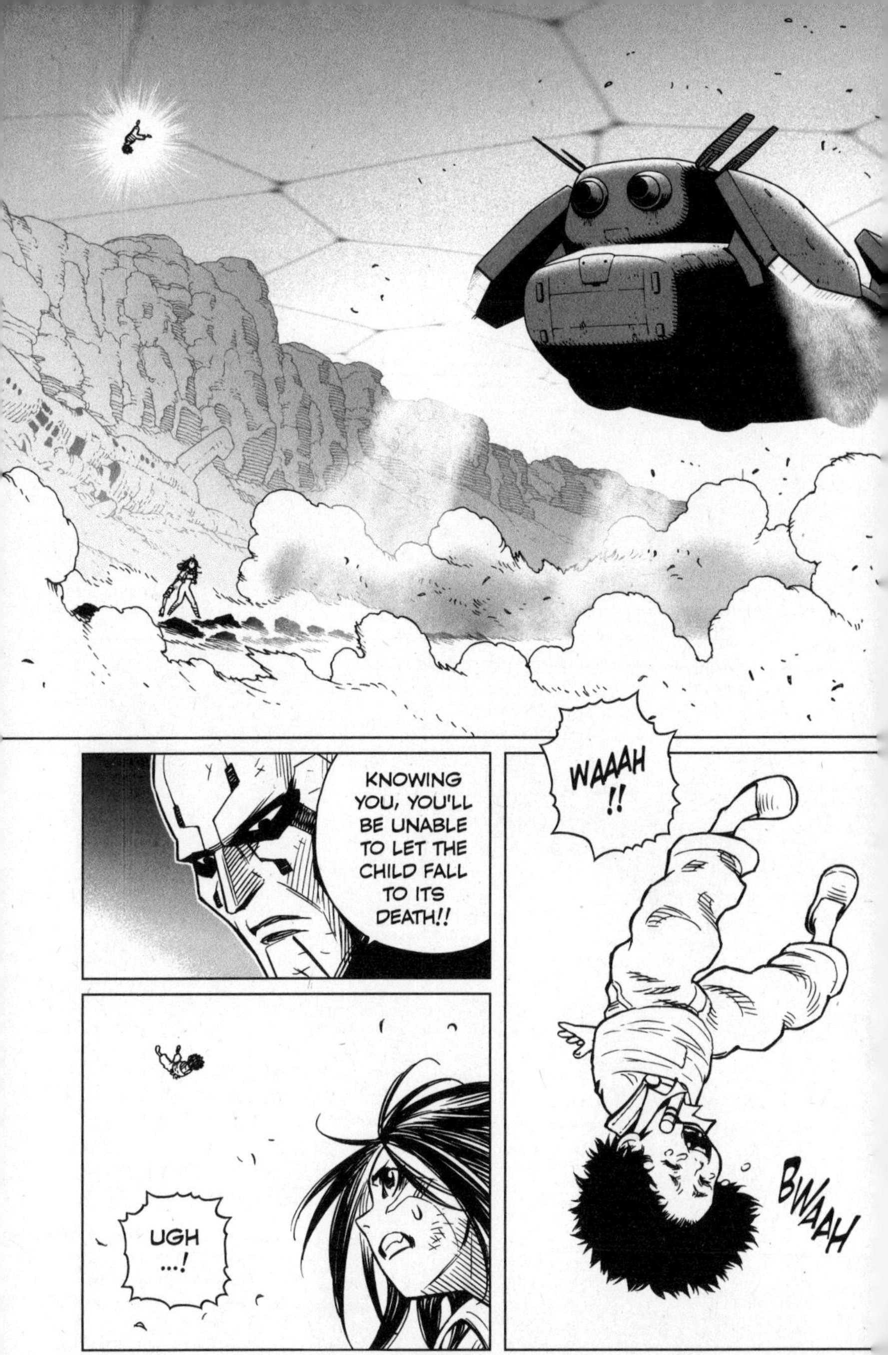
WAAAH !!
BWAAH
KNOWING YOU, YOU'LL BE UNABLE TO LET THE CHILD FALL TO ITS DEATH!!
UGH ...!

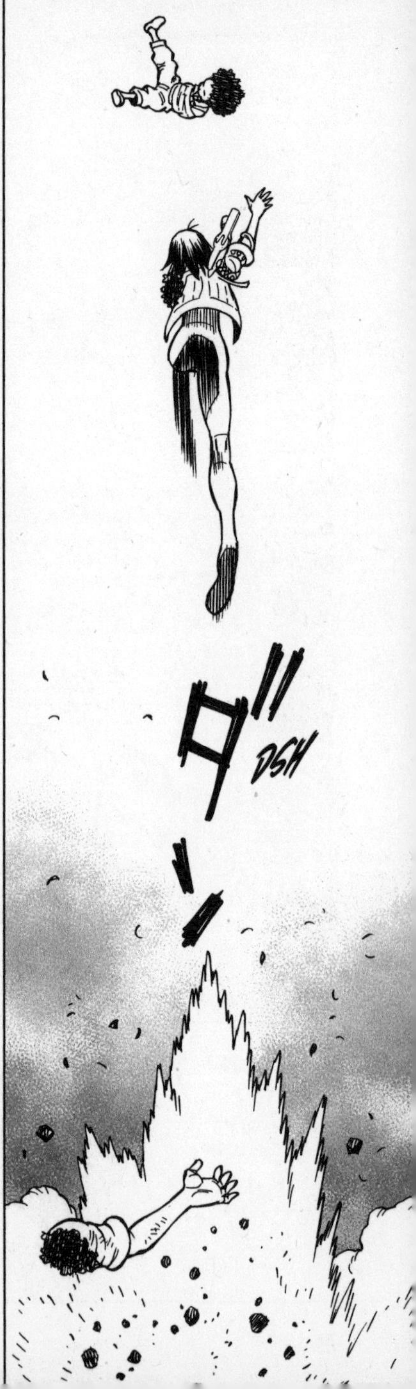
DSH

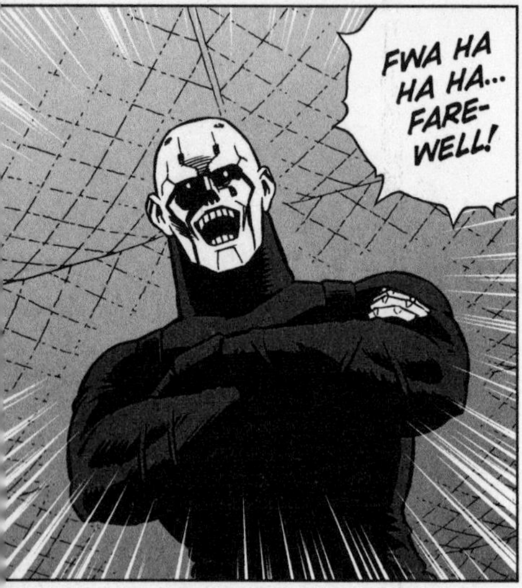
FWA HA HA HA... FARE-WELL!

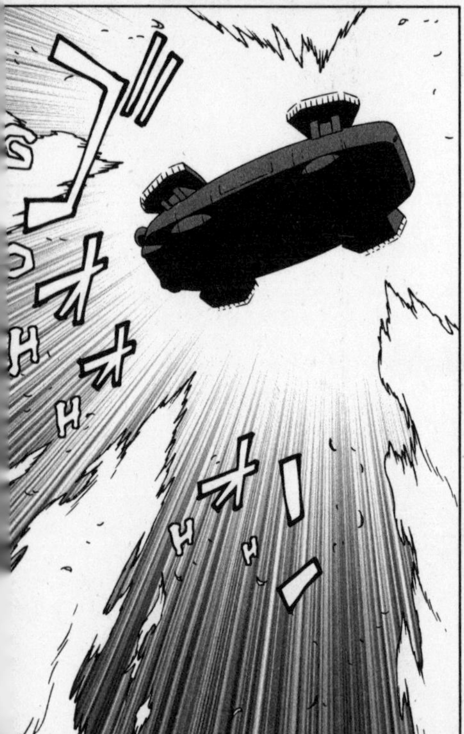

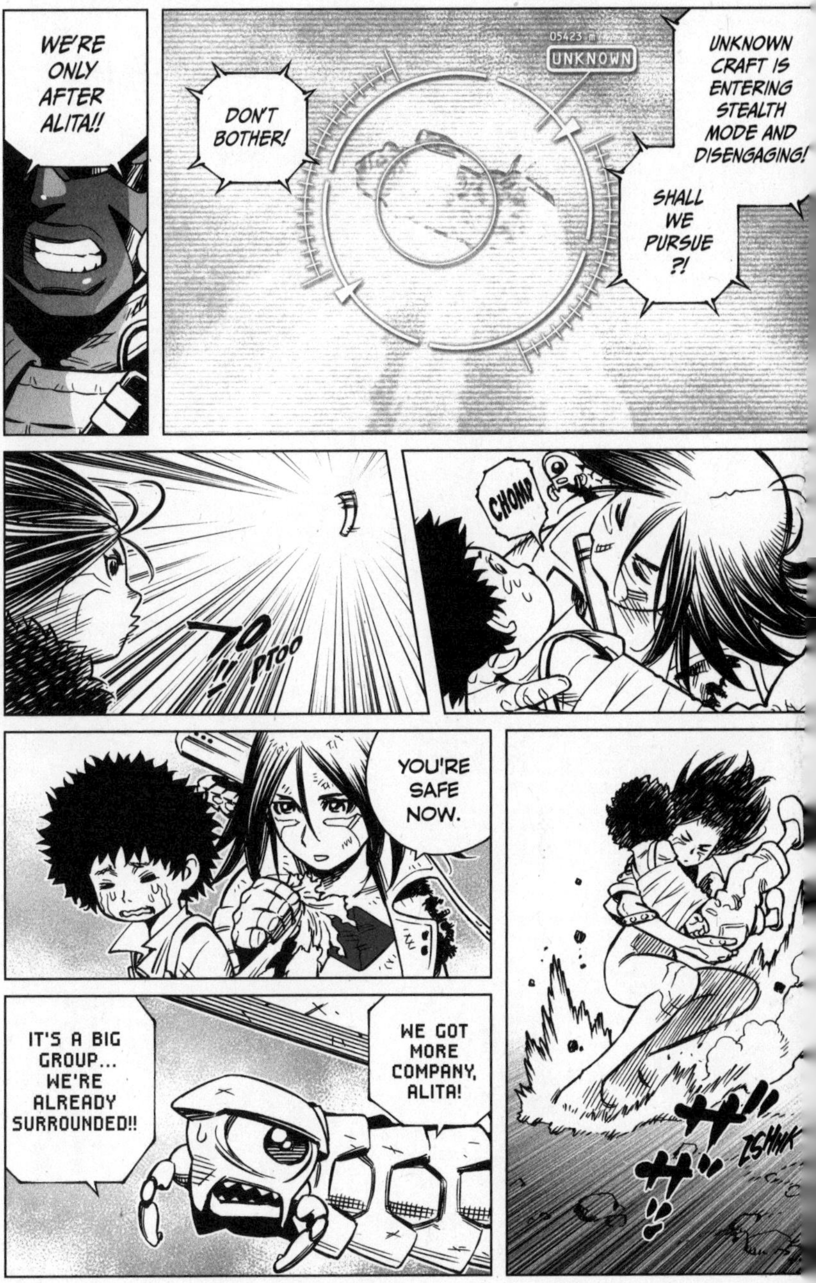
05423 m
UNKNOWN
UNKNOWN CRAFT IS ENTERING STEALTH MODE AND DISENGAGING!
SHALL WE PURSUE ?!
DON'T BOTHER!
WE'RE ONLY AFTER ALITA!!
CHOMP
PTOO
ZSHNK
YOU'RE SAFE NOW.
WE GOT MORE COMPANY, ALITA!
IT'S A BIG GROUP... WE'RE ALREADY SURROUNDED!!

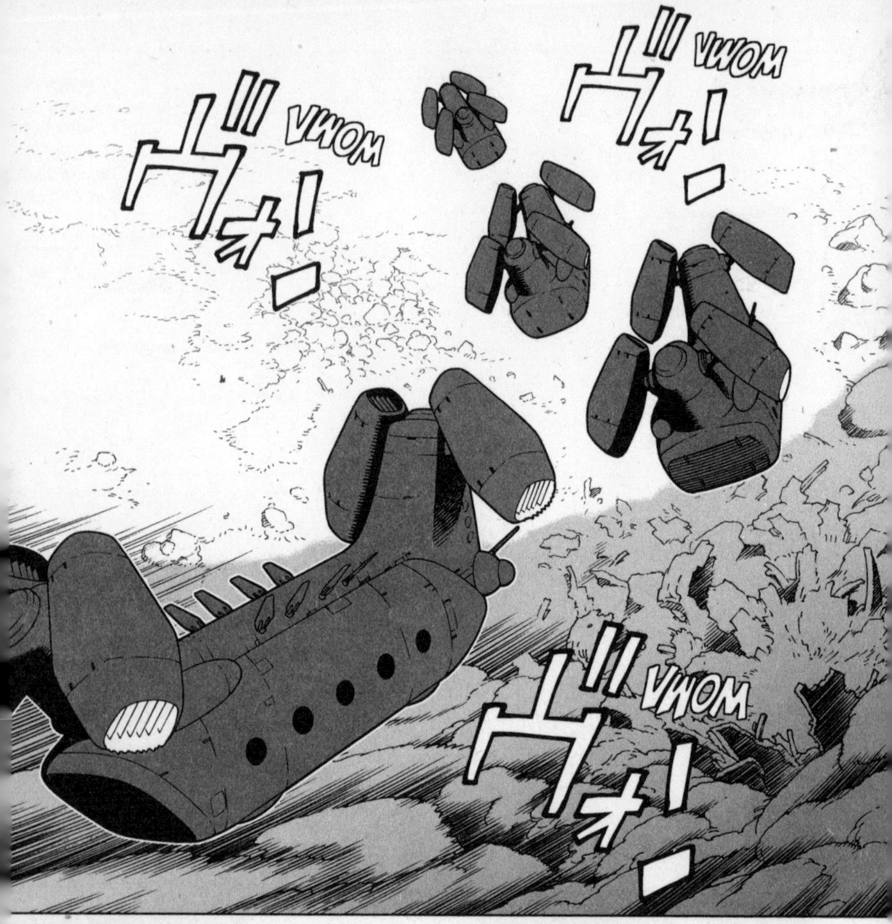
ヴォー
VWOM
ヴォー
VWOM
ヴォー
VWOM

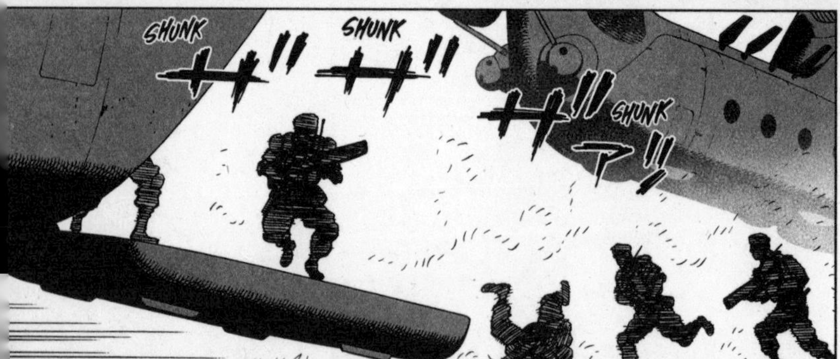
SHUNK
SHUNK
SHUNK

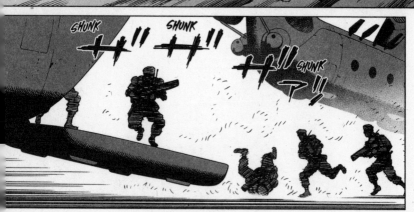

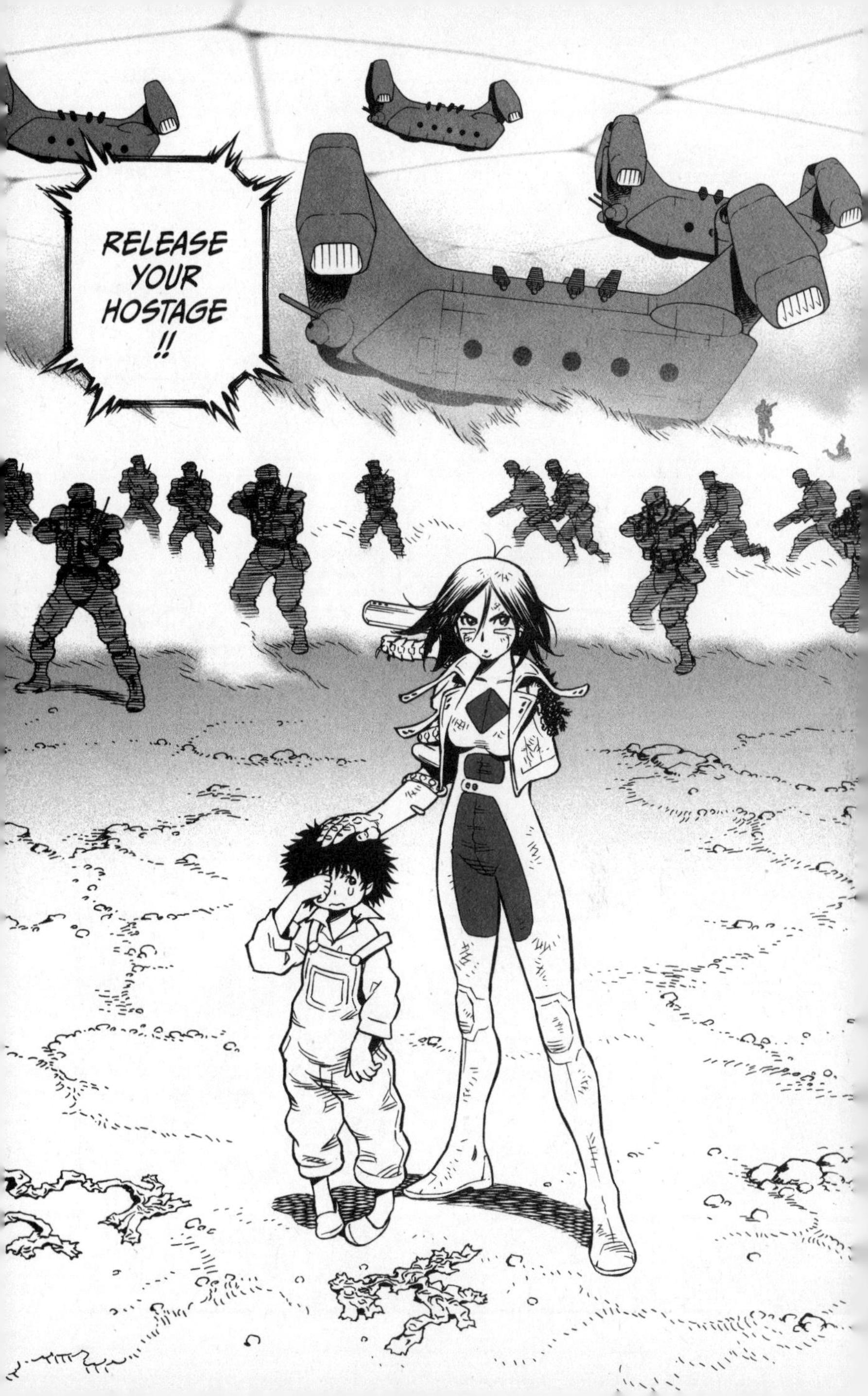
RELEASE YOUR HOSTAGE !!

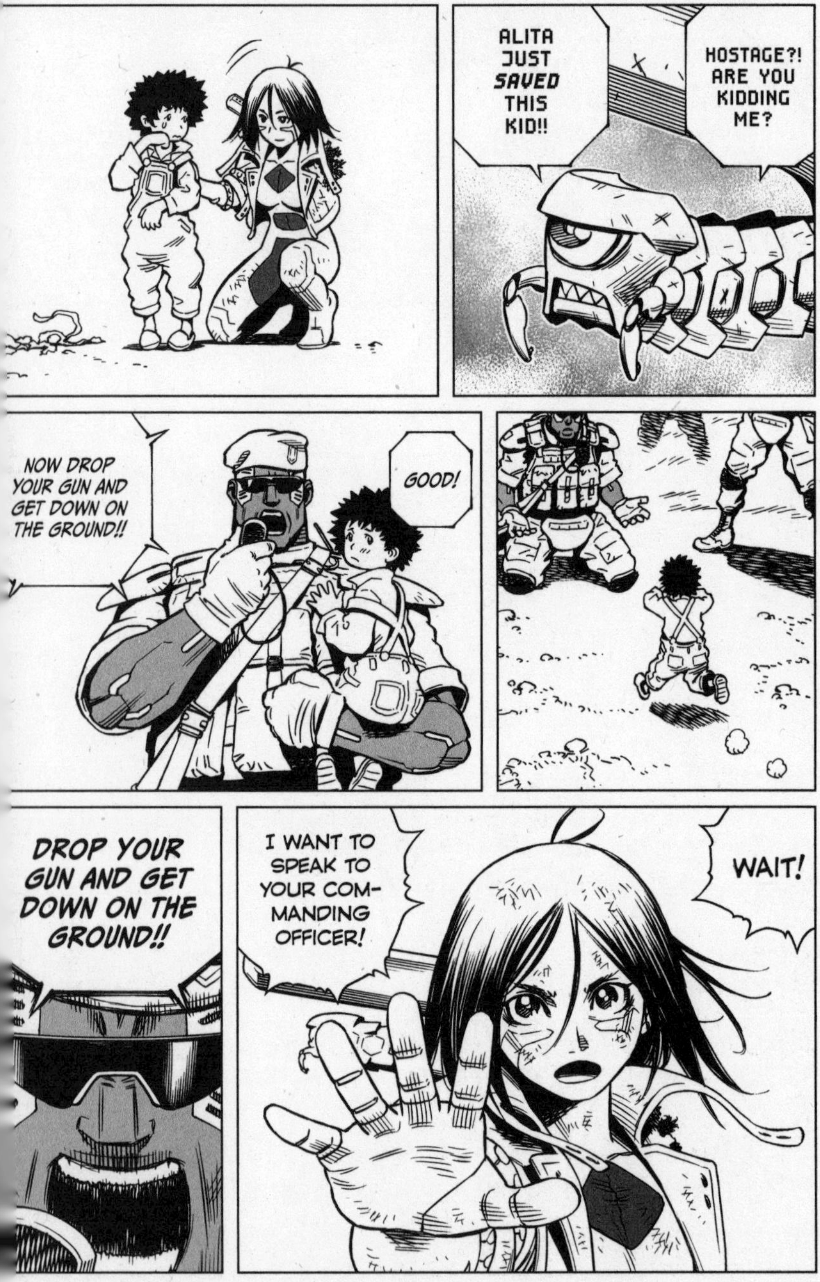
HOSTAGE?! ARE YOU KIDDING ME?
ALITA JUST *SAVED* THIS KID!!
GOOD!
NOW DROP YOUR GUN AND GET DOWN ON THE GROUND!!
WAIT!
I WANT TO SPEAK TO YOUR COM-MANDING OFFICER!
DROP YOUR GUN AND GET DOWN ON THE GROUND!!

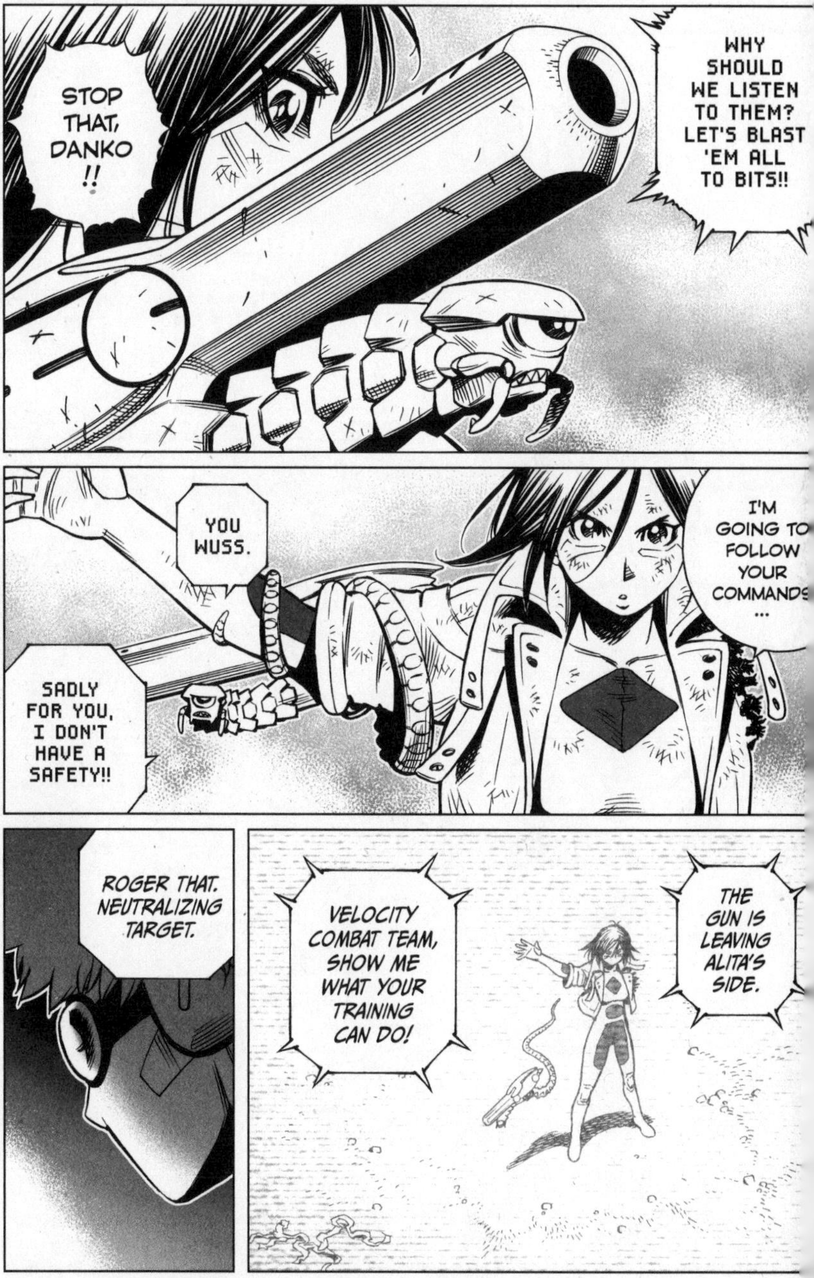
WHY SHOULD WE LISTEN TO THEM? LET'S BLAST 'EM ALL TO BITS!!
STOP THAT, DANKO!!
I'M GOING TO FOLLOW YOUR COMMANDS...
YOU WUSS.
SADLY FOR YOU, I DON'T HAVE A SAFETY!!
THE GUN IS LEAVING ALITA'S SIDE.
VELOCITY COMBAT TEAM, SHOW ME WHAT YOUR TRAINING CAN DO!
ROGER THAT. NEUTRALIZING TARGET.

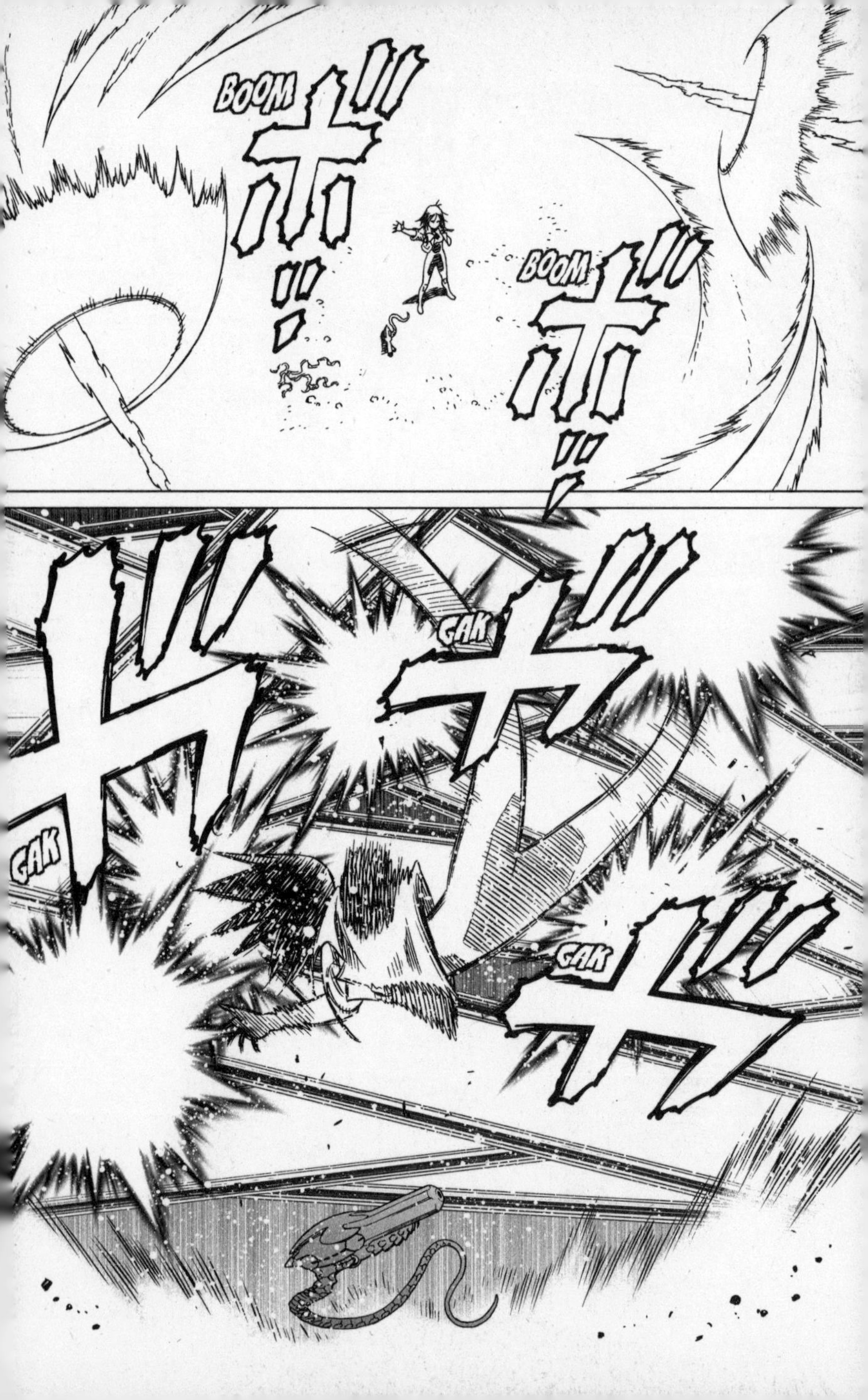
BOOM
BOOM
GAK
GAK
GAK

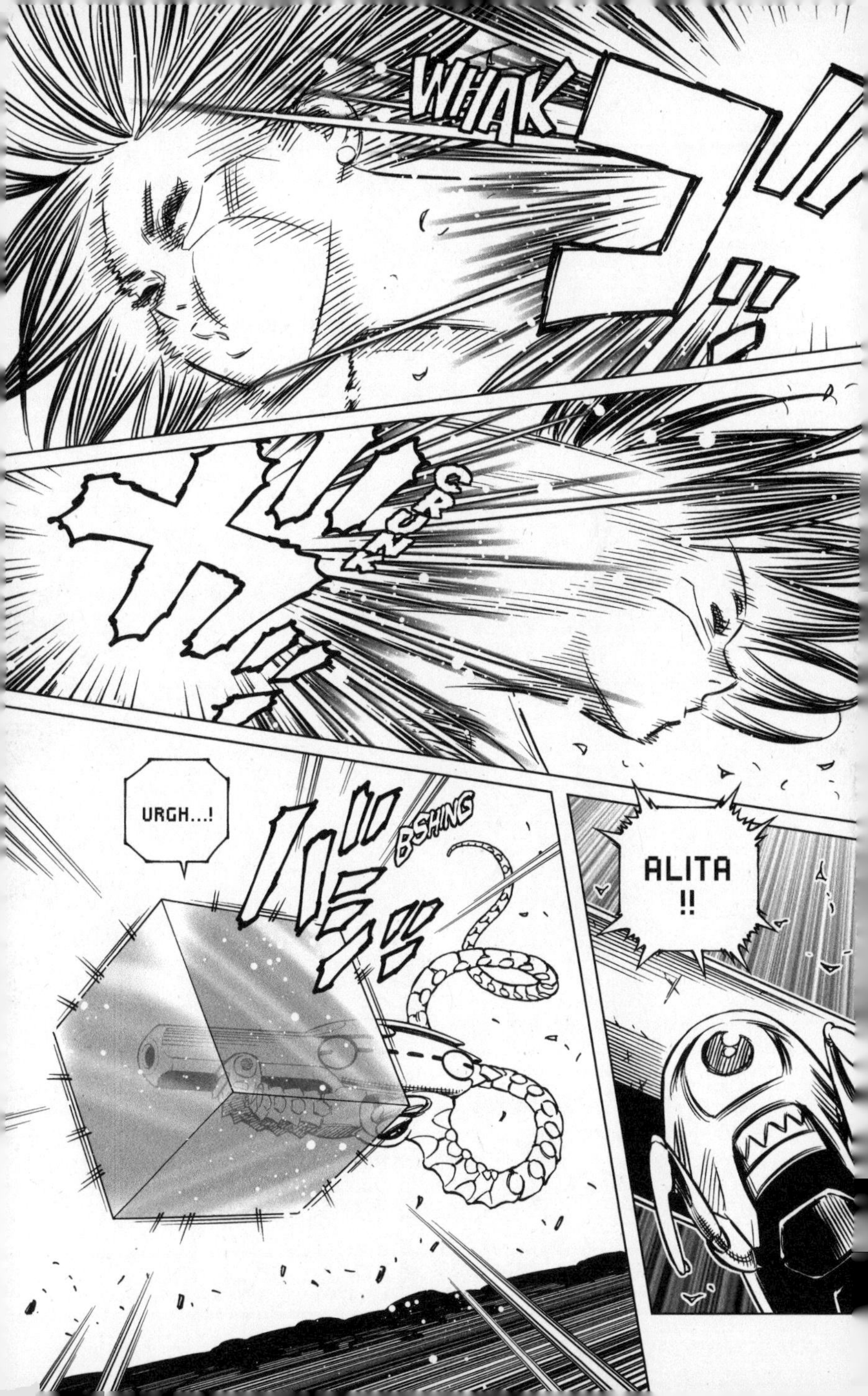
WHAK
CRUNK
ALITA
!!
BSHING
URGH...!

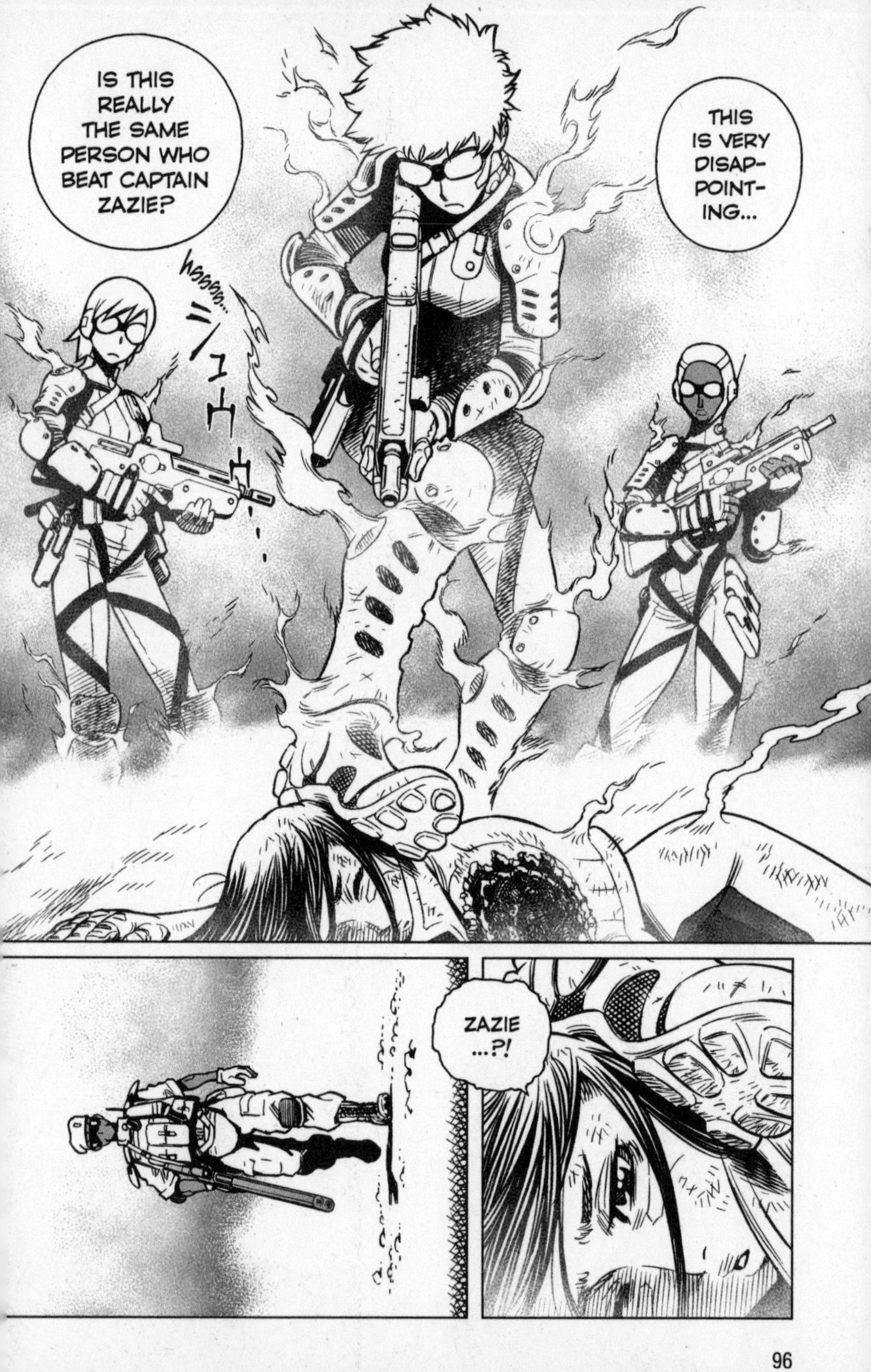

THIS IS VERY DISAP-POINTING...
IS THIS REALLY THE SAME PERSON WHO BEAT CAPTAIN ZAZIE?
hssss...
ZAZIE ...?!

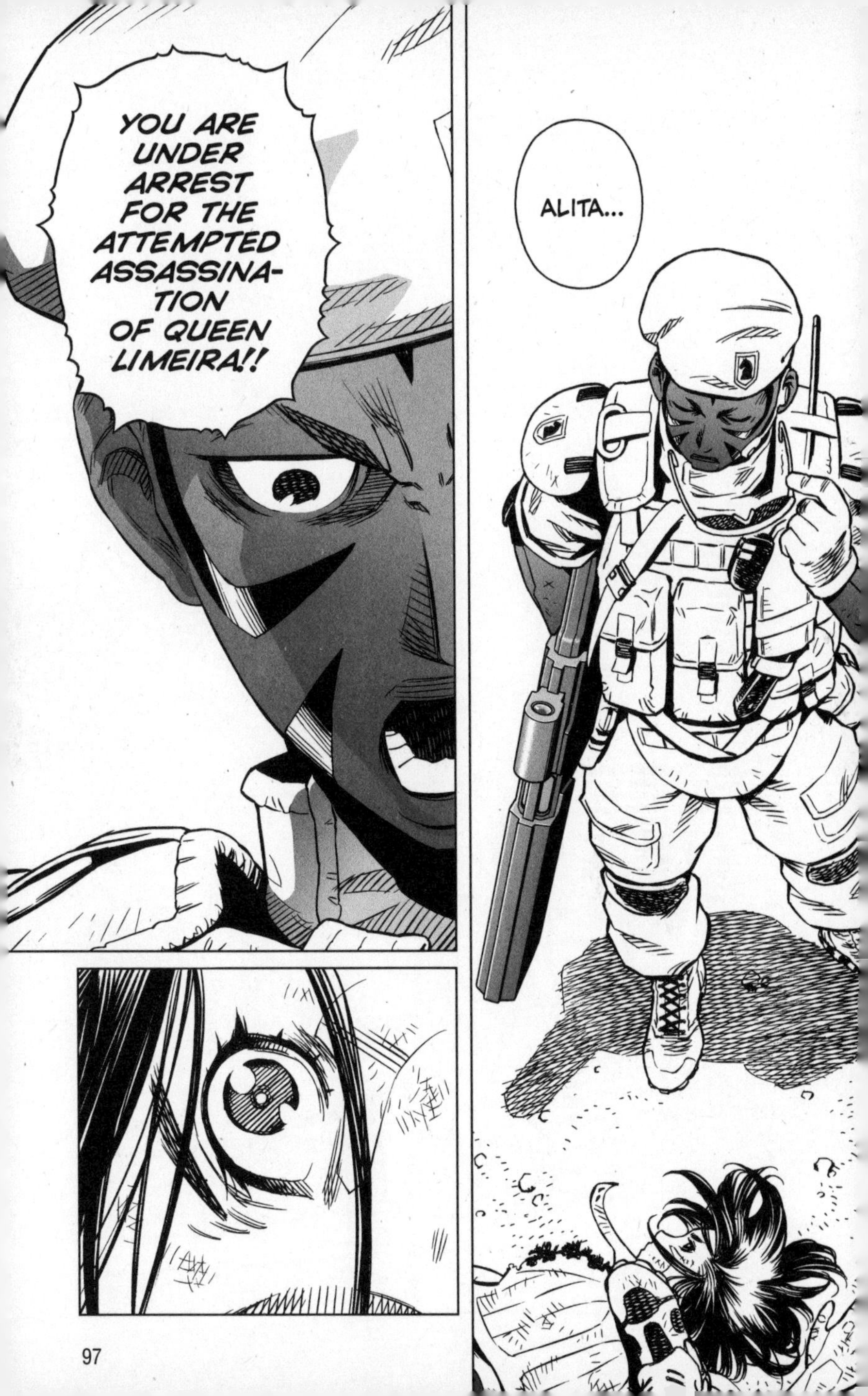
ALITA...
YOU ARE UNDER ARREST FOR THE ATTEMPTED ASSASSINATION OF QUEEN LIMEIRA!!

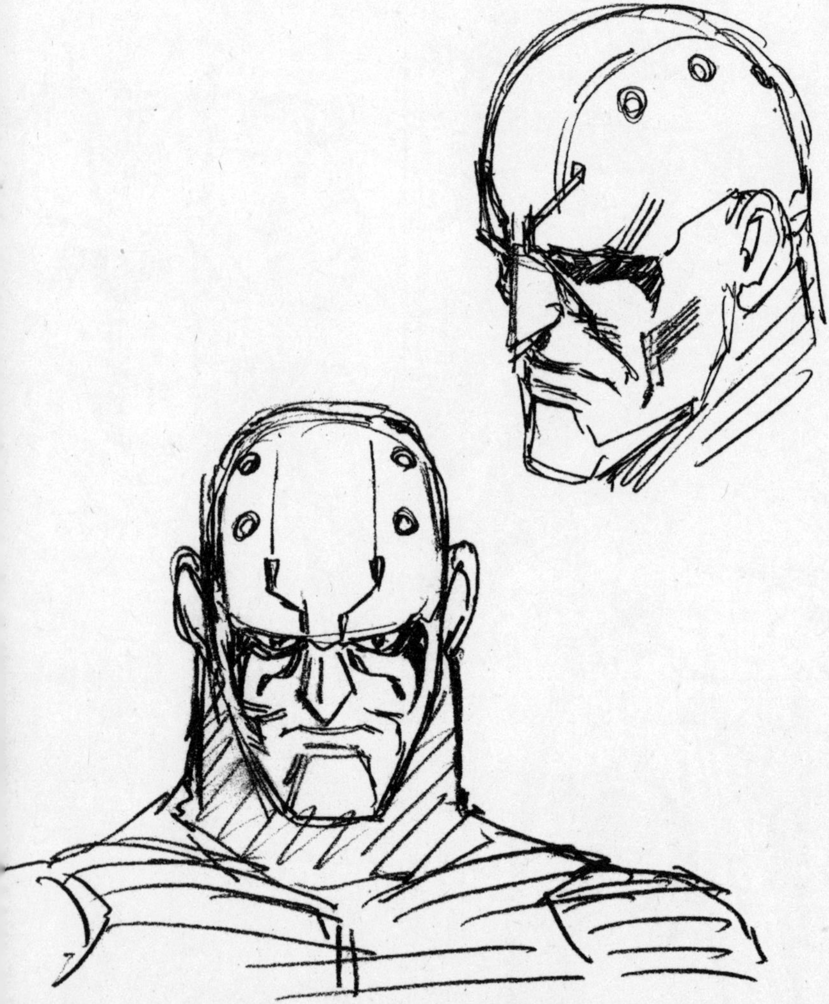

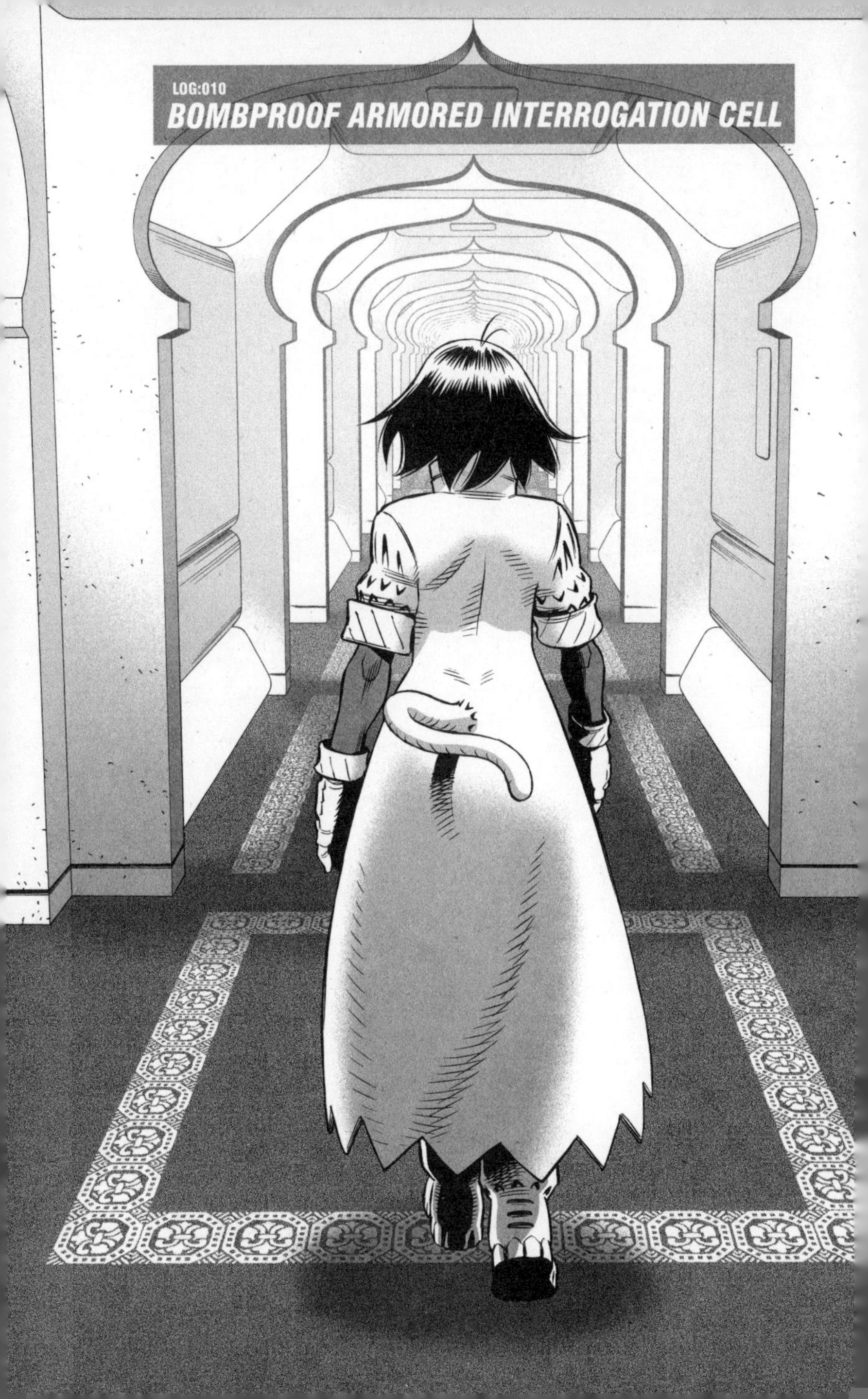
LOG:010
BOMBPROOF ARMORED INTERROGATION CELL

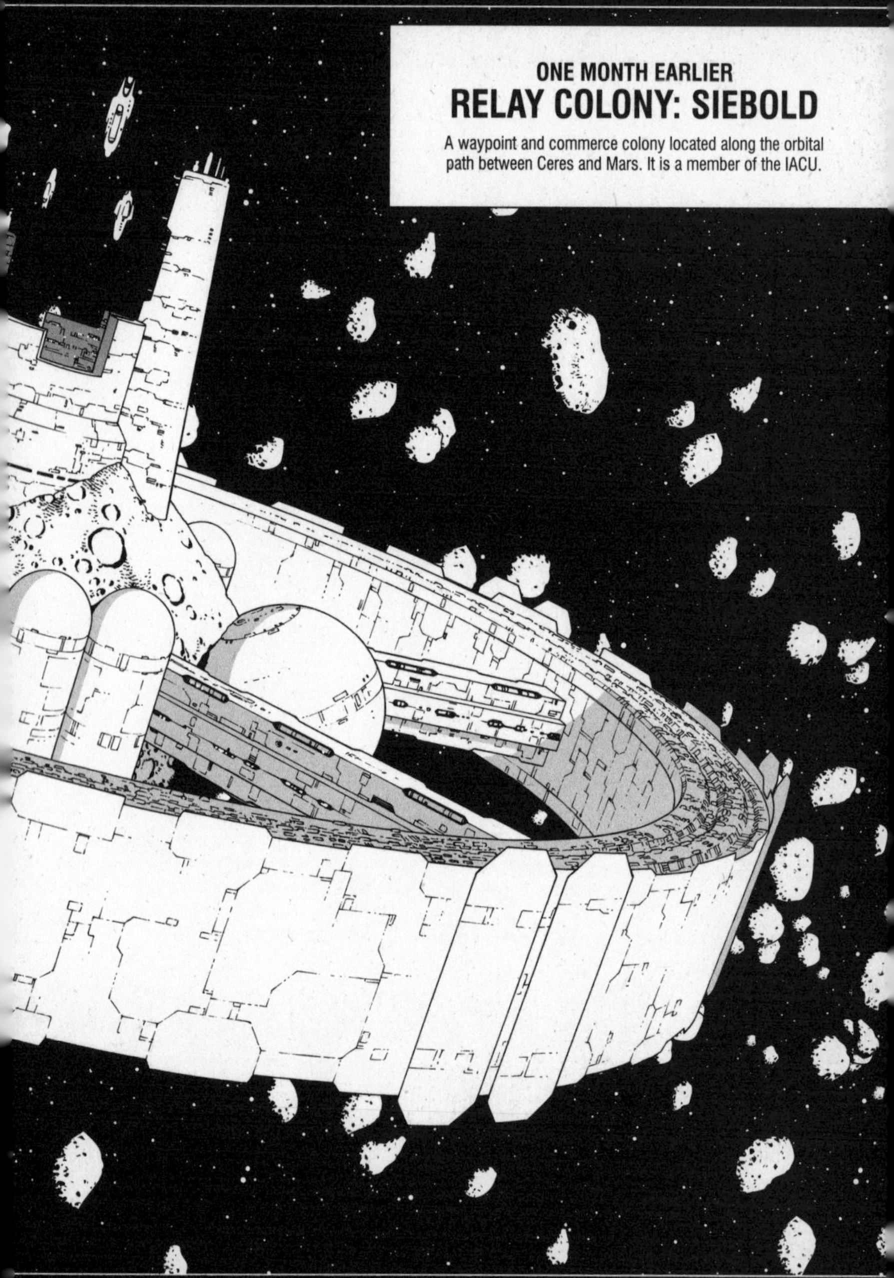
ONE MONTH EARLIER
RELAY COLONY: SIEBOLD
A waypoint and commerce colony located along the orbital path between Ceres and Mars. It is a member of the IACU.

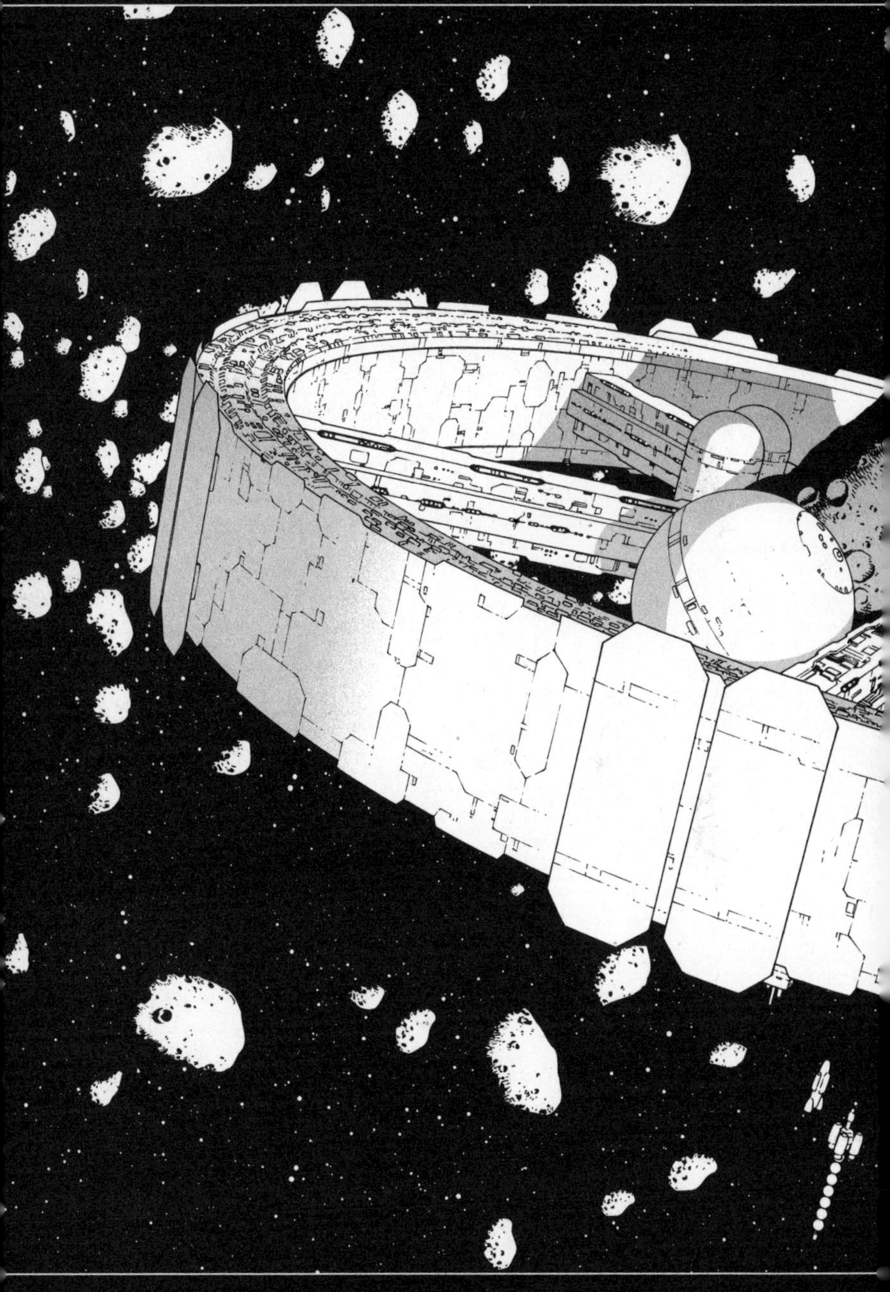

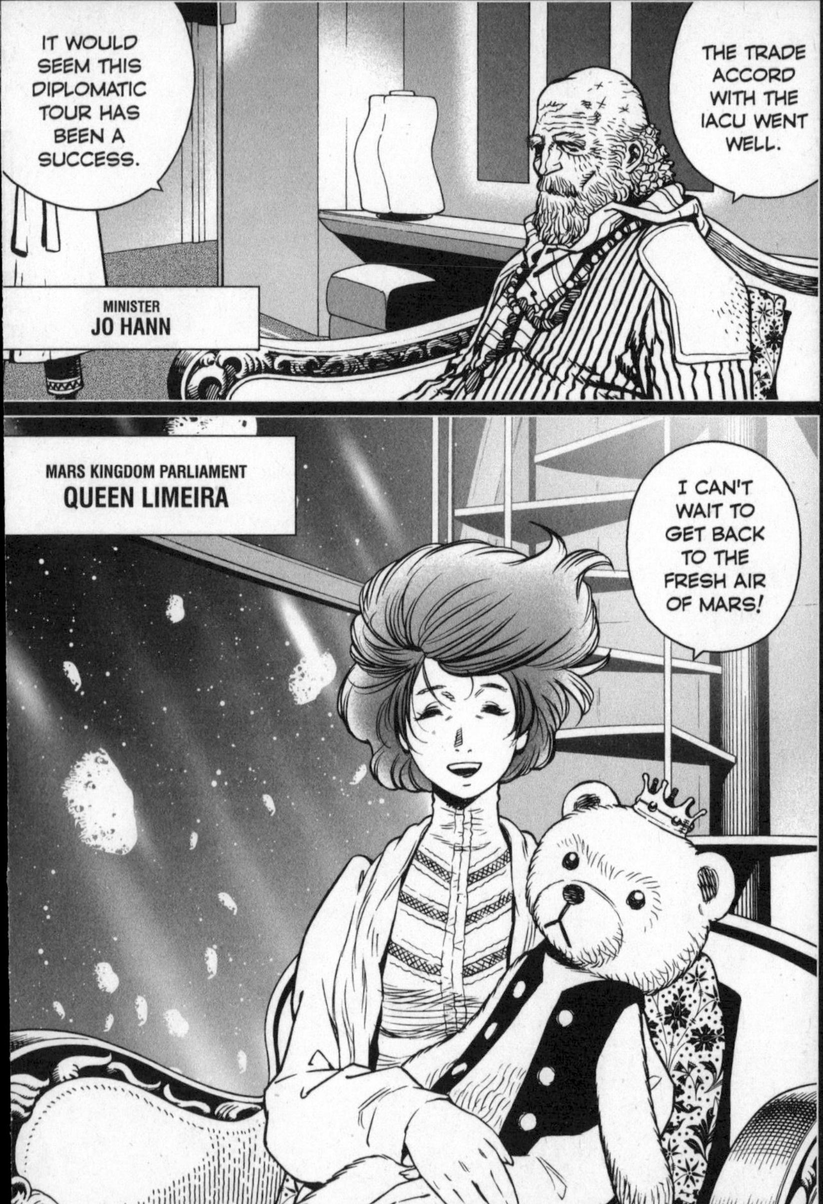
THE TRADE ACCORD WITH THE IACU WENT WELL.
IT WOULD SEEM THIS DIPLOMATIC TOUR HAS BEEN A SUCCESS.
MINISTER
JO HANN
MARS KINGDOM PARLIAMENT
QUEEN LIMEIRA
I CAN'T WAIT TO GET BACK TO THE FRESH AIR OF MARS!

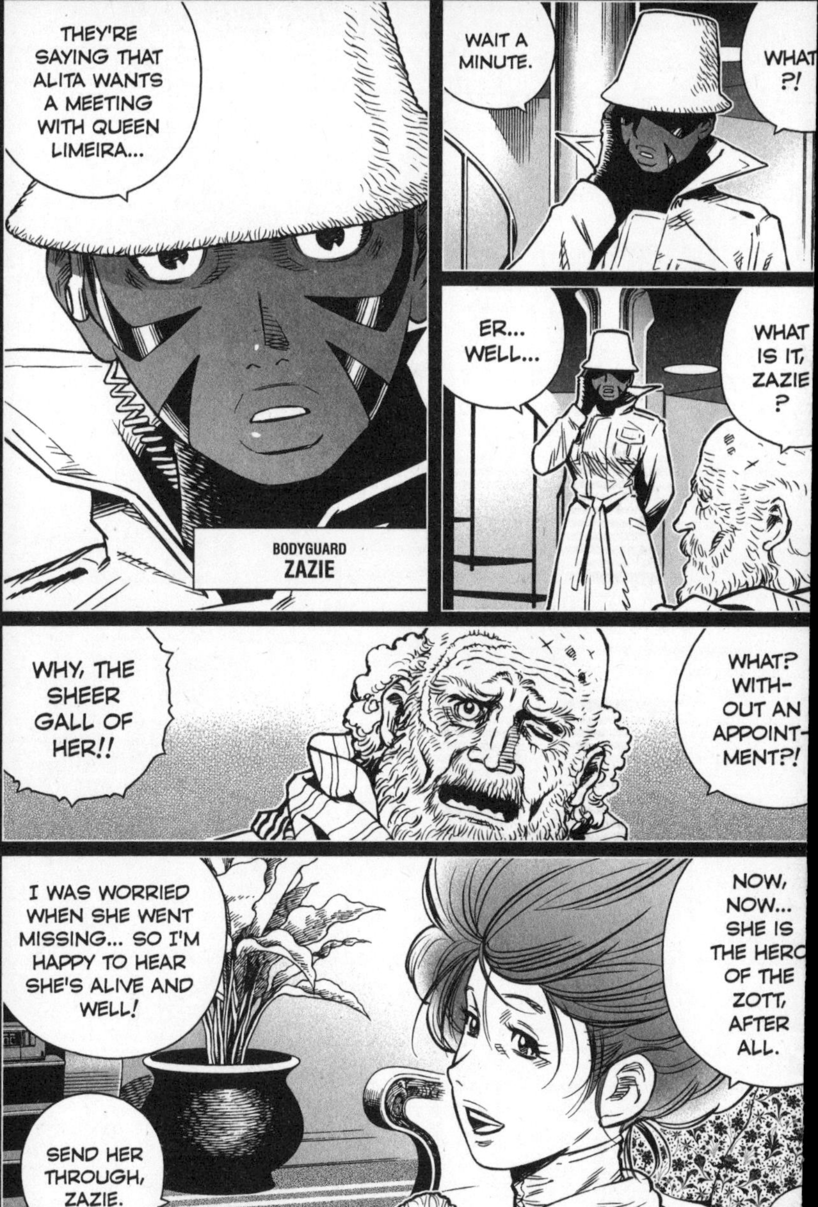
WHAT?!
WAIT A MINUTE.
WHAT IS IT, ZAZIE?
ER... WELL...
THEY'RE SAYING THAT ALITA WANTS A MEETING WITH QUEEN LIMEIRA...
BODYGUARD
ZAZIE
WHAT? WITH-OUT AN APPOINT-MENT?!
WHY, THE SHEER GALL OF HER!!
NOW, NOW... SHE IS THE HERO OF THE ZOTT, AFTER ALL.
I WAS WORRIED WHEN SHE WENT MISSING... SO I'M HAPPY TO HEAR SHE'S ALIVE AND WELL!
SEND HER THROUGH, ZAZIE.

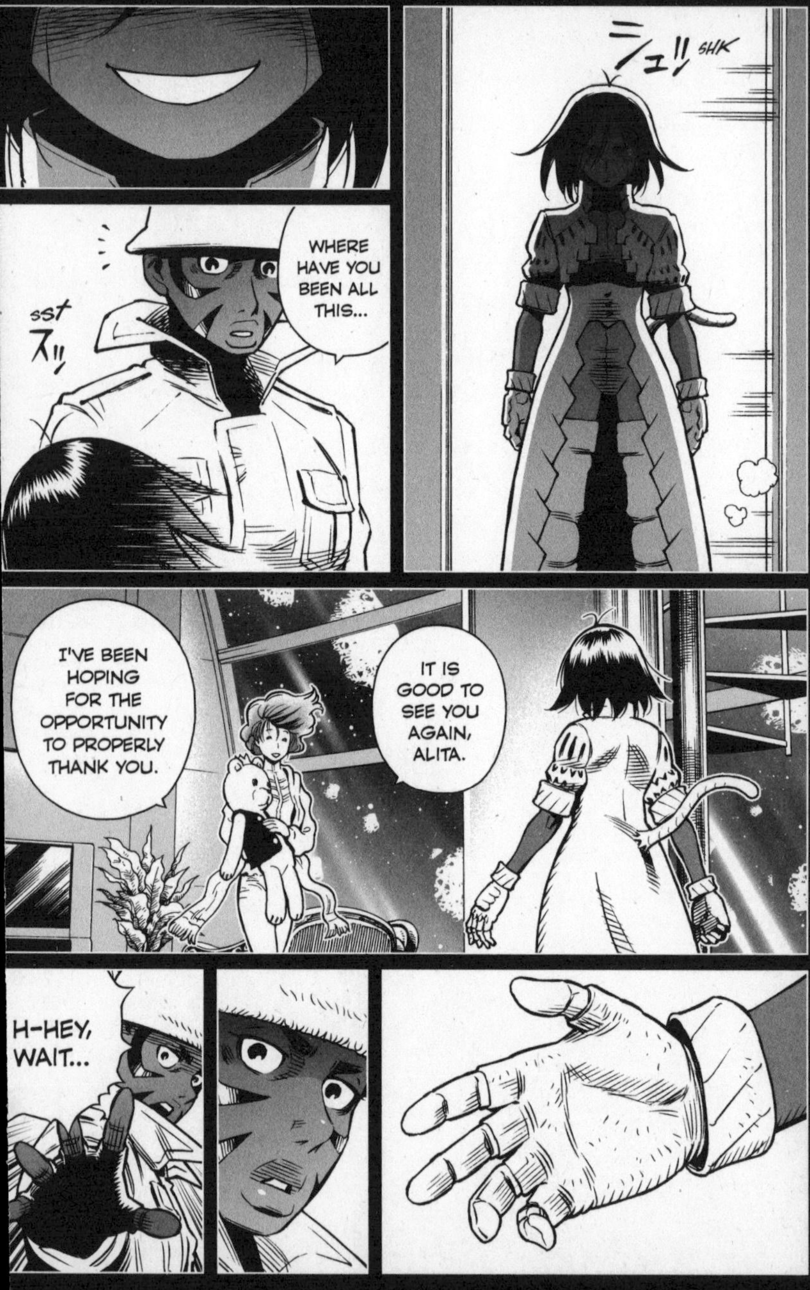
シュ!!
SHK
ス!!
sst
WHERE HAVE YOU BEEN ALL THIS...
IT IS GOOD TO SEE YOU AGAIN, ALITA.
I'VE BEEN HOPING FOR THE OPPORTUNITY TO PROPERLY THANK YOU.
H-HEY, WAIT...

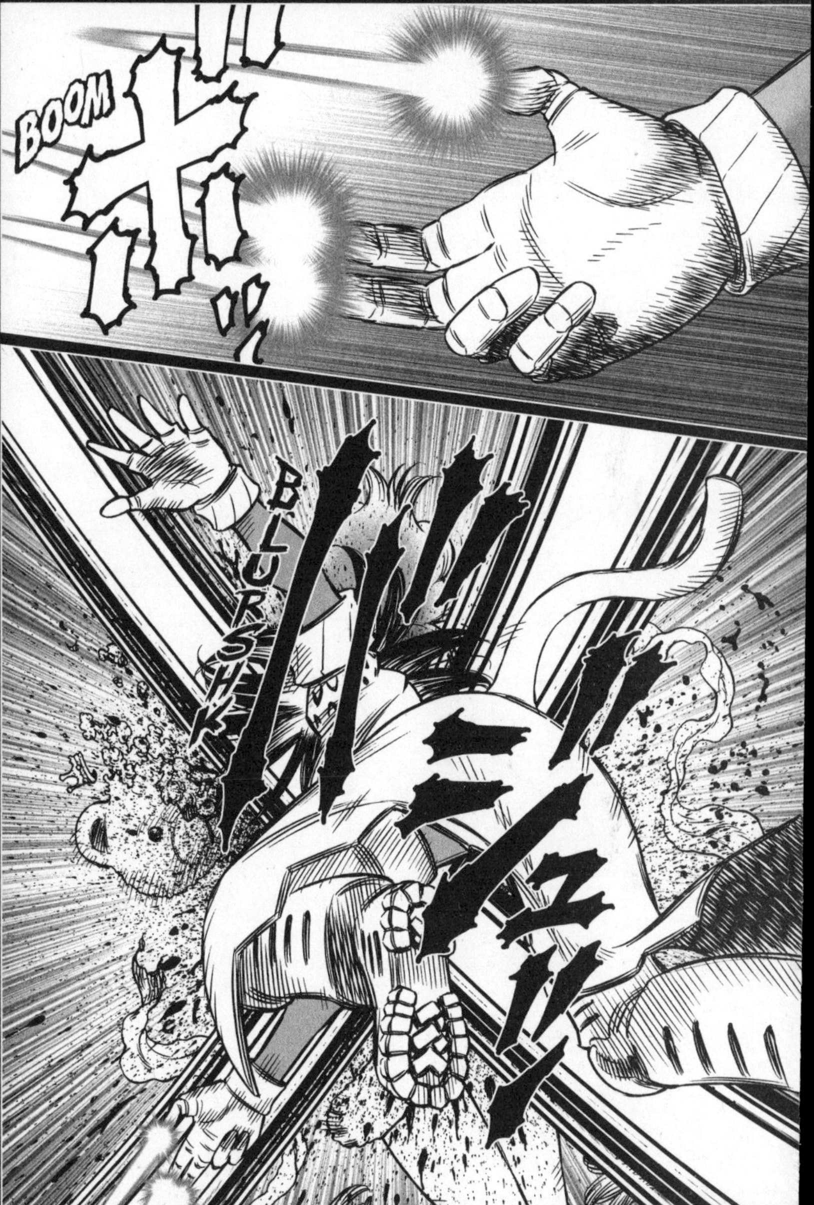
BOOM
BLURSHK

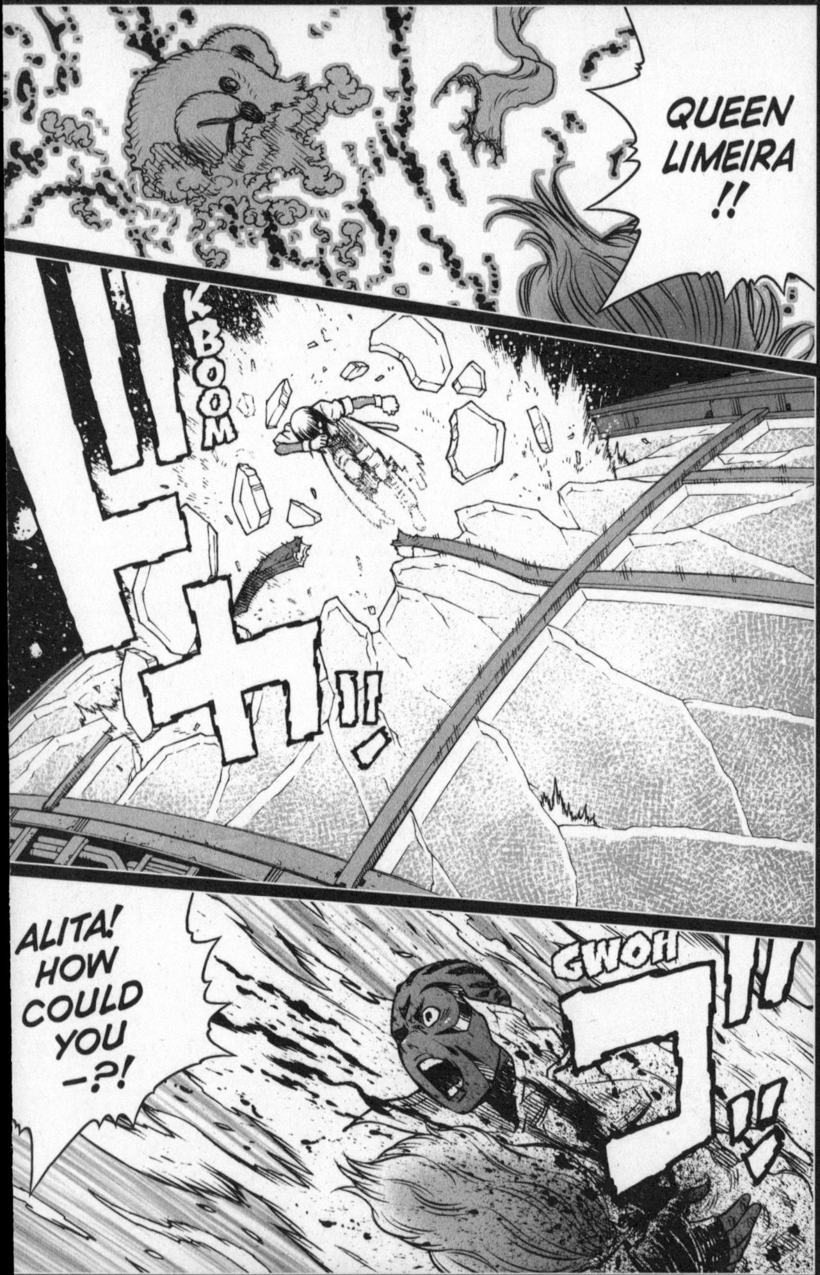
QUEEN LIMEIRA !!
KBOOM
GWOH
ALITA! HOW COULD YOU —?!

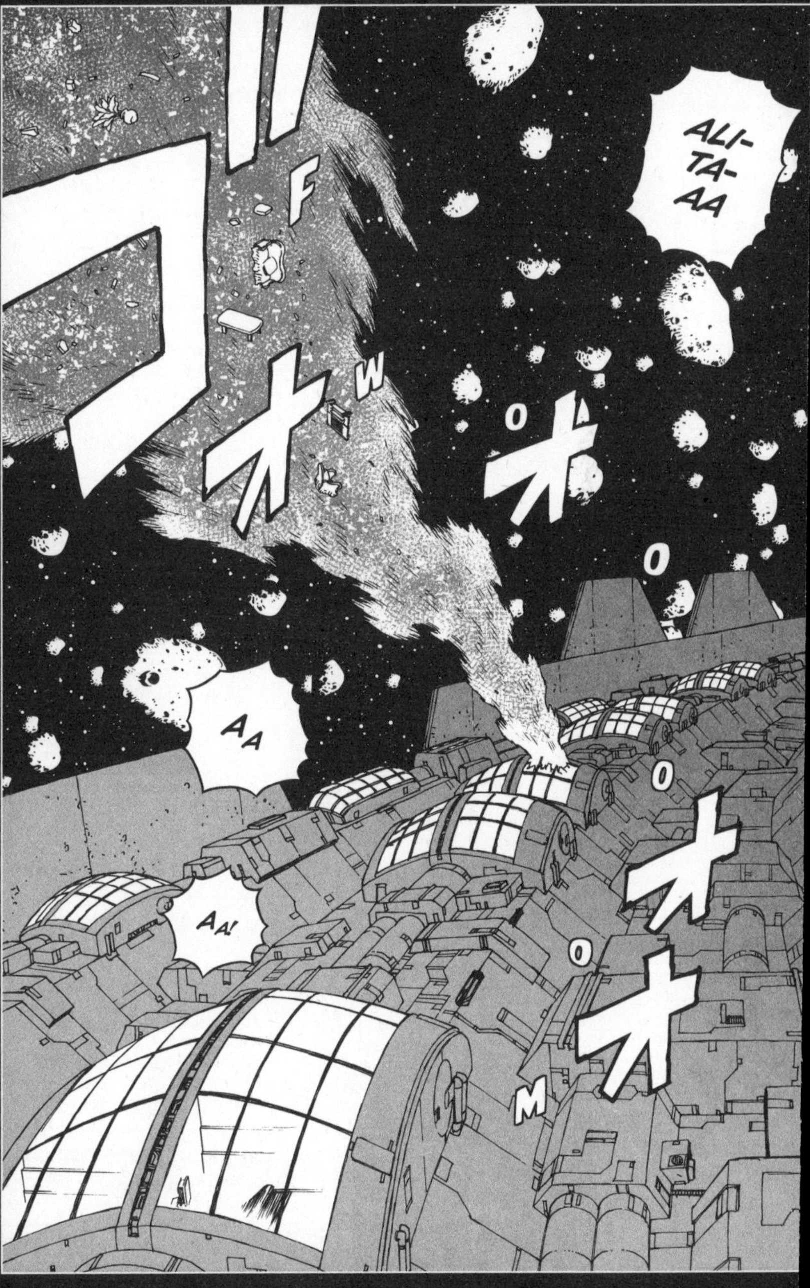
ALI-TA-AA
AA
AA!
ゴオオオオ
FWOOOOM

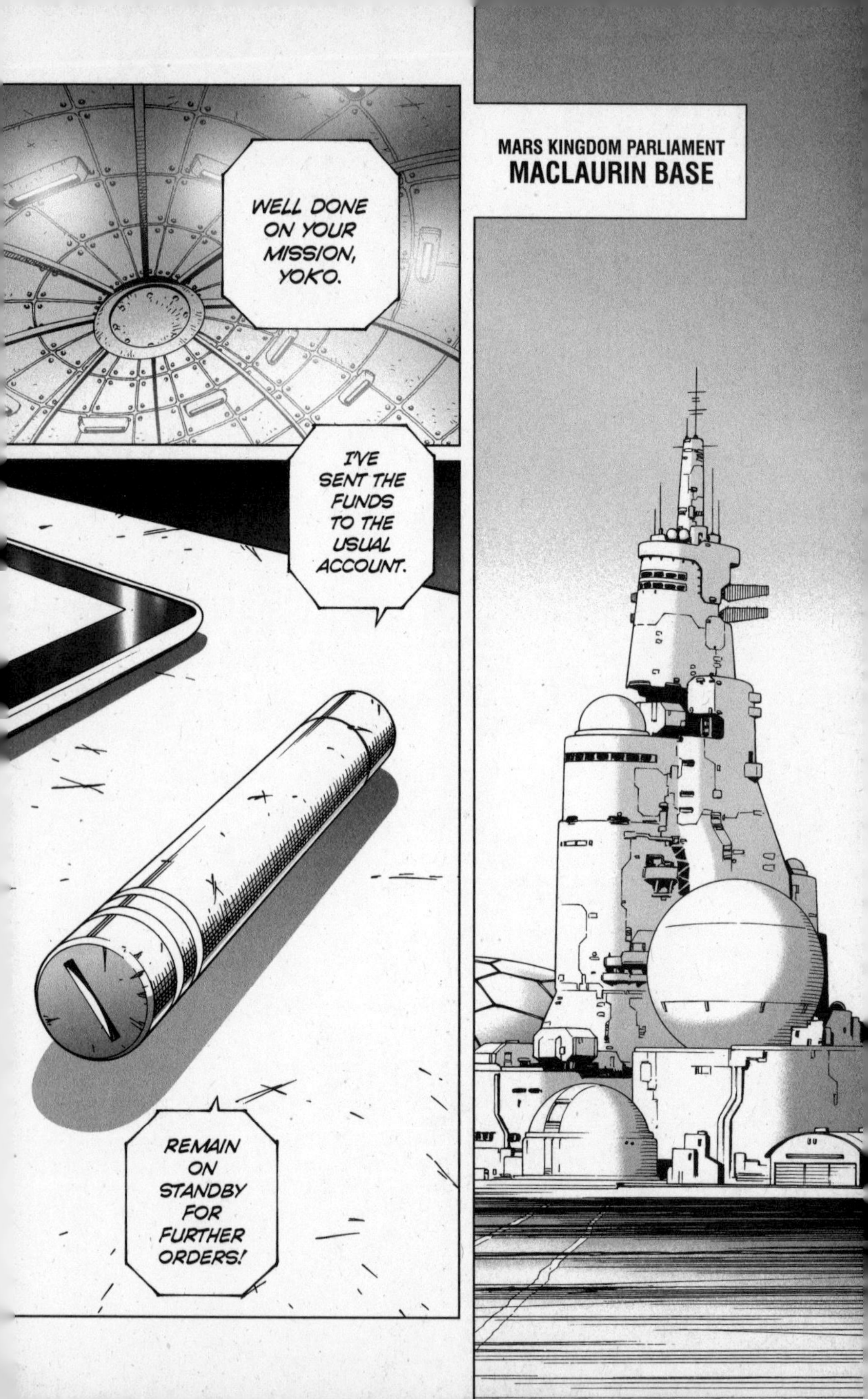
MARS KINGDOM PARLIAMENT
MACLAURIN BASE
WELL DONE ON YOUR MISSION, YOKO.
I'VE SENT THE FUNDS TO THE USUAL ACCOUNT.
REMAIN ON STANDBY FOR FURTHER ORDERS!

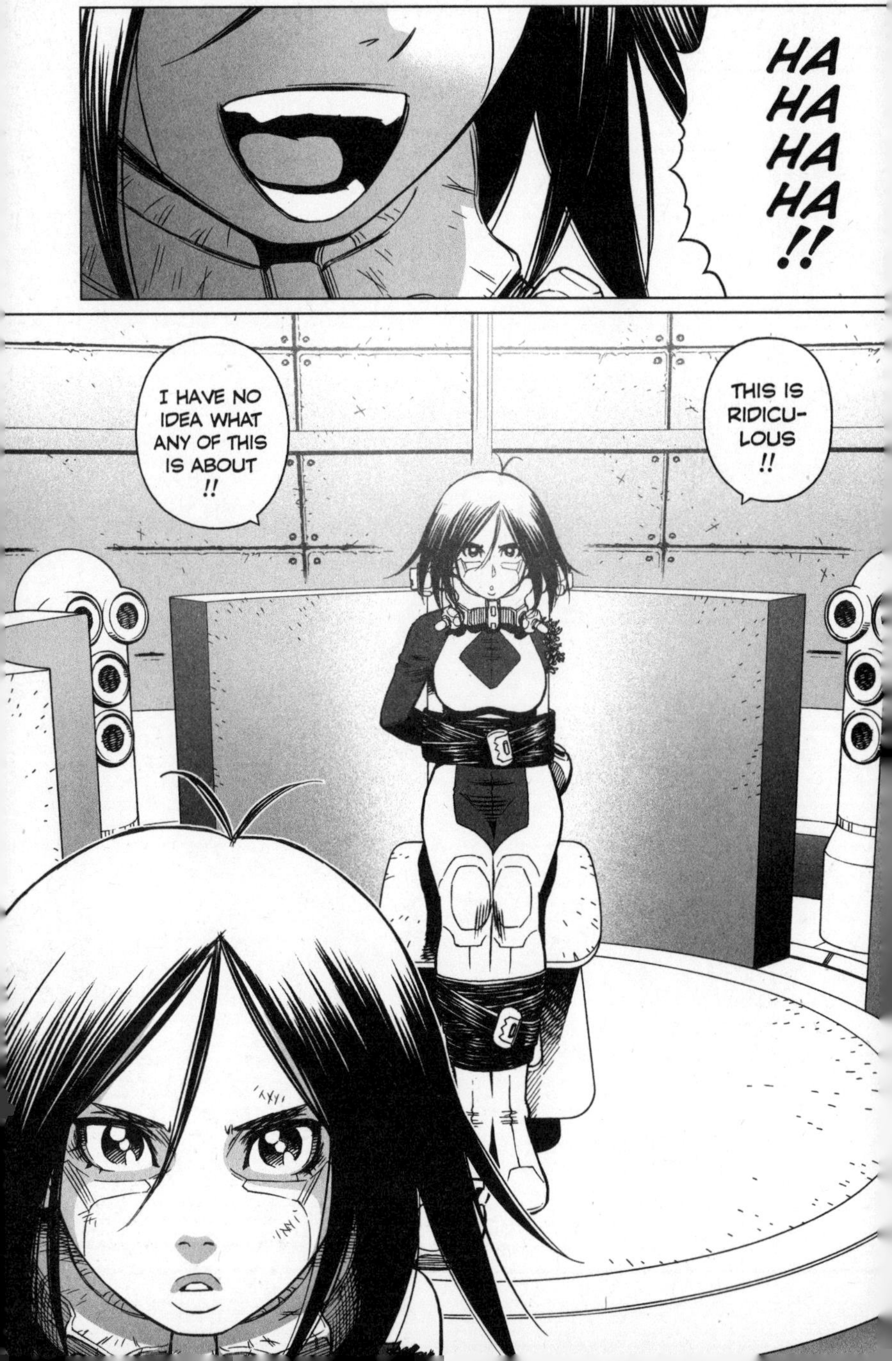
HA HA HA HA!!
THIS IS RIDICULOUS!!
I HAVE NO IDEA WHAT ANY OF THIS IS ABOUT!!

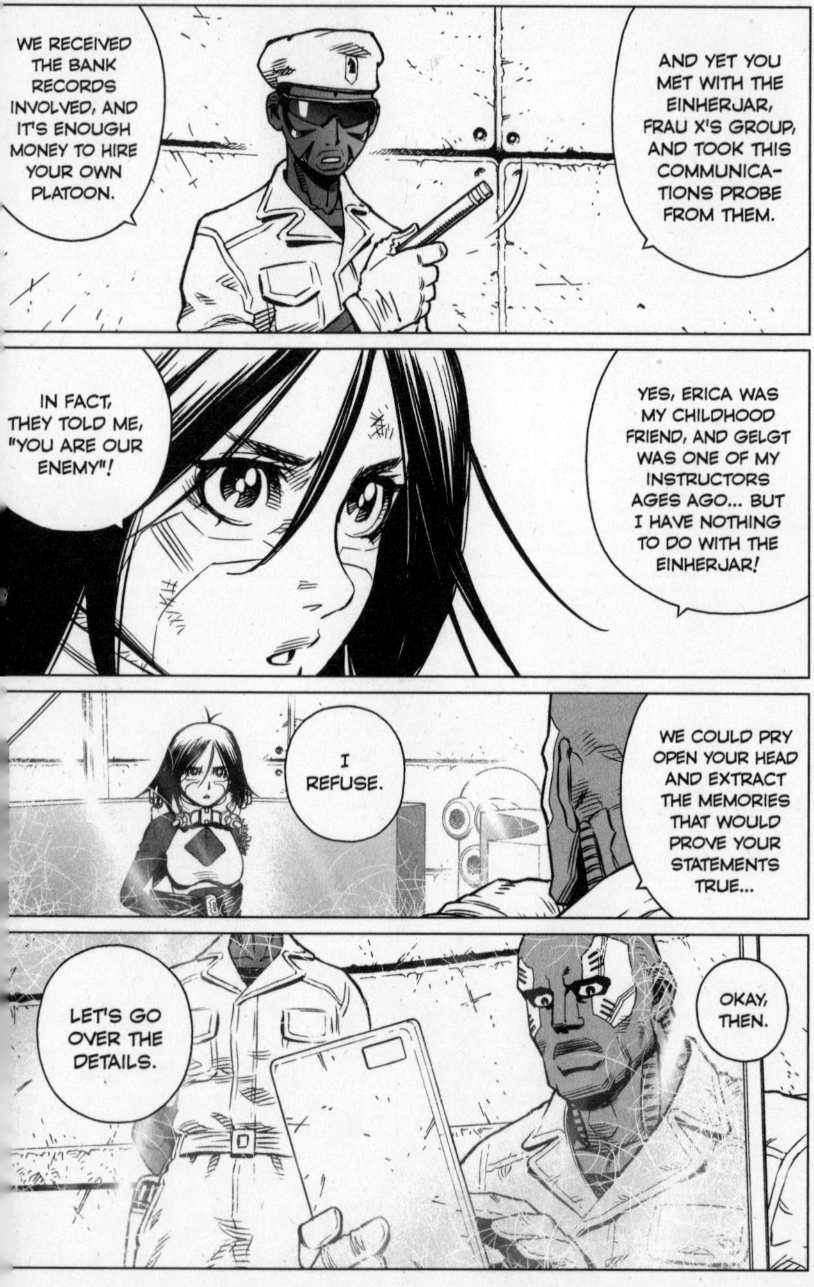
AND YET YOU MET WITH THE EINHERJAR, FRAU X'S GROUP, AND TOOK THIS COMMUNICATIONS PROBE FROM THEM.
WE RECEIVED THE BANK RECORDS INVOLVED, AND IT'S ENOUGH MONEY TO HIRE YOUR OWN PLATOON.
YES, ERICA WAS MY CHILDHOOD FRIEND, AND GELGT WAS ONE OF MY INSTRUCTORS AGES AGO... BUT I HAVE NOTHING TO DO WITH THE EINHERJAR!
IN FACT, THEY TOLD ME, "YOU ARE OUR ENEMY"!
WE COULD PRY OPEN YOUR HEAD AND EXTRACT THE MEMORIES THAT WOULD PROVE YOUR STATEMENTS TRUE...
I REFUSE.
OKAY, THEN.
LET'S GO OVER THE DETAILS.

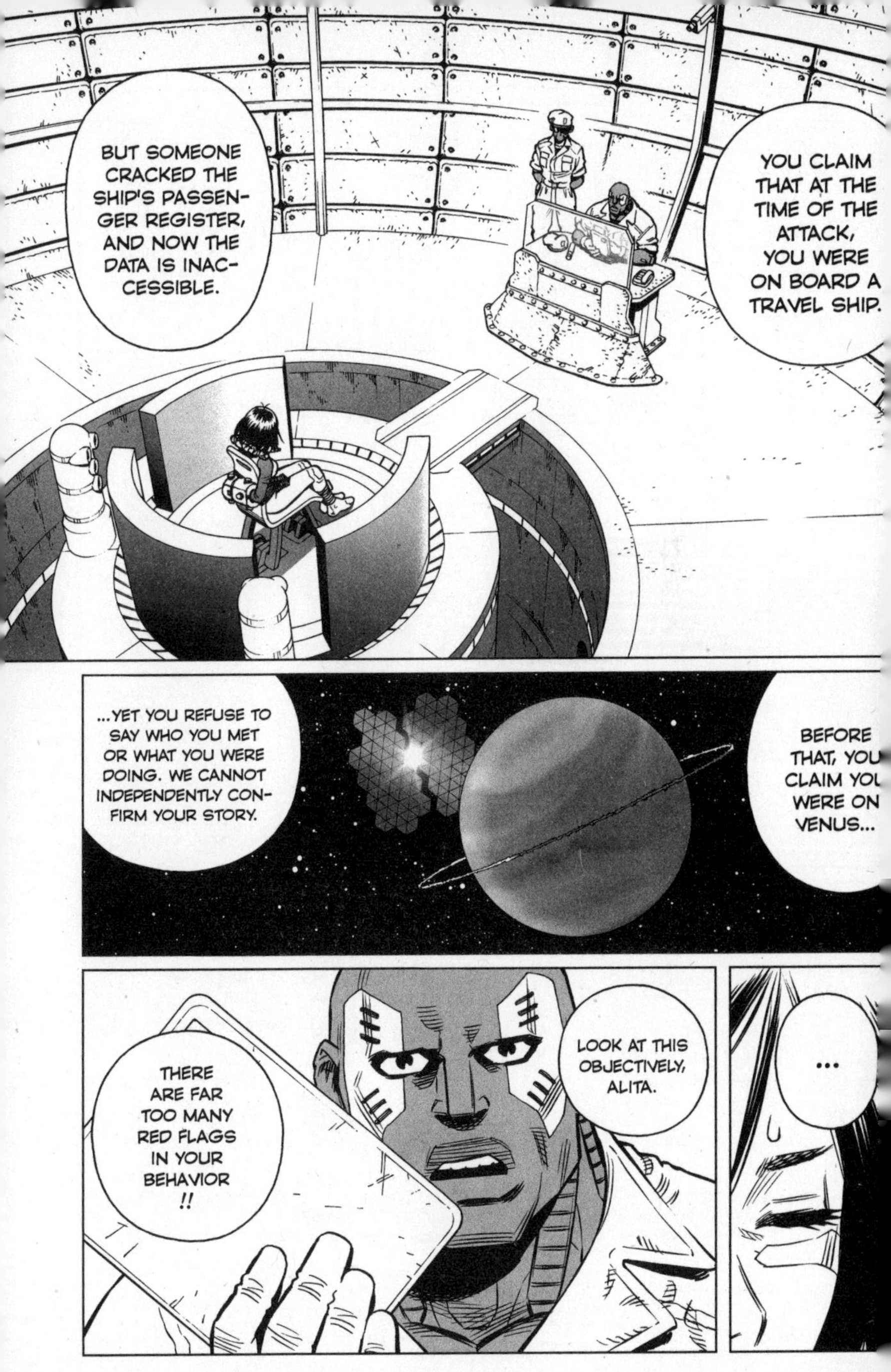
YOU CLAIM THAT AT THE TIME OF THE ATTACK, YOU WERE ON BOARD A TRAVEL SHIP.
BUT SOMEONE CRACKED THE SHIP'S PASSENGER REGISTER, AND NOW THE DATA IS INACCESSIBLE.
BEFORE THAT, YOU CLAIM YOU WERE ON VENUS...
...YET YOU REFUSE TO SAY WHO YOU MET OR WHAT YOU WERE DOING. WE CANNOT INDEPENDENTLY CONFIRM YOUR STORY.
...
LOOK AT THIS OBJECTIVELY, ALITA.
THERE ARE FAR TOO MANY RED FLAGS IN YOUR BEHAVIOR !!

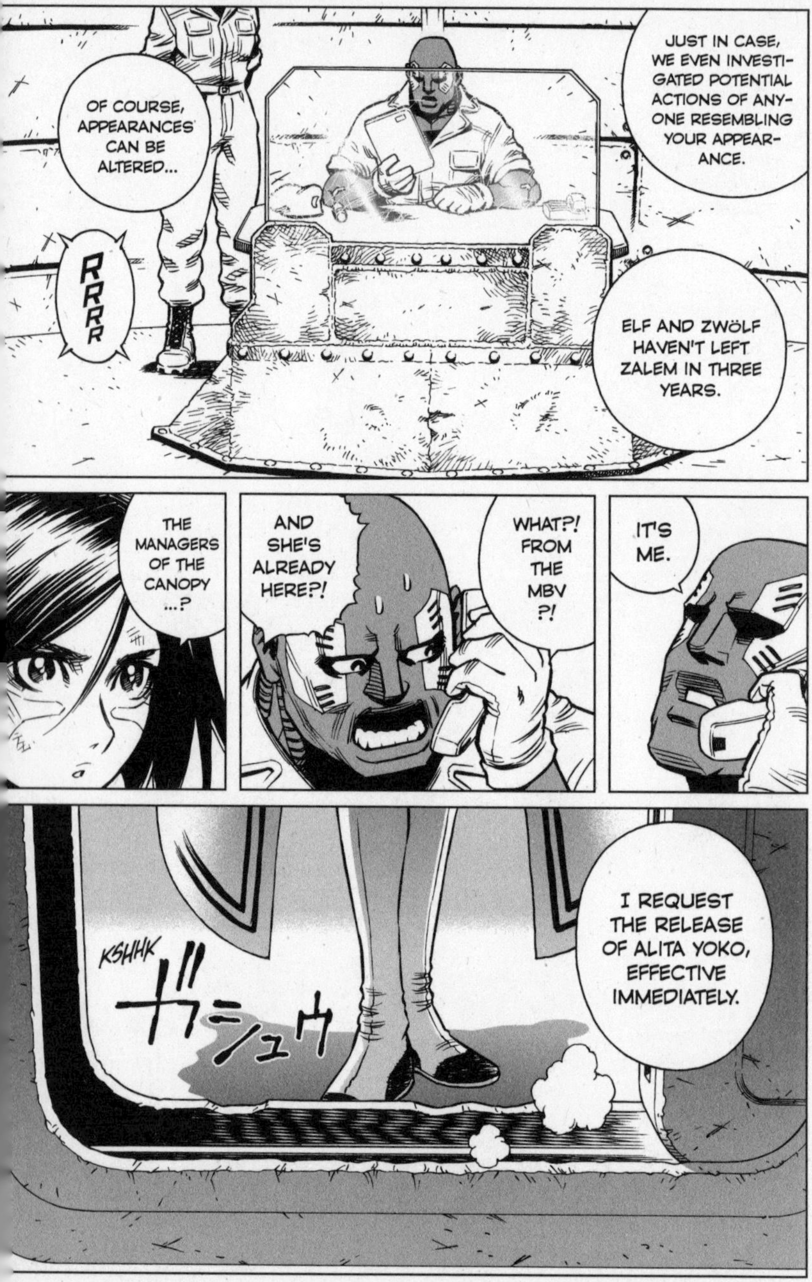
OF COURSE, APPEARANCES CAN BE ALTERED...
JUST IN CASE, WE EVEN INVESTIGATED POTENTIAL ACTIONS OF ANYONE RESEMBLING YOUR APPEARANCE.
ELF AND ZWÖLF HAVEN'T LEFT ZALEM IN THREE YEARS.
RRRR
IT'S ME.
WHAT?! FROM THE MBV ?!
AND SHE'S ALREADY HERE?!
THE MANAGERS OF THE CANOPY ...?
I REQUEST THE RELEASE OF ALITA YOKO, EFFECTIVE IMMEDIATELY.
KSHHK

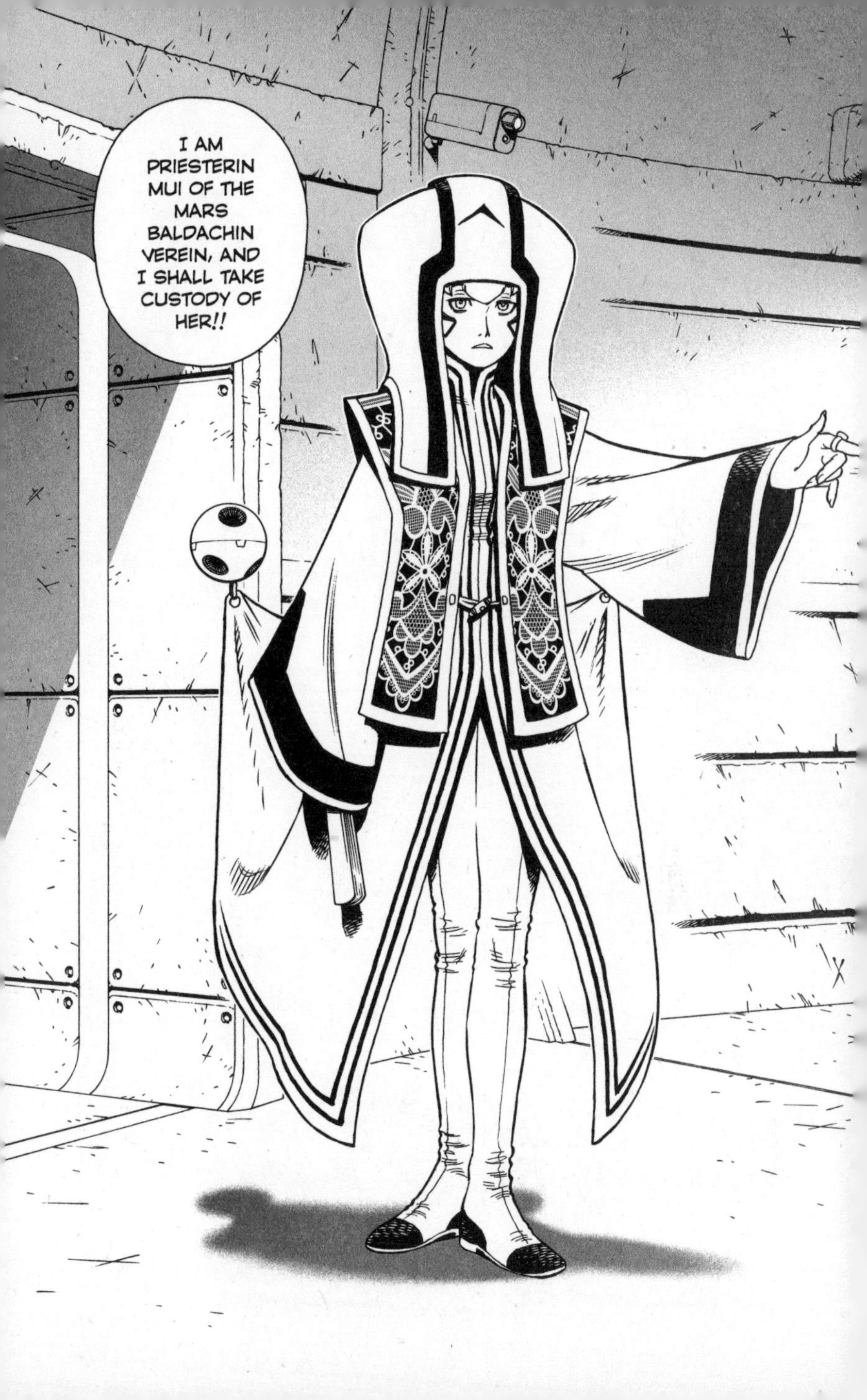
I AM PRIESTERIN MUI OF THE MARS BALDACHIN VEREIN, AND I SHALL TAKE CUSTODY OF HER!!

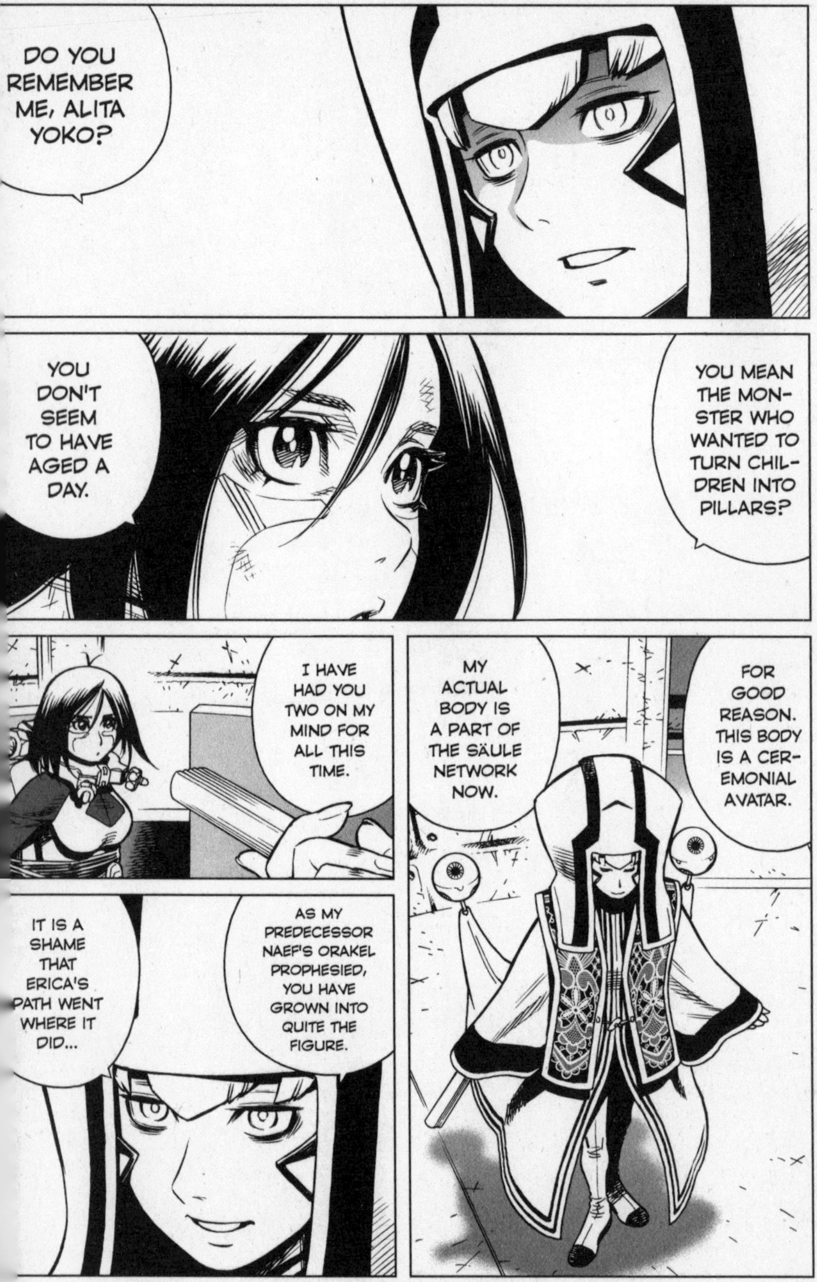
DO YOU REMEMBER ME, ALITA YOKO?
YOU MEAN THE MONSTER WHO WANTED TO TURN CHILDREN INTO PILLARS?
YOU DON'T SEEM TO HAVE AGED A DAY.
FOR GOOD REASON. THIS BODY IS A CEREMONIAL AVATAR.
MY ACTUAL BODY IS A PART OF THE SÄULE NETWORK NOW.
I HAVE HAD YOU TWO ON MY MIND FOR ALL THIS TIME.
AS MY PREDECESSOR NAEF'S ORAKEL PROPHESIED, YOU HAVE GROWN INTO QUITE THE FIGURE.
IT IS A SHAME THAT ERICA'S PATH WENT WHERE IT DID...

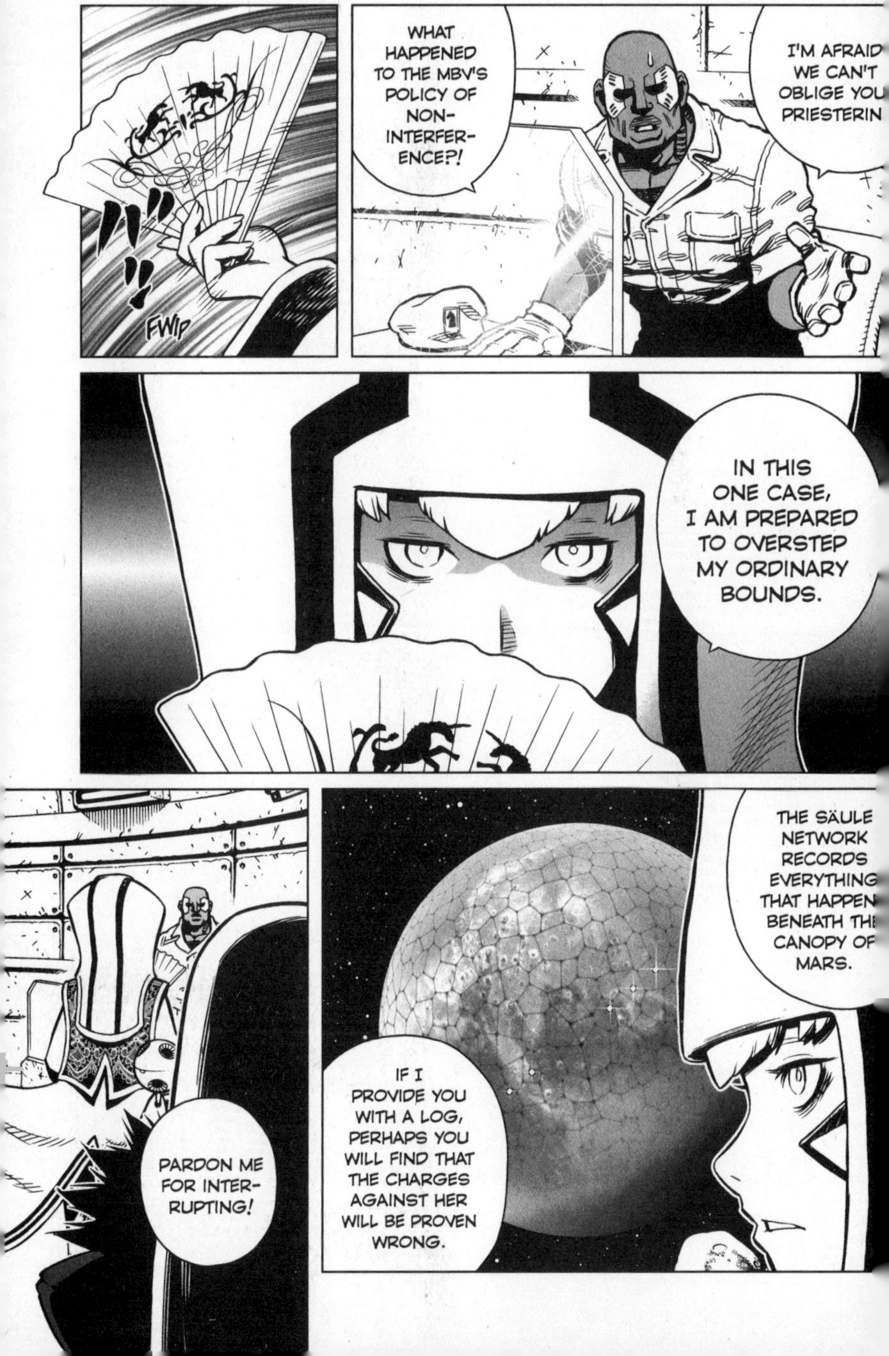
I'M AFRAID WE CAN'T OBLIGE YOU PRIESTERIN
WHAT HAPPENED TO THE MBV'S POLICY OF NON-INTERFERENCE?!
FWIP
IN THIS ONE CASE, I AM PREPARED TO OVERSTEP MY ORDINARY BOUNDS.
THE SÄULE NETWORK RECORDS EVERYTHING THAT HAPPEN BENEATH THE CANOPY OF MARS.
IF I PROVIDE YOU WITH A LOG, PERHAPS YOU WILL FIND THAT THE CHARGES AGAINST HER WILL BE PROVEN WRONG.
PARDON ME FOR INTERRUPTING!

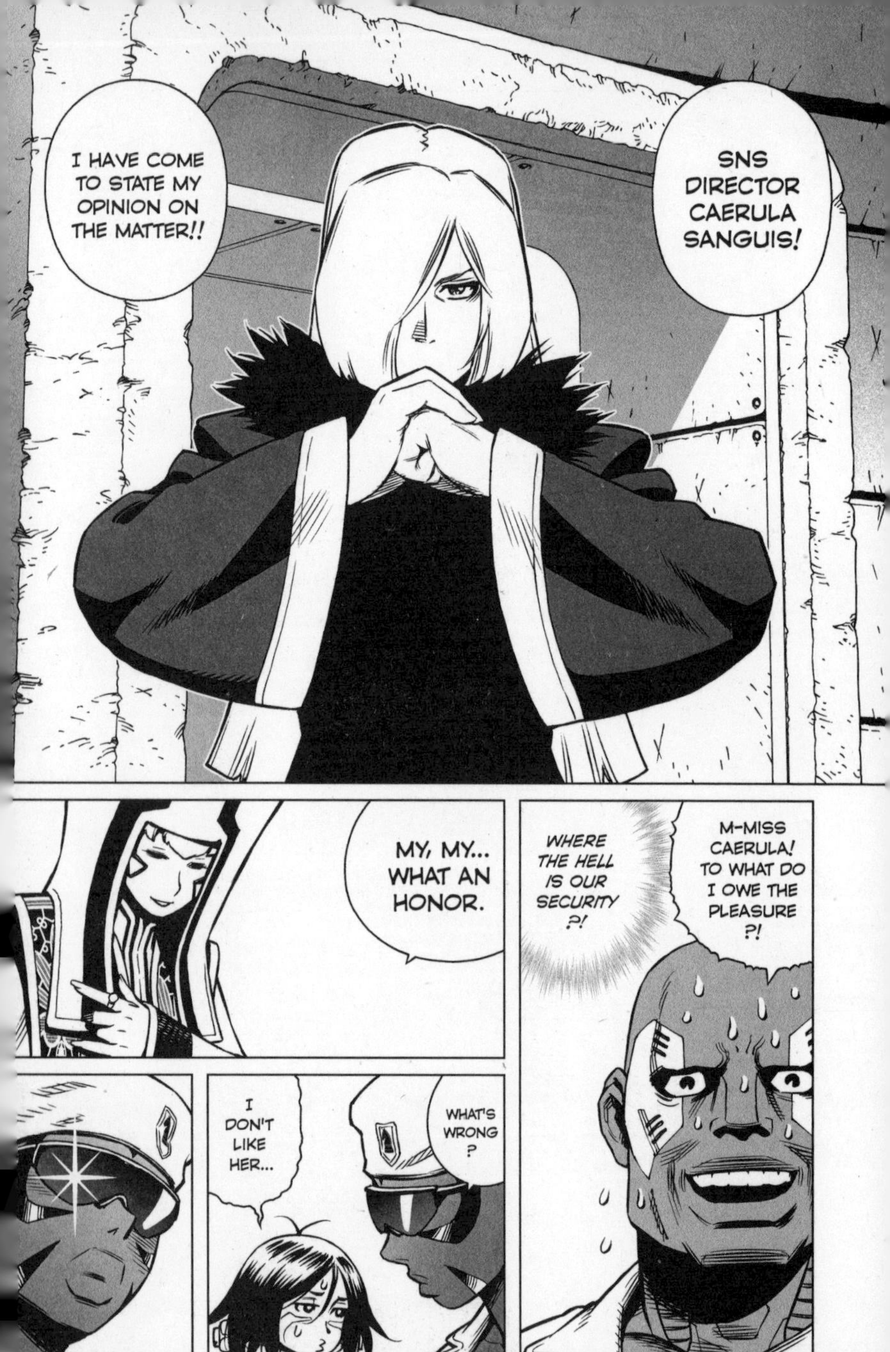
SNS DIRECTOR CAERULA SANGUIS!
I HAVE COME TO STATE MY OPINION ON THE MATTER!!
M-MISS CAERULA! TO WHAT DO I OWE THE PLEASURE ?!
WHERE THE HELL IS OUR SECURITY ?!
MY, MY... WHAT AN HONOR.
WHAT'S WRONG ?
I DON'T LIKE HER...

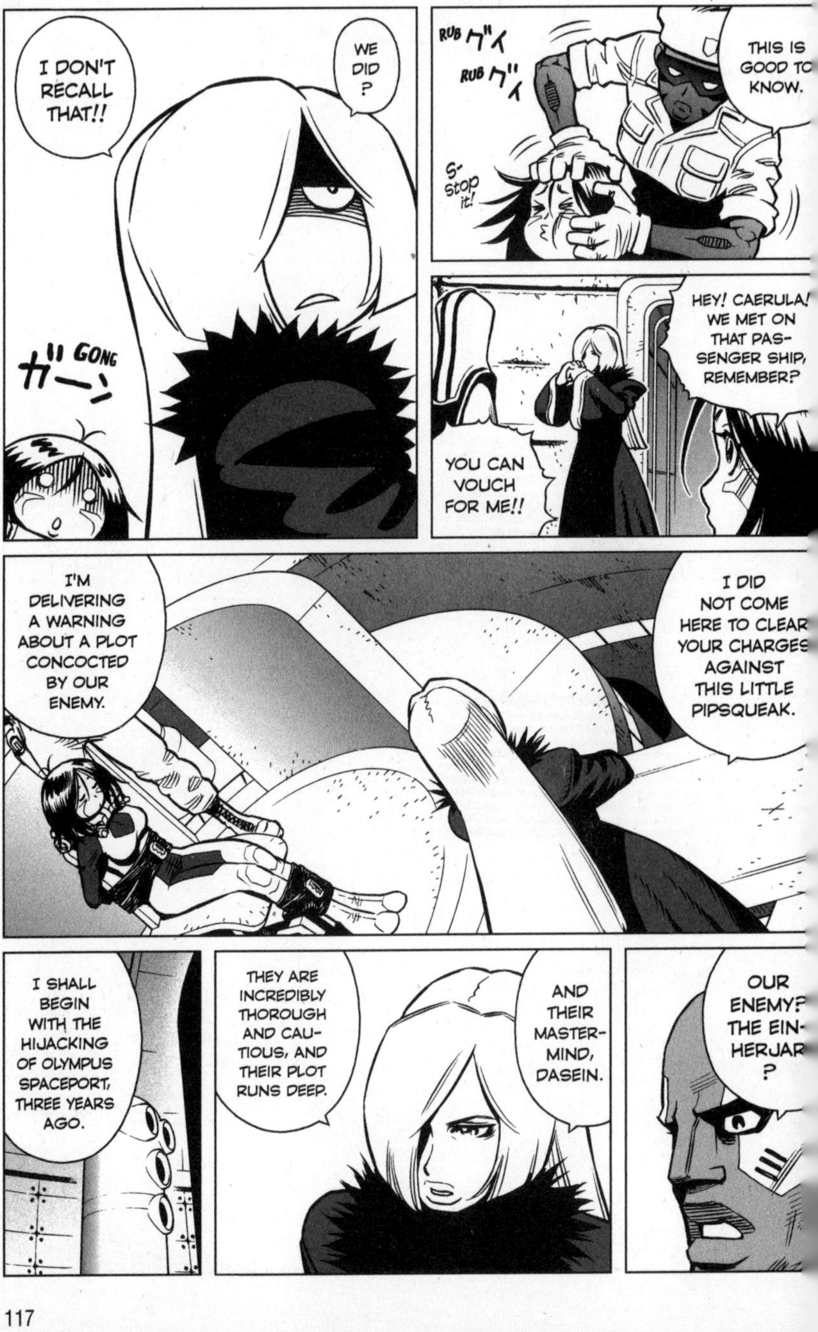
THIS IS GOOD TO KNOW.
RUB グイ
RUB グイ
S-Stop it!
HEY! CAERULA! WE MET ON THAT PAS-SENGER SHIP, REMEMBER?
YOU CAN VOUCH FOR ME!!
WE DID?
I DON'T RECALL THAT!!
GONG ガーン
I DID NOT COME HERE TO CLEAR YOUR CHARGES AGAINST THIS LITTLE PIPSQUEAK.
I'M DELIVERING A WARNING ABOUT A PLOT CONCOCTED BY OUR ENEMY.
OUR ENEMY? THE EIN-HERJAR?
AND THEIR MASTER-MIND, DASEIN.
THEY ARE INCREDIBLY THOROUGH AND CAU-TIOUS, AND THEIR PLOT RUNS DEEP.
I SHALL BEGIN WITH THE HIJACKING OF OLYMPUS SPACEPORT, THREE YEARS AGO.

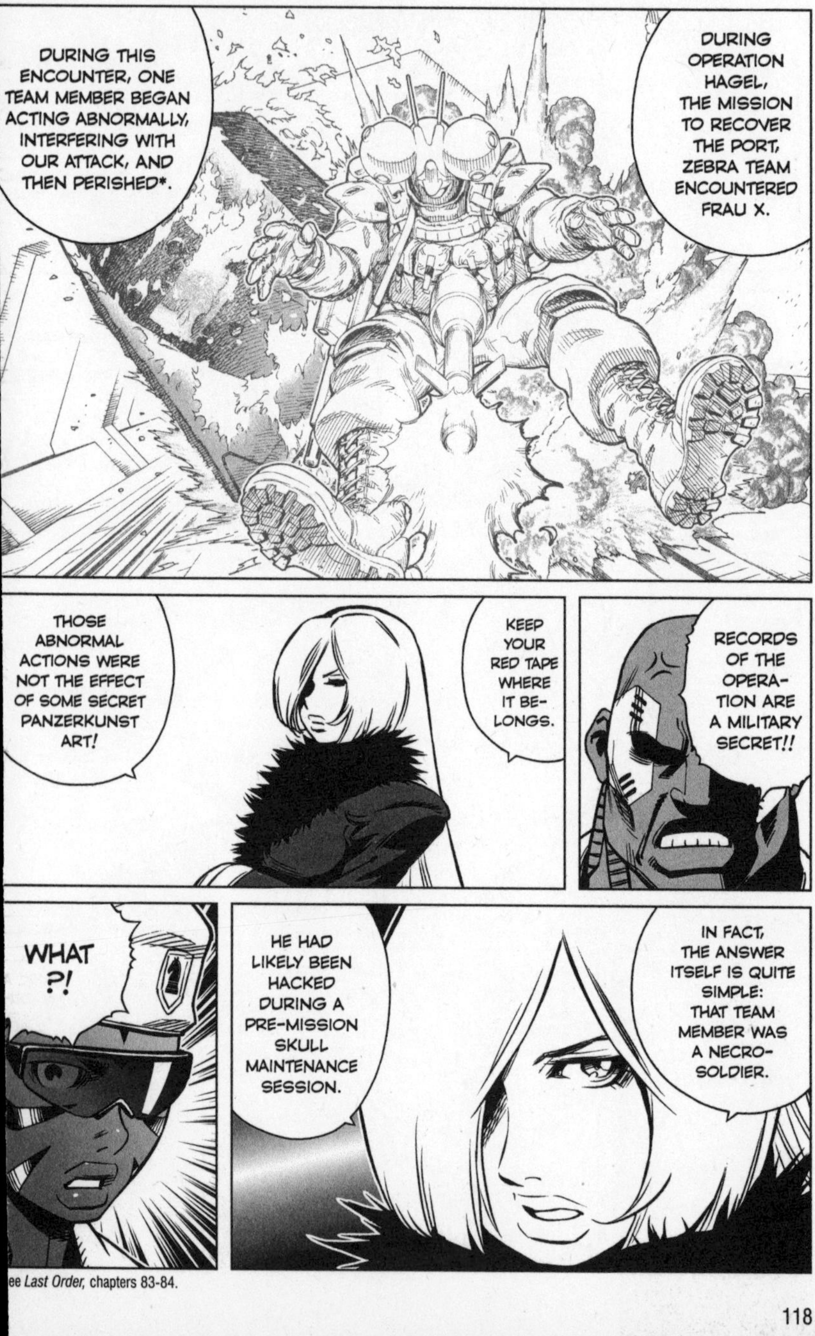
DURING OPERATION HAGEL, THE MISSION TO RECOVER THE PORT, ZEBRA TEAM ENCOUNTERED FRAU X.
DURING THIS ENCOUNTER, ONE TEAM MEMBER BEGAN ACTING ABNORMALLY, INTERFERING WITH OUR ATTACK, AND THEN PERISHED*.
RECORDS OF THE OPERA-TION ARE A MILITARY SECRET!!
KEEP YOUR RED TAPE WHERE IT BE-LONGS.
THOSE ABNORMAL ACTIONS WERE NOT THE EFFECT OF SOME SECRET PANZERKUNST ART!
IN FACT, THE ANSWER ITSELF IS QUITE SIMPLE: THAT TEAM MEMBER WAS A NECRO-SOLDIER.
HE HAD LIKELY BEEN HACKED DURING A PRE-MISSION SKULL MAINTENANCE SESSION.
WHAT?!

ee *Last Order*, chapters 83-84.

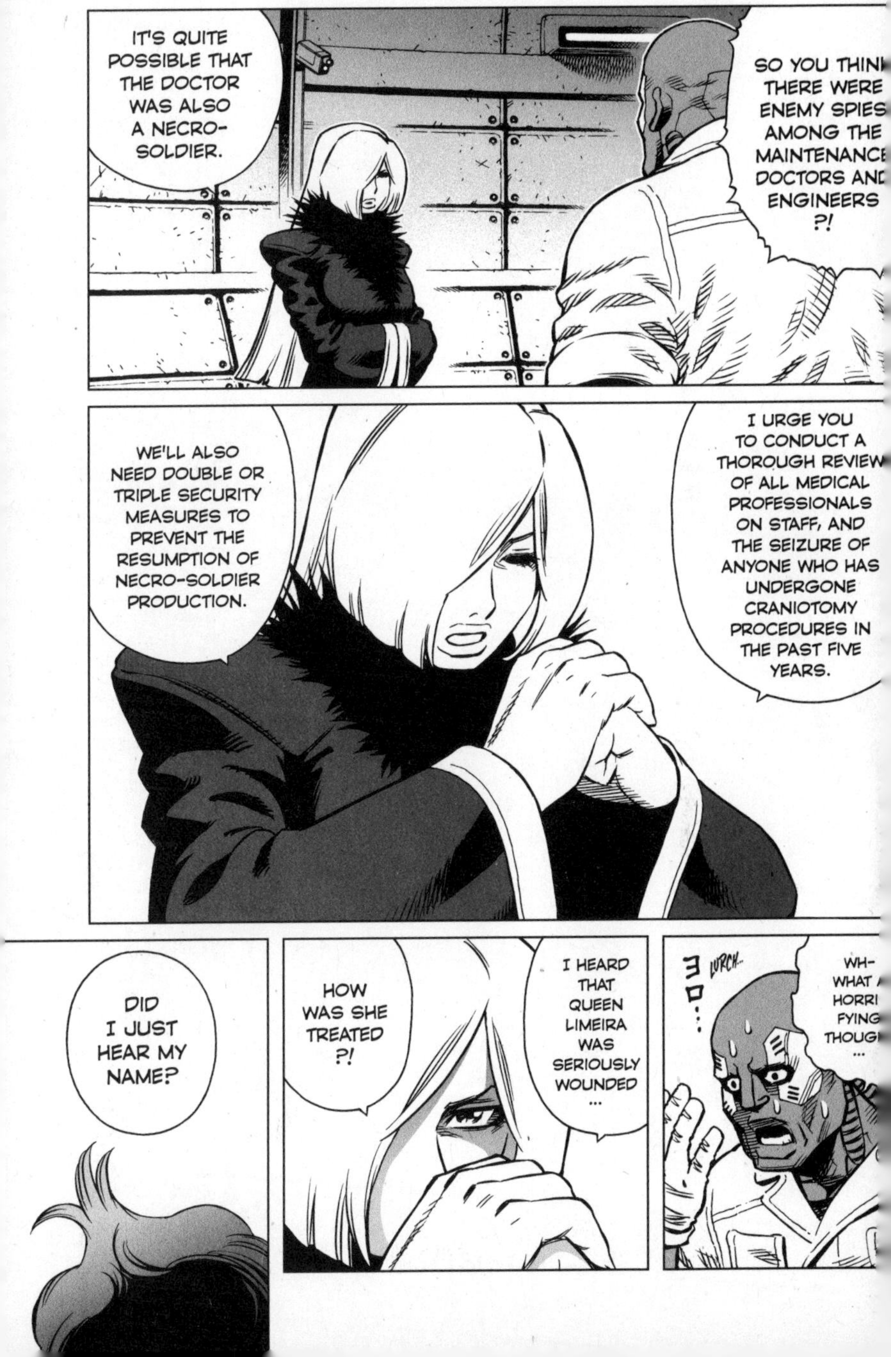
SO YOU THINK THERE WERE ENEMY SPIES AMONG THE MAINTENANCE DOCTORS AND ENGINEERS ?!
IT'S QUITE POSSIBLE THAT THE DOCTOR WAS ALSO A NECRO-SOLDIER.
I URGE YOU TO CONDUCT A THOROUGH REVIEW OF ALL MEDICAL PROFESSIONALS ON STAFF, AND THE SEIZURE OF ANYONE WHO HAS UNDERGONE CRANIOTOMY PROCEDURES IN THE PAST FIVE YEARS.
WE'LL ALSO NEED DOUBLE OR TRIPLE SECURITY MEASURES TO PREVENT THE RESUMPTION OF NECRO-SOLDIER PRODUCTION.
WH- WHAT A HORRIFYING THOUGHT ...
ヨロ…
LURCH...
I HEARD THAT QUEEN LIMEIRA WAS SERIOUSLY WOUNDED ...
HOW WAS SHE TREATED ?!
DID I JUST HEAR MY NAME?

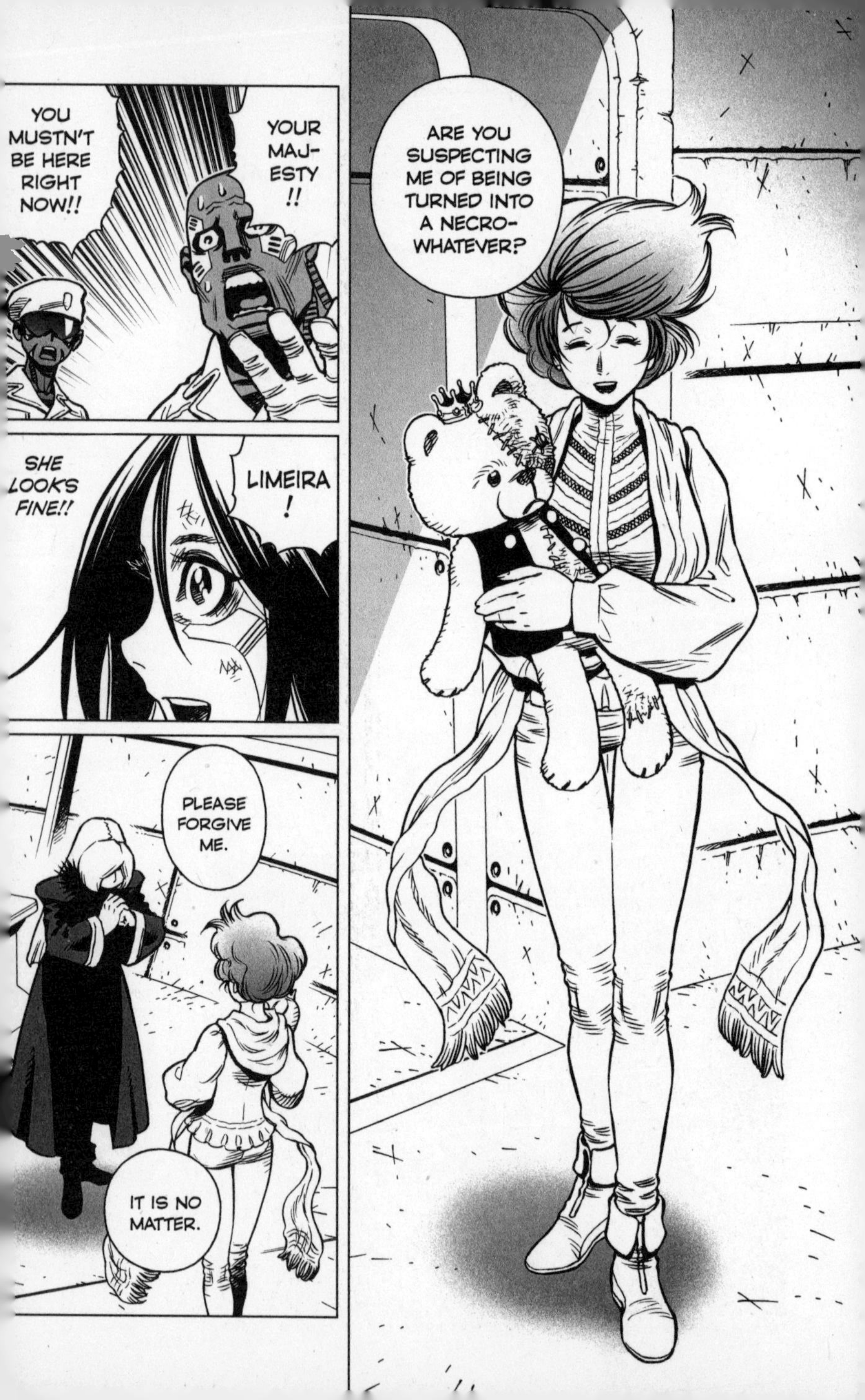
ARE YOU SUSPECTING ME OF BEING TURNED INTO A NECRO-WHATEVER?
YOUR MAJ-ESTY!!
YOU MUSTN'T BE HERE RIGHT NOW!!
LIMEIRA!
SHE LOOKS FINE!!
PLEASE FORGIVE ME.
IT IS NO MATTER.

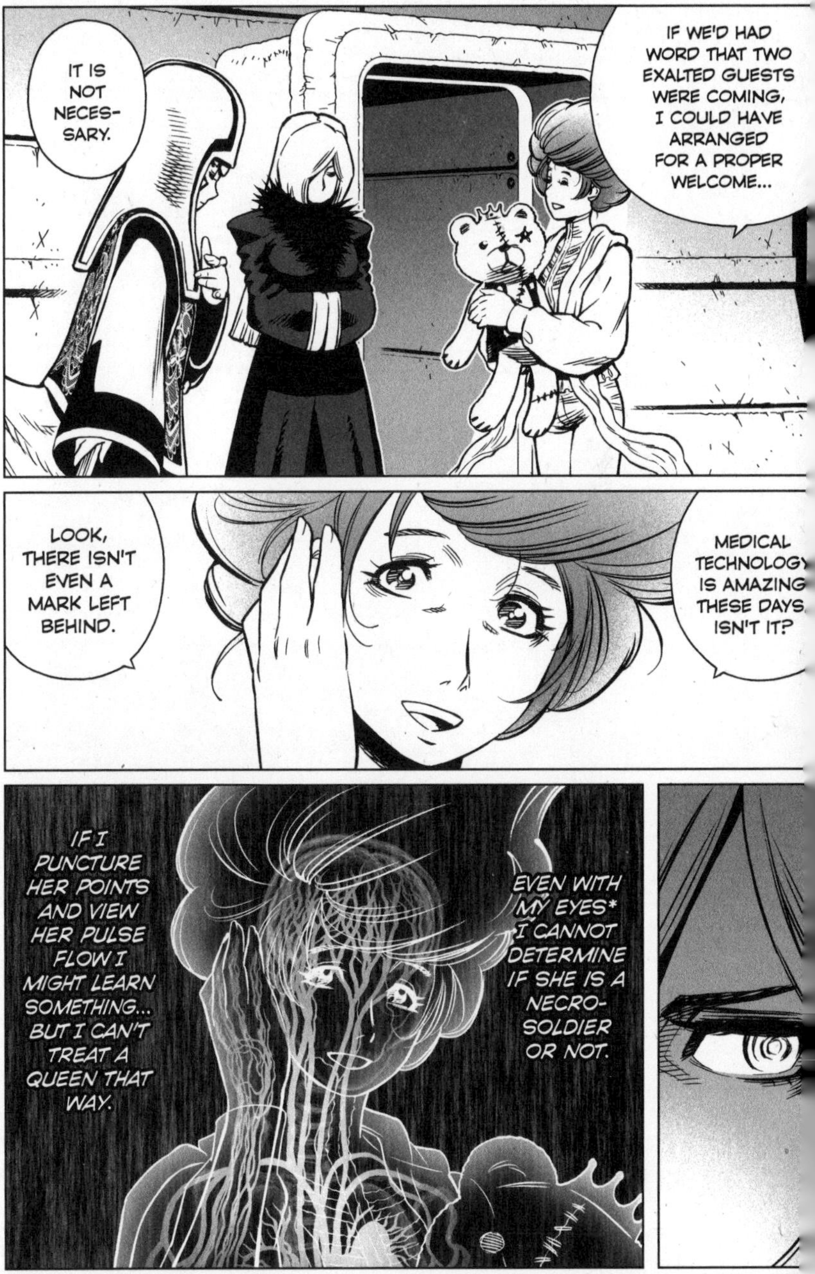
IF WE'D HAD WORD THAT TWO EXALTED GUESTS WERE COMING, I COULD HAVE ARRANGED FOR A PROPER WELCOME...
IT IS NOT NECES-SARY.
MEDICAL TECHNOLOGY IS AMAZING THESE DAYS, ISN'T IT?
LOOK, THERE ISN'T EVEN A MARK LEFT BEHIND.
EVEN WITH MY EYES* I CANNOT DETERMINE IF SHE IS A NECRO-SOLDIER OR NOT.
IF I PUNCTURE HER POINTS AND VIEW HER PULSE FLOW I MIGHT LEARN SOMETHING... BUT I CAN'T TREAT A QUEEN THAT WAY.

***My eyes:** Caerula has vampire eyes that allow her to view nerve pulses and blood flow beneath the skin.

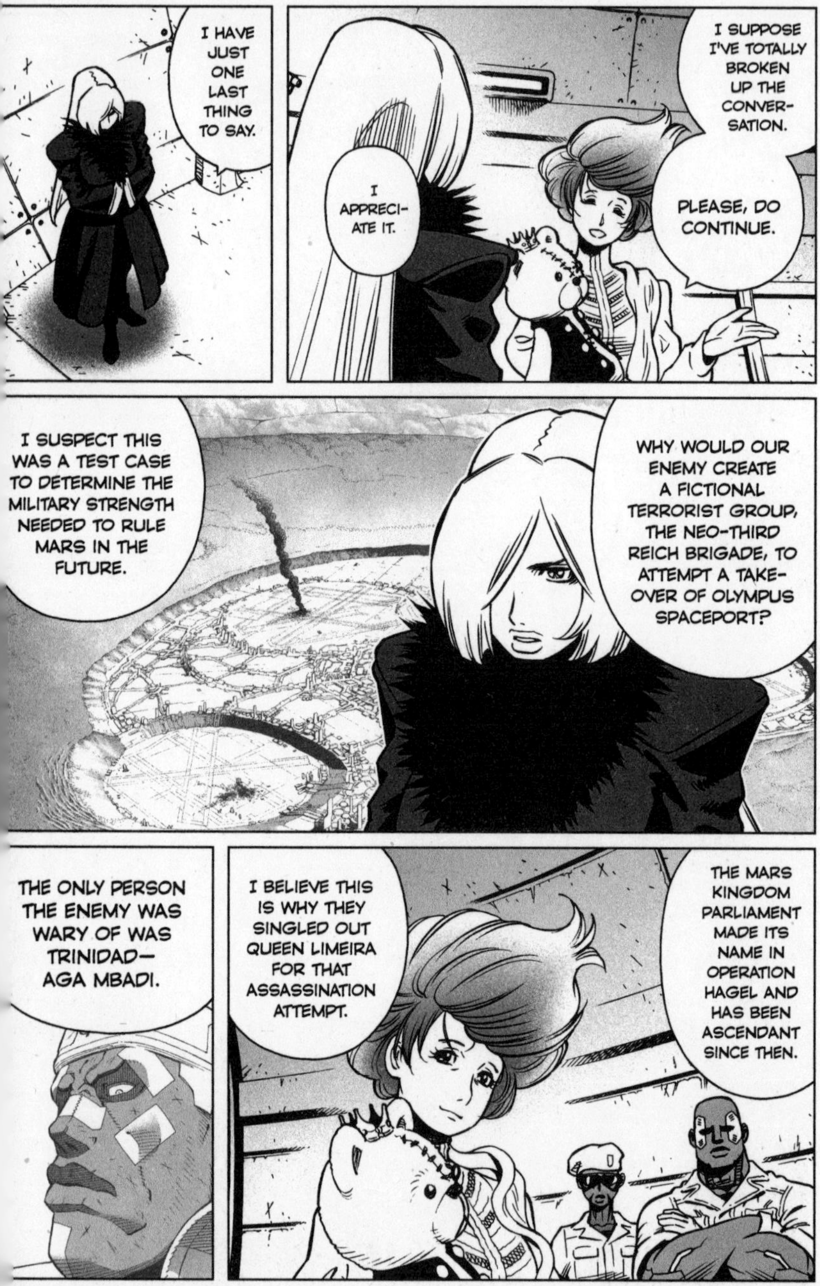
I SUPPOSE I'VE TOTALLY BROKEN UP THE CONVERSATION.
PLEASE, DO CONTINUE.
I APPRECIATE IT.
I HAVE JUST ONE LAST THING TO SAY.
WHY WOULD OUR ENEMY CREATE A FICTIONAL TERRORIST GROUP, THE NEO-THIRD REICH BRIGADE, TO ATTEMPT A TAKE-OVER OF OLYMPUS SPACEPORT?
I SUSPECT THIS WAS A TEST CASE TO DETERMINE THE MILITARY STRENGTH NEEDED TO RULE MARS IN THE FUTURE.
THE MARS KINGDOM PARLIAMENT MADE ITS NAME IN OPERATION HAGEL AND HAS BEEN ASCENDANT SINCE THEN.
I BELIEVE THIS IS WHY THEY SINGLED OUT QUEEN LIMEIRA FOR THAT ASSASSINATION ATTEMPT.
THE ONLY PERSON THE ENEMY WAS WARY OF WAS TRINIDAD—AGA MBADI.

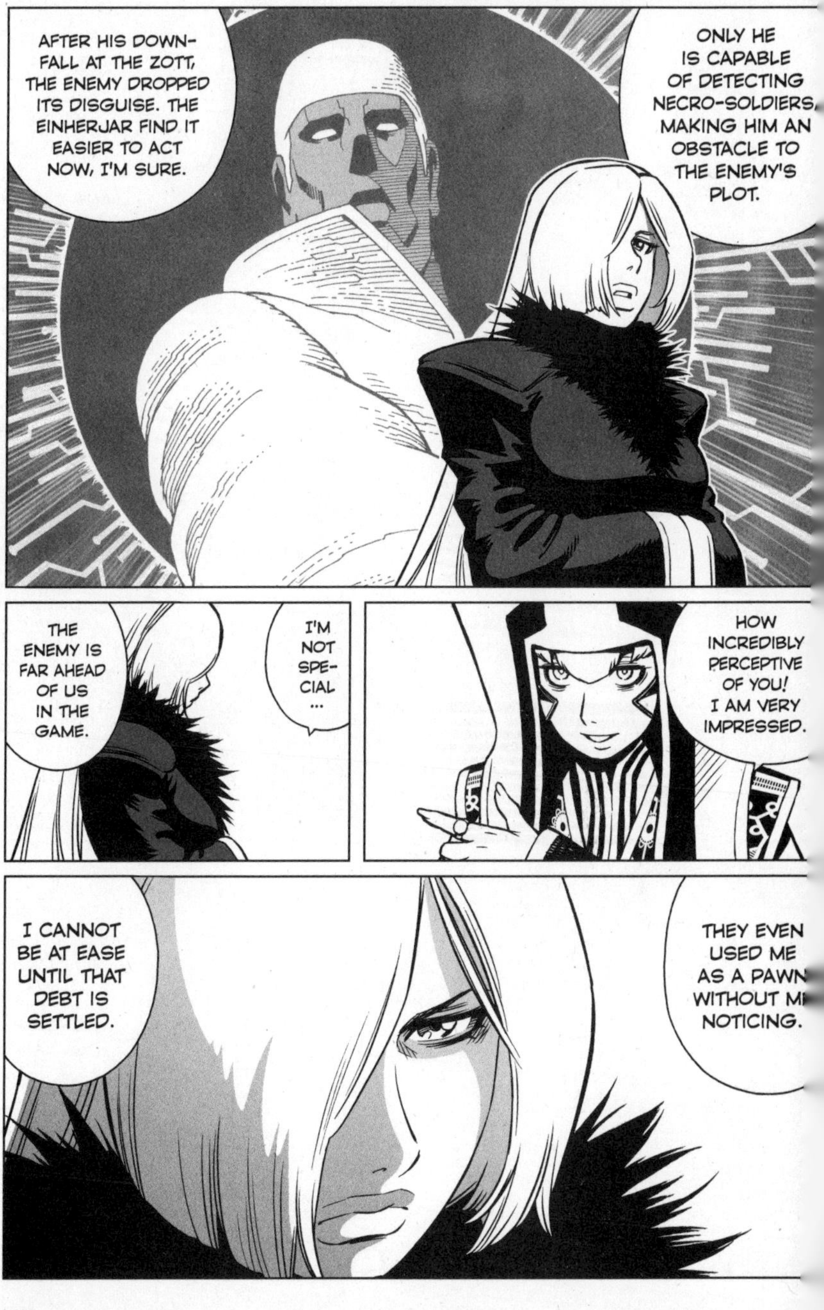
ONLY HE IS CAPABLE OF DETECTING NECRO-SOLDIERS, MAKING HIM AN OBSTACLE TO THE ENEMY'S PLOT.
AFTER HIS DOWN-FALL AT THE ZOTT, THE ENEMY DROPPED ITS DISGUISE. THE EINHERJAR FIND IT EASIER TO ACT NOW, I'M SURE.
HOW INCREDIBLY PERCEPTIVE OF YOU! I AM VERY IMPRESSED.
I'M NOT SPE-CIAL ...
THE ENEMY IS FAR AHEAD OF US IN THE GAME.
THEY EVEN USED ME AS A PAWN WITHOUT M NOTICING.
I CANNOT BE AT EASE UNTIL THAT DEBT IS SETTLED.

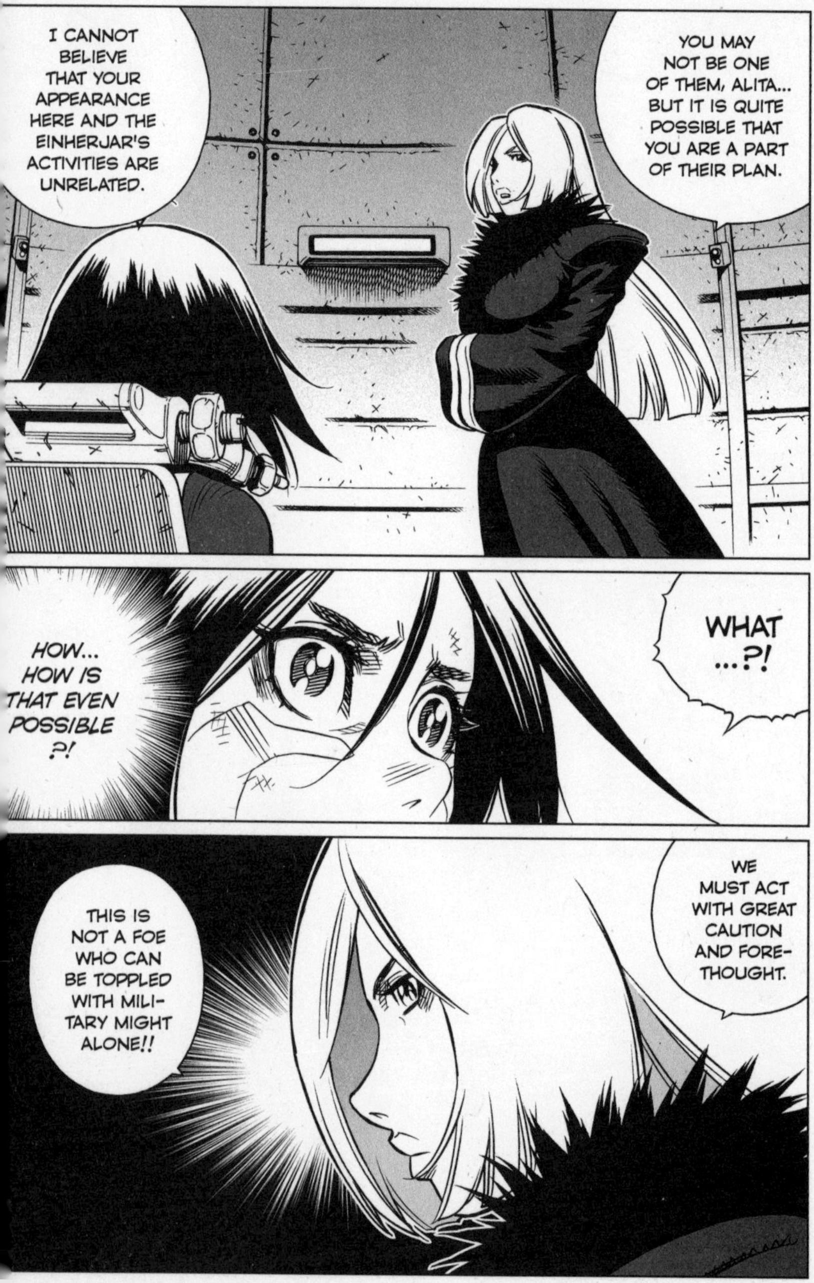
YOU MAY NOT BE ONE OF THEM, ALITA... BUT IT IS QUITE POSSIBLE THAT YOU ARE A PART OF THEIR PLAN.
I CANNOT BELIEVE THAT YOUR APPEARANCE HERE AND THE EINHERJAR'S ACTIVITIES ARE UNRELATED.
WHAT ...?!
HOW... HOW IS THAT EVEN POSSIBLE ?!
WE MUST ACT WITH GREAT CAUTION AND FORE-THOUGHT.
THIS IS NOT A FOE WHO CAN BE TOPPLED WITH MILI-TARY MIGHT ALONE!!

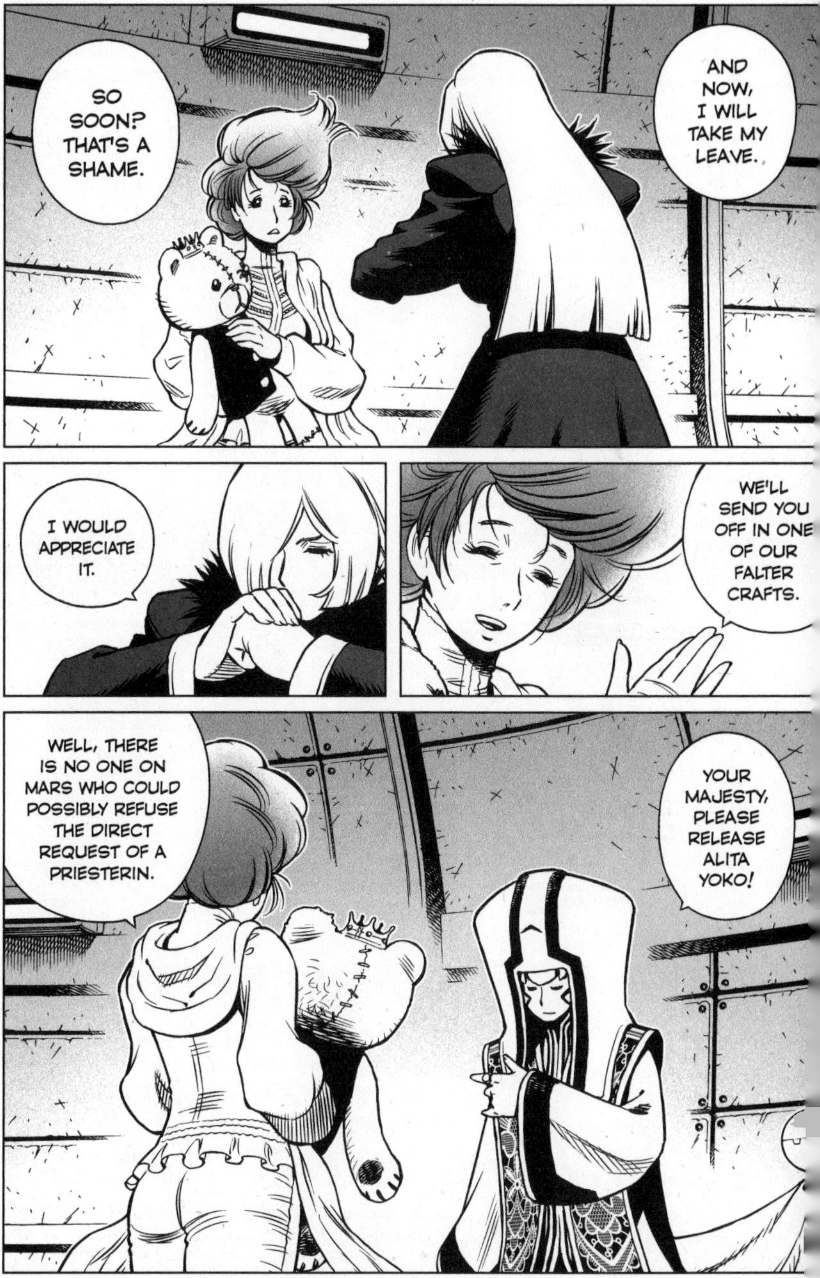
AND NOW, I WILL TAKE MY LEAVE.
SO SOON? THAT'S A SHAME.
WE'LL SEND YOU OFF IN ONE OF OUR FALTER CRAFTS.
I WOULD APPRECIATE IT.
YOUR MAJESTY, PLEASE RELEASE ALITA YOKO!
WELL, THERE IS NO ONE ON MARS WHO COULD POSSIBLY REFUSE THE DIRECT REQUEST OF A PRIESTERIN.

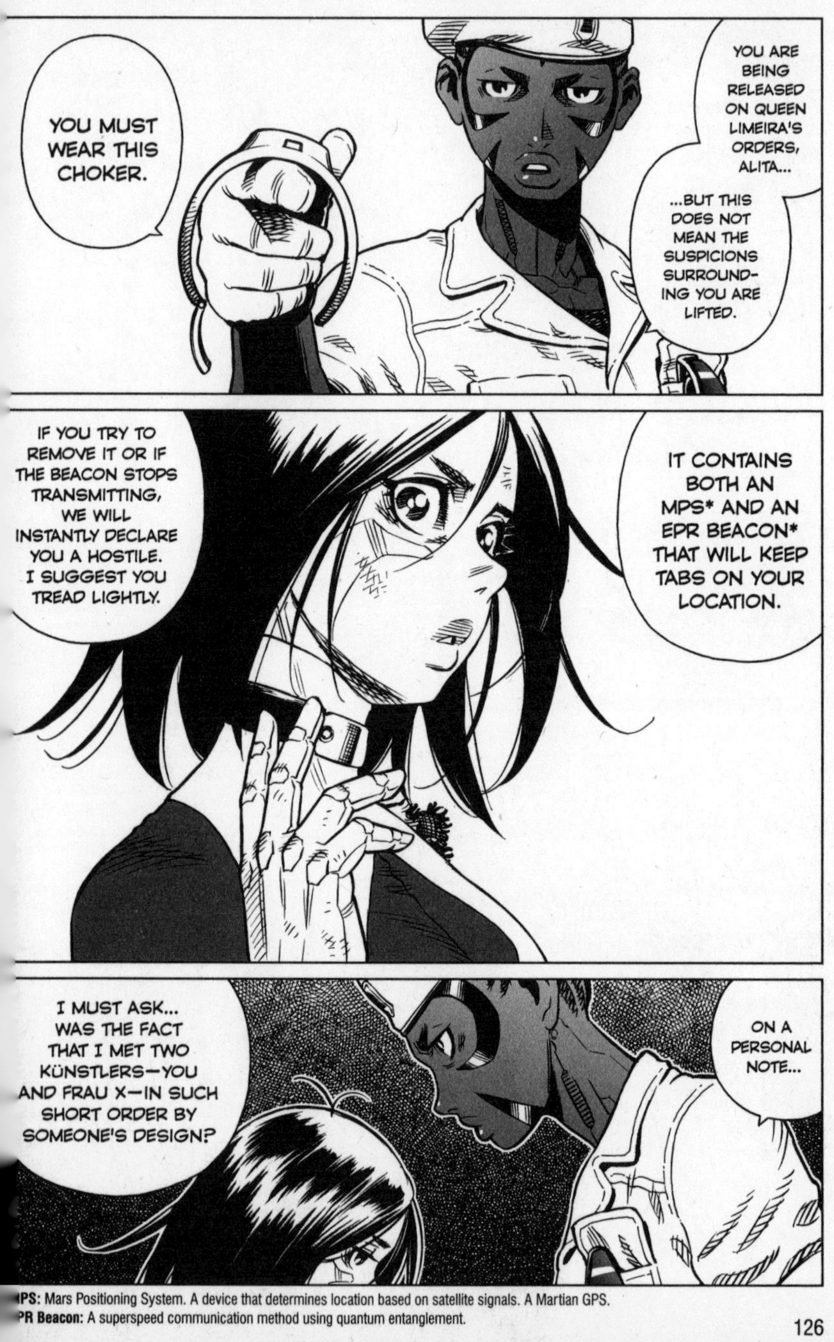
YOU ARE BEING RELEASED ON QUEEN LIMEIRA'S ORDERS, ALITA...
...BUT THIS DOES NOT MEAN THE SUSPICIONS SURROUND-ING YOU ARE LIFTED.
YOU MUST WEAR THIS CHOKER.
IT CONTAINS BOTH AN MPS* AND AN EPR BEACON* THAT WILL KEEP TABS ON YOUR LOCATION.
IF YOU TRY TO REMOVE IT OR IF THE BEACON STOPS TRANSMITTING, WE WILL INSTANTLY DECLARE YOU A HOSTILE. I SUGGEST YOU TREAD LIGHTLY.
ON A PERSONAL NOTE...
I MUST ASK... WAS THE FACT THAT I MET TWO KÜNSTLERS—YOU AND FRAU X—IN SUCH SHORT ORDER BY SOMEONE'S DESIGN?

**MPS:** Mars Positioning System. A device that determines location based on satellite signals. A Martian GPS.
**EPR Beacon:** A superspeed communication method using quantum entanglement.

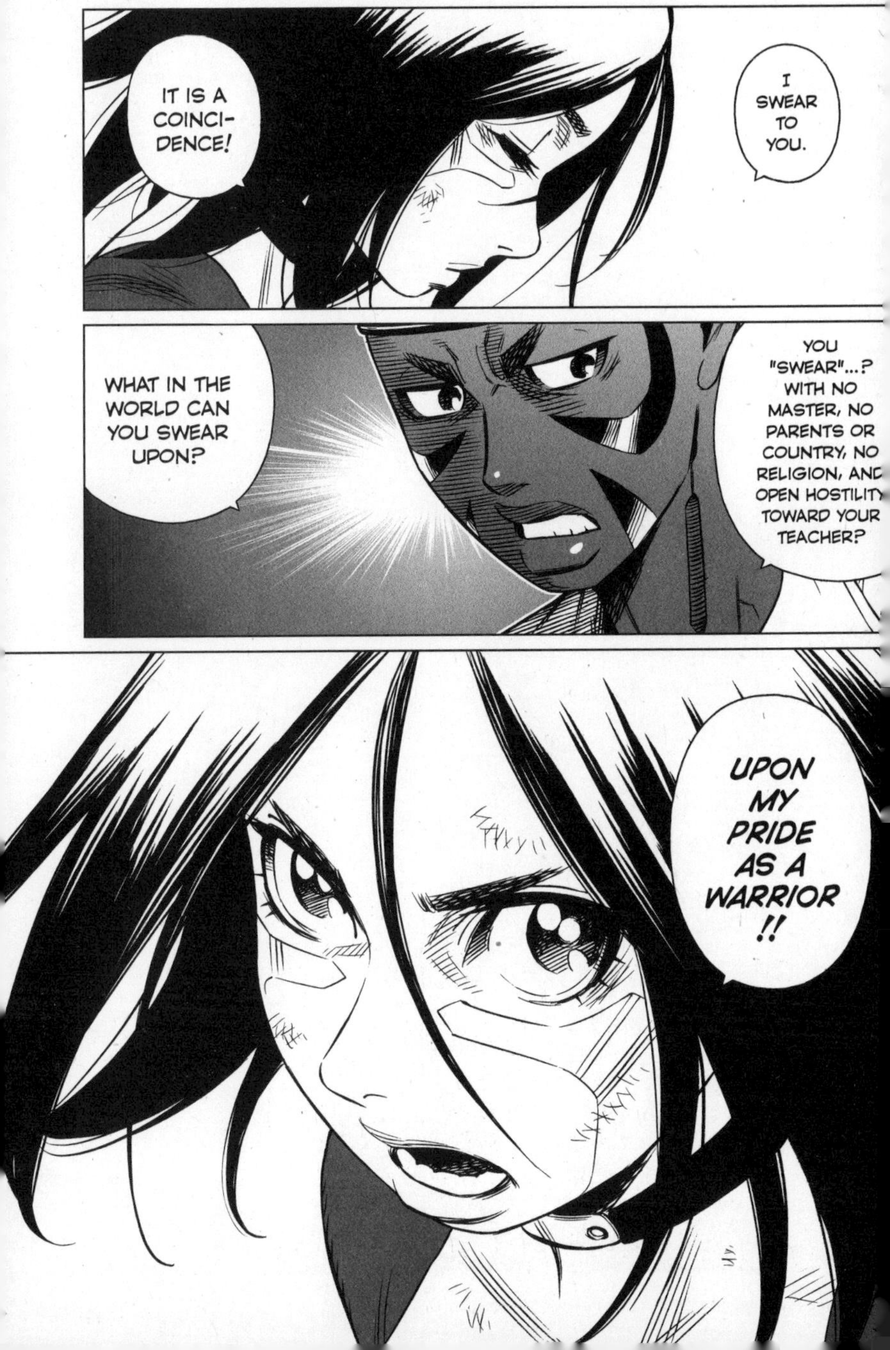
I SWEAR TO YOU.
IT IS A COINCIDENCE!
YOU "SWEAR"...? WITH NO MASTER, NO PARENTS OR COUNTRY, NO RELIGION, AND OPEN HOSTILITY TOWARD YOUR TEACHER?
WHAT IN THE WORLD CAN YOU SWEAR UPON?
UPON MY PRIDE AS A WARRIOR!!

HMM ...?

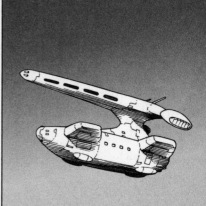

YOUR BEARING IS IN-CORRECT, PILOT.

!!

KEEEE

SHIT! IT'S A SET-UP!!

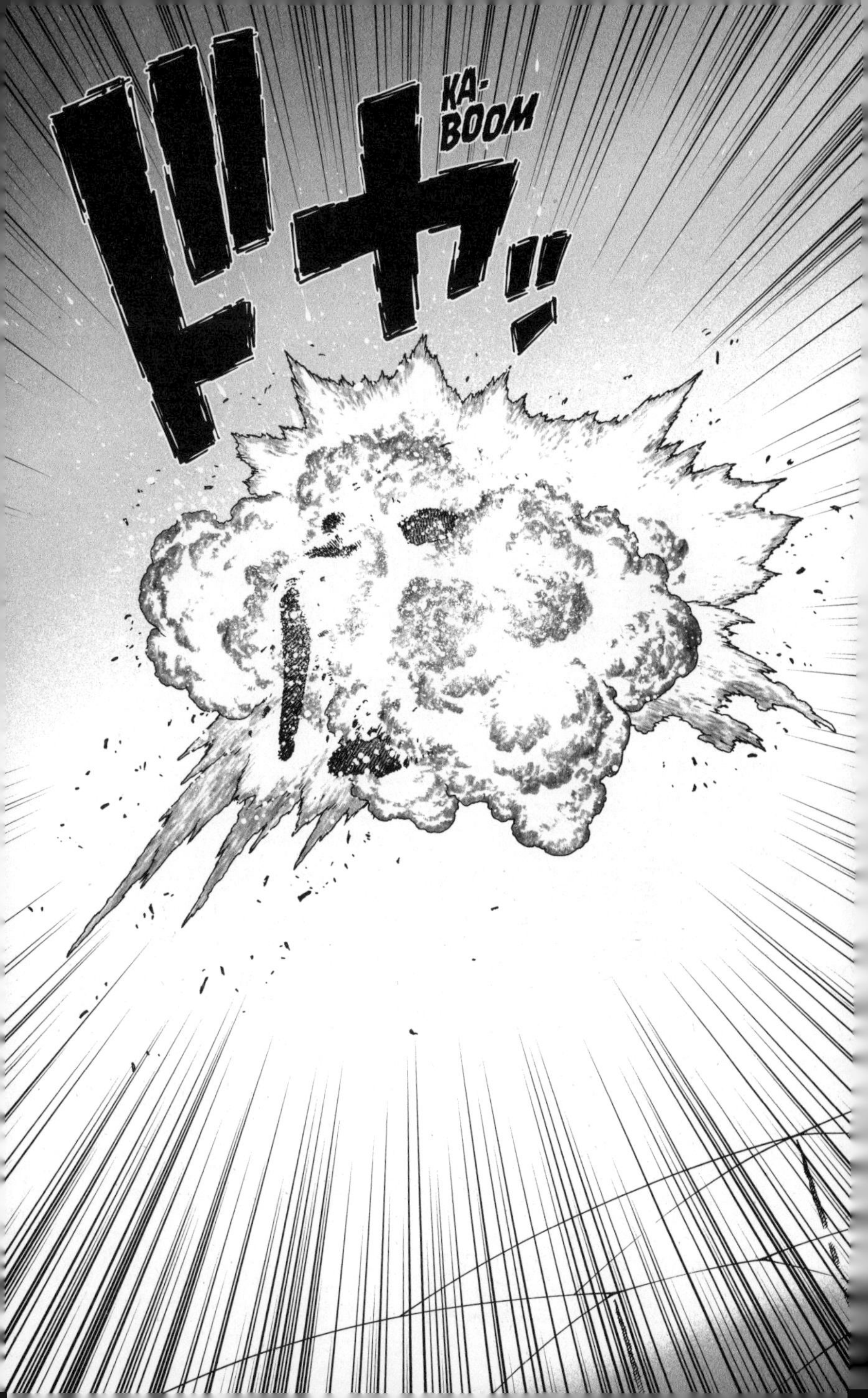
ドゴォ!!
KA-
BOOM

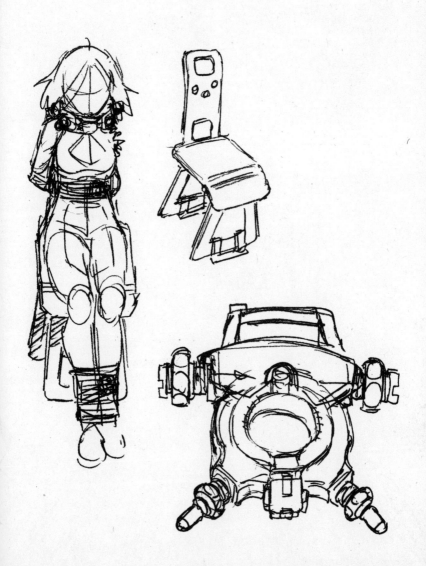

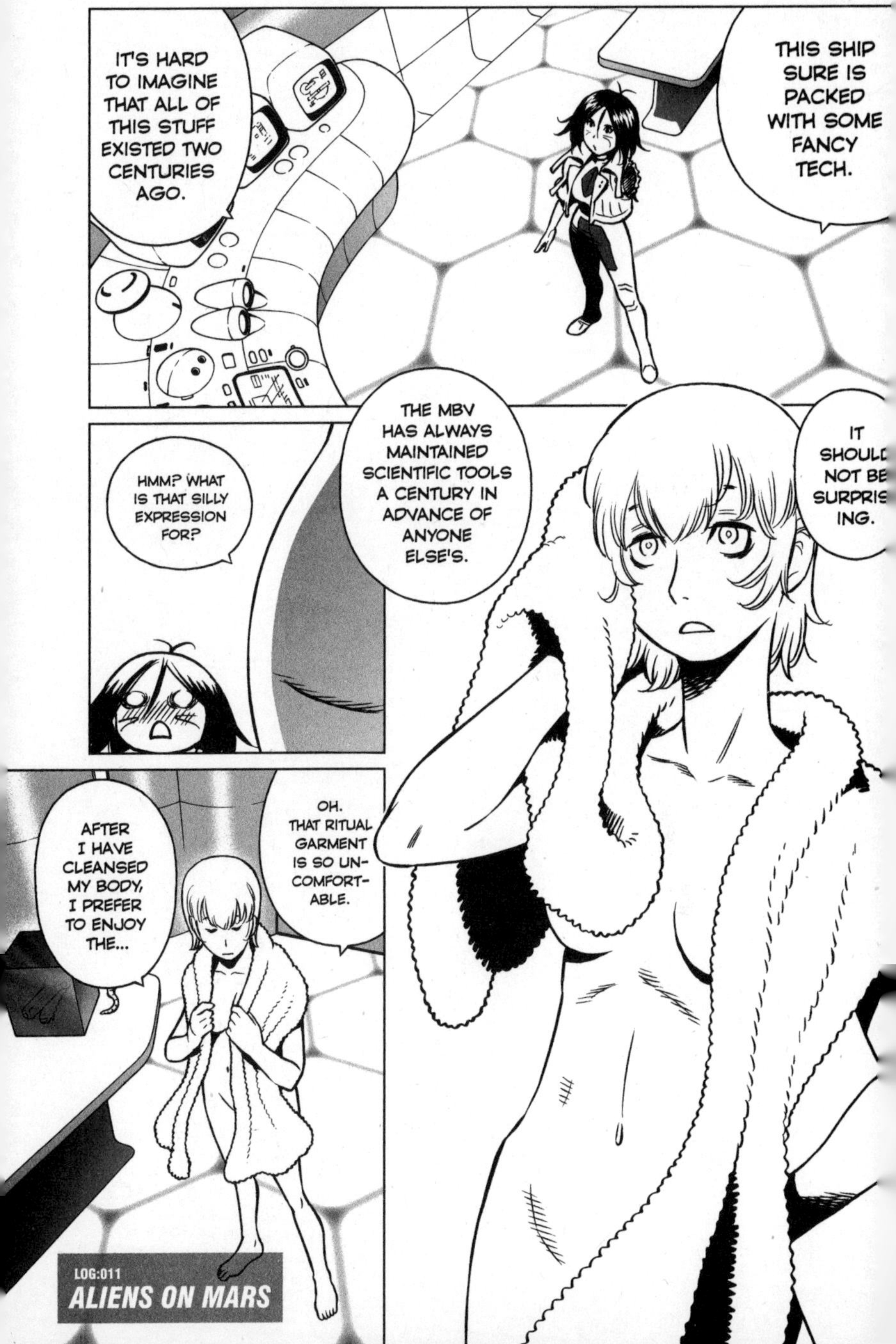
THIS SHIP SURE IS PACKED WITH SOME FANCY TECH.
IT'S HARD TO IMAGINE THAT ALL OF THIS STUFF EXISTED TWO CENTURIES AGO.
IT SHOULD NOT BE SURPRISING.
THE MBV HAS ALWAYS MAINTAINED SCIENTIFIC TOOLS A CENTURY IN ADVANCE OF ANYONE ELSE'S.
HMM? WHAT IS THAT SILLY EXPRESSION FOR?
OH. THAT RITUAL GARMENT IS SO UN-COMFORT-ABLE.
AFTER I HAVE CLEANSED MY BODY, I PREFER TO ENJOY THE...
LOG:011
ALIENS ON MARS

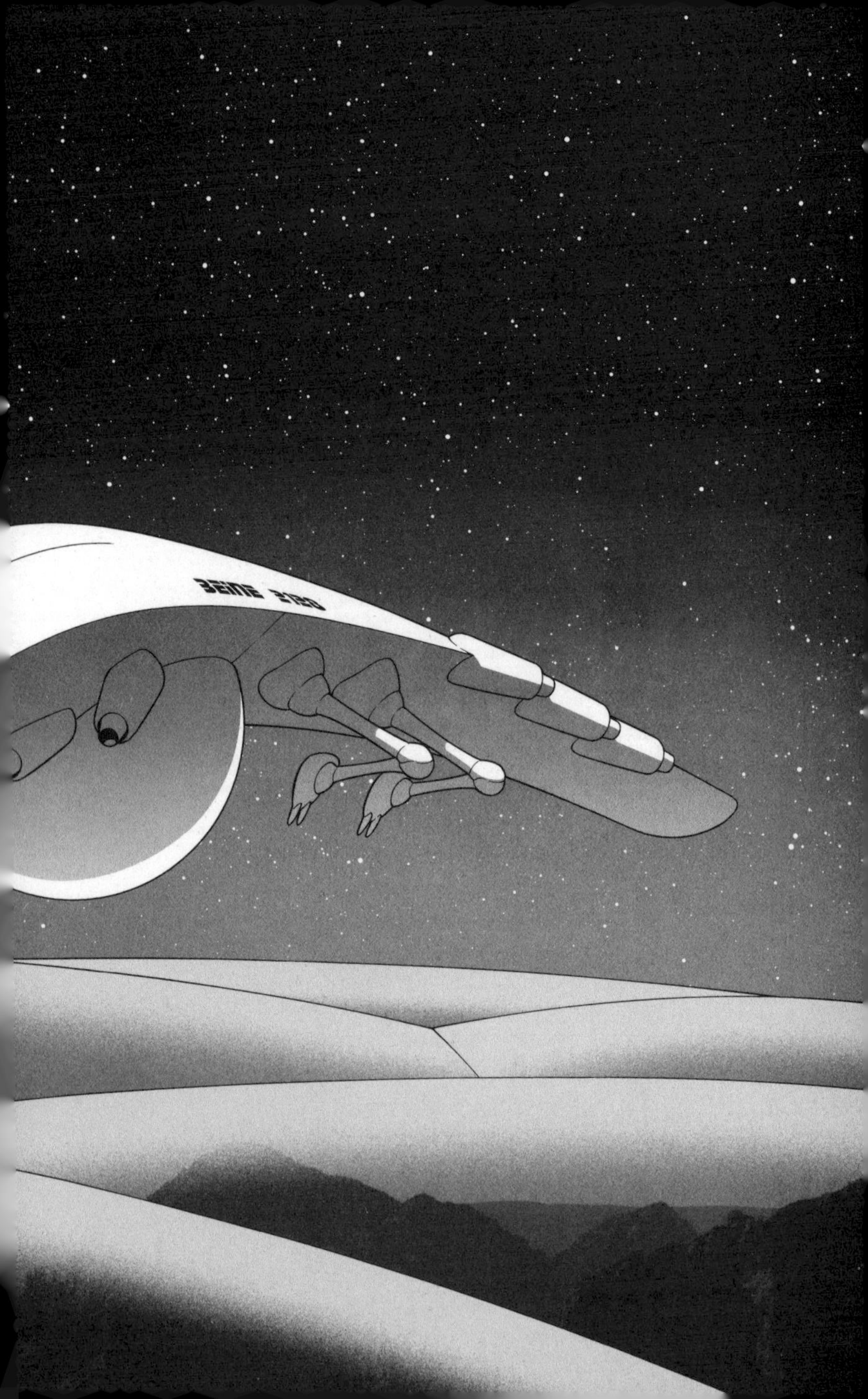

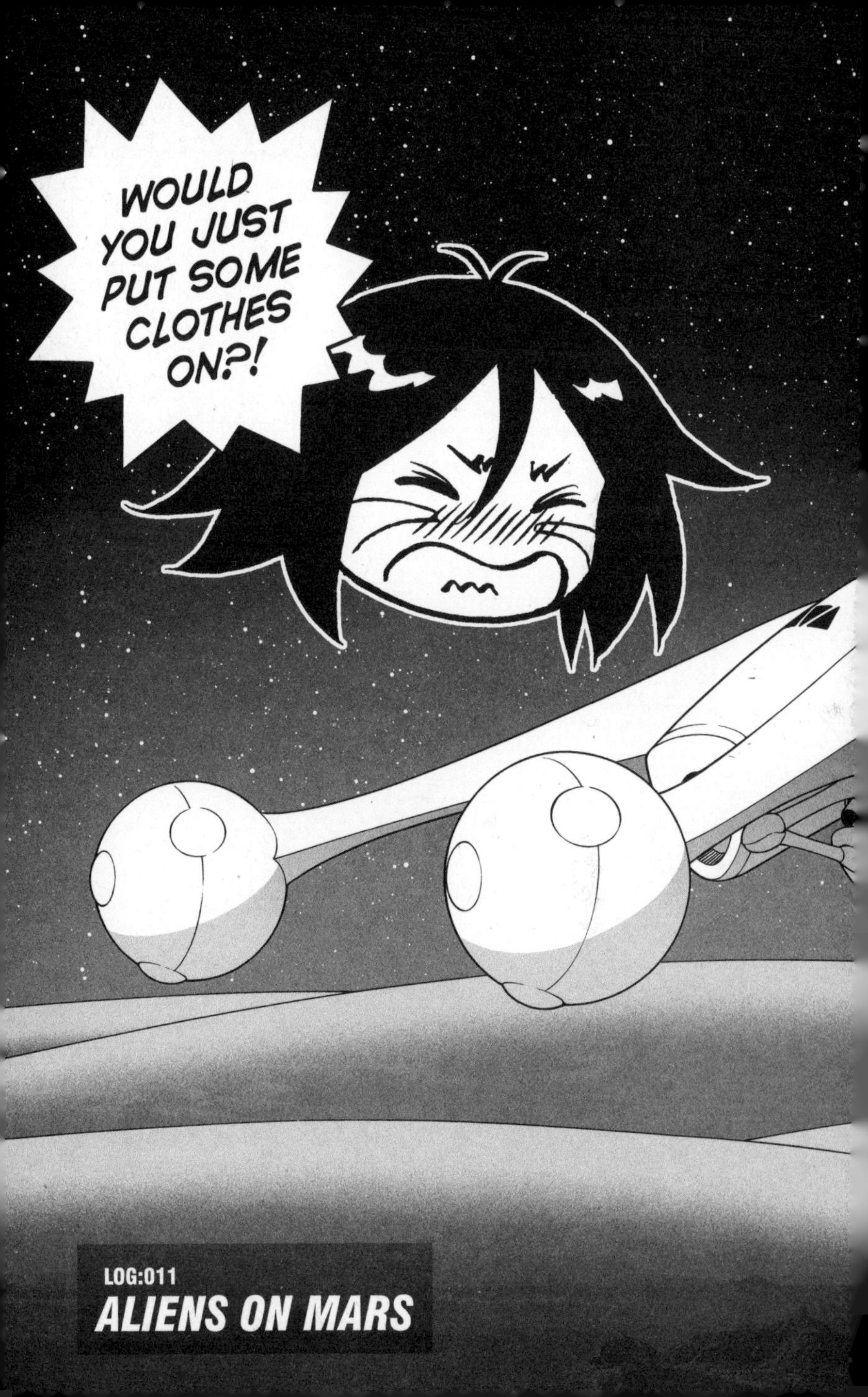
WOULD YOU JUST PUT SOME CLOTHES ON?!

LOG:011

## ALIENS ON MARS

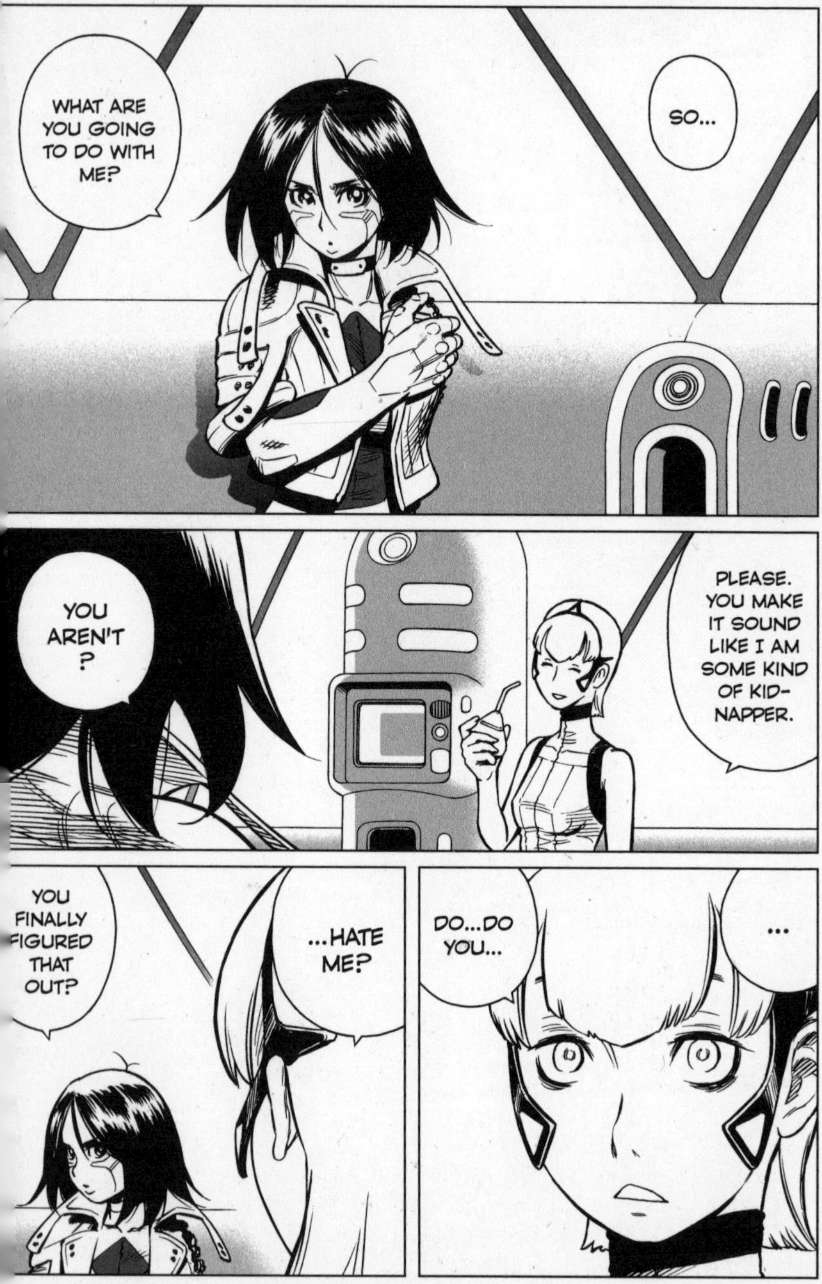
SO...
WHAT ARE YOU GOING TO DO WITH ME?
PLEASE. YOU MAKE IT SOUND LIKE I AM SOME KIND OF KID-NAPPER.
YOU AREN'T ?
...
DO...DO YOU...
...HATE ME?
YOU FINALLY FIGURED THAT OUT?

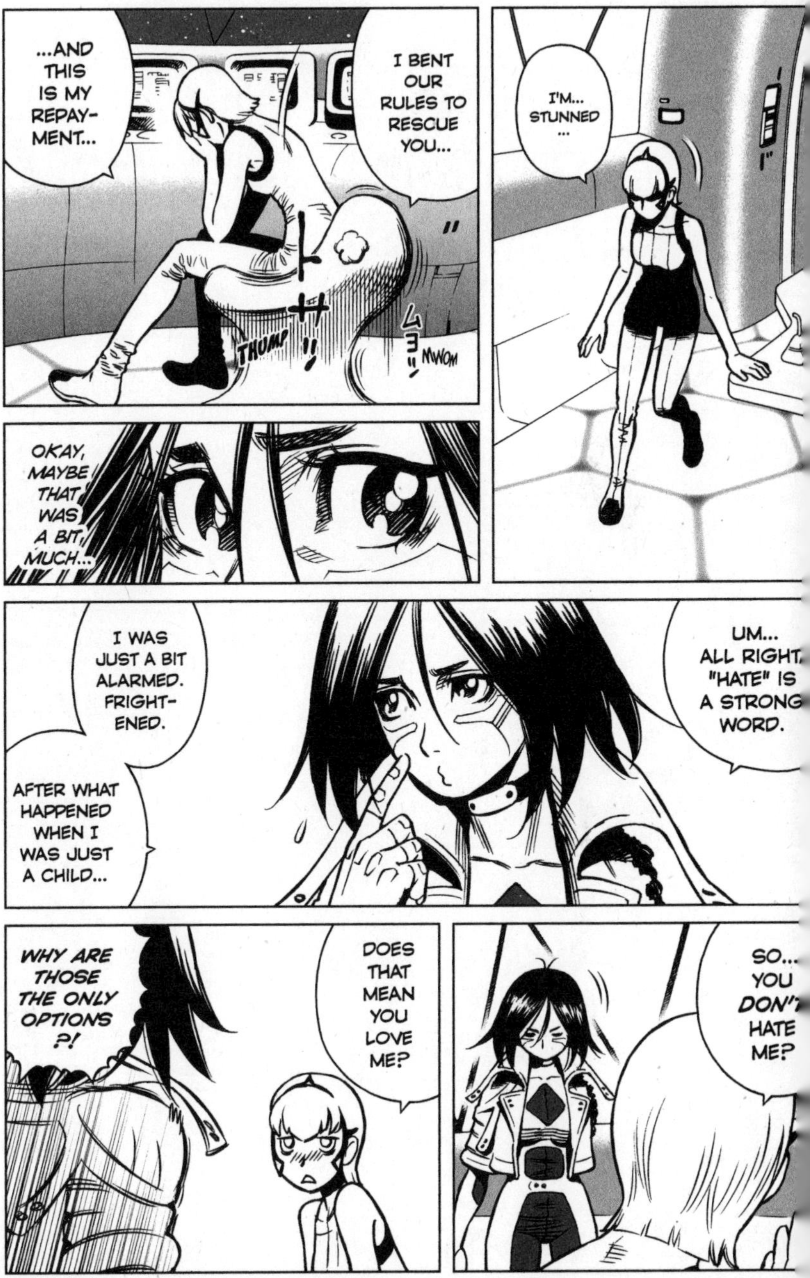
I'M... STUNNED ...
I BENT OUR RULES TO RESCUE YOU...
...AND THIS IS MY REPAY- MENT...
THUMP
ムニ
MWOM
OKAY, MAYBE THAT WAS A BIT MUCH...
UM... ALL RIGHT. "HATE" IS A STRONG WORD.
I WAS JUST A BIT ALARMED. FRIGHT- ENED.
AFTER WHAT HAPPENED WHEN I WAS JUST A CHILD...
SO... YOU DON'T HATE ME?
DOES THAT MEAN YOU LOVE ME?
WHY ARE THOSE THE ONLY OPTIONS ?!

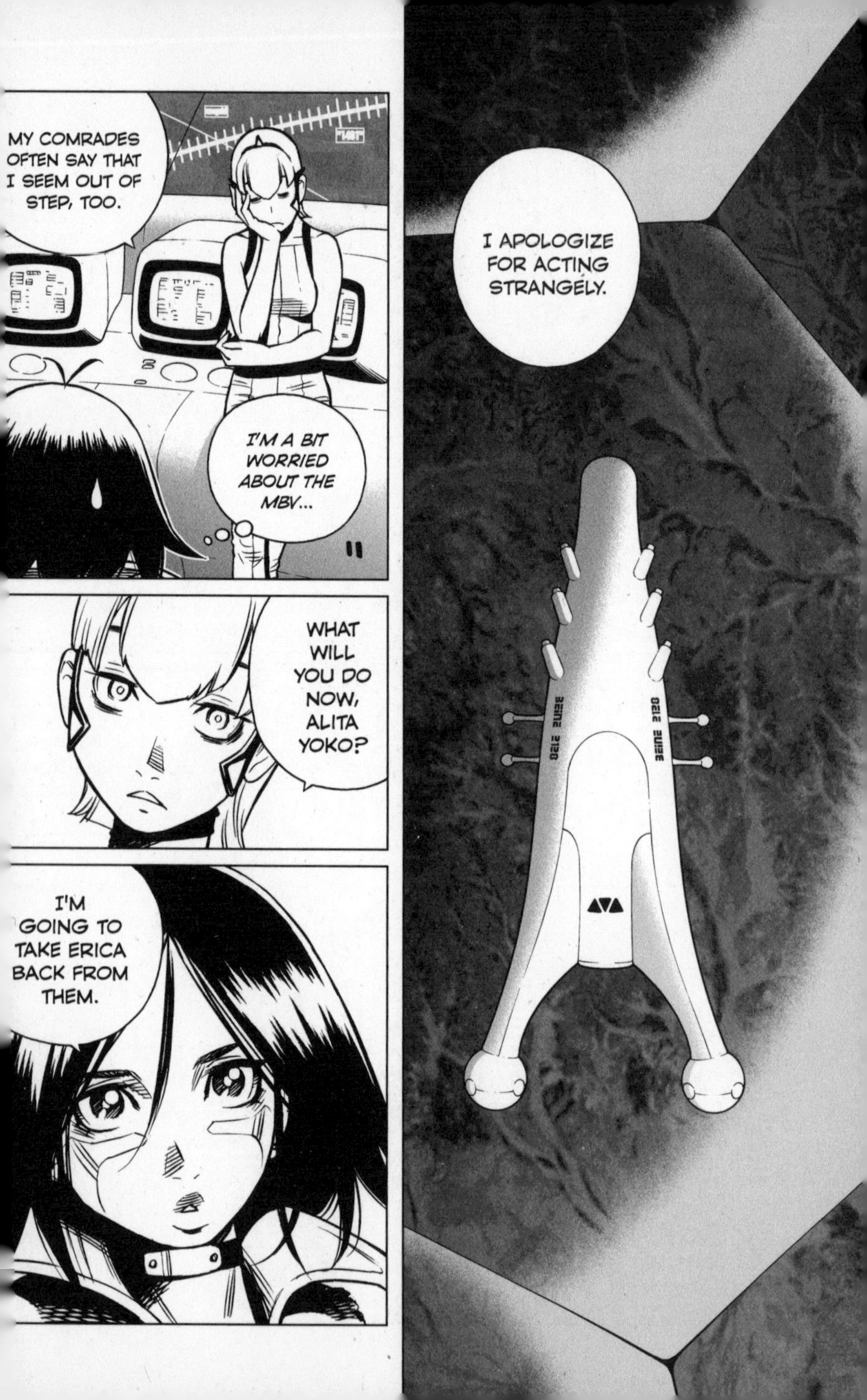
I APOLOGIZE FOR ACTING STRANGELY.
MY COMRADES OFTEN SAY THAT I SEEM OUT OF STEP, TOO.
I'M A BIT WORRIED ABOUT THE MBV...
WHAT WILL YOU DO NOW, ALITA YOKO?
I'M GOING TO TAKE ERICA BACK FROM THEM.

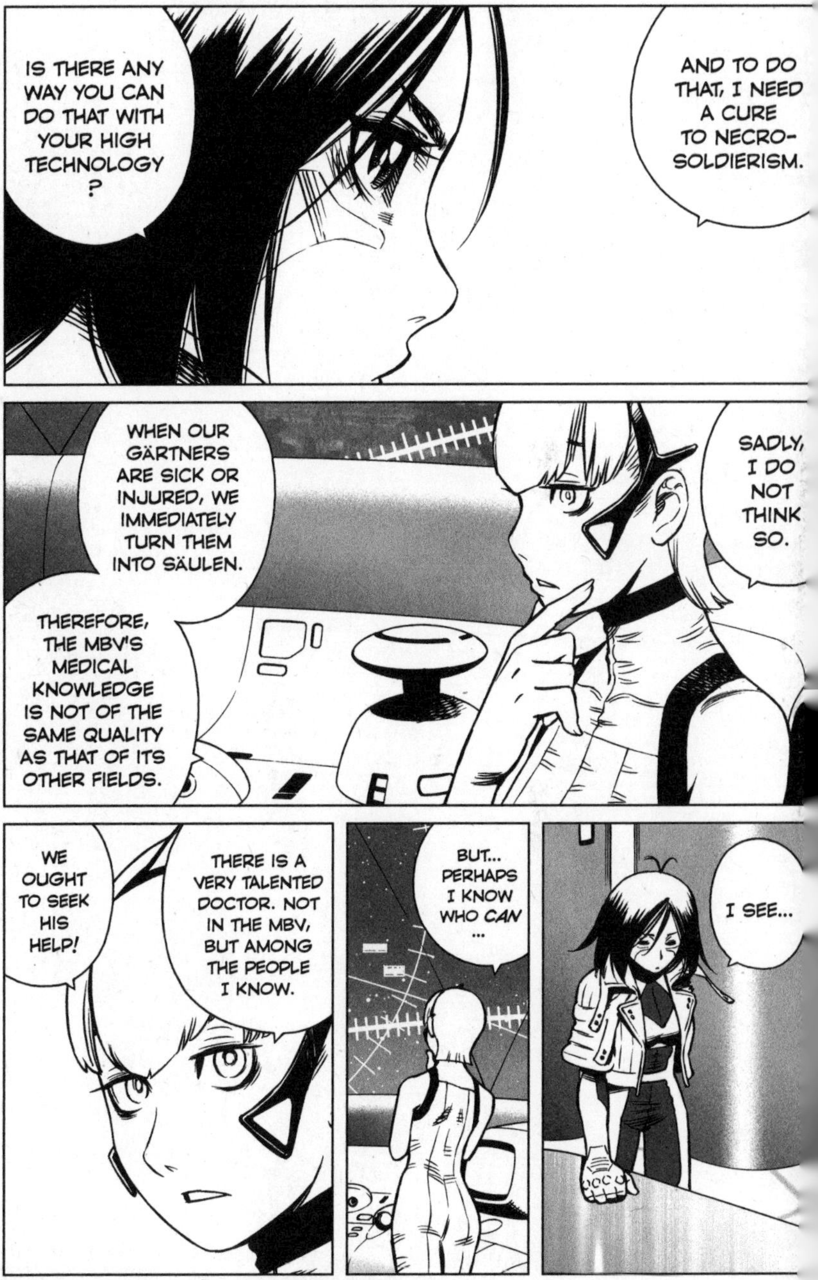
AND TO DO THAT, I NEED A CURE TO NECRO-SOLDIERISM.
IS THERE ANY WAY YOU CAN DO THAT WITH YOUR HIGH TECHNOLOGY ?
SADLY, I DO NOT THINK SO.
WHEN OUR GÄRTNERS ARE SICK OR INJURED, WE IMMEDIATELY TURN THEM INTO SÄULEN.
THEREFORE, THE MBV'S MEDICAL KNOWLEDGE IS NOT OF THE SAME QUALITY AS THAT OF ITS OTHER FIELDS.
I SEE...
BUT... PERHAPS I KNOW WHO *CAN* ...
THERE IS A VERY TALENTED DOCTOR. NOT IN THE MBV, BUT AMONG THE PEOPLE I KNOW.
WE OUGHT TO SEEK HIS HELP!

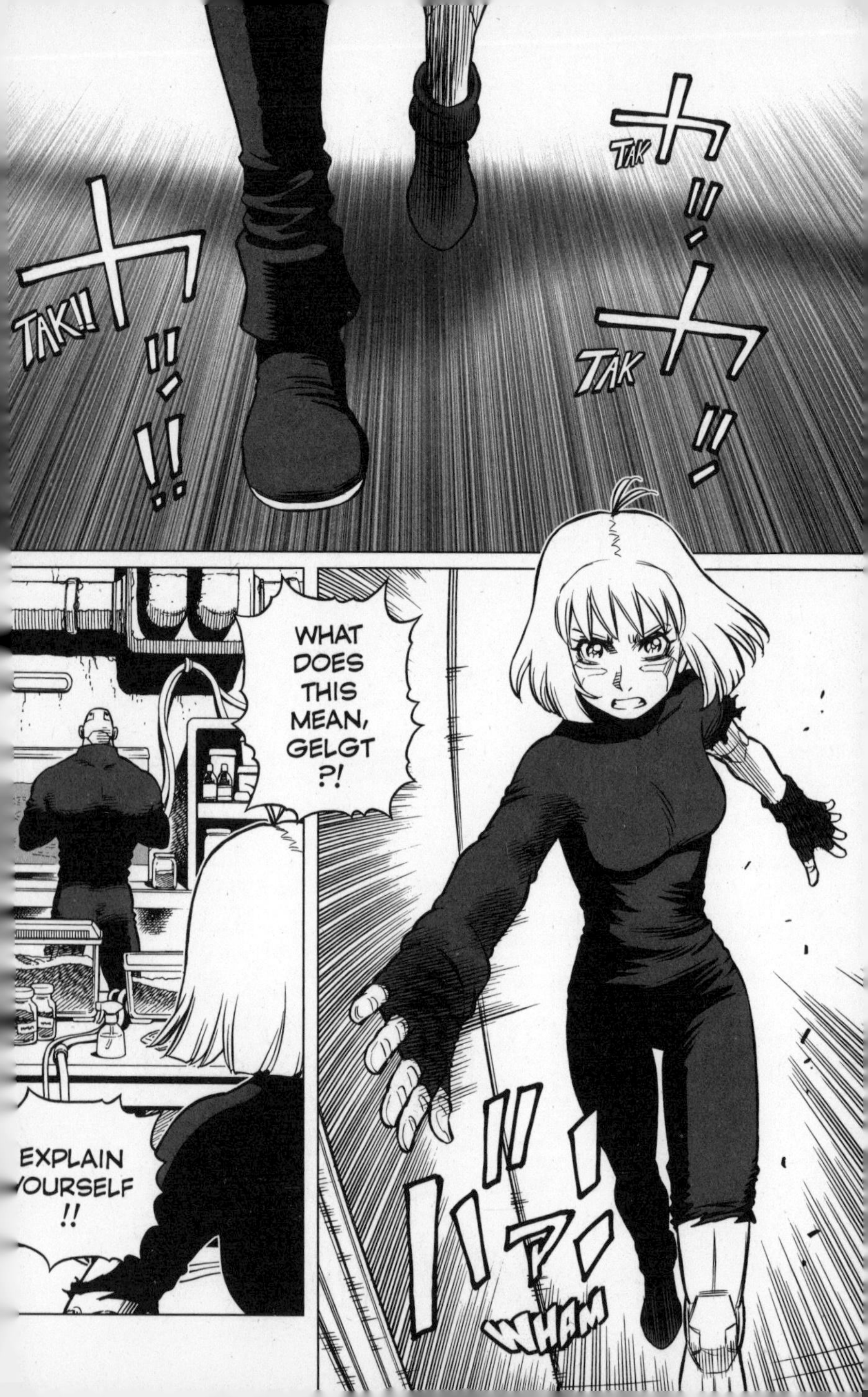
TAK
TAK
TAK!!
WHAT DOES THIS MEAN, GELGT ?!
WHAM
EXPLAIN YOURSELF !!

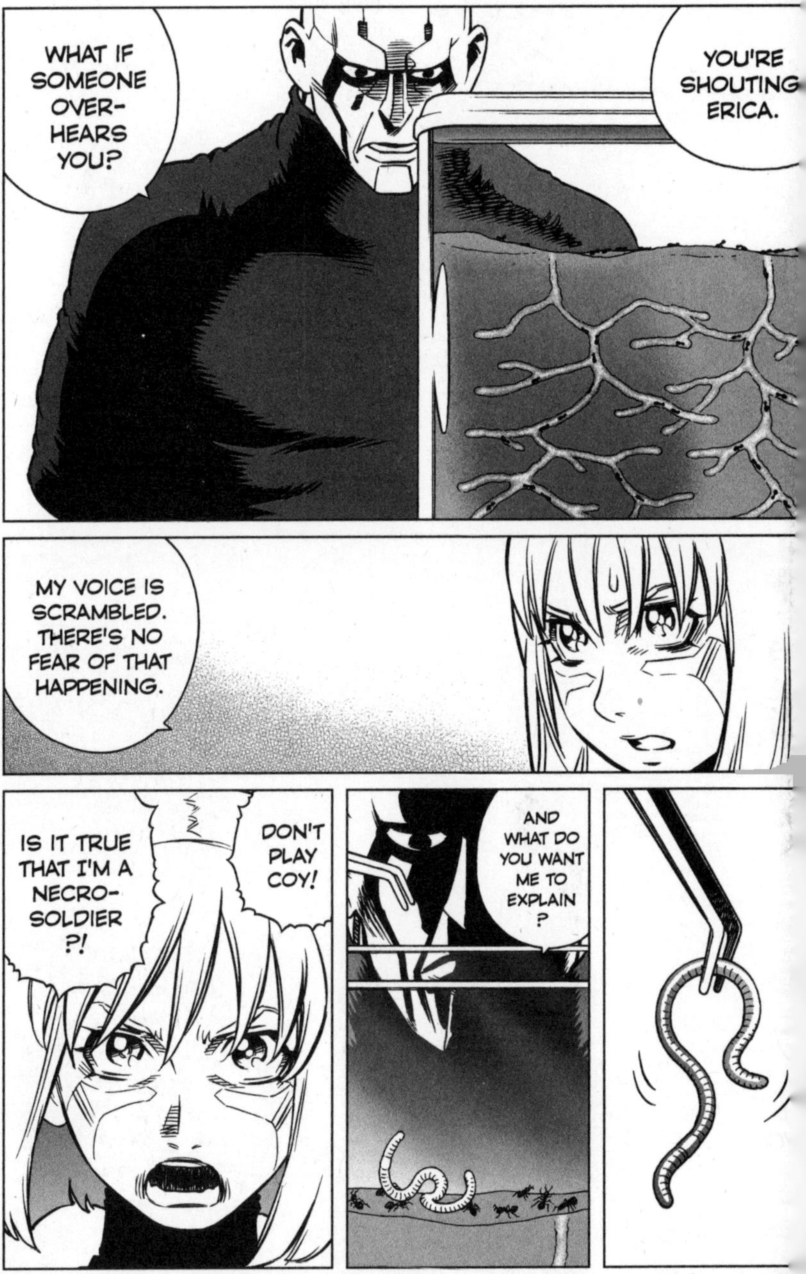
YOU'RE SHOUTING ERICA.
WHAT IF SOMEONE OVER-HEARS YOU?
MY VOICE IS SCRAMBLED. THERE'S NO FEAR OF THAT HAPPENING.
AND WHAT DO YOU WANT ME TO EXPLAIN?
DON'T PLAY COY!
IS IT TRUE THAT I'M A NECRO-SOLDIER?!

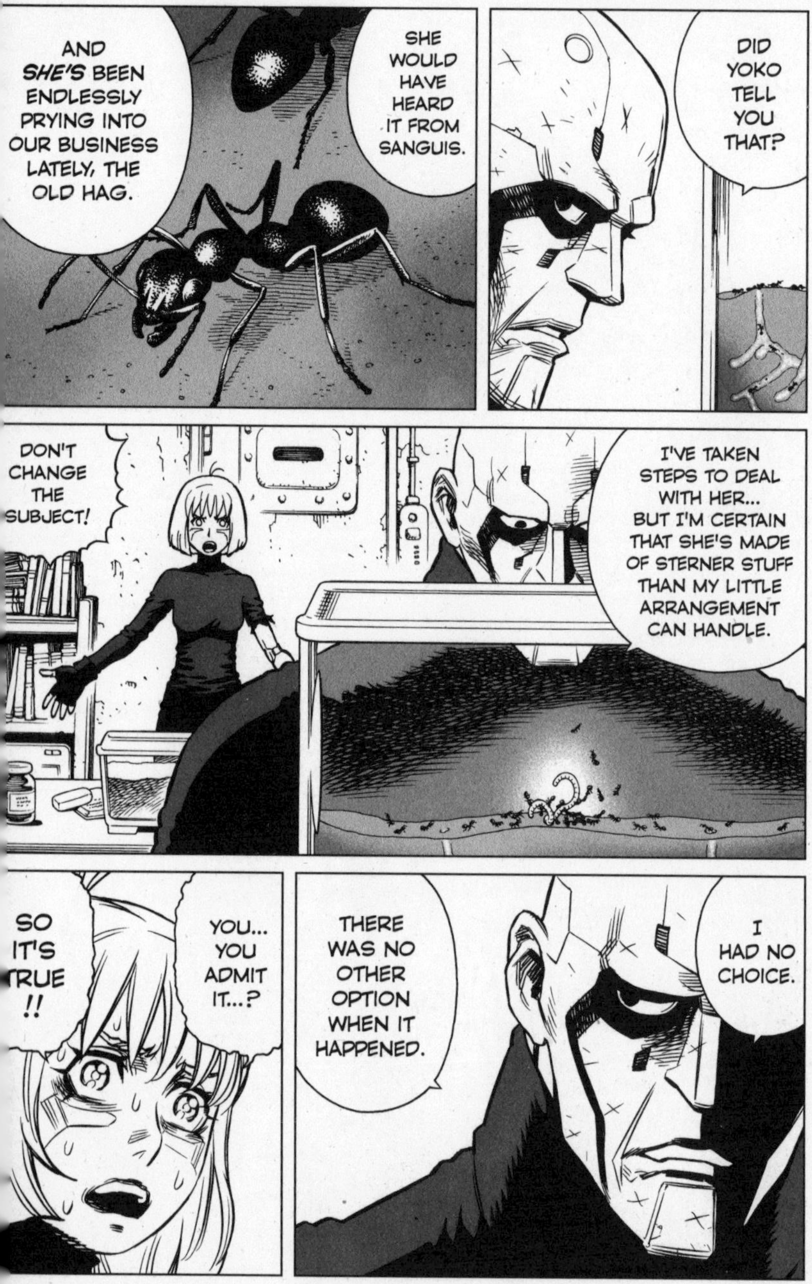
DID YOKO TELL YOU THAT?
SHE WOULD HAVE HEARD IT FROM SANGUIS.
AND *SHE'S* BEEN ENDLESSLY PRYING INTO OUR BUSINESS LATELY, THE OLD HAG.
I'VE TAKEN STEPS TO DEAL WITH HER... BUT I'M CERTAIN THAT SHE'S MADE OF STERNER STUFF THAN MY LITTLE ARRANGEMENT CAN HANDLE.
DON'T CHANGE THE SUBJECT!
I HAD NO CHOICE.
THERE WAS NO OTHER OPTION WHEN IT HAPPENED.
YOU... YOU ADMIT IT...?
SO IT'S TRUE !!

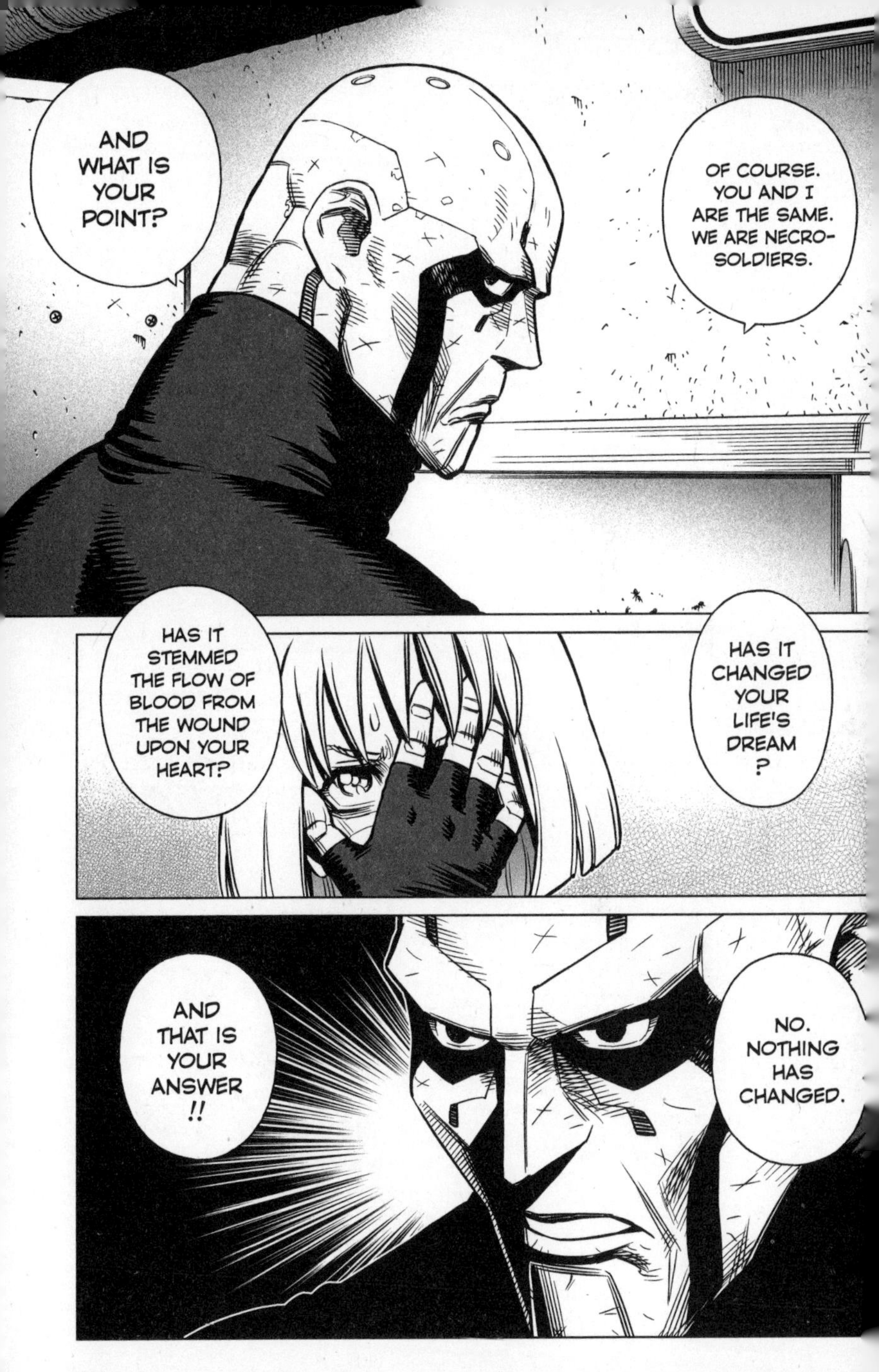
OF COURSE. YOU AND I ARE THE SAME. WE ARE NECRO-SOLDIERS.
AND WHAT IS YOUR POINT?
HAS IT CHANGED YOUR LIFE'S DREAM ?
HAS IT STEMMED THE FLOW OF BLOOD FROM THE WOUND UPON YOUR HEART?
NO. NOTHING HAS CHANGED.
AND THAT IS YOUR ANSWER !!

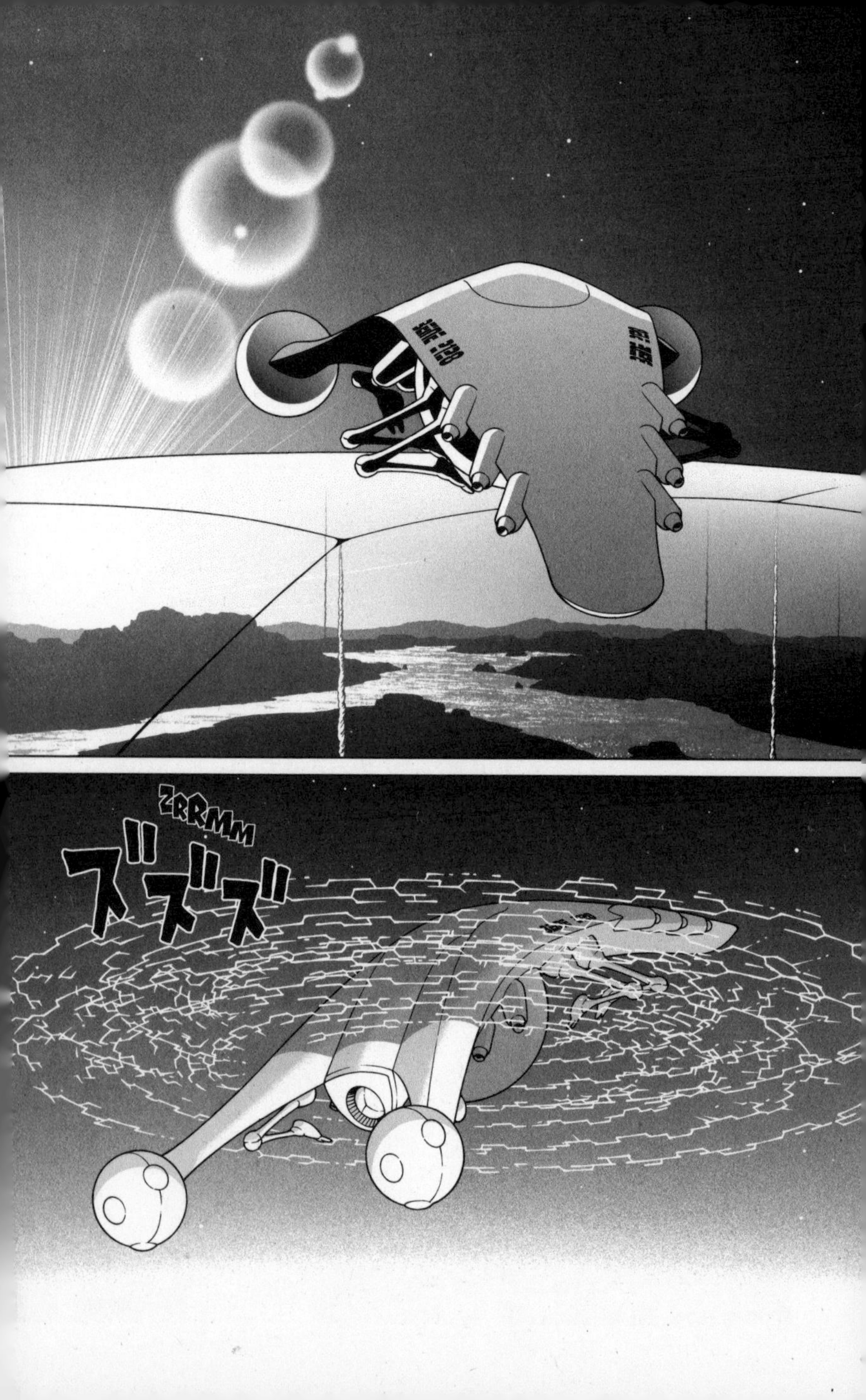
ズズズ
ZRRMM

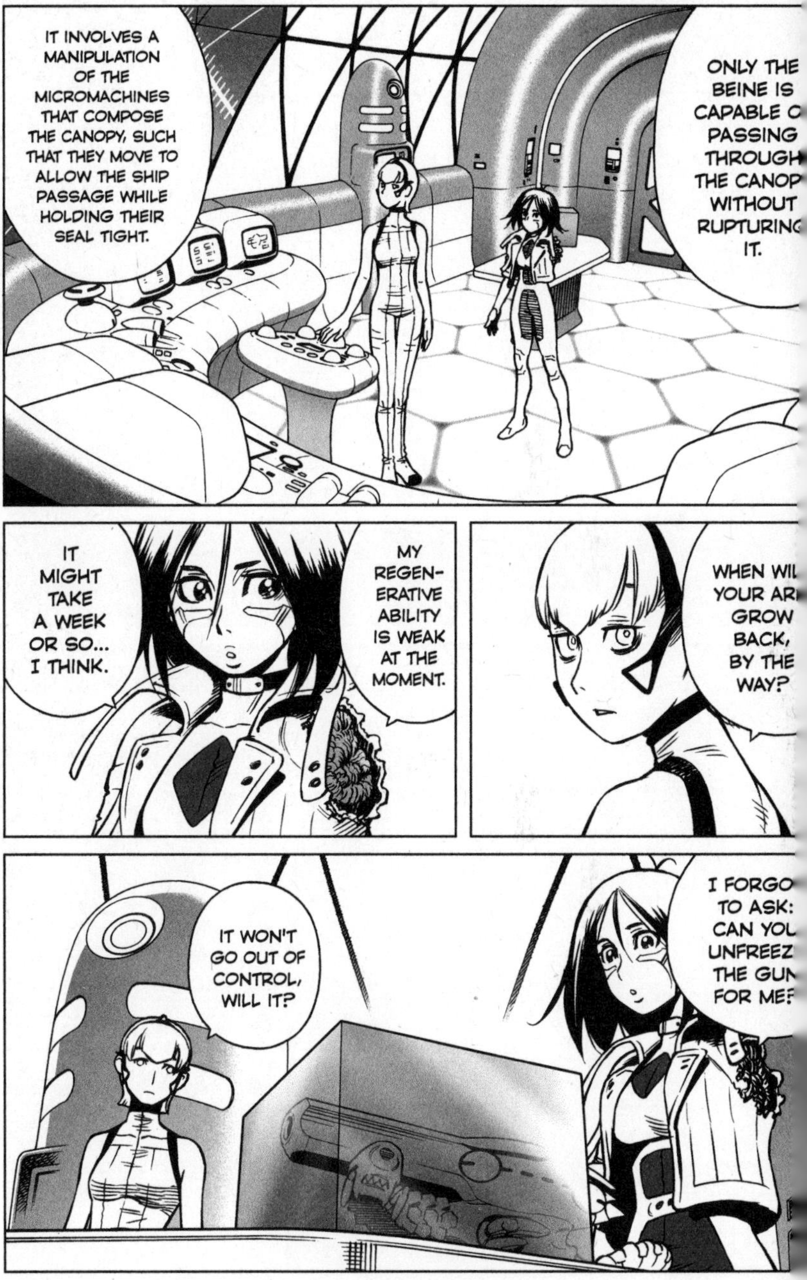
ONLY THE BEINE IS CAPABLE O PASSING THROUGH THE CANOP WITHOUT RUPTURING IT.
IT INVOLVES A MANIPULATION OF THE MICROMACHINES THAT COMPOSE THE CANOPY, SUCH THAT THEY MOVE TO ALLOW THE SHIP PASSAGE WHILE HOLDING THEIR SEAL TIGHT.
WHEN WI YOUR AR GROW BACK, BY THE WAY?
MY REGEN- ERATIVE ABILITY IS WEAK AT THE MOMENT.
IT MIGHT TAKE A WEEK OR SO... I THINK.
I FORGO TO ASK: CAN YOU UNFREEZ THE GUN FOR ME?
IT WON'T GO OUT OF CONTROL, WILL IT?

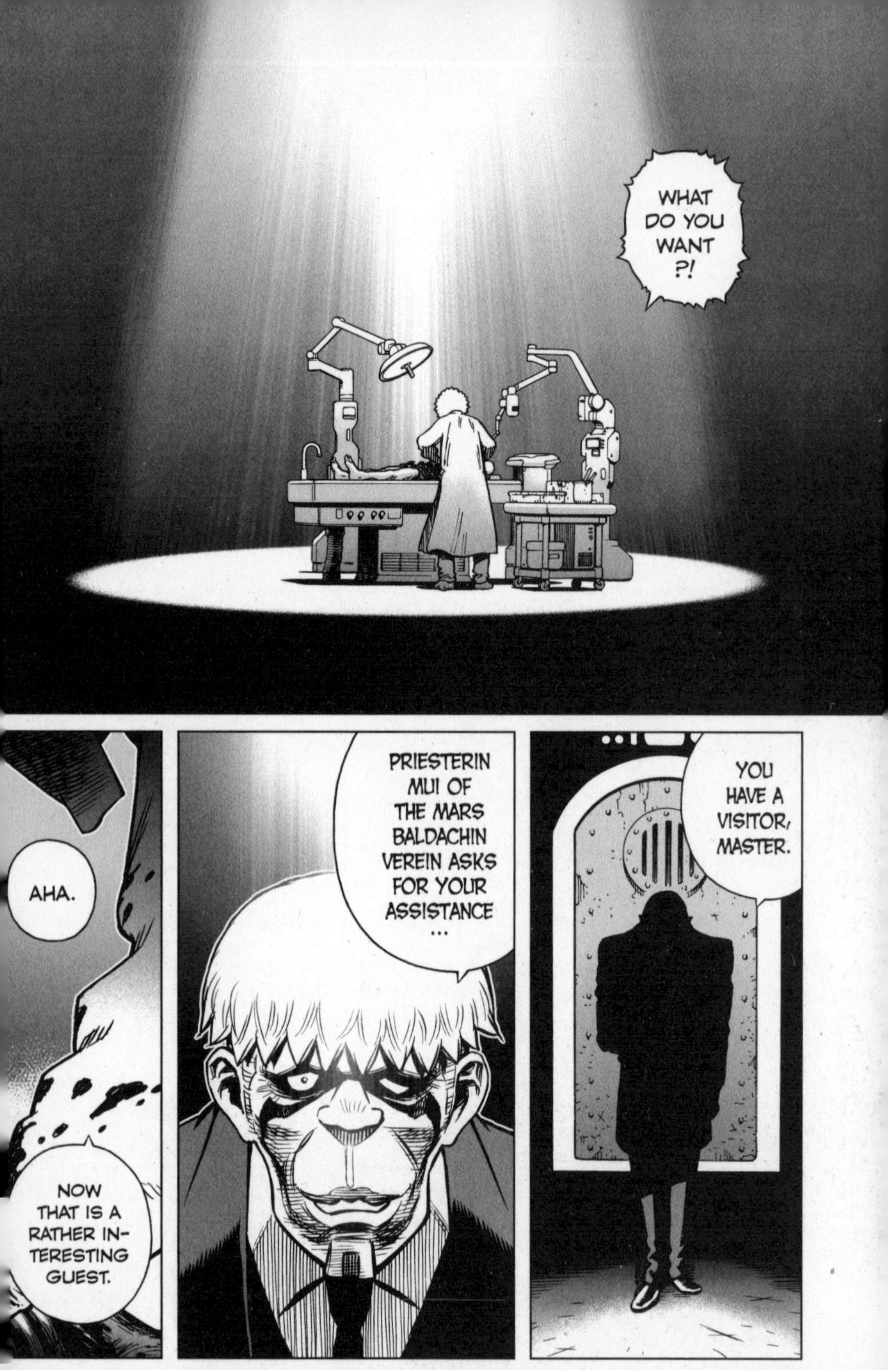
WHAT DO YOU WANT ?!
YOU HAVE A VISITOR, MASTER.
PRIESTERIN MUI OF THE MARS BALDACHIN VEREIN ASKS FOR YOUR ASSISTANCE ...
AHA.
NOW THAT IS A RATHER IN-TERESTING GUEST.

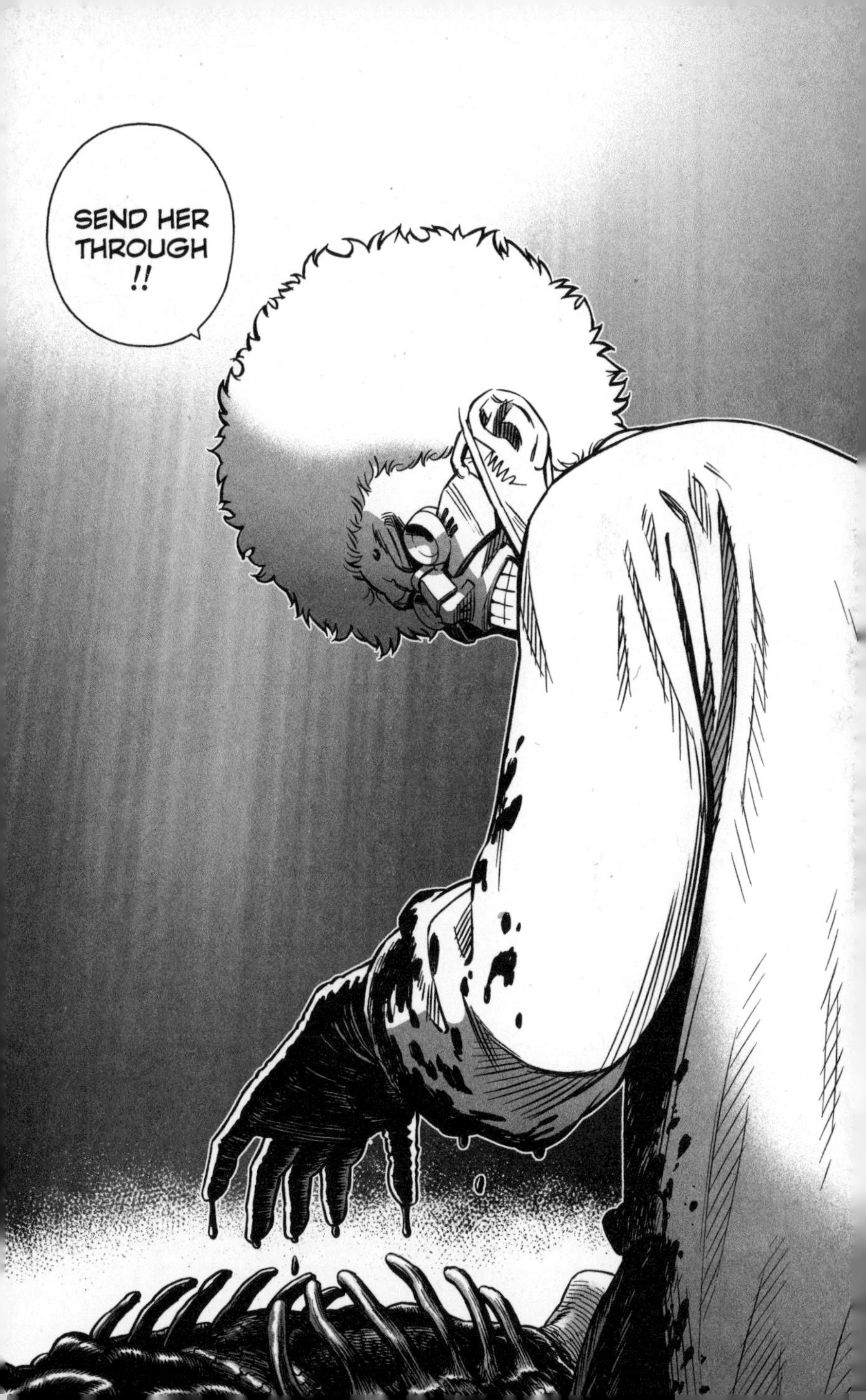
SEND HER THROUGH !!

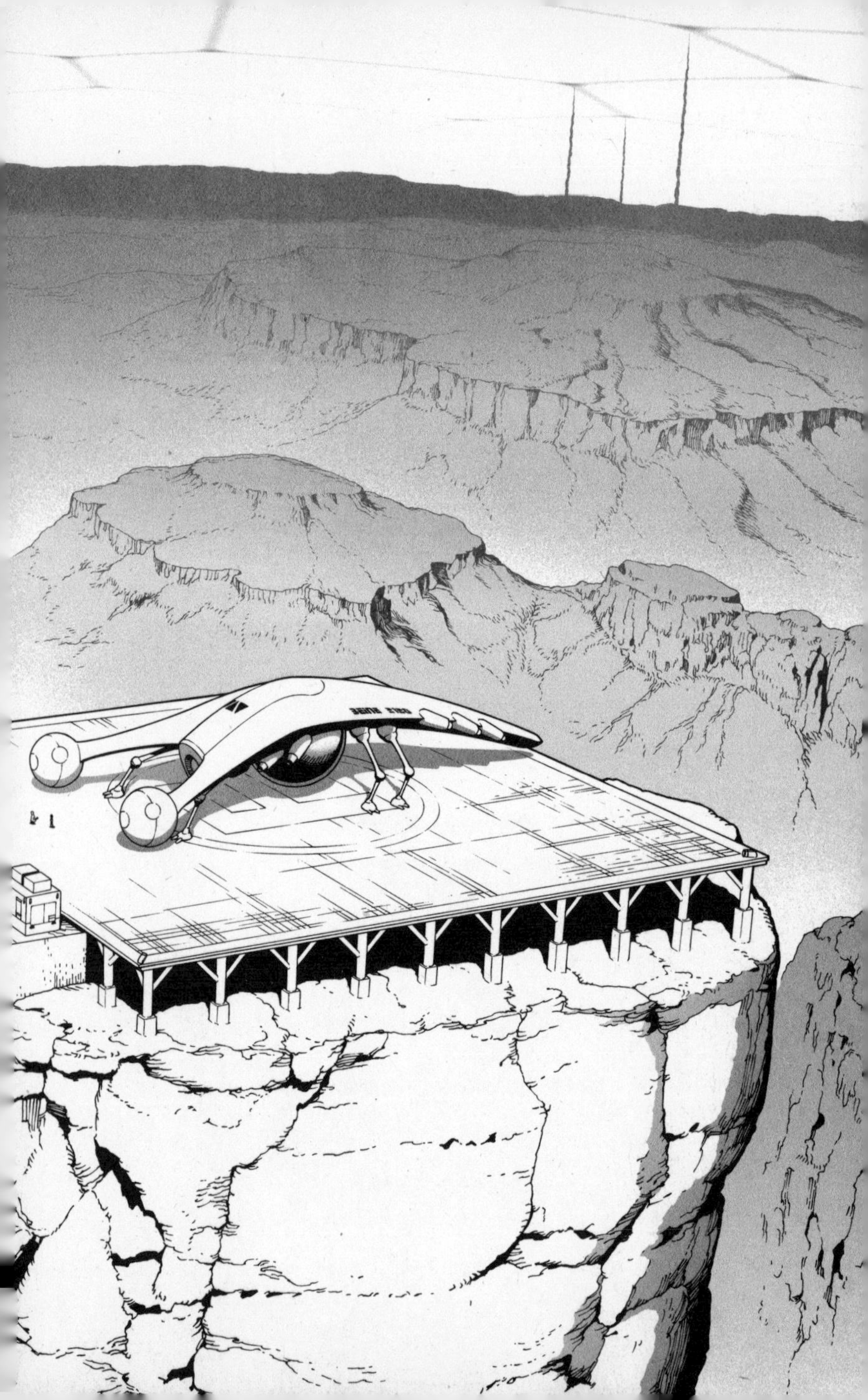

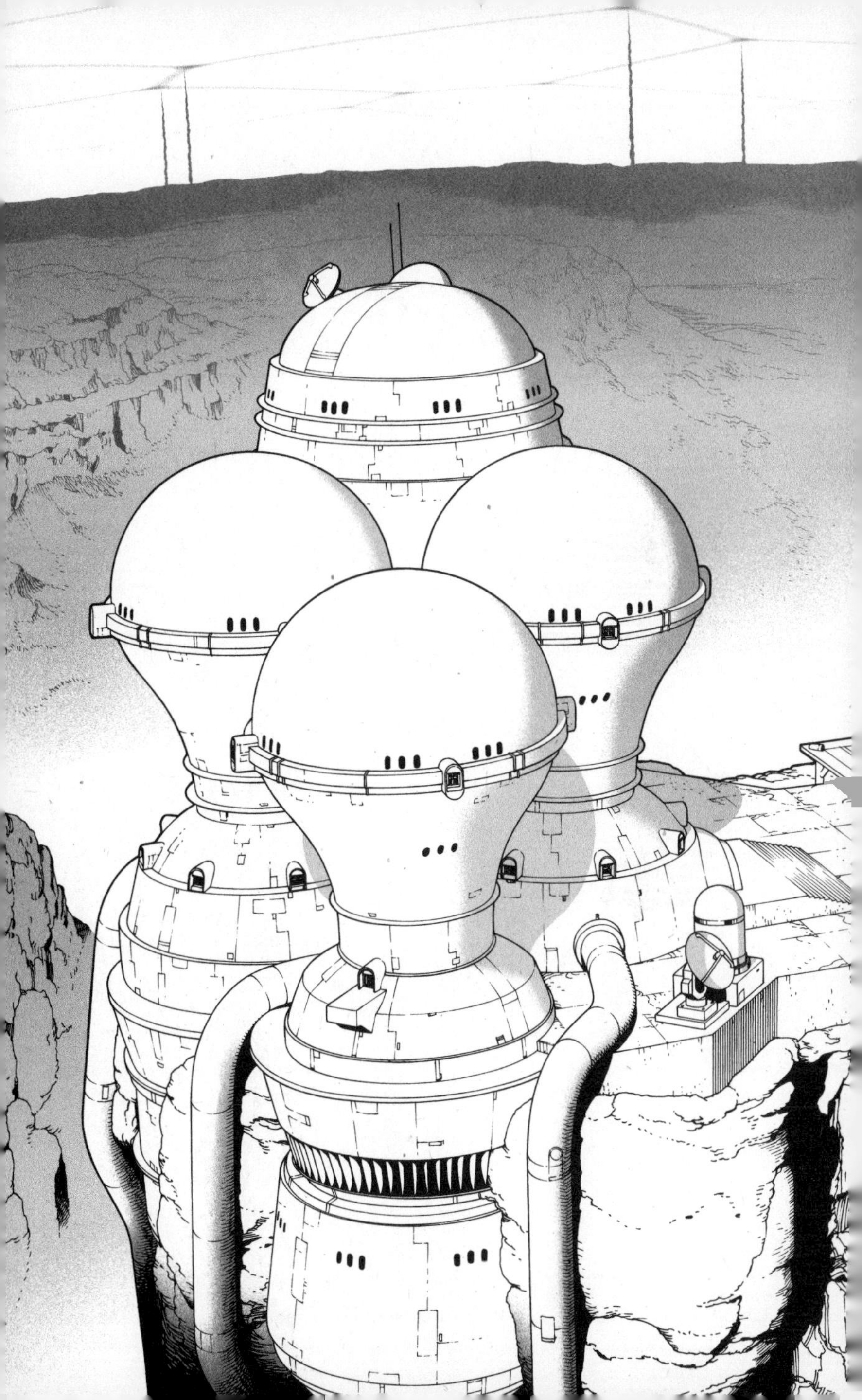

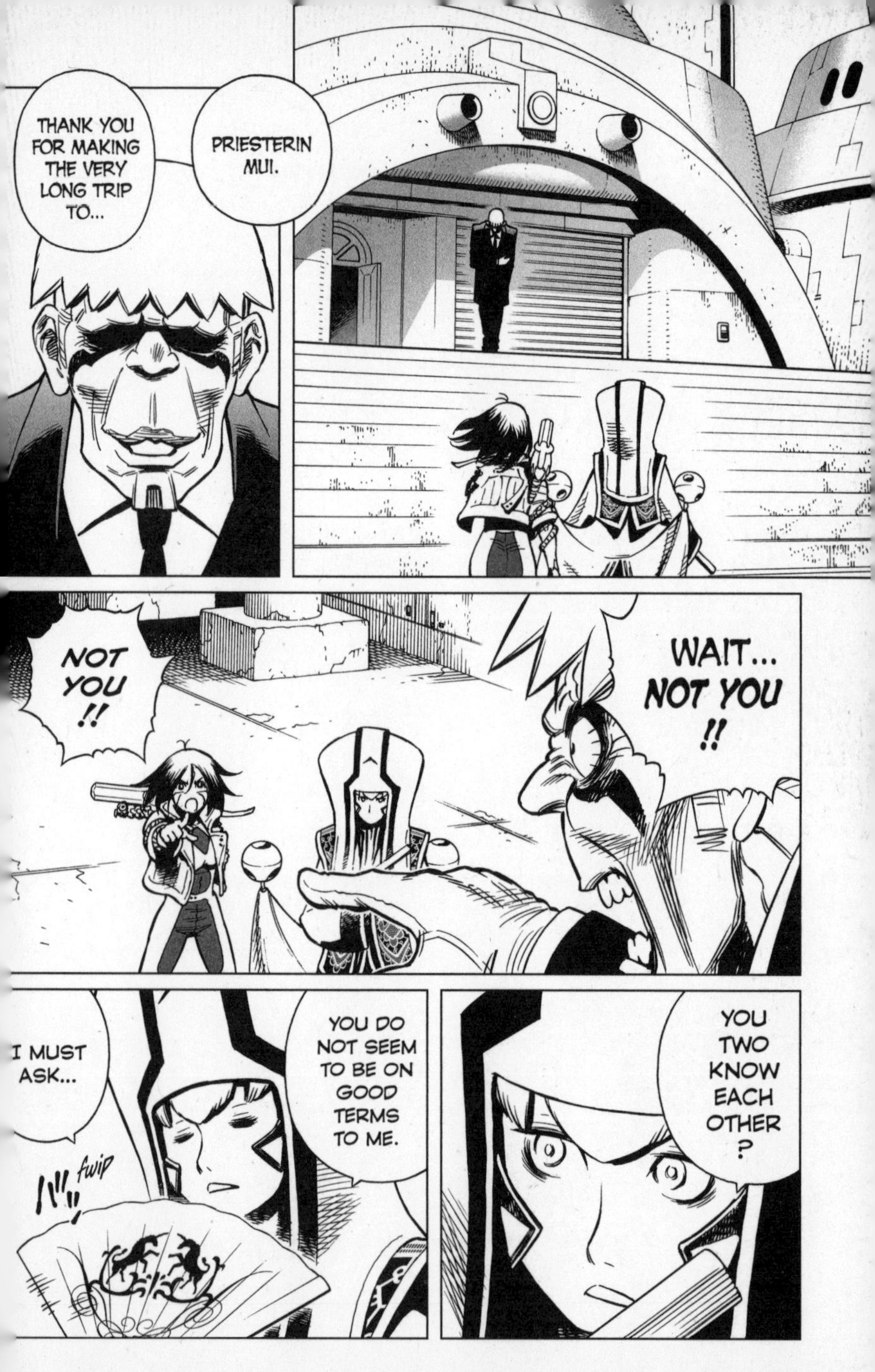
THANK YOU FOR MAKING THE VERY LONG TRIP TO...
PRIESTERIN MUI.
NOT YOU !!
WAIT... NOT YOU !!
I MUST ASK...
fwip
YOU DO NOT SEEM TO BE ON GOOD TERMS TO ME.
YOU TWO KNOW EACH OTHER ?

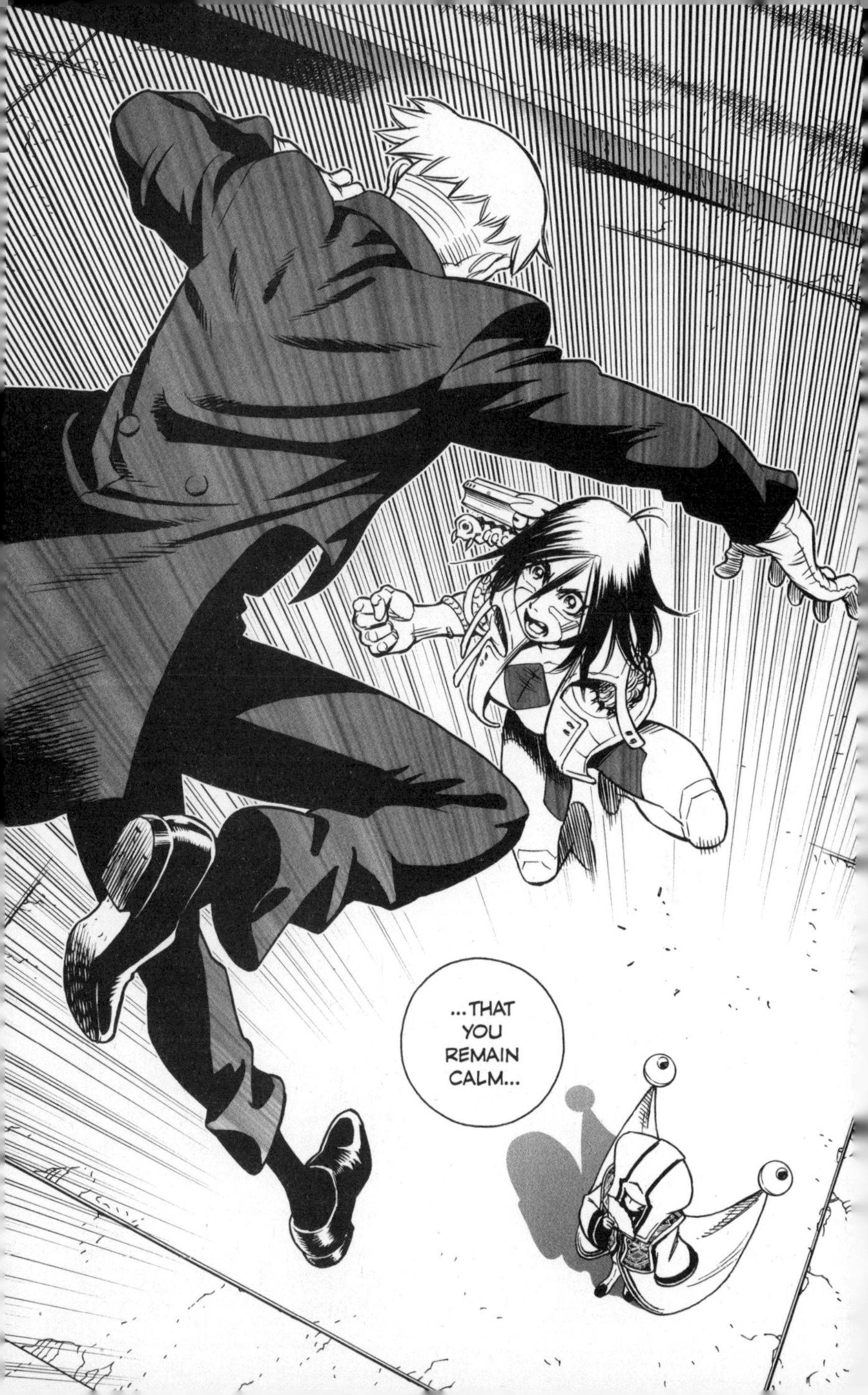
...THAT YOU REMAIN CALM...

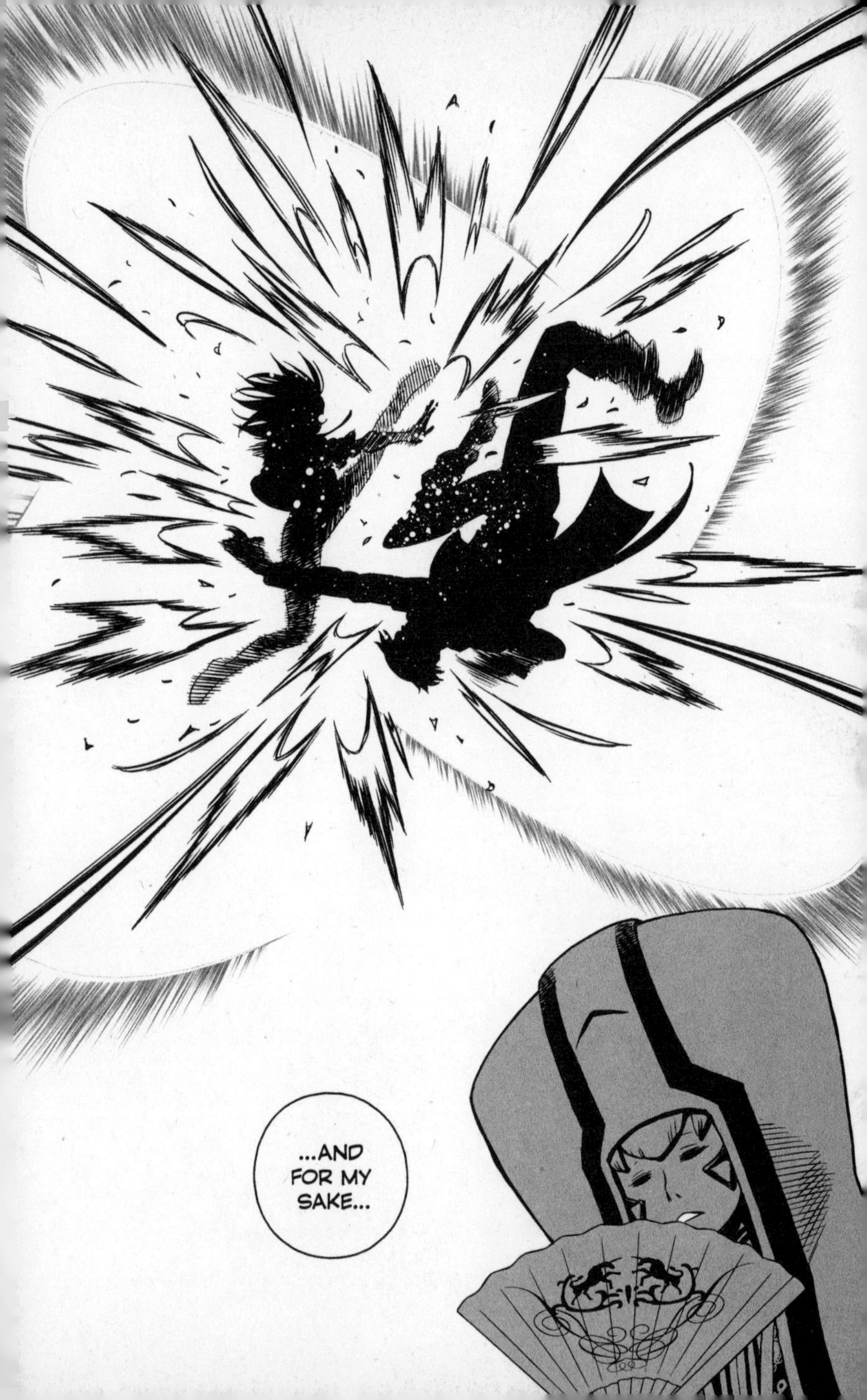
...AND FOR MY SAKE...

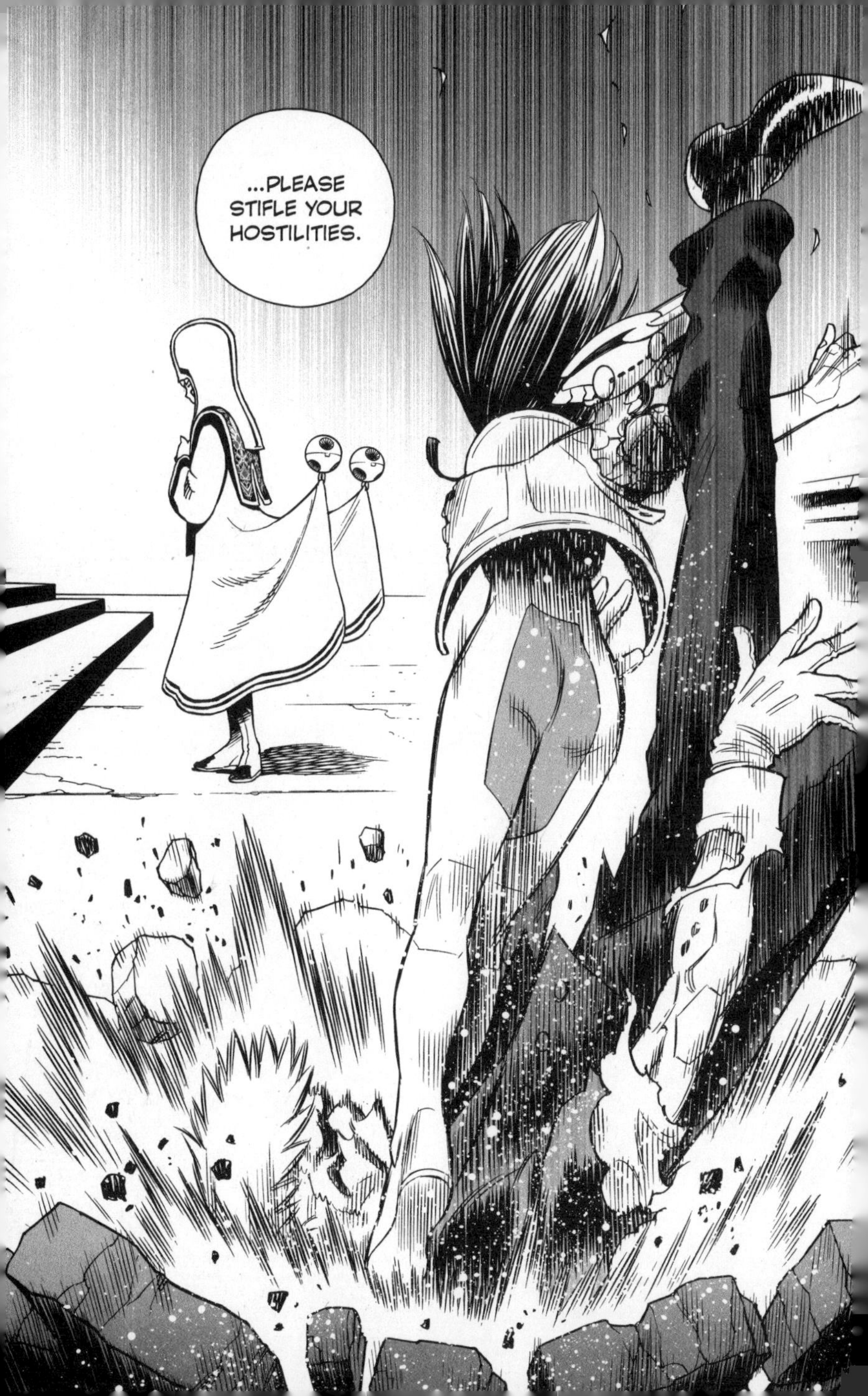
...PLEASE STIFLE YOUR HOSTILITIES.

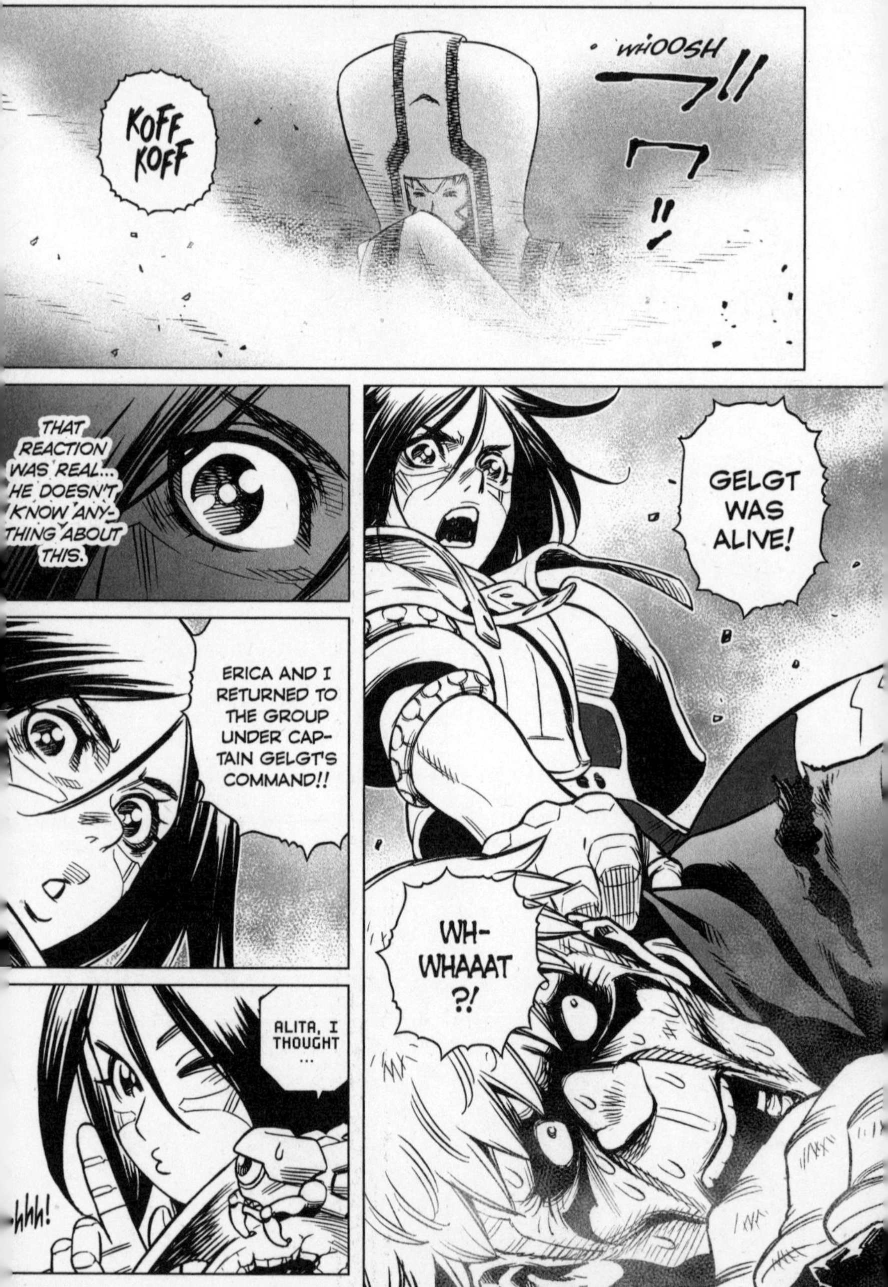
WHOOSH
KOFF KOFF
GELGT WAS ALIVE!
WH-WHAAAT?!
THAT REACTION WAS REAL... HE DOESN'T KNOW ANYTHING ABOUT THIS.
ERICA AND I RETURNED TO THE GROUP UNDER CAPTAIN GELGT'S COMMAND!!
ALITA, I THOUGHT...

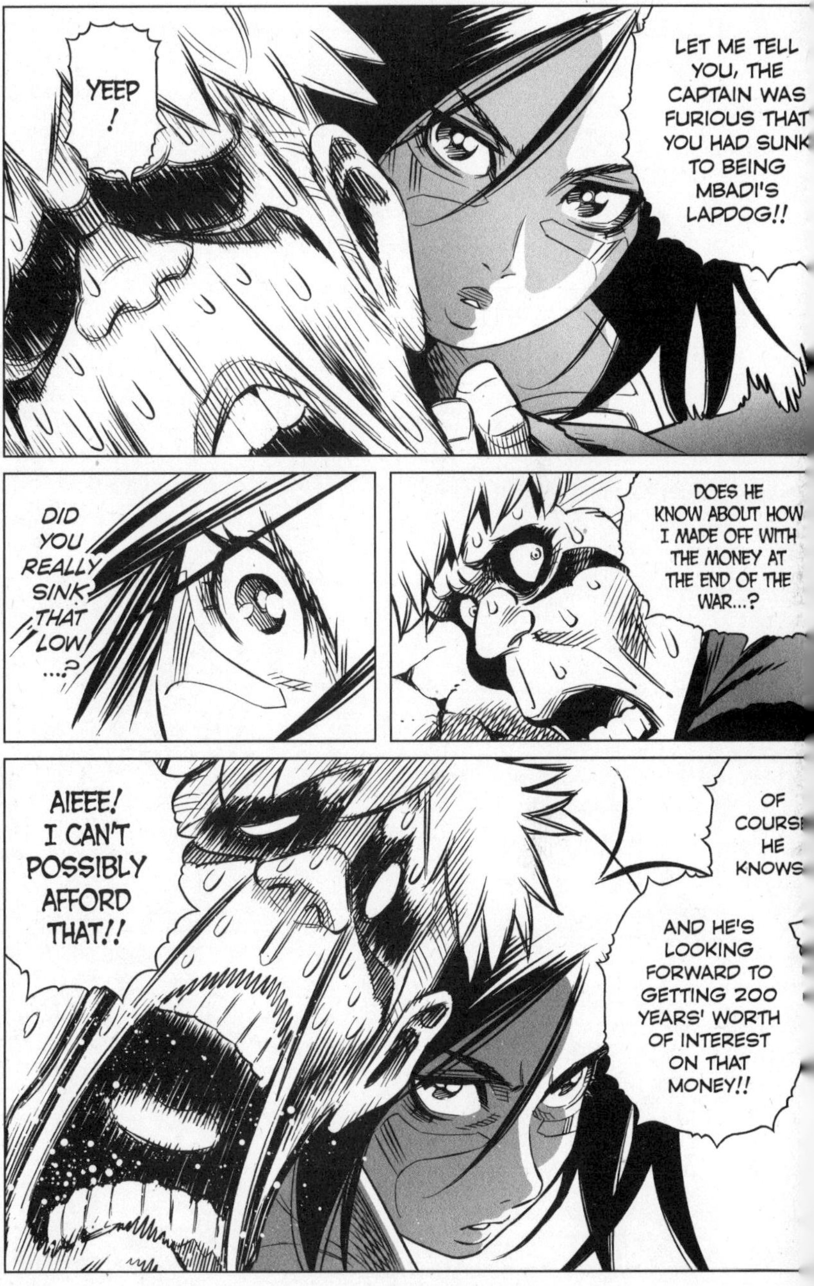
LET ME TELL YOU, THE CAPTAIN WAS FURIOUS THAT YOU HAD SUNK TO BEING MBADI'S LAPDOG!!
YEEP!
DOES HE KNOW ABOUT HOW I MADE OFF WITH THE MONEY AT THE END OF THE WAR...?
DID YOU REALLY SINK THAT LOW...?
OF COURSE HE KNOWS
AND HE'S LOOKING FORWARD TO GETTING 200 YEARS' WORTH OF INTEREST ON THAT MONEY!!
AIEEE! I CAN'T POSSIBLY AFFORD THAT!!

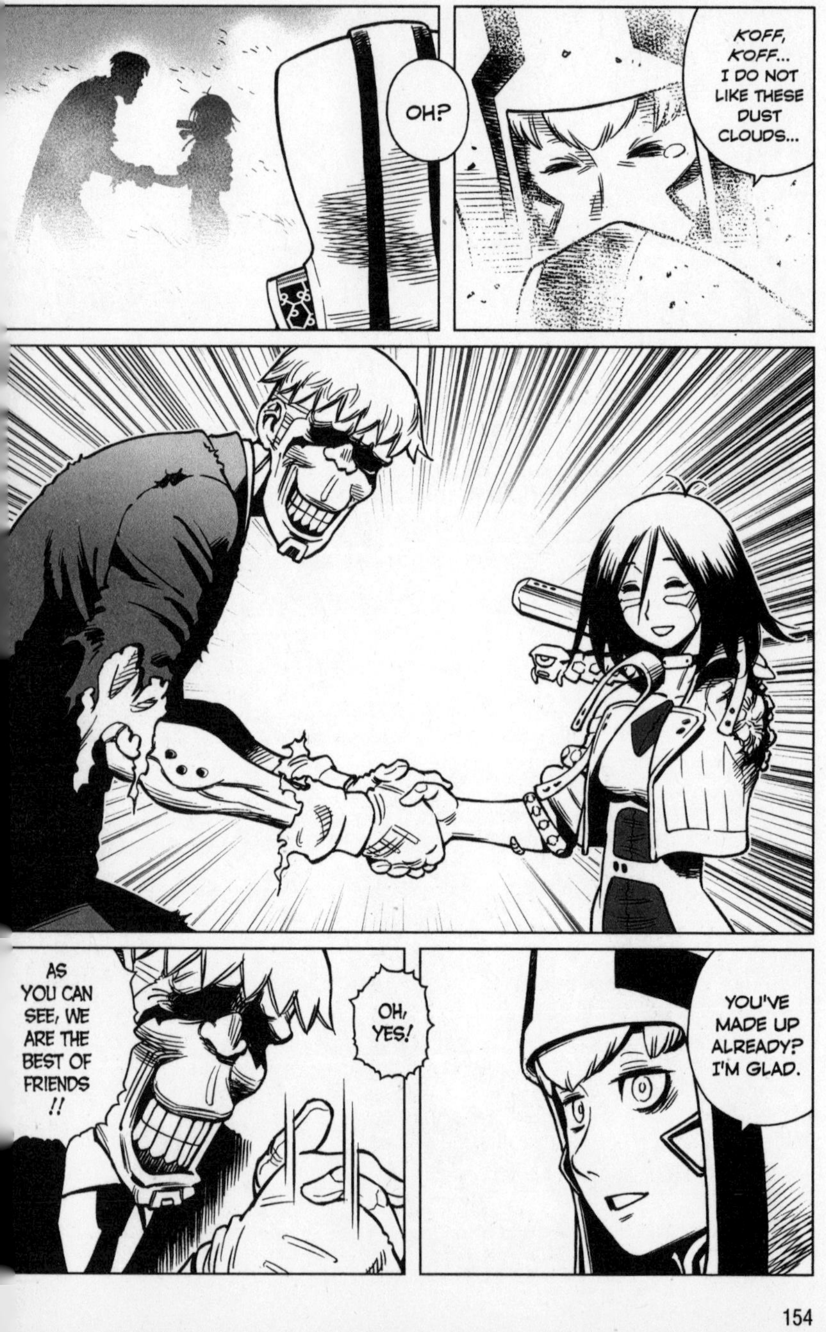
KOFF, KOFF... I DO NOT LIKE THESE DUST CLOUDS...
OH?
YOU'VE MADE UP ALREADY? I'M GLAD.
OH, YES!
AS YOU CAN SEE, WE ARE THE BEST OF FRIENDS !!

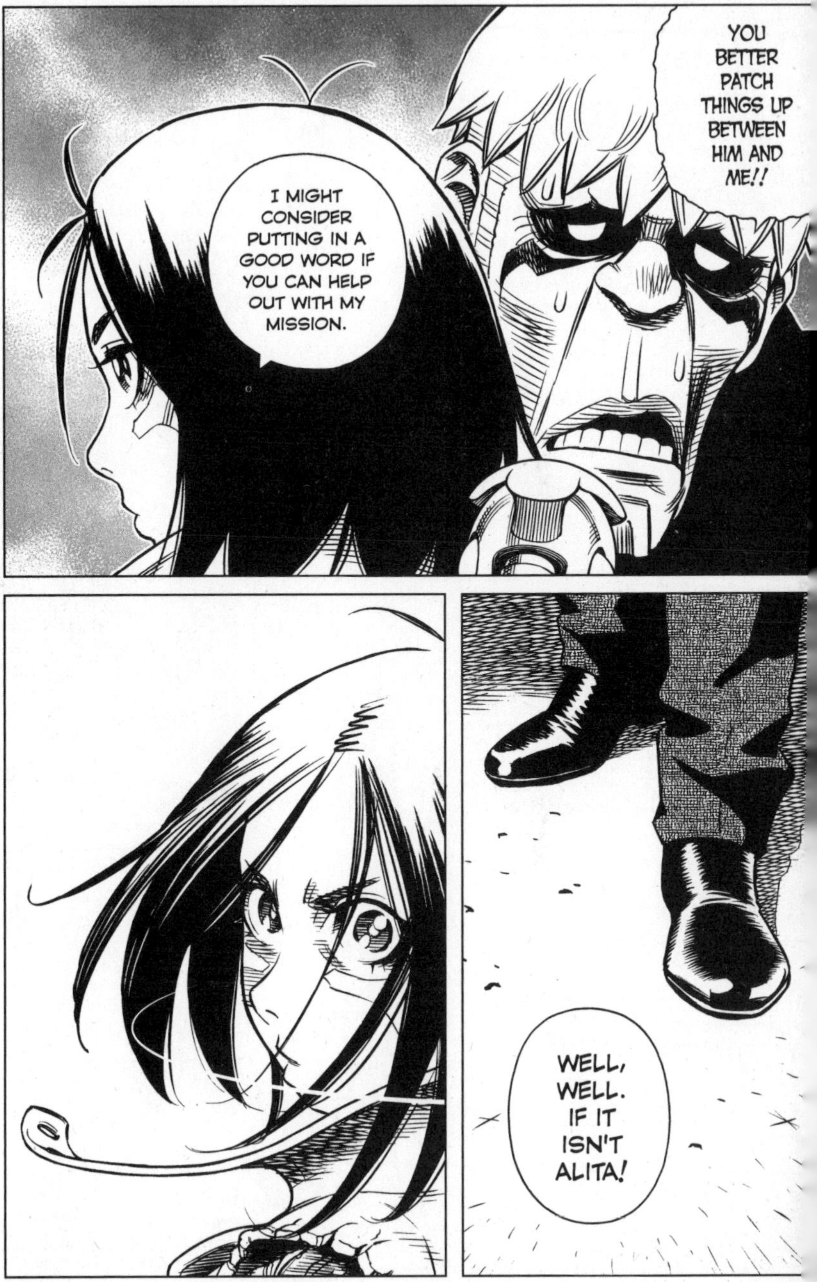
YOU BETTER PATCH THINGS UP BETWEEN HIM AND ME!!
I MIGHT CONSIDER PUTTING IN A GOOD WORD IF YOU CAN HELP OUT WITH MY MISSION.
WELL, WELL. IF IT ISN'T ALITA!

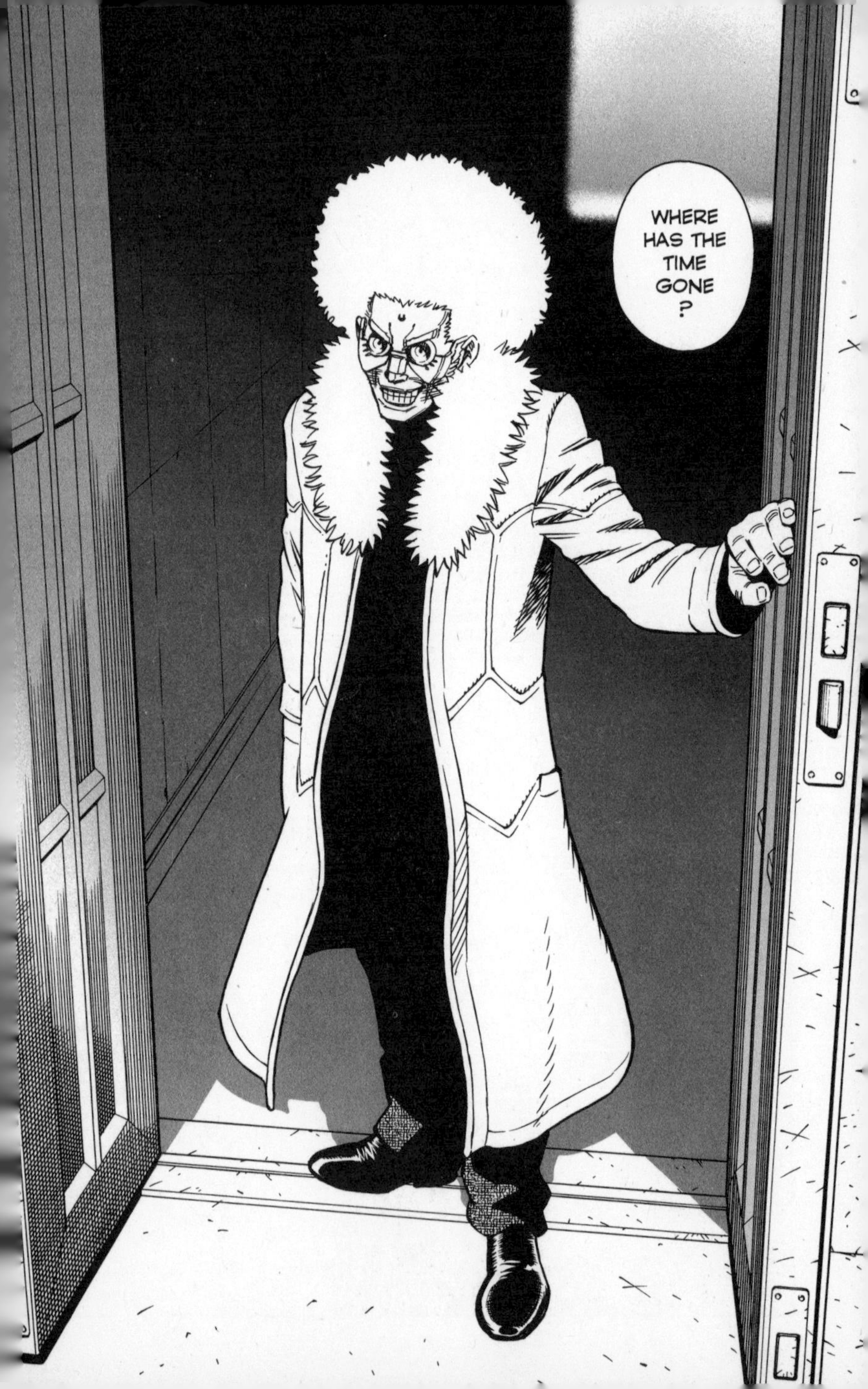
WHERE HAS THE TIME GONE ?

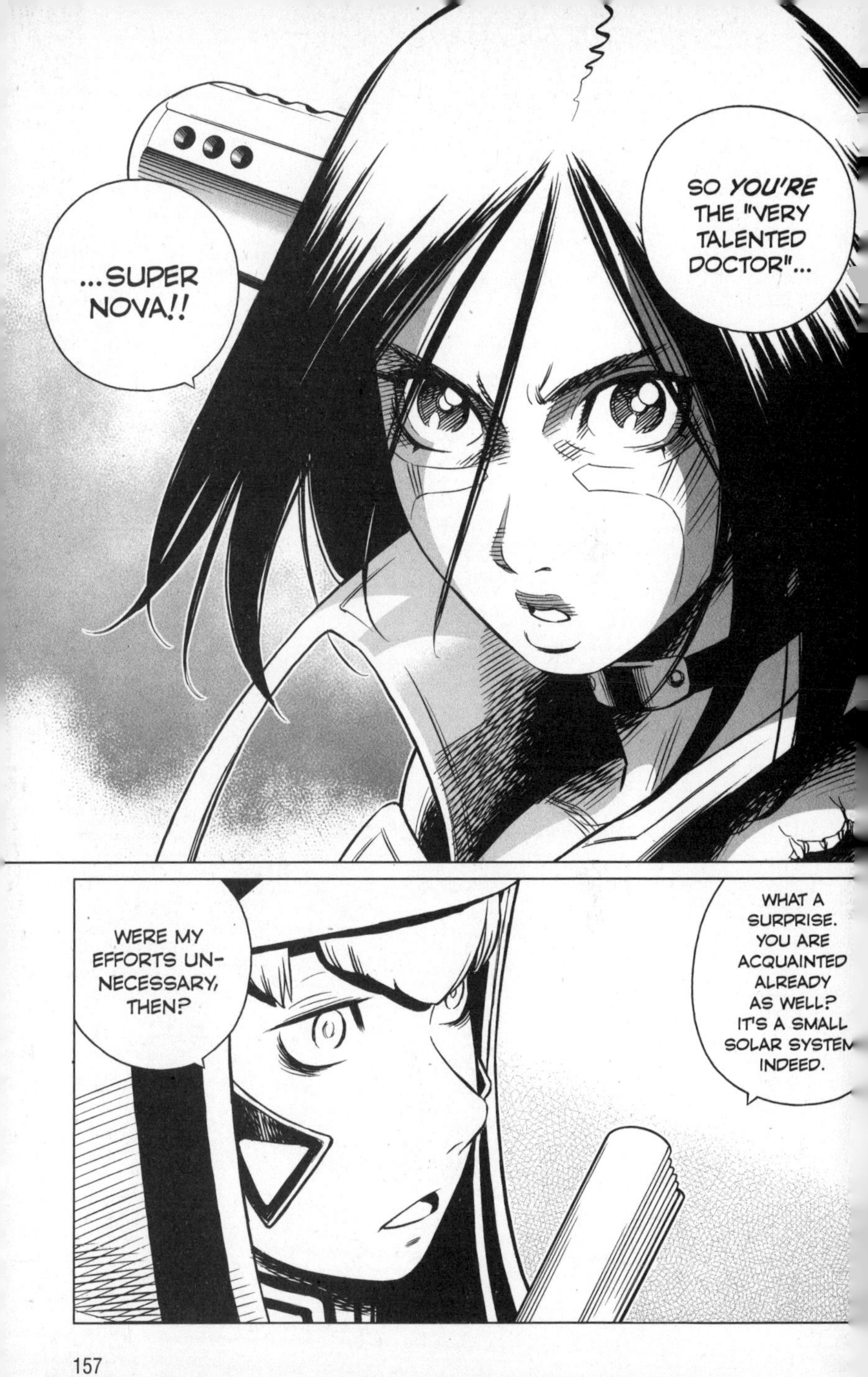
SO *YOU'RE* THE "VERY TALENTED DOCTOR"...
...SUPER NOVA!!
WHAT A SURPRISE. YOU ARE ACQUAINTED ALREADY AS WELL? IT'S A SMALL SOLAR SYSTEM INDEED.
WERE MY EFFORTS UN-NECESSARY, THEN?

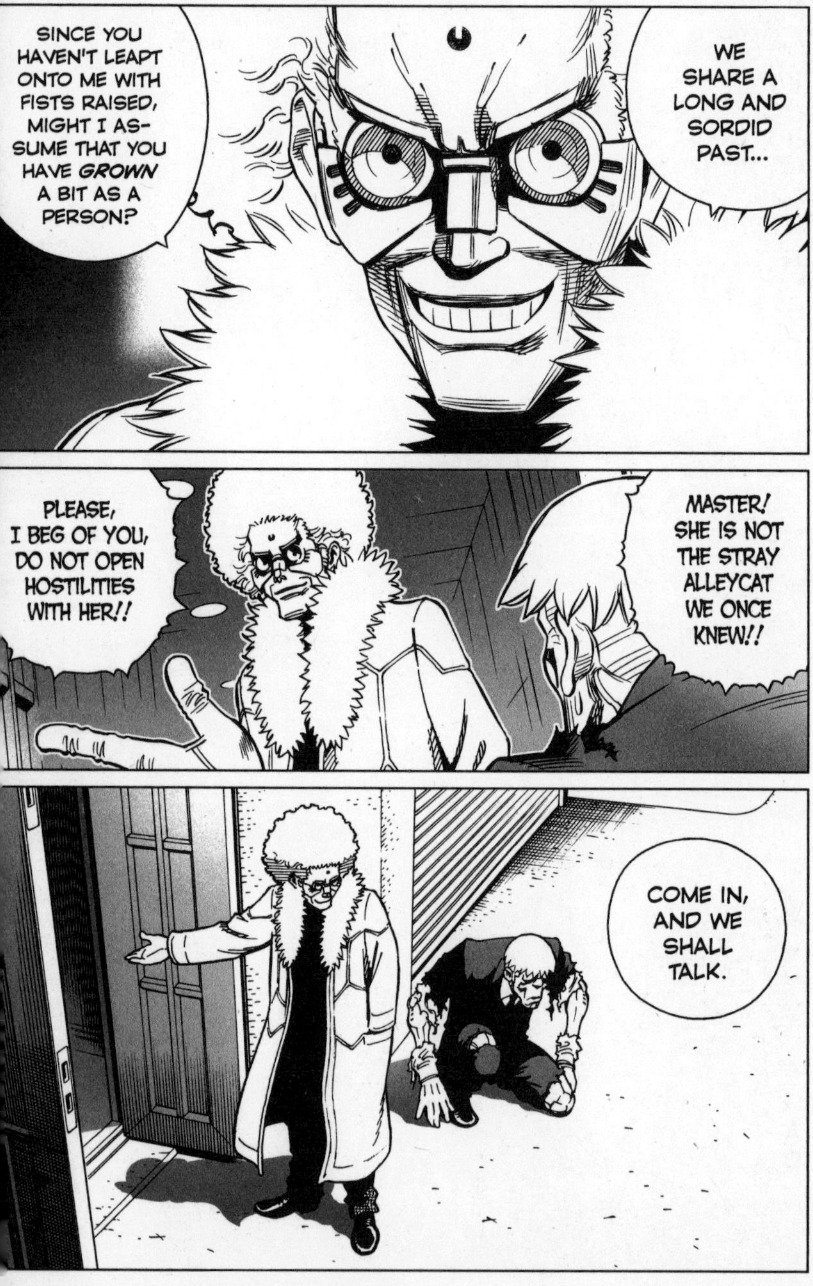
WE SHARE A LONG AND SORDID PAST...
SINCE YOU HAVEN'T LEAPT ONTO ME WITH FISTS RAISED, MIGHT I AS-SUME THAT YOU HAVE *GROWN* A BIT AS A PERSON?
MASTER! SHE IS NOT THE STRAY ALLEYCAT WE ONCE KNEW!!
PLEASE, I BEG OF YOU, DO NOT OPEN HOSTILITIES WITH HER!!
COME IN, AND WE SHALL TALK.

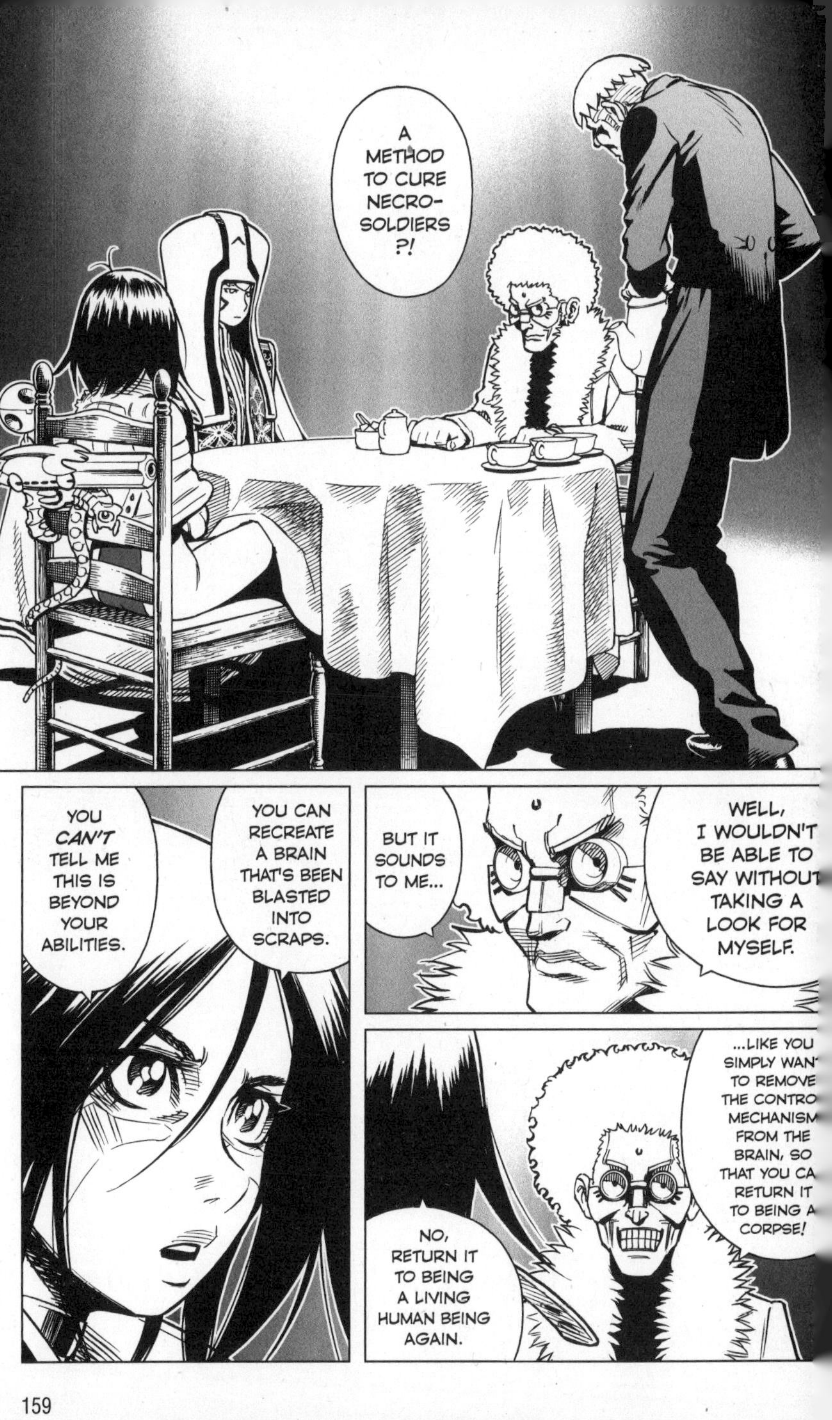
A METHOD TO CURE NECRO-SOLDIERS ?!
WELL, I WOULDN'T BE ABLE TO SAY WITHOUT TAKING A LOOK FOR MYSELF.
BUT IT SOUNDS TO ME...
...LIKE YOU SIMPLY WAN TO REMOVE THE CONTRO MECHANISM FROM THE BRAIN, SO THAT YOU CA RETURN IT TO BEING A CORPSE!
NO, RETURN IT TO BEING A LIVING HUMAN BEING AGAIN.
YOU CAN RECREATE A BRAIN THAT'S BEEN BLASTED INTO SCRAPS.
YOU *CAN'T* TELL ME THIS IS BEYOND YOUR ABILITIES.

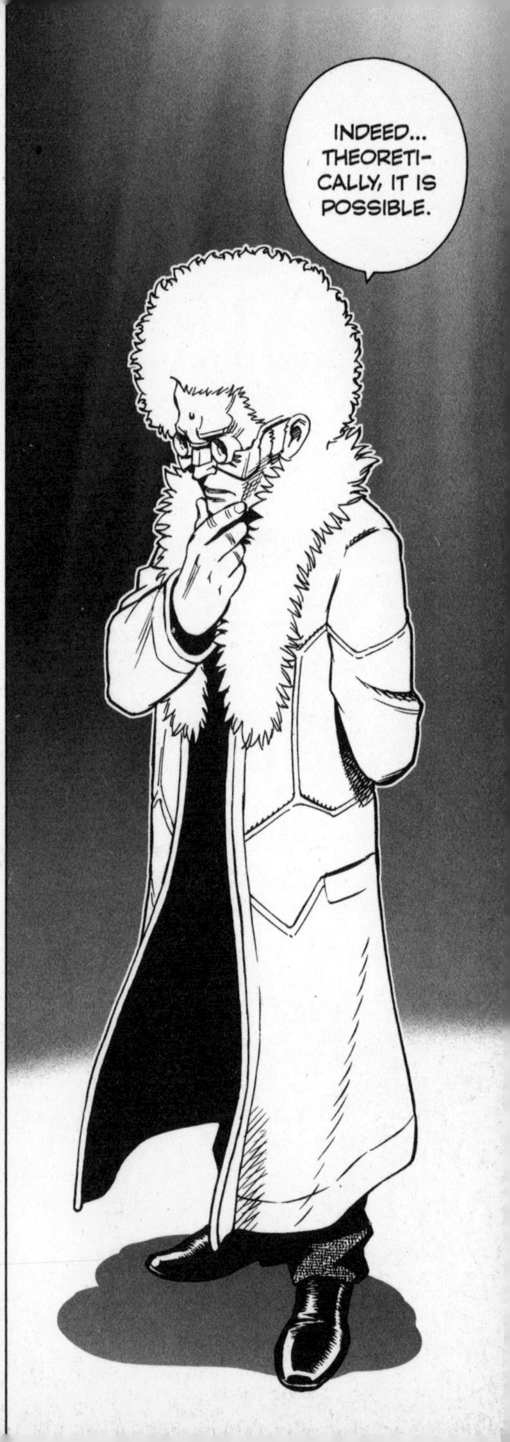
INDEED... THEORETICALLY, IT IS POSSIBLE.

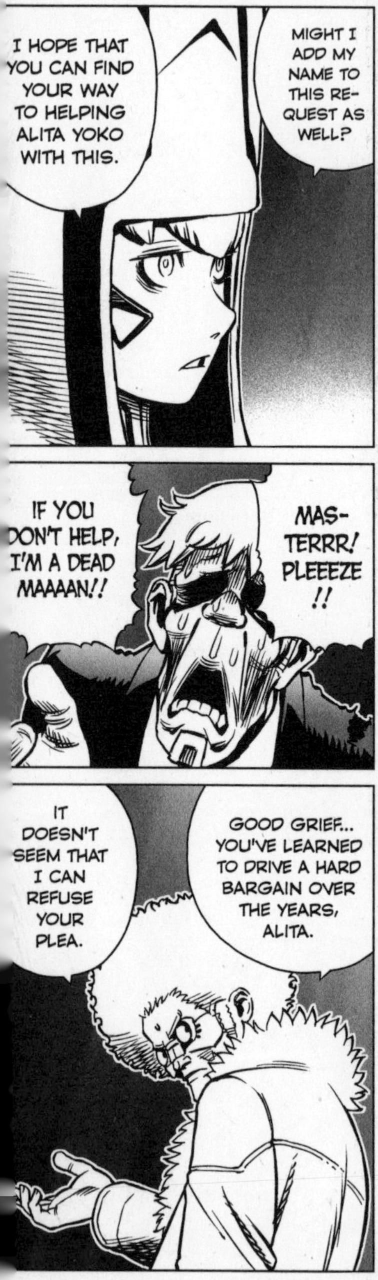
MIGHT I ADD MY NAME TO THIS REQUEST AS WELL?
I HOPE THAT YOU CAN FIND YOUR WAY TO HELPING ALITA YOKO WITH THIS.
MAS-TERRR! PLEEEZE!!
IF YOU DON'T HELP, I'M A DEAD MAAAAN!!
GOOD GRIEF... YOU'VE LEARNED TO DRIVE A HARD BARGAIN OVER THE YEARS, ALITA.
IT DOESN'T SEEM THAT I CAN REFUSE YOUR PLEA.

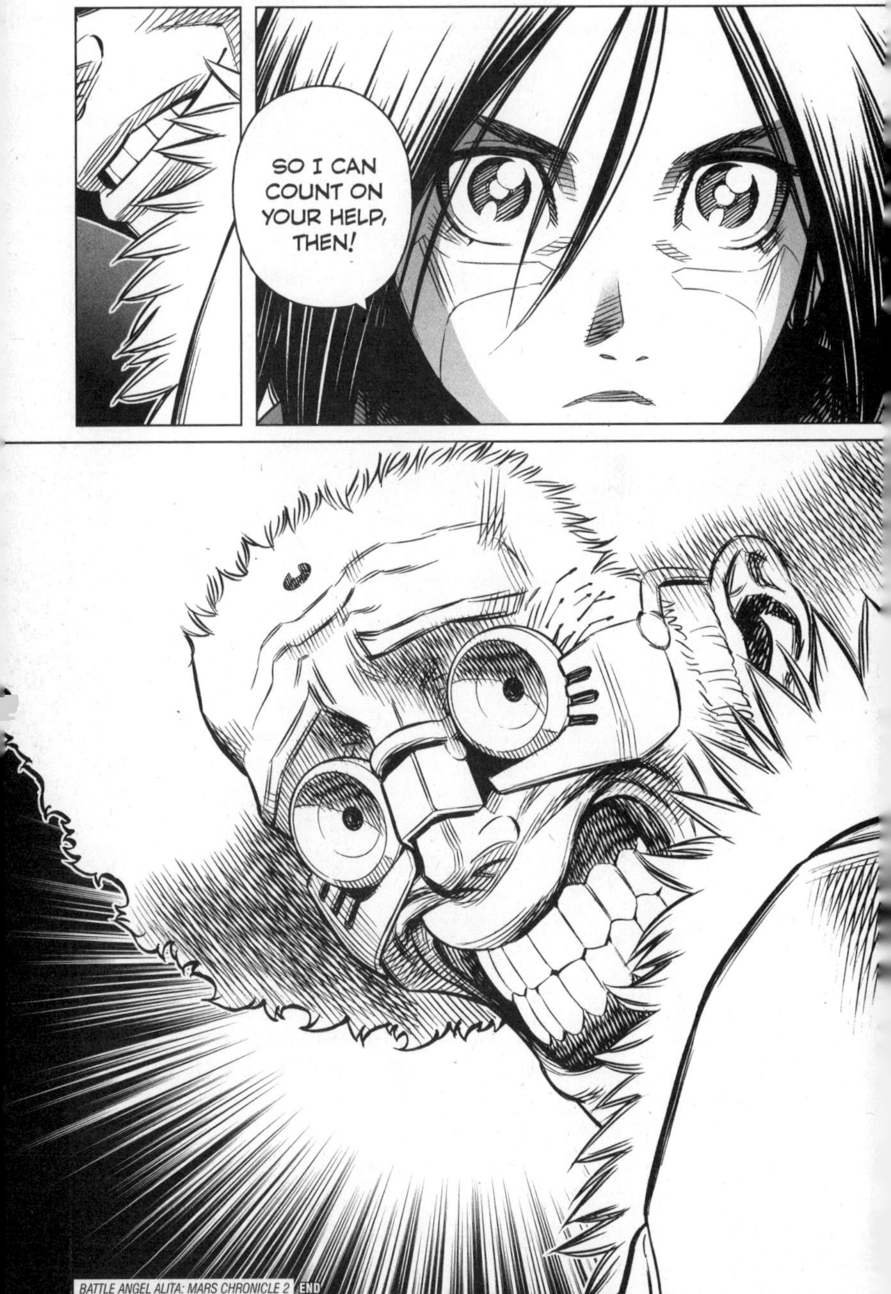
SO I CAN COUNT ON YOUR HELP, THEN!
BATTLE ANGEL ALITA: MARS CHRONICLE 2 END

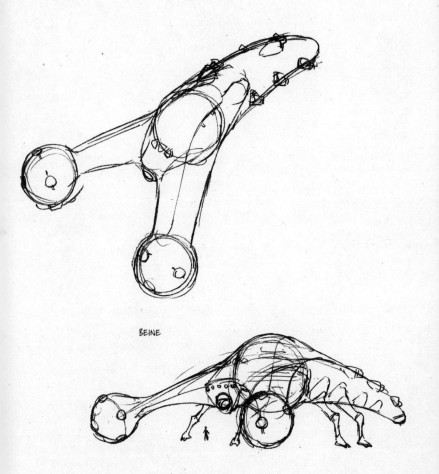

BEINE

A MANGA EDITION OF THE 46TH SEIUN AWARD WINNER FOR BEST JAPANESE SCI-FI SHORT STORY!

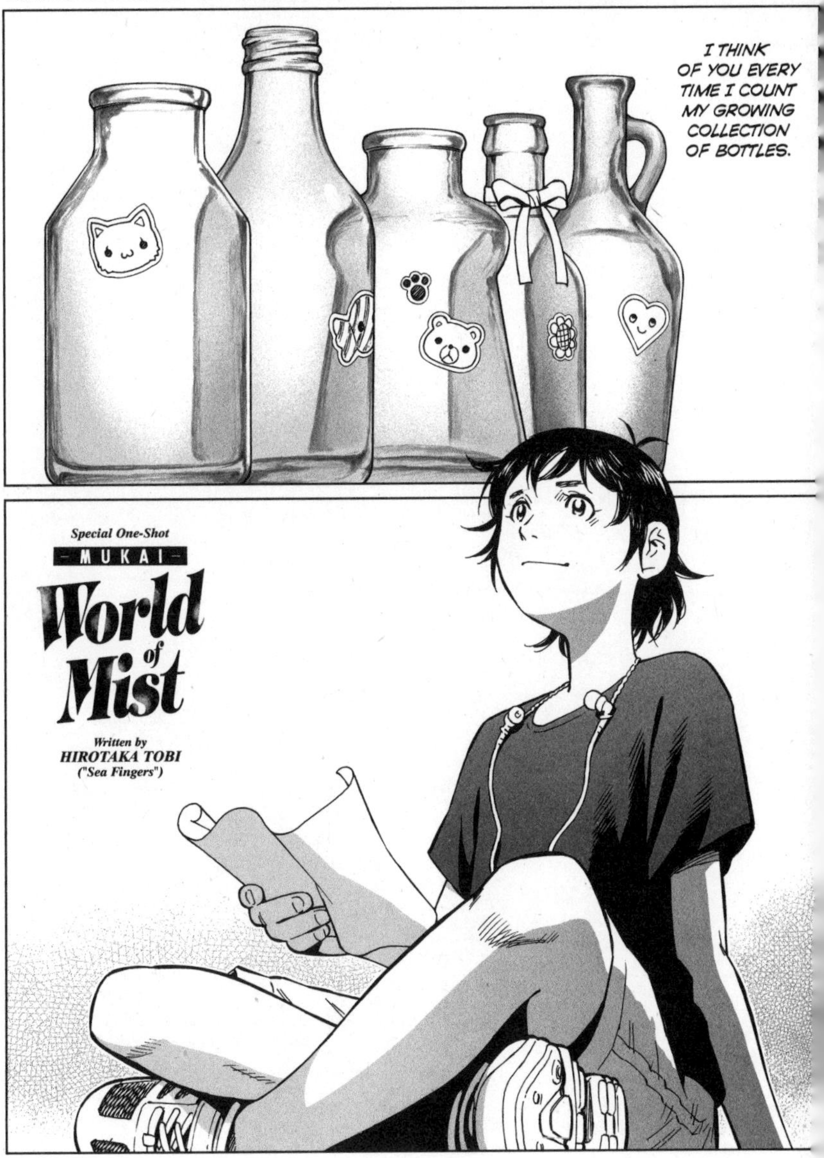
I THINK OF YOU EVERY TIME I COUNT MY GROWING COLLECTION OF BOTTLES.
Special One-Shot
MUKAI
World of Mist
Written by
HIROTAKA TOBI
("Sea Fingers")

I MET YOU ON THE DAY AFTER A STORM.

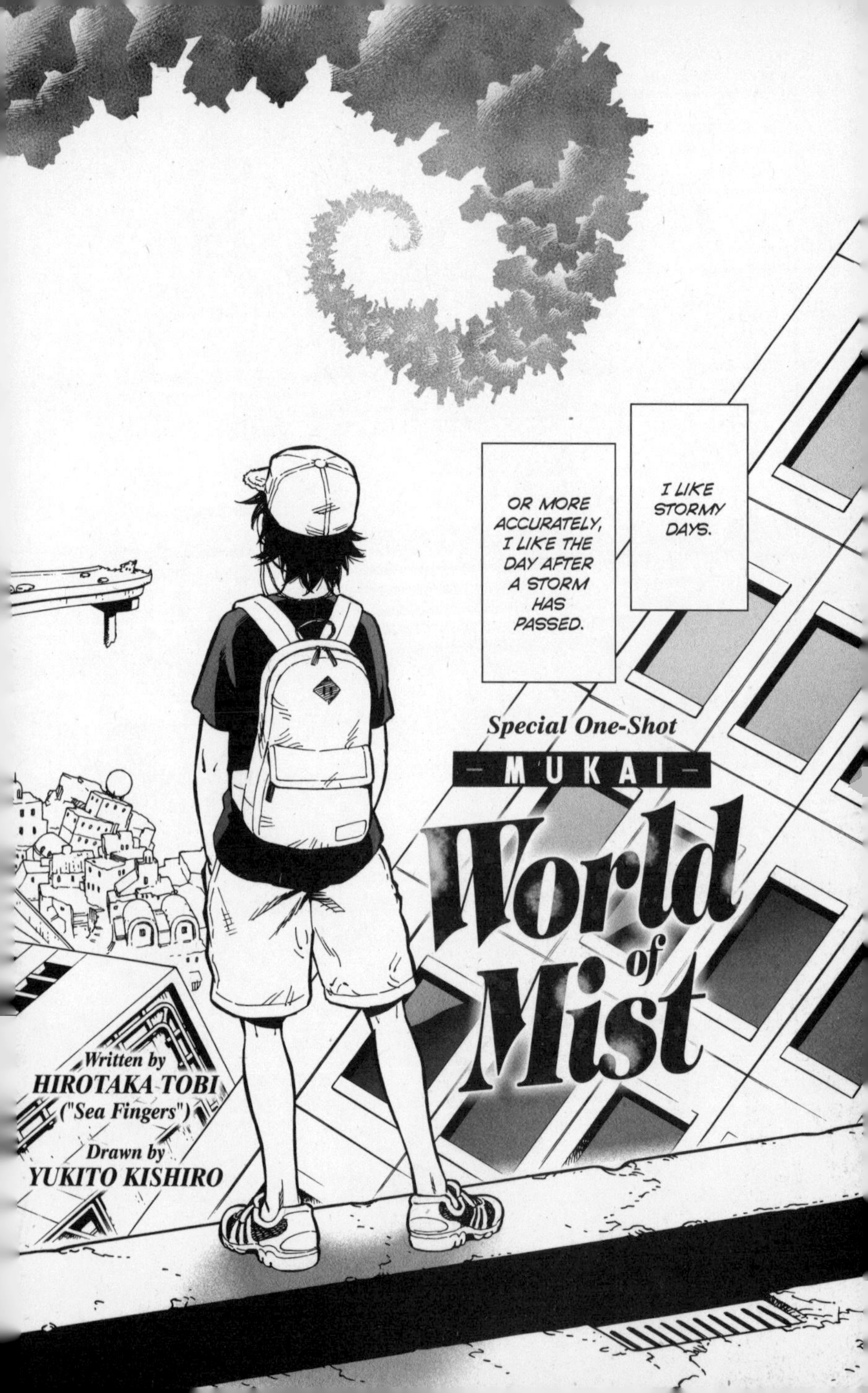
I LIKE STORMY DAYS.
OR MORE ACCURATELY, I LIKE THE DAY AFTER A STORM HAS PASSED.
Special One-Shot
MUKAI
World of Mist
Written by
HIROTAKA TOBI
("Sea Fingers")
Drawn by
YUKITO KISHIRO

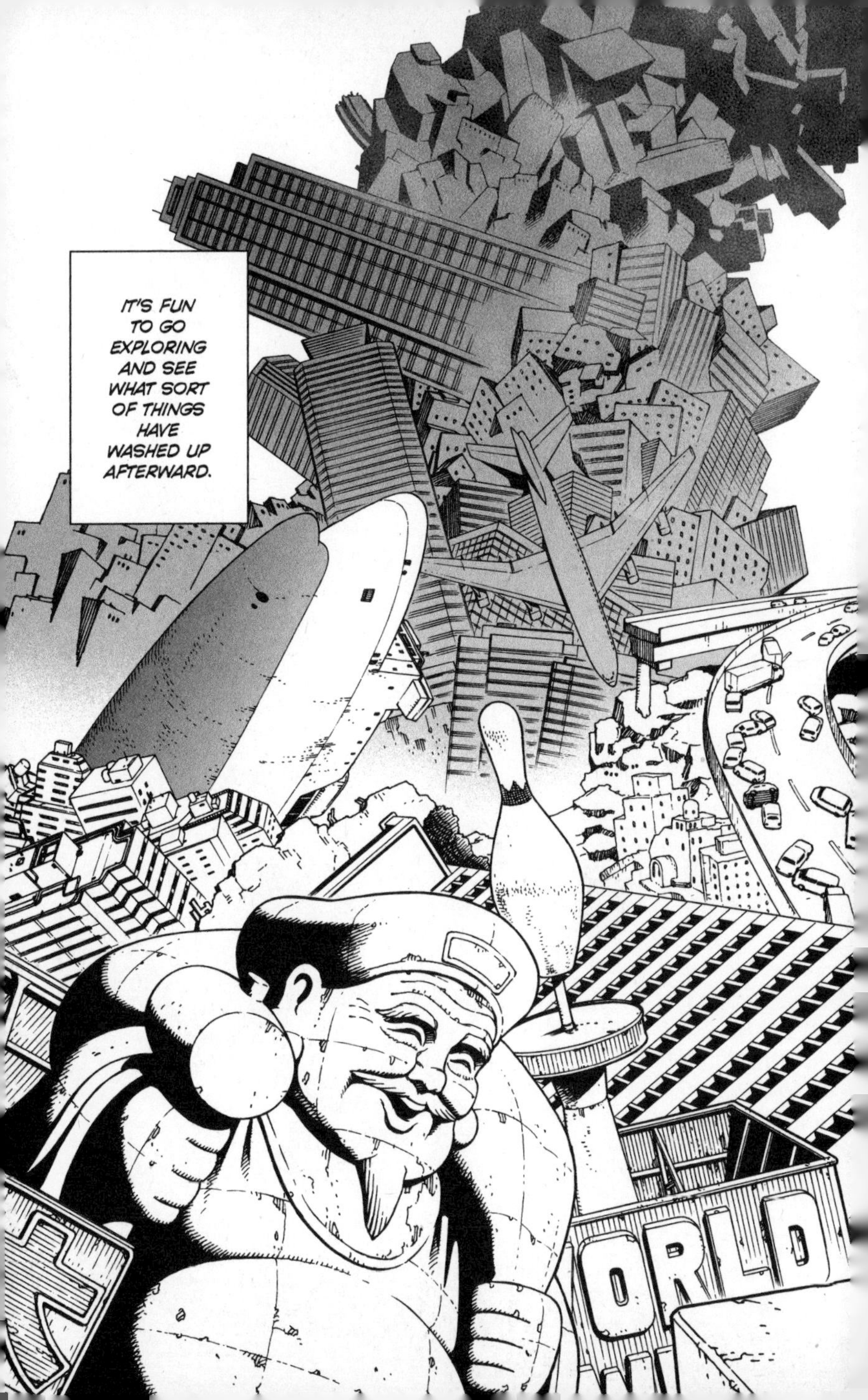
IT'S FUN TO GO EXPLORING AND SEE WHAT SORT OF THINGS HAVE WASHED UP AFTERWARD.
ORLD

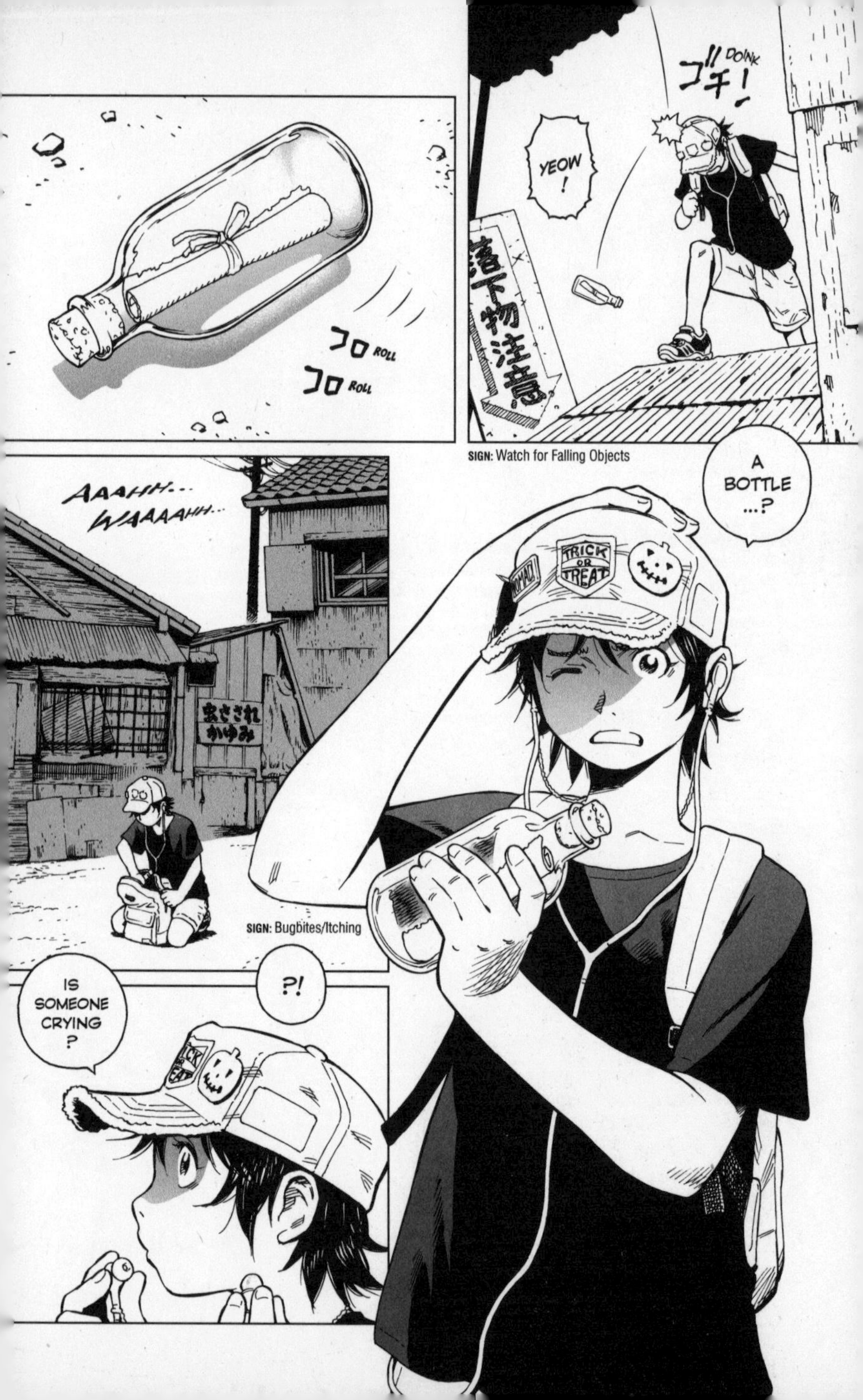
ゴチ! DOINK
YEOW!
落下物注意
SIGN: Watch for Falling Objects
コロ ROLL
コロ ROLL
A BOTTLE...?
TRICK OR TREAT
AAAHH... WAAAAHH...
あせされ かゆみ
SIGN: Bugbites/Itching
?!
IS SOMEONE CRYING?

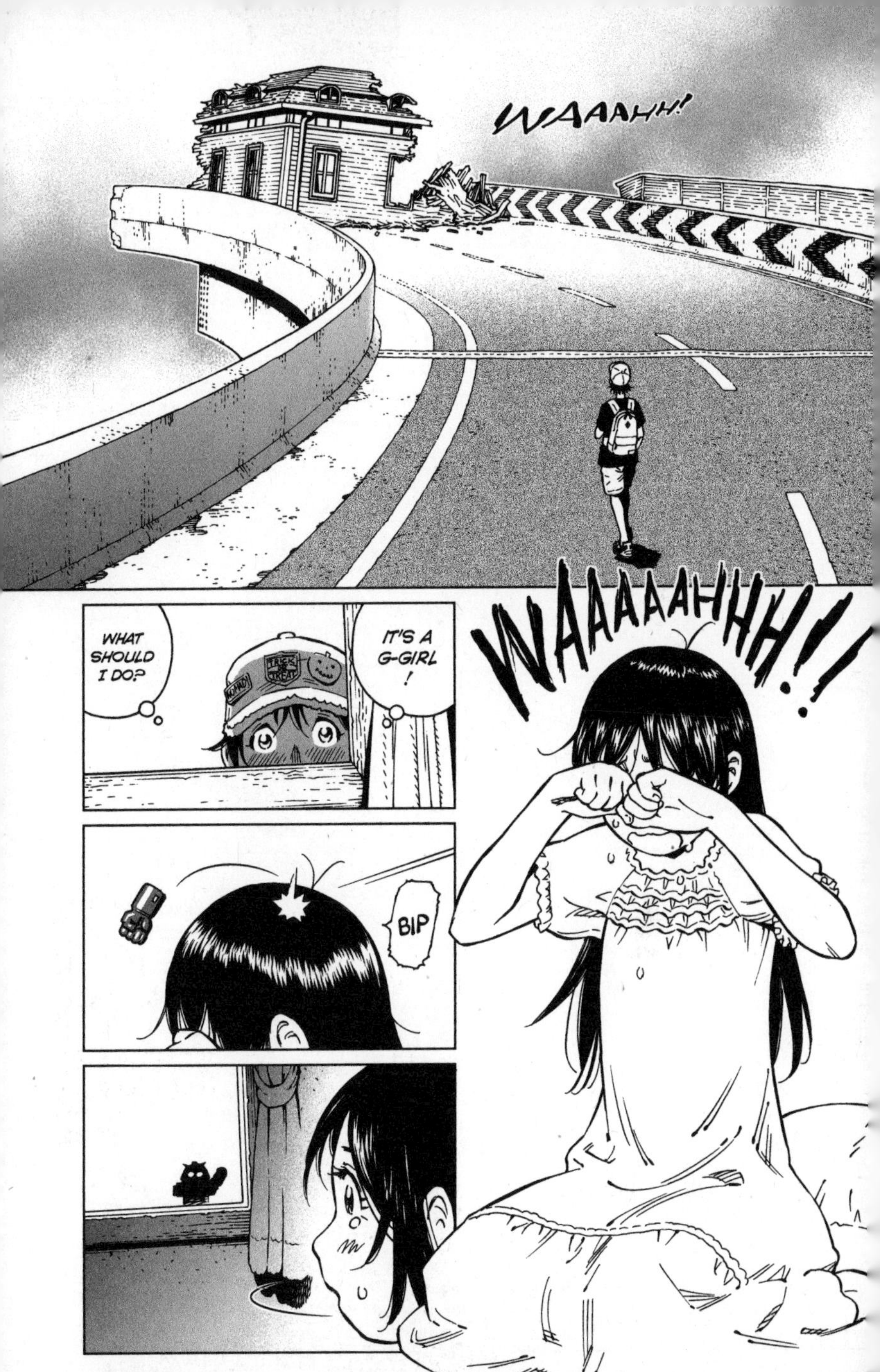
WAAAHH!
WAAAAAHHH!!
IT'S A G-GIRL!
WHAT SHOULD I DO?
BIP

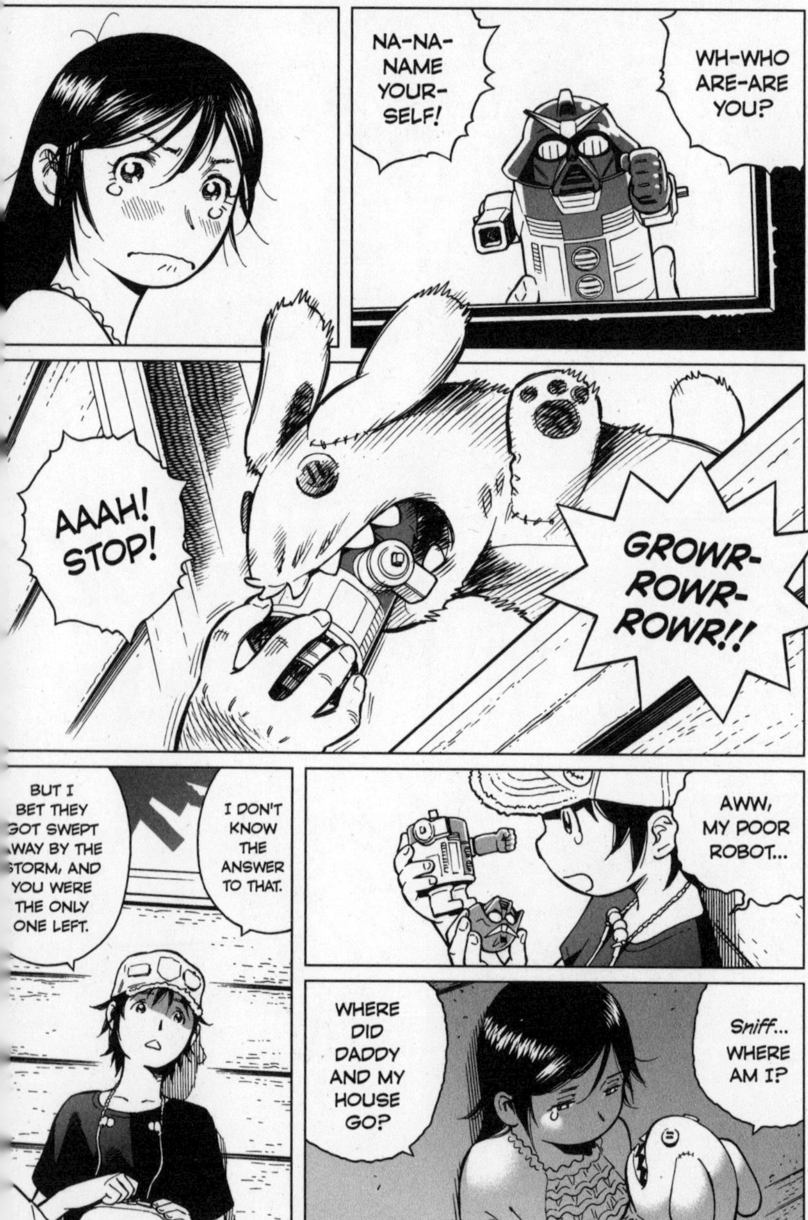

WH-WHO ARE-ARE YOU?
NA-NA-NAME YOUR-SELF!
GROWR-ROWR-ROWR!!
AAAH! STOP!
AWW, MY POOR ROBOT...
*Sniff*... WHERE AM I?
WHERE DID DADDY AND MY HOUSE GO?
I DON'T KNOW THE ANSWER TO THAT.
BUT I BET THEY GOT SWEPT AWAY BY THE STORM, AND YOU WERE THE ONLY ONE LEFT.

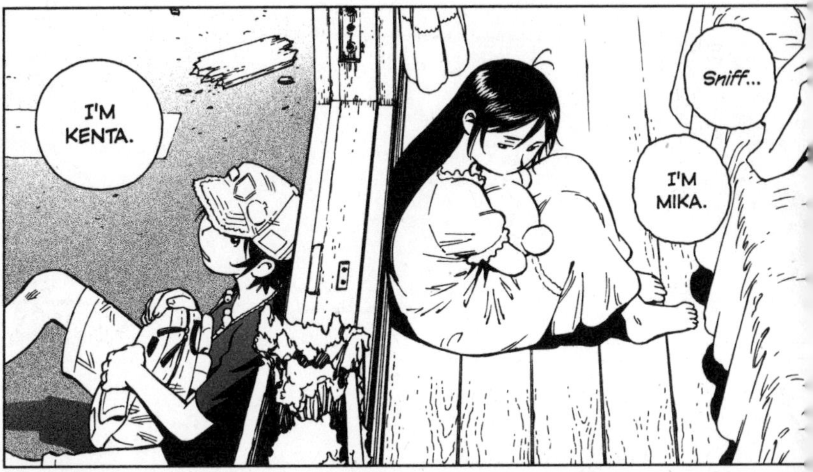
Sniff...
I'M MIKA.
I'M KENTA.

*THIS IS HOW I BECAME FRIENDS WITH MIKA THE CRYBABY.*

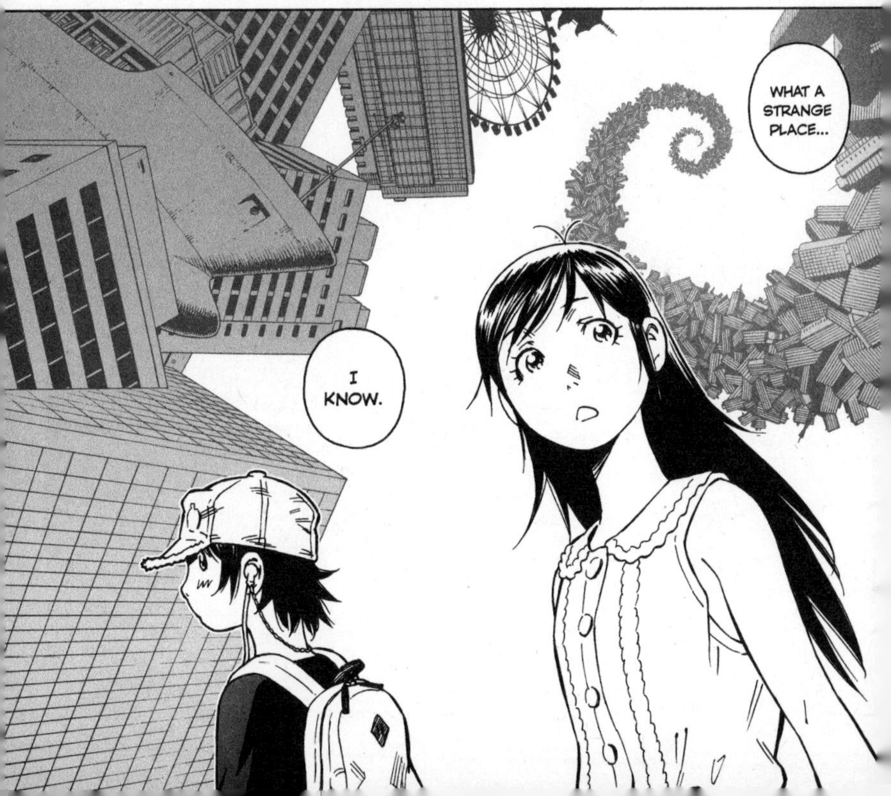
WHAT A STRANGE PLACE...
I KNOW.

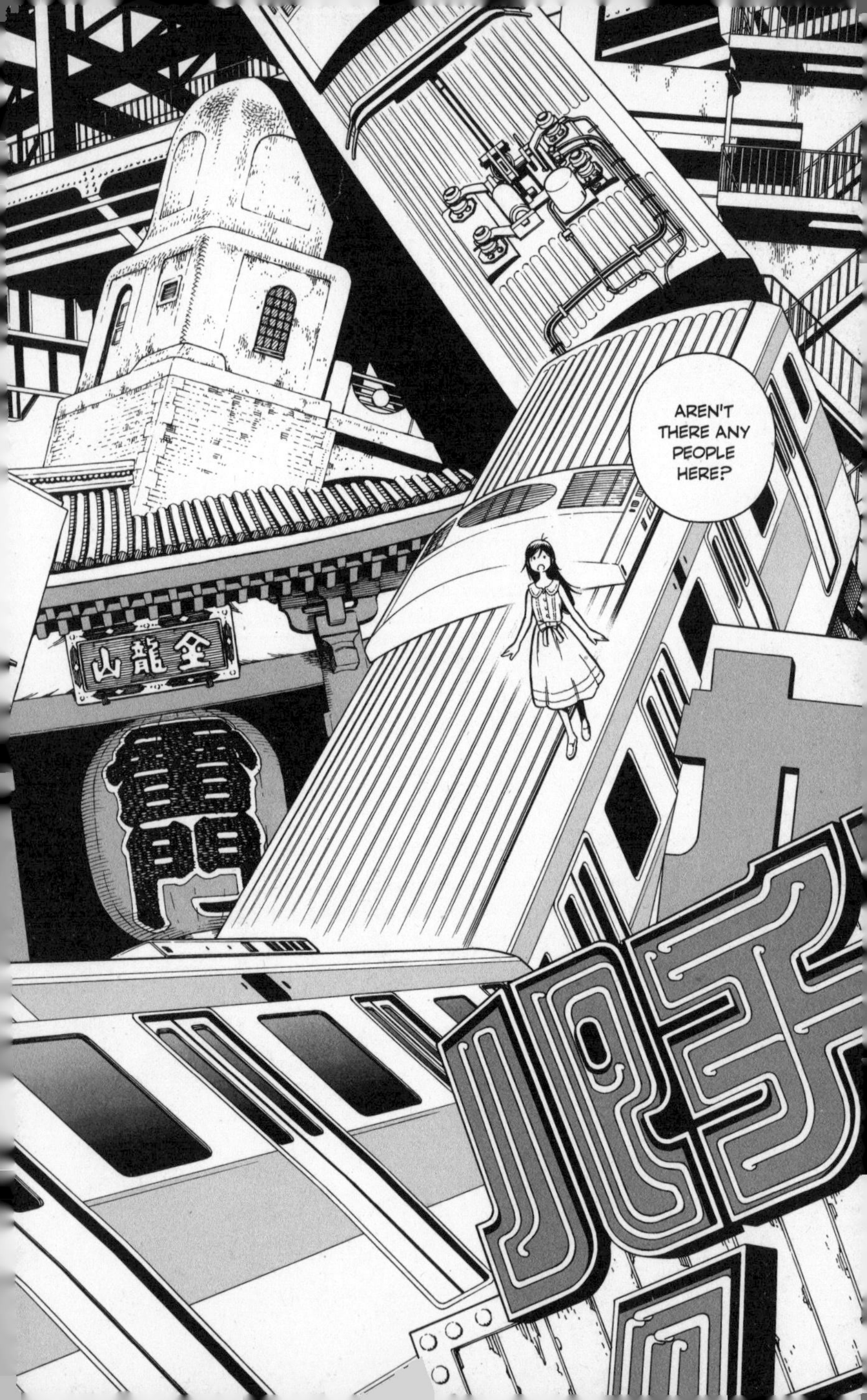
AREN'T THERE ANY PEOPLE HERE?
金龍山
雷門

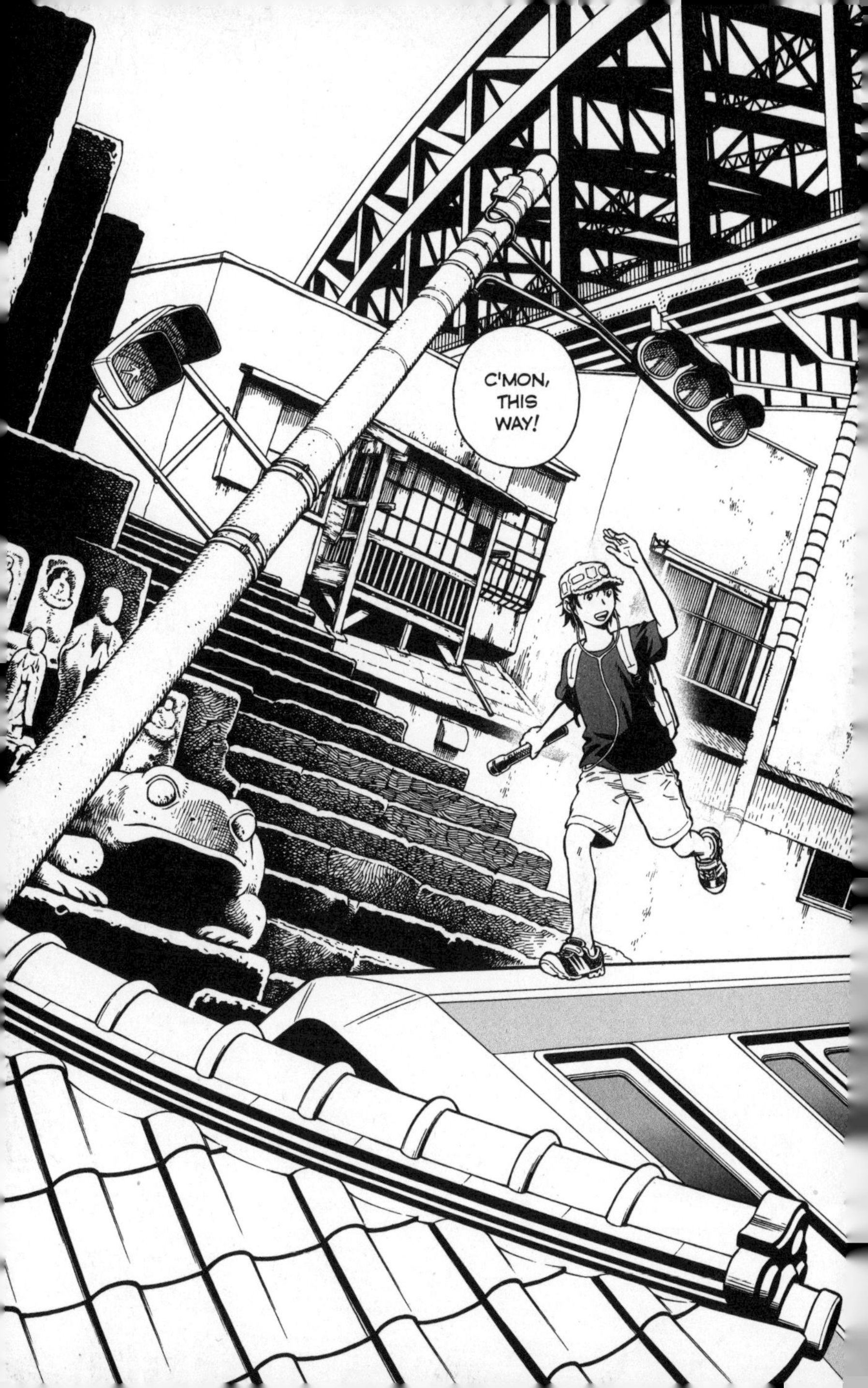
C'MON, THIS WAY!

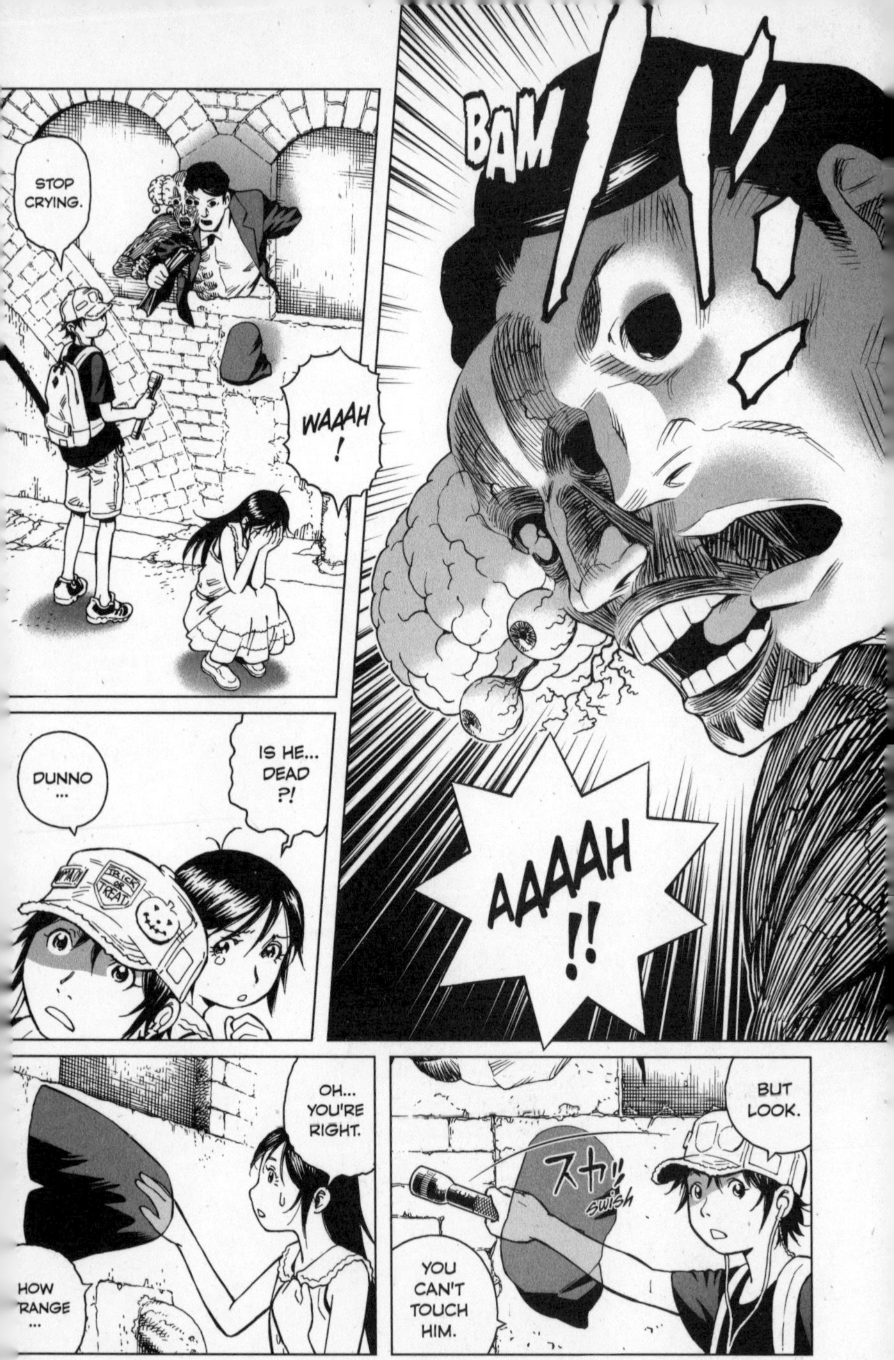
BAM
AAAAH !!
WAAAH !
STOP CRYING.
IS HE... DEAD ?!
DUNNO ...
BUT LOOK.
スカ!! swish
YOU CAN'T TOUCH HIM.
OH... YOU'RE RIGHT.
HOW RANGE ...

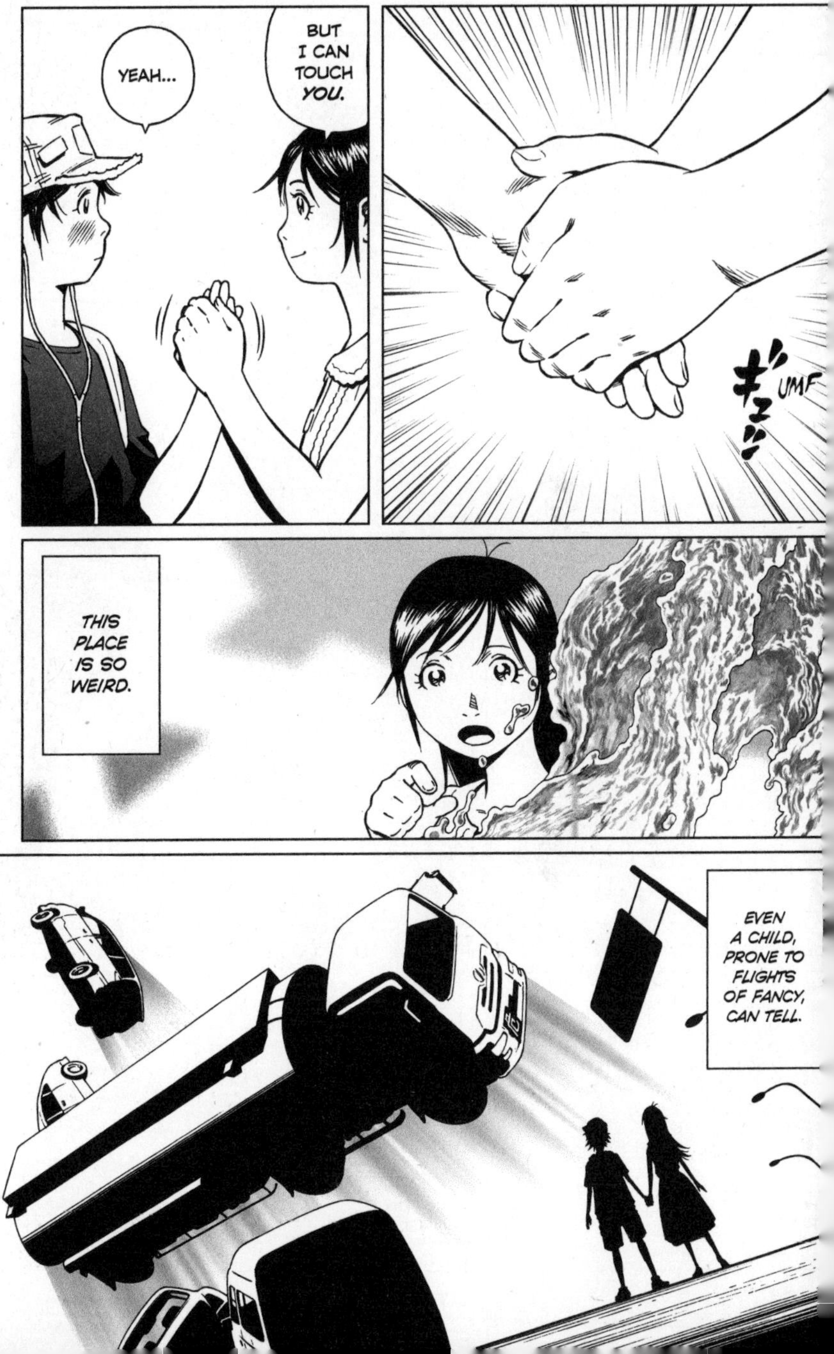
UMF
BUT I CAN TOUCH YOU.
YEAH...
THIS PLACE IS SO WEIRD.
EVEN A CHILD, PRONE TO FLIGHTS OF FANCY, CAN TELL.

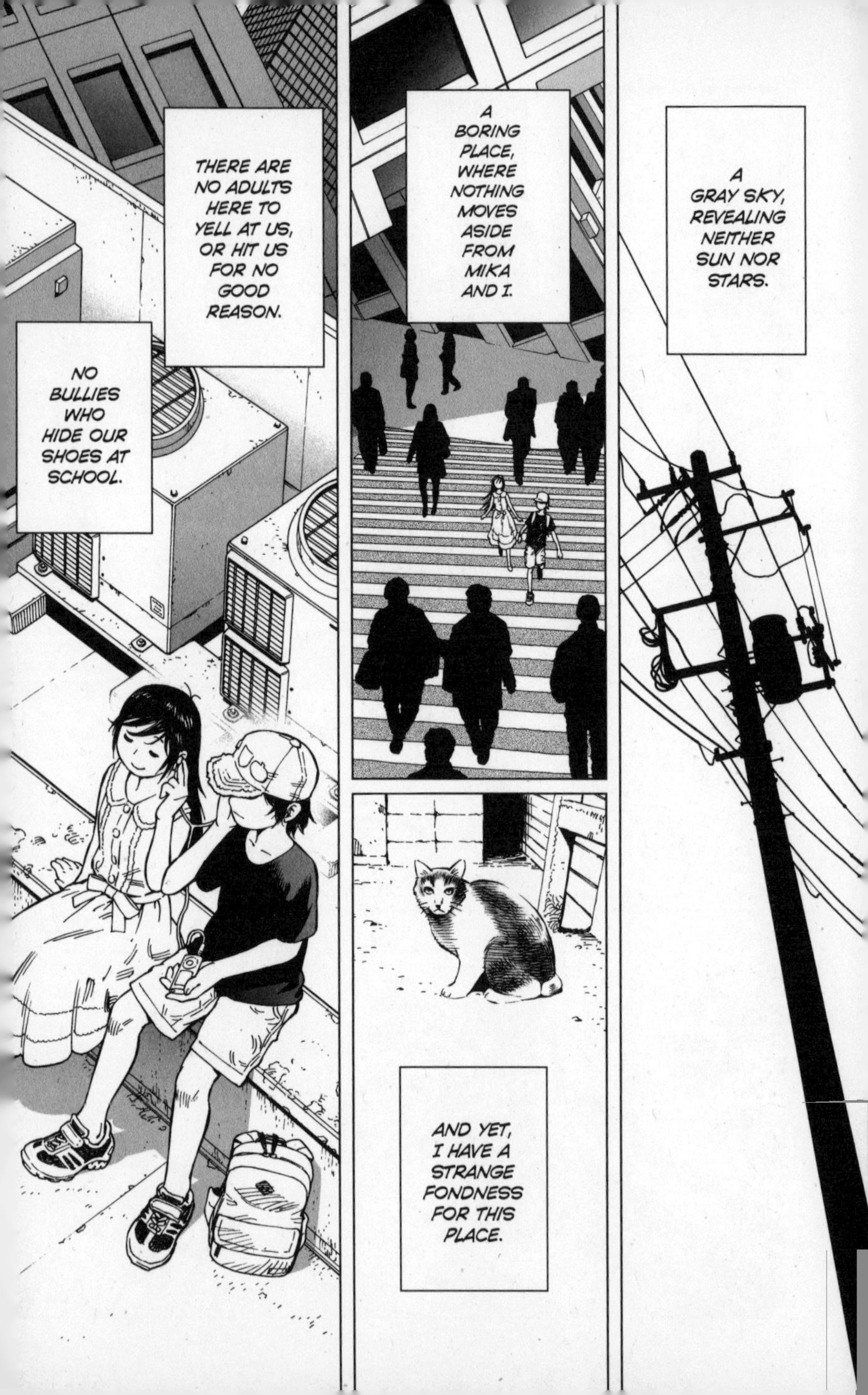
A GRAY SKY, REVEALING NEITHER SUN NOR STARS.
A BORING PLACE, WHERE NOTHING MOVES ASIDE FROM MIKA AND I.
AND YET, I HAVE A STRANGE FONDNESS FOR THIS PLACE.
THERE ARE NO ADULTS HERE TO YELL AT US, OR HIT US FOR NO GOOD REASON.
NO BULLIES WHO HIDE OUR SHOES AT SCHOOL.

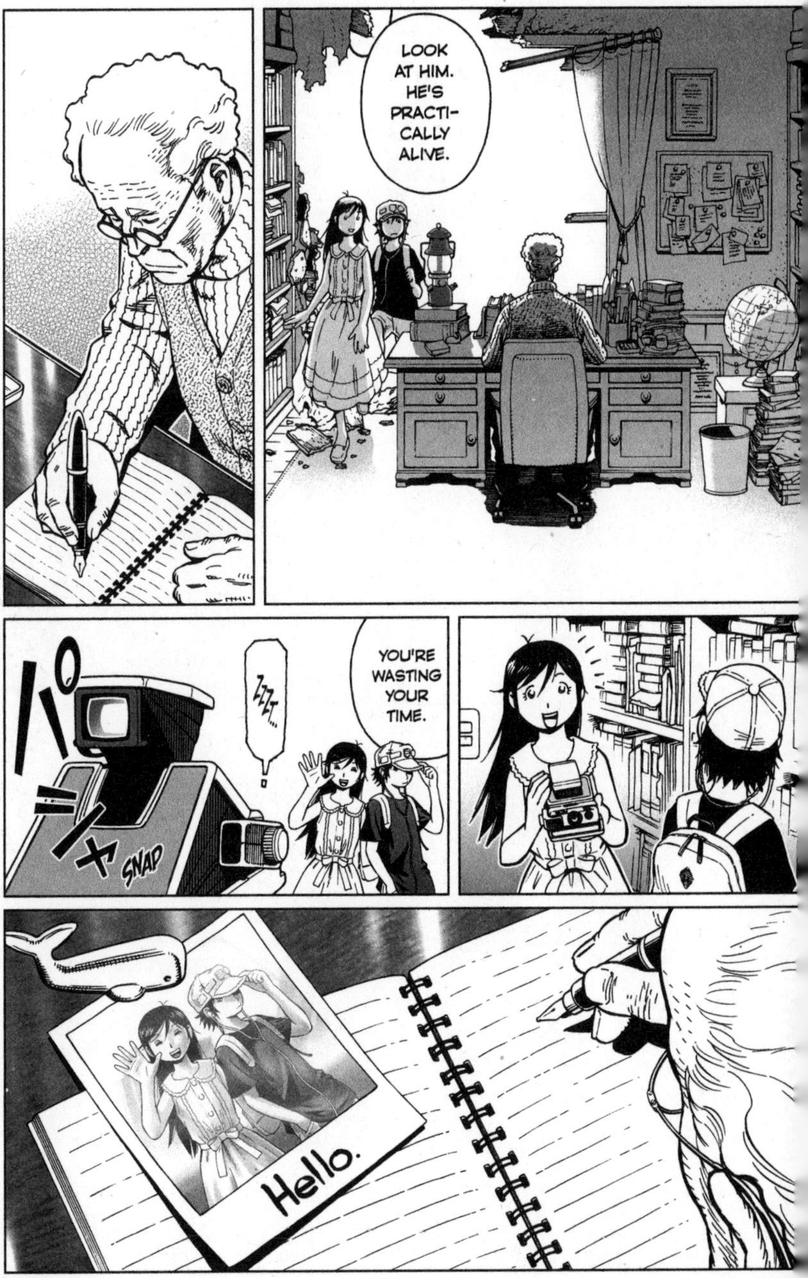
LOOK AT HIM. HE'S PRACTI- CALLY ALIVE.
YOU'RE WASTING YOUR TIME.
ZZZT...!
パシャ
SNAP
Hello.

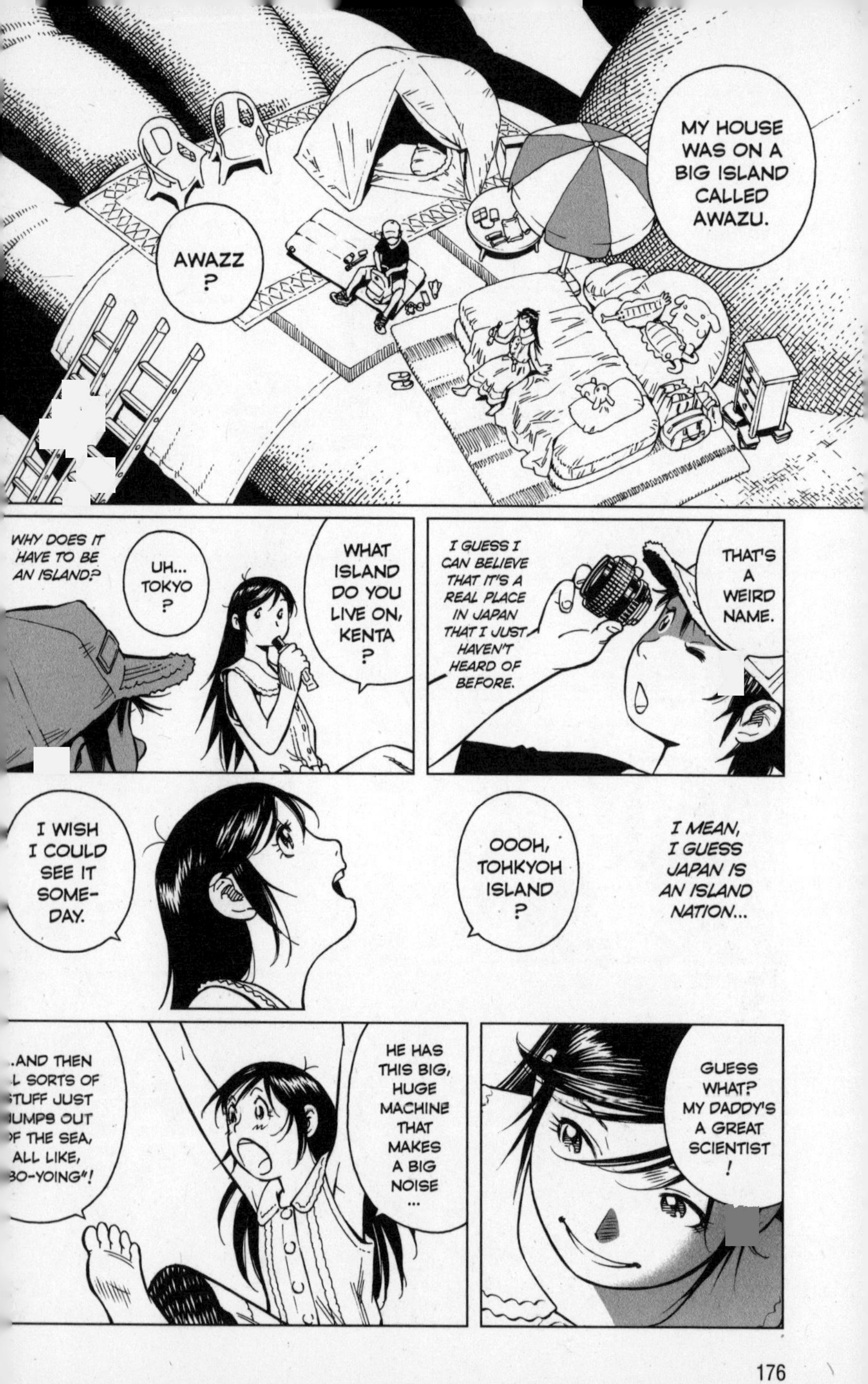
MY HOUSE WAS ON A BIG ISLAND CALLED AWAZU.
AWAZZ ?
THAT'S A WEIRD NAME.
I GUESS I CAN BELIEVE THAT IT'S A REAL PLACE IN JAPAN THAT I JUST HAVEN'T HEARD OF BEFORE.
WHAT ISLAND DO YOU LIVE ON, KENTA ?
UH... TOKYO ?
WHY DOES IT HAVE TO BE AN ISLAND?
I MEAN, I GUESS JAPAN IS AN ISLAND NATION...
OOOH, TOHKYOH ISLAND ?
I WISH I COULD SEE IT SOME-DAY.
GUESS WHAT? MY DADDY'S A GREAT SCIENTIST !
HE HAS THIS BIG, HUGE MACHINE THAT MAKES A BIG NOISE ...
.AND THEN L SORTS OF TUFF JUST UMPS OUT F THE SEA, ALL LIKE, BO-YOING"!

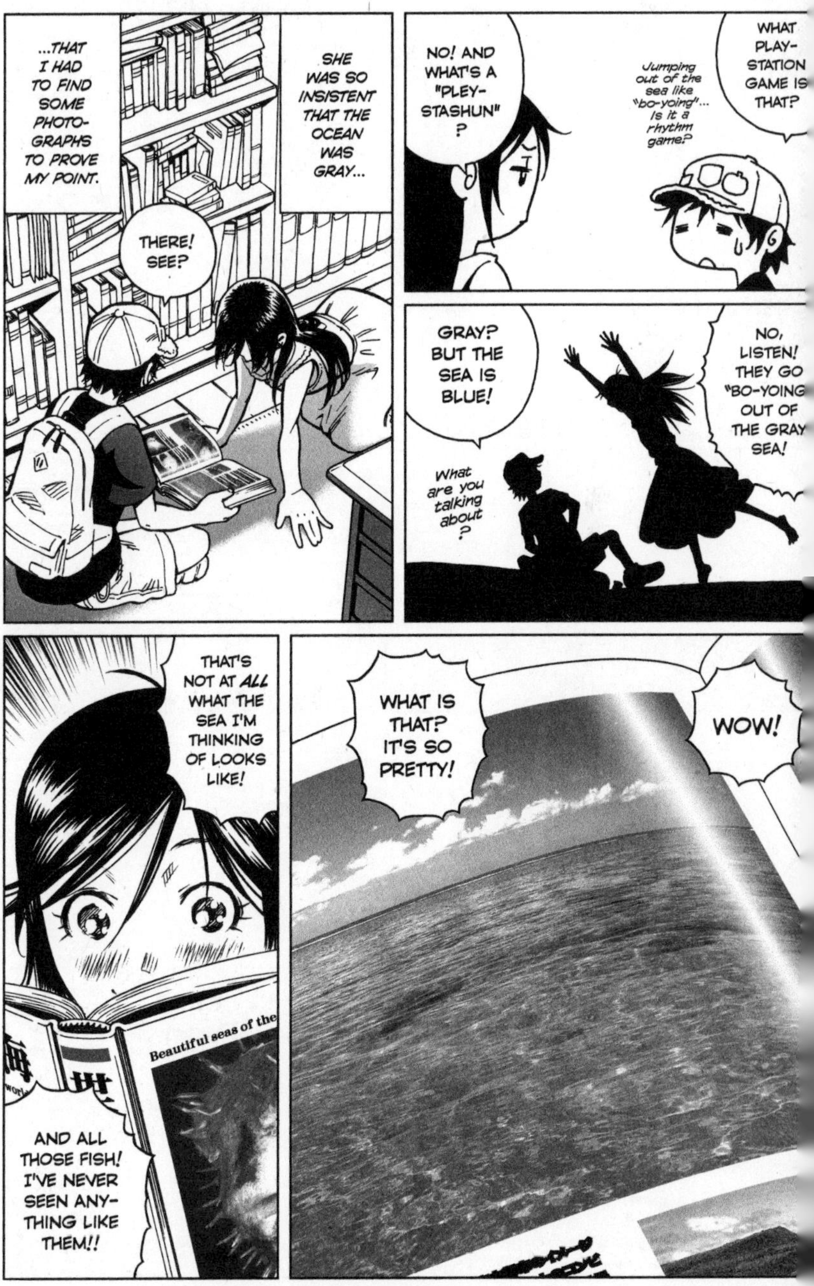
WHAT PLAY-STATION GAME IS THAT?
Jumping out of the sea like "bo-yoing"... Is it a rhythm game?
NO! AND WHAT'S A "PLEY-STASHUN"?
NO, LISTEN! THEY GO "BO-YOING OUT OF THE GRAY SEA!
GRAY? BUT THE SEA IS BLUE!
What are you talking about?
SHE WAS SO INSISTENT THAT THE OCEAN WAS GRAY...
...THAT I HAD TO FIND SOME PHOTOGRAPHS TO PROVE MY POINT.
THERE! SEE?
WOW!
WHAT IS THAT? IT'S SO PRETTY!
THAT'S NOT AT *ALL* WHAT THE SEA I'M THINKING OF LOOKS LIKE!
Beautiful seas of the
AND ALL THOSE FISH! I'VE NEVER SEEN ANYTHING LIKE THEM!!

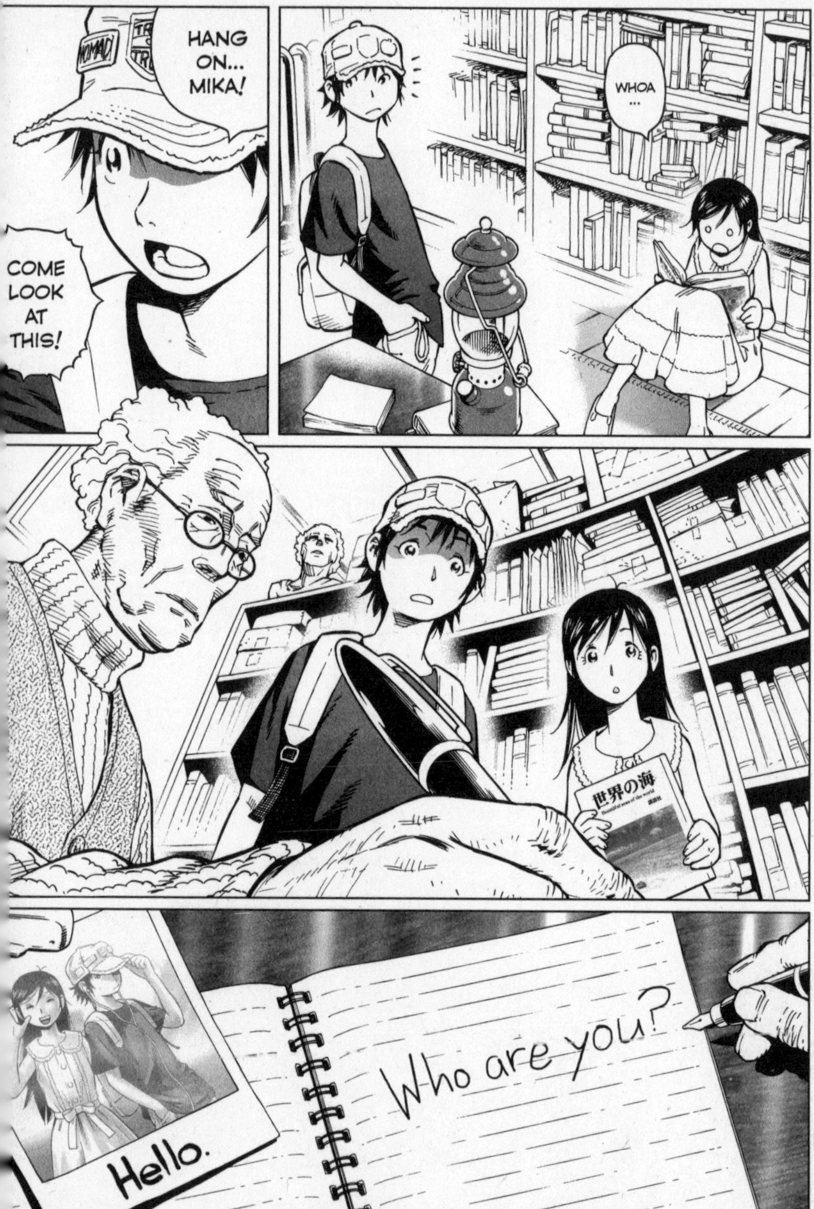
WHOA ...
HANG ON... MIKA!
COME LOOK AT THIS!
世界の海
Who are you?
Hello.

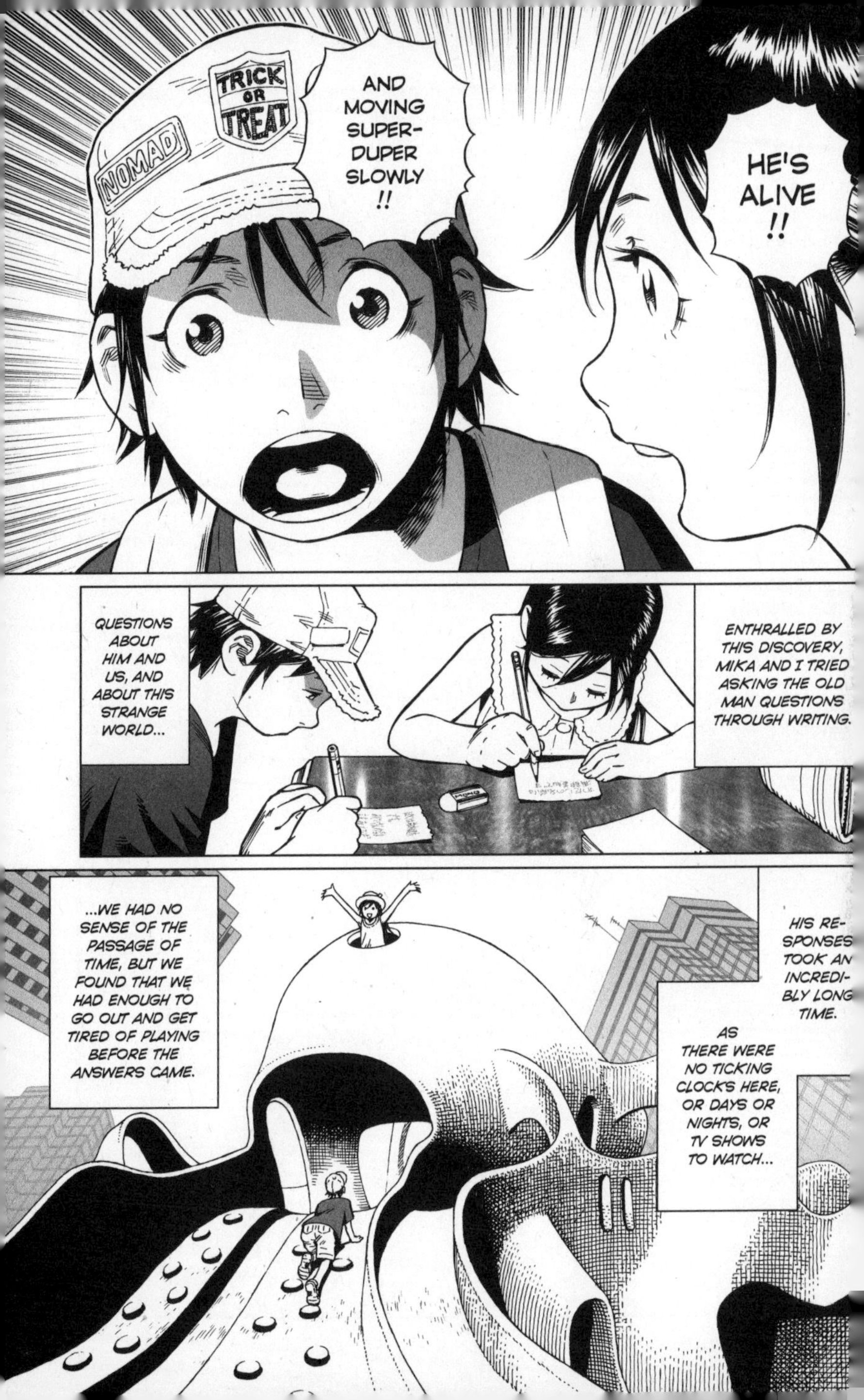
HE'S ALIVE !!
AND MOVING SUPER-DUPER SLOWLY !!
ENTHRALLED BY THIS DISCOVERY, MIKA AND I TRIED ASKING THE OLD MAN QUESTIONS THROUGH WRITING.
QUESTIONS ABOUT HIM AND US, AND ABOUT THIS STRANGE WORLD...
HIS RE-SPONSES TOOK AN INCREDI-BLY LONG TIME.
AS THERE WERE NO TICKING CLOCKS HERE, OR DAYS OR NIGHTS, OR TV SHOWS TO WATCH...
...WE HAD NO SENSE OF THE PASSAGE OF TIME, BUT WE FOUND THAT WE HAD ENOUGH TO GO OUT AND GET TIRED OF PLAYING BEFORE THE ANSWERS CAME.

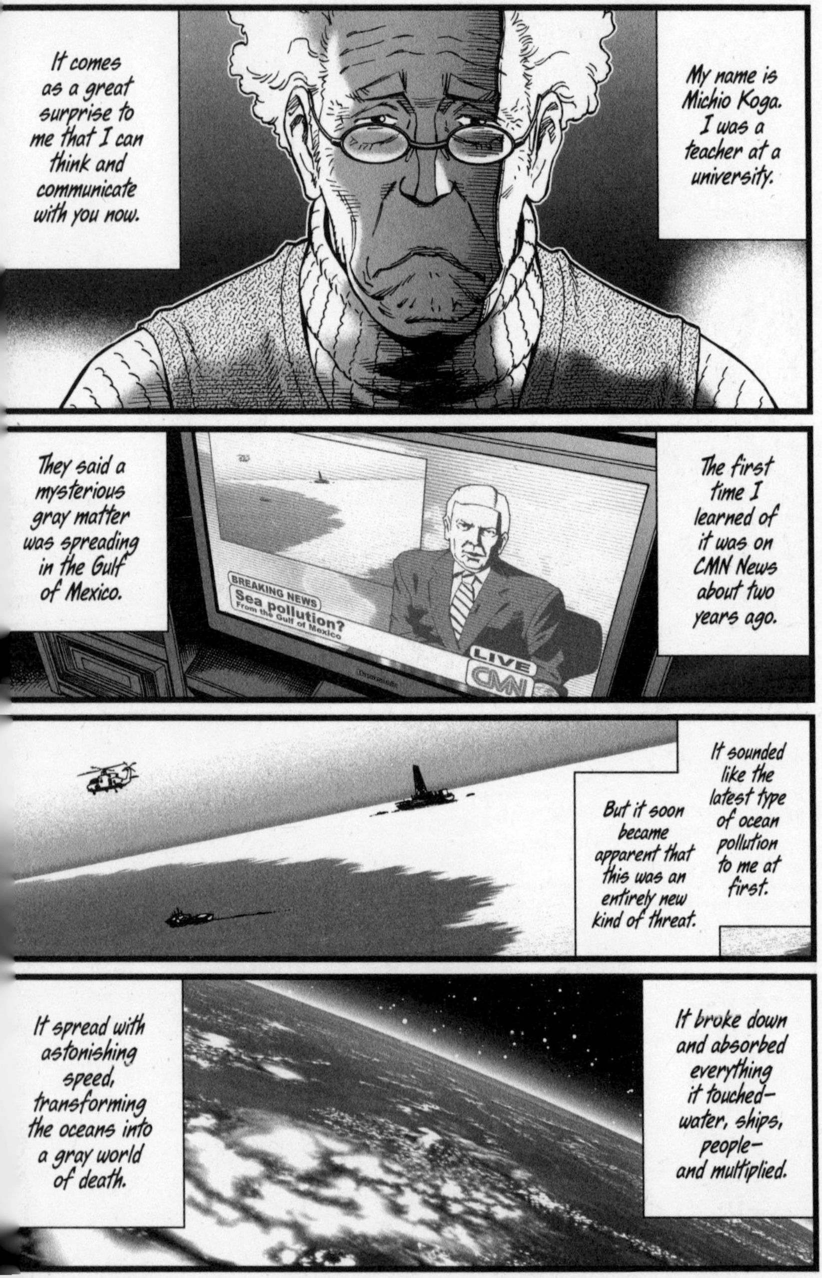
My name is Michio Koga. I was a teacher at a university.
It comes as a great surprise to me that I can think and communicate with you now.
The first time I learned of it was on CMN News about two years ago.
BREAKING NEWS
Sea pollution?
From the Gulf of Mexico
LIVE
CMN
They said a mysterious gray matter was spreading in the Gulf of Mexico.
It sounded like the latest type of ocean pollution to me at first.
But it soon became apparent that this was an entirely new kind of threat.
It broke down and absorbed everything it touched—water, ships, people—and multiplied.
It spread with astonishing speed, transforming the oceans into a gray world of death.

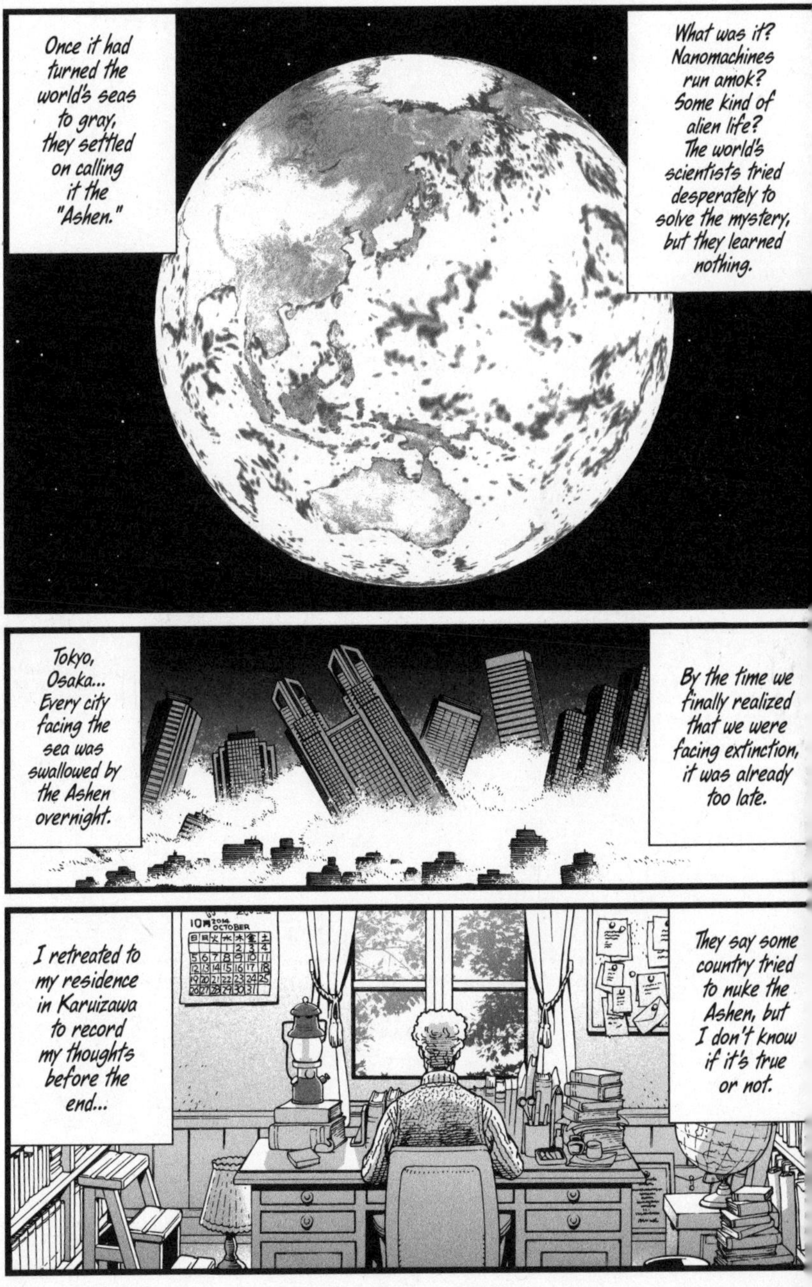
What was it? Nanomachines run amok? Some kind of alien life? The world's scientists tried desperately to solve the mystery, but they learned nothing.
Once it had turned the world's seas to gray, they settled on calling it the "Ashen."
By the time we finally realized that we were facing extinction, it was already too late.
Tokyo, Osaka... Every city facing the sea was swallowed by the Ashen overnight.
They say some country tried to nuke the Ashen, but I don't know if it's true or not.
I retreated to my residence in Karuizawa to record my thoughts before the end...
10月 2014 OCTOBER

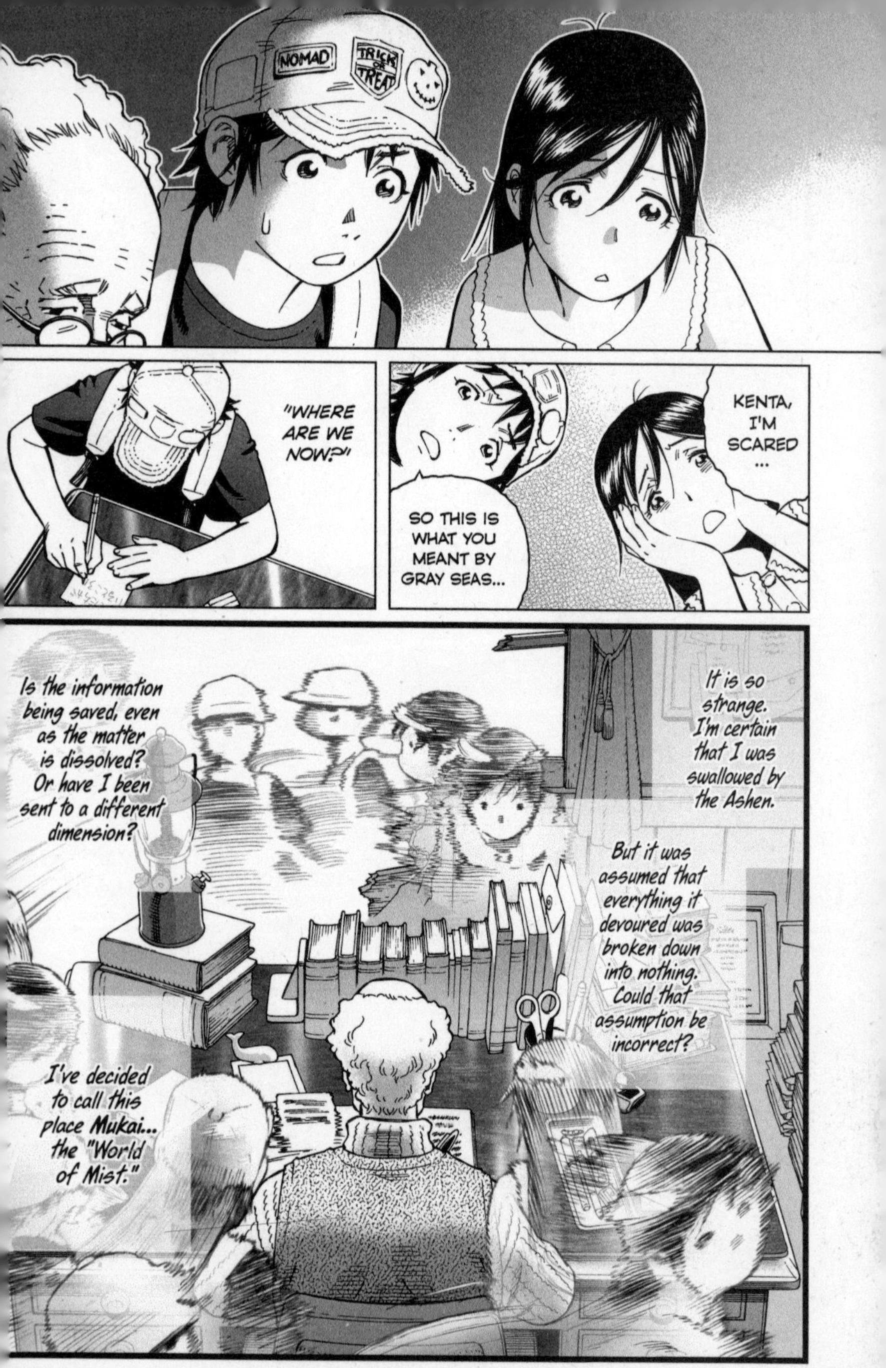
NOMAD
TRICK OR TREAT
KENTA, I'M SCARED ...
SO THIS IS WHAT YOU MEANT BY GRAY SEAS...
"WHERE ARE WE NOW?"
It is so strange. I'm certain that I was swallowed by the Ashen.
But it was assumed that everything it devoured was broken down into nothing. Could that assumption be incorrect?
Is the information being saved, even as the matter is dissolved? Or have I been sent to a different dimension?
I've decided to call this place Mukai... the "World of Mist."

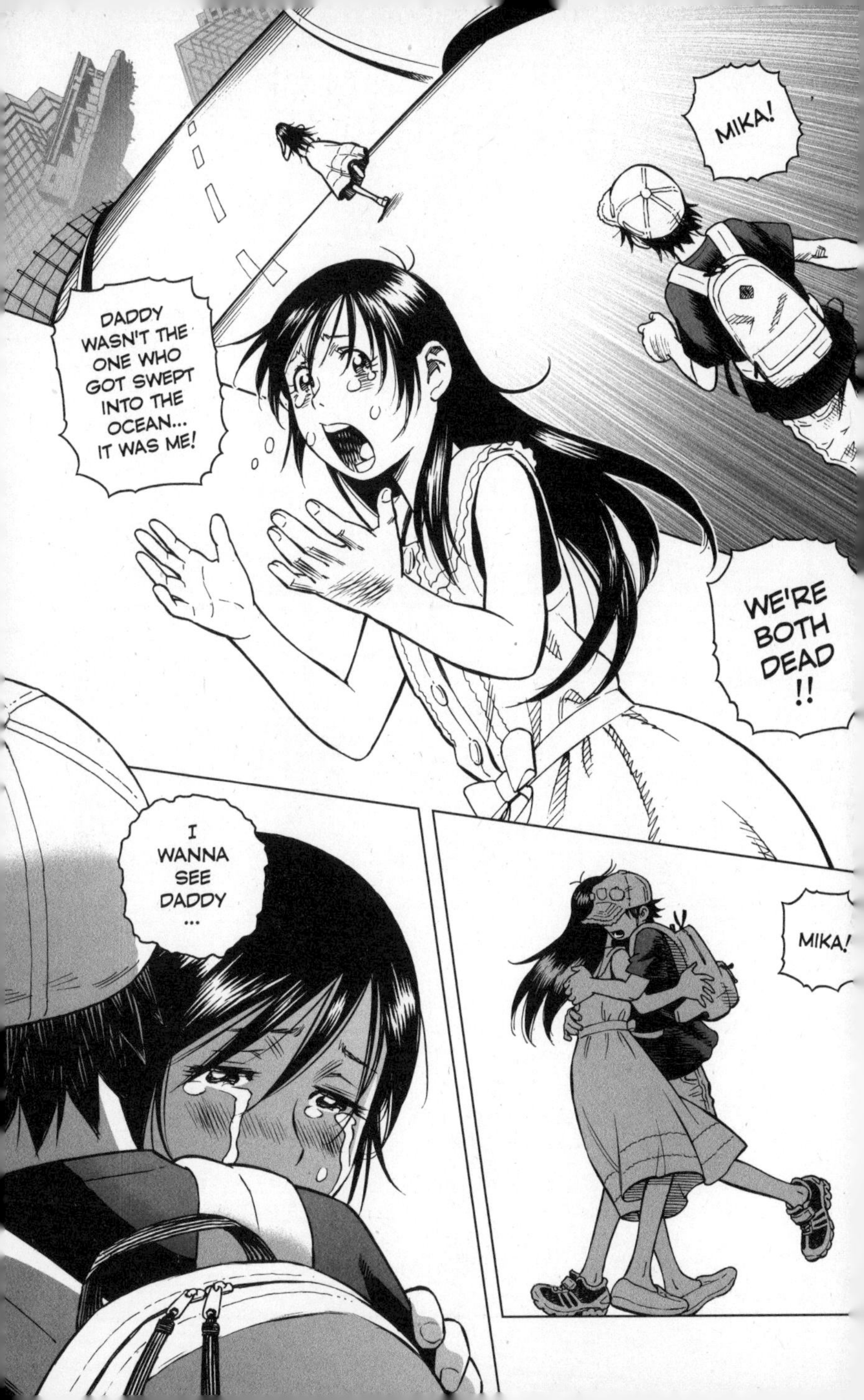
MIKA!
DADDY WASN'T THE ONE WHO GOT SWEPT INTO THE OCEAN... IT WAS ME!
WE'RE BOTH DEAD !!
MIKA!
I WANNA SEE DADDY ...

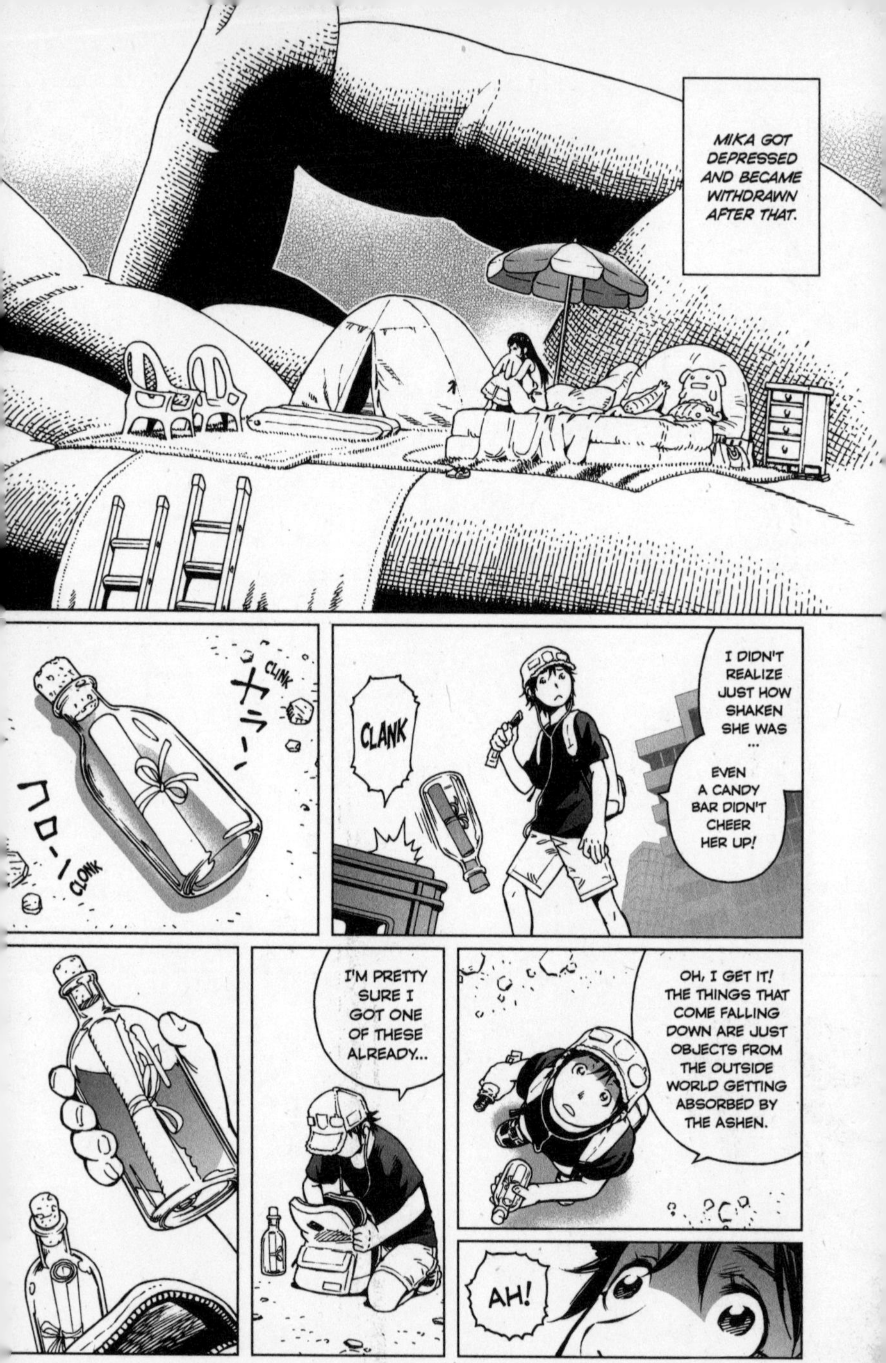
MIKA GOT DEPRESSED AND BECAME WITHDRAWN AFTER THAT.
I DIDN'T REALIZE JUST HOW SHAKEN SHE WAS ...
EVEN A CANDY BAR DIDN'T CHEER HER UP!
CLANK
CLINK
CLONK
OH, I GET IT! THE THINGS THAT COME FALLING DOWN ARE JUST OBJECTS FROM THE OUTSIDE WORLD GETTING ABSORBED BY THE ASHEN.
AH!
I'M PRETTY SURE I GOT ONE OF THESE ALREADY...

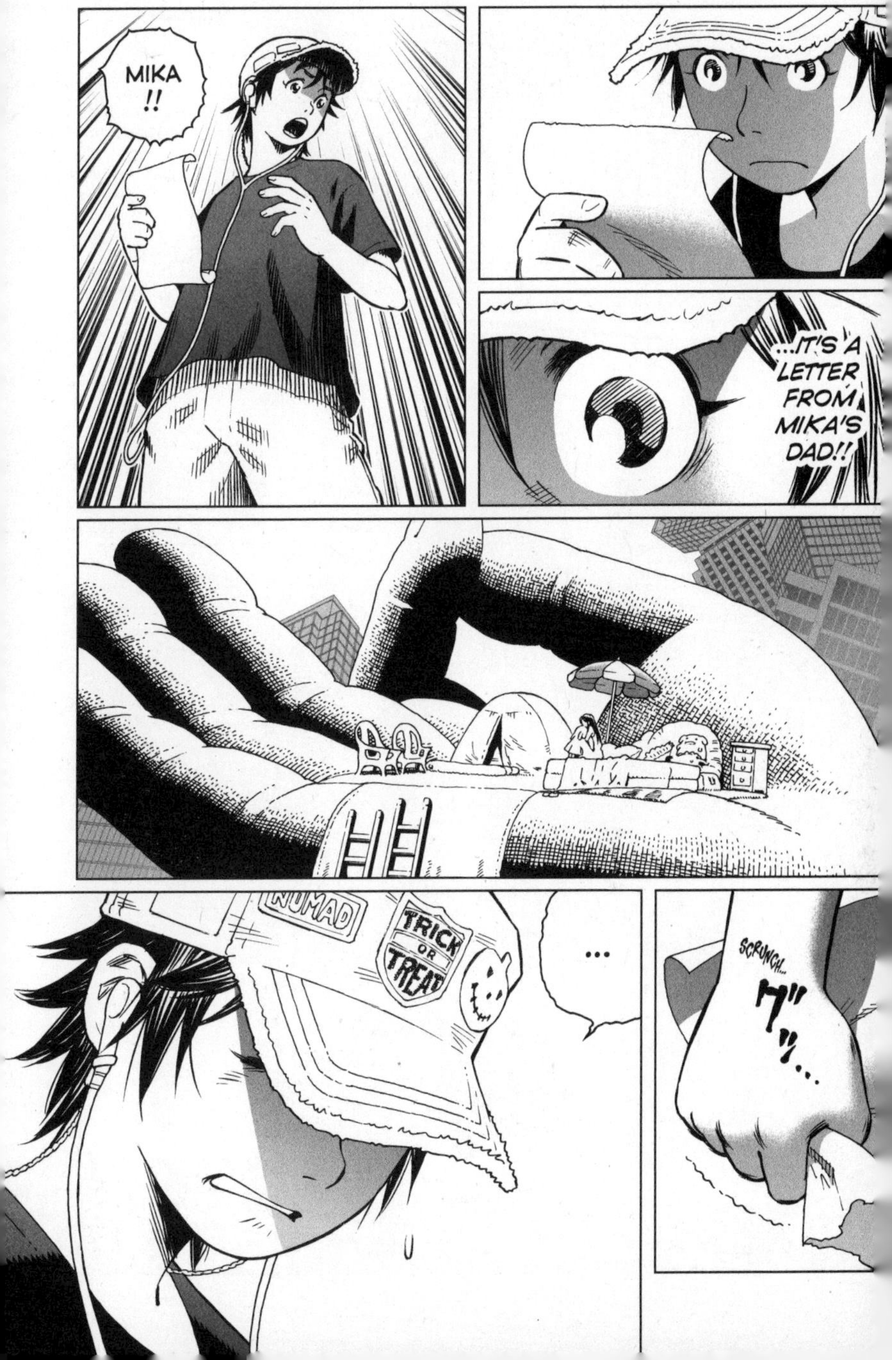
...IT'S A LETTER FROM MIKA'S DAD!!
MIKA !!
SCRUNCH...
グッ...
...
NOMAD
TRICK OR TREAT

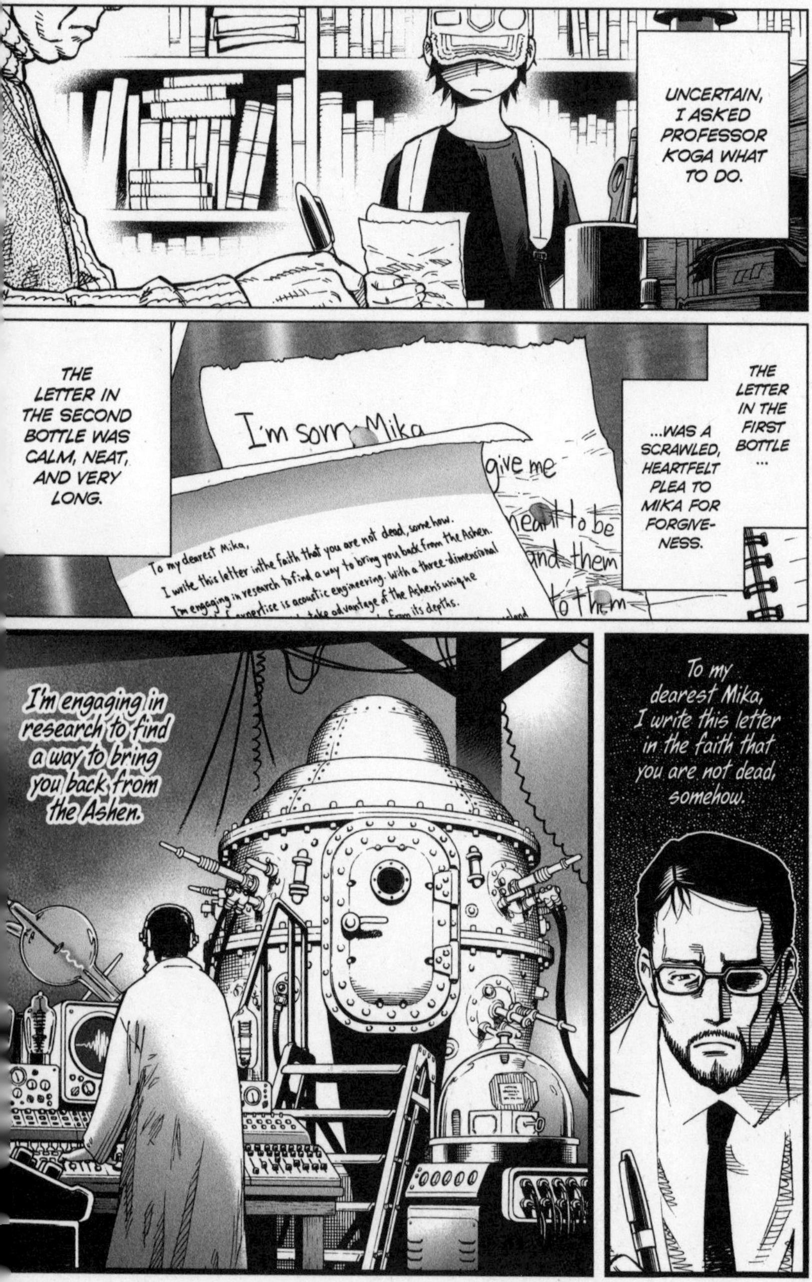
UNCERTAIN, I ASKED PROFESSOR KOGA WHAT TO DO.
THE LETTER IN THE FIRST BOTTLE...
...WAS A SCRAWLED, HEARTFELT PLEA TO MIKA FOR FORGIVE-NESS.
I'm sorr Mika
give me
and them
to them
THE LETTER IN THE SECOND BOTTLE WAS CALM, NEAT, AND VERY LONG.
To my dearest Mika,
I write this letter in the faith that you are not dead, somehow.
I'm engaging in research to find a way to bring you back from the Ashen.
expertise is acoustic engineering. with a three-dimensional
take advantage of the Ashen's unique
from its depths.
To my dearest Mika, I write this letter in the faith that you are not dead, somehow.
I'm engaging in research to find a way to bring you back from the Ashen.

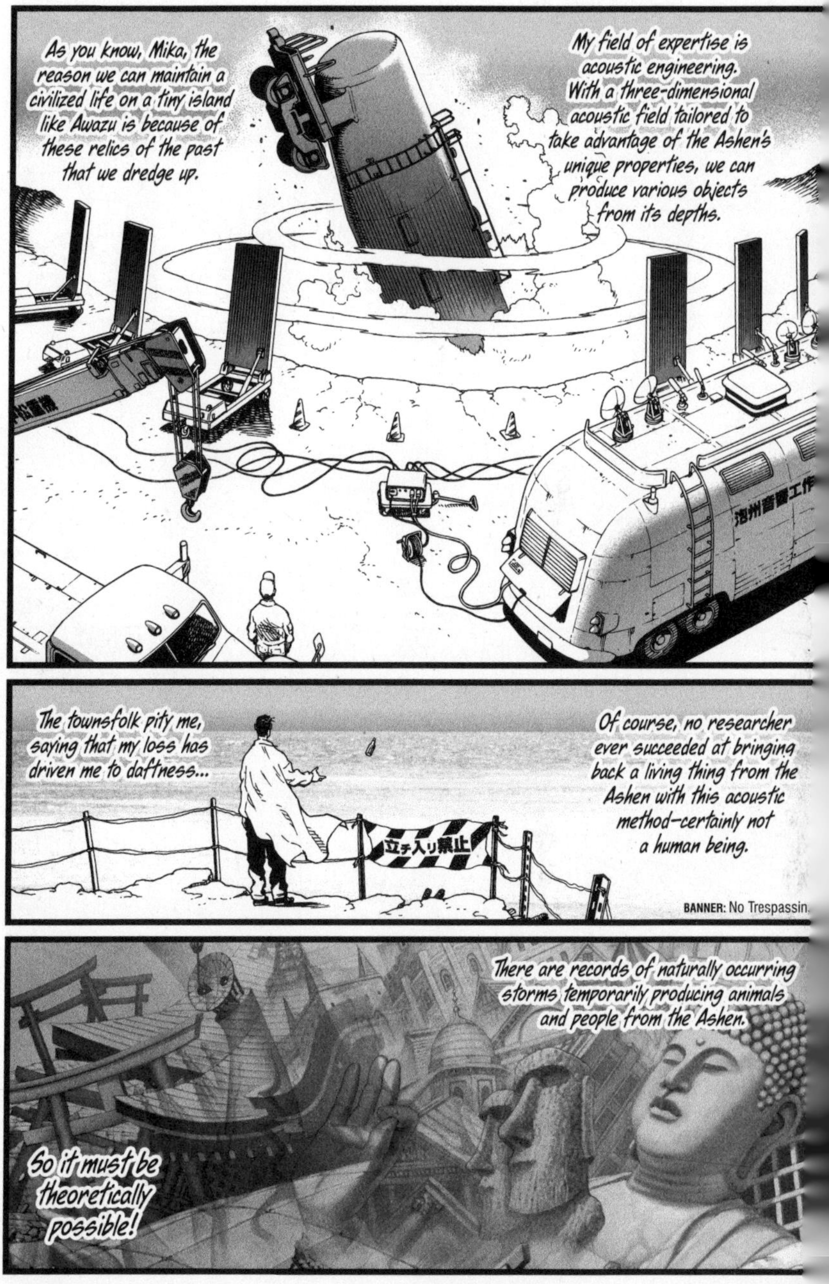
My field of expertise is acoustic engineering. With a three-dimensional acoustic field tailored to take advantage of the Ashen's unique properties, we can produce various objects from its depths.
As you know, Mika, the reason we can maintain a civilized life on a tiny island like Awazu is because of these relics of the past that we dredge up.
Of course, no researcher ever succeeded at bringing back a living thing from the Ashen with this acoustic method—certainly not a human being.
The townsfolk pity me, saying that my loss has driven me to daftness...
立チ入リ禁止
BANNER: No Trespassin.
There are records of naturally occurring storms temporarily producing animals and people from the Ashen.
So it must be theoretically possible!

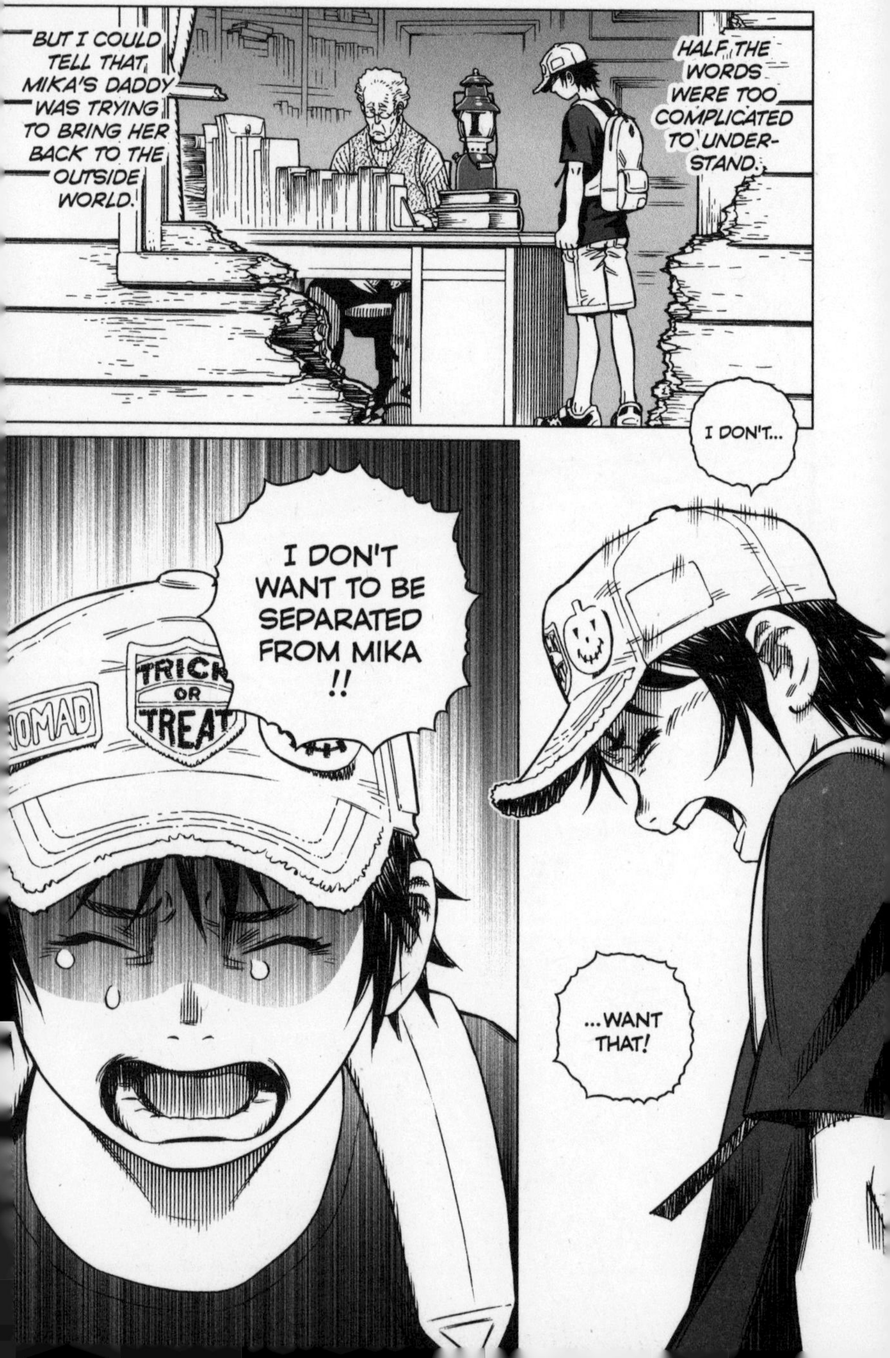
HALF THE WORDS WERE TOO COMPLICATED TO UNDER-STAND.
BUT I COULD TELL THAT MIKA'S DADDY WAS TRYING TO BRING HER BACK TO THE OUTSIDE WORLD.
I DON'T...
...WANT THAT!
I DON'T WANT TO BE SEPARATED FROM MIKA !!

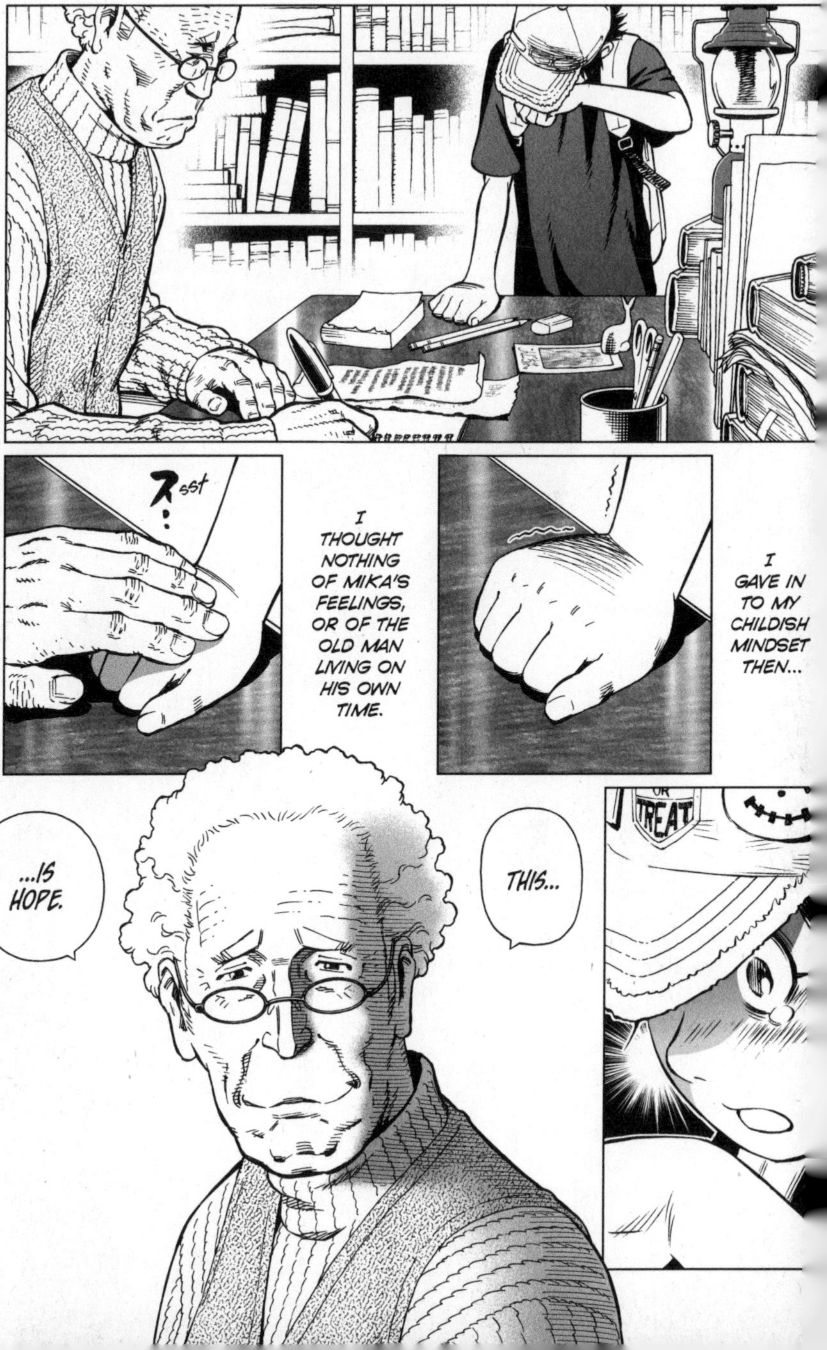

I GAVE IN TO MY CHILDISH MINDSET THEN...
I THOUGHT NOTHING OF MIKA'S FEELINGS, OR OF THE OLD MAN LIVING ON HIS OWN TIME.
sst
OR TREAT
THIS...
...IS HOPE.

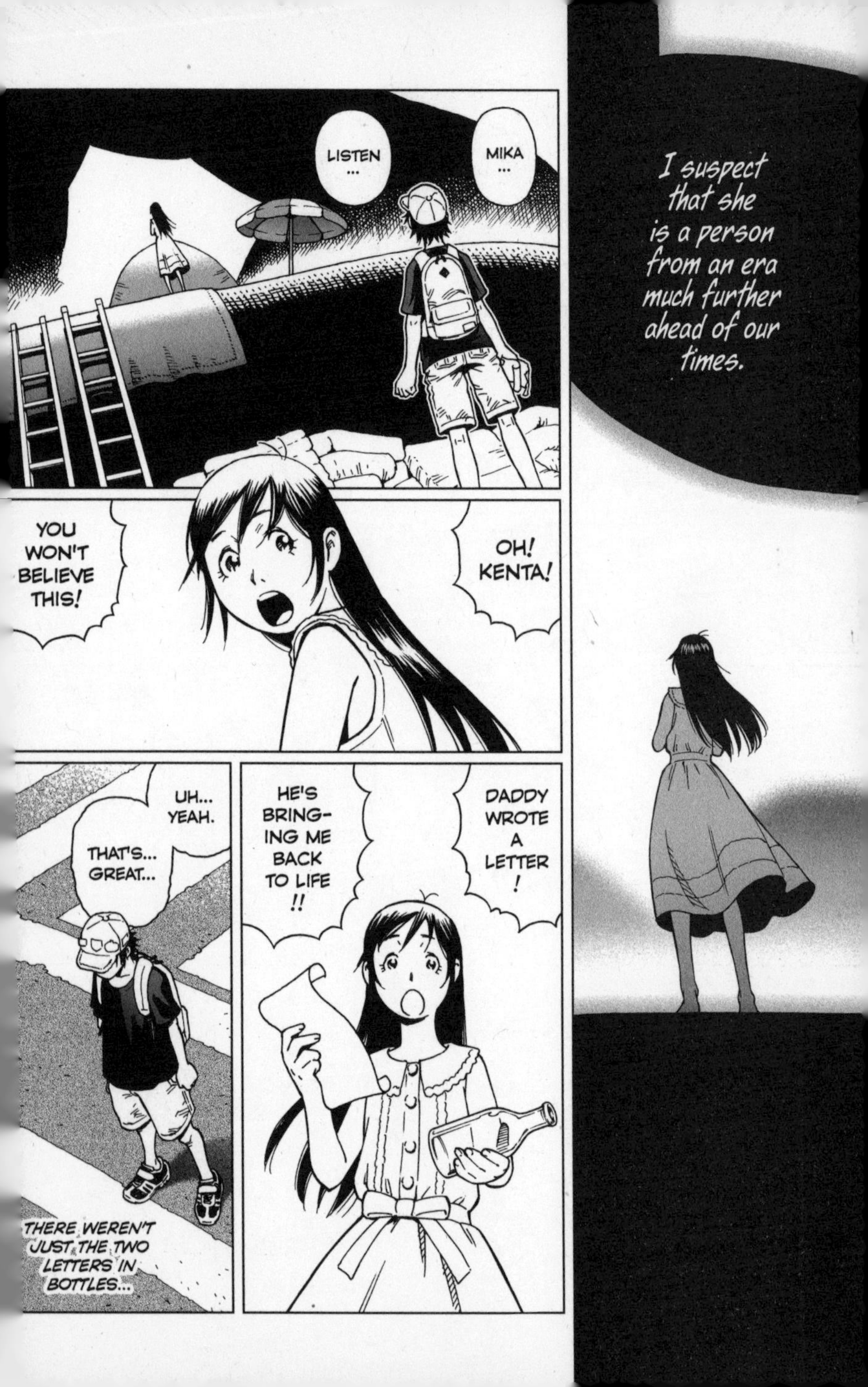
I suspect that she is a person from an era much further ahead of our times.
MIKA...
LISTEN...
OH! KENTA!
YOU WON'T BELIEVE THIS!
DADDY WROTE A LETTER!
HE'S BRING-ING ME BACK TO LIFE!!
UH... YEAH.
THAT'S... GREAT...
THERE WEREN'T JUST THE TWO LETTERS IN BOTTLES...

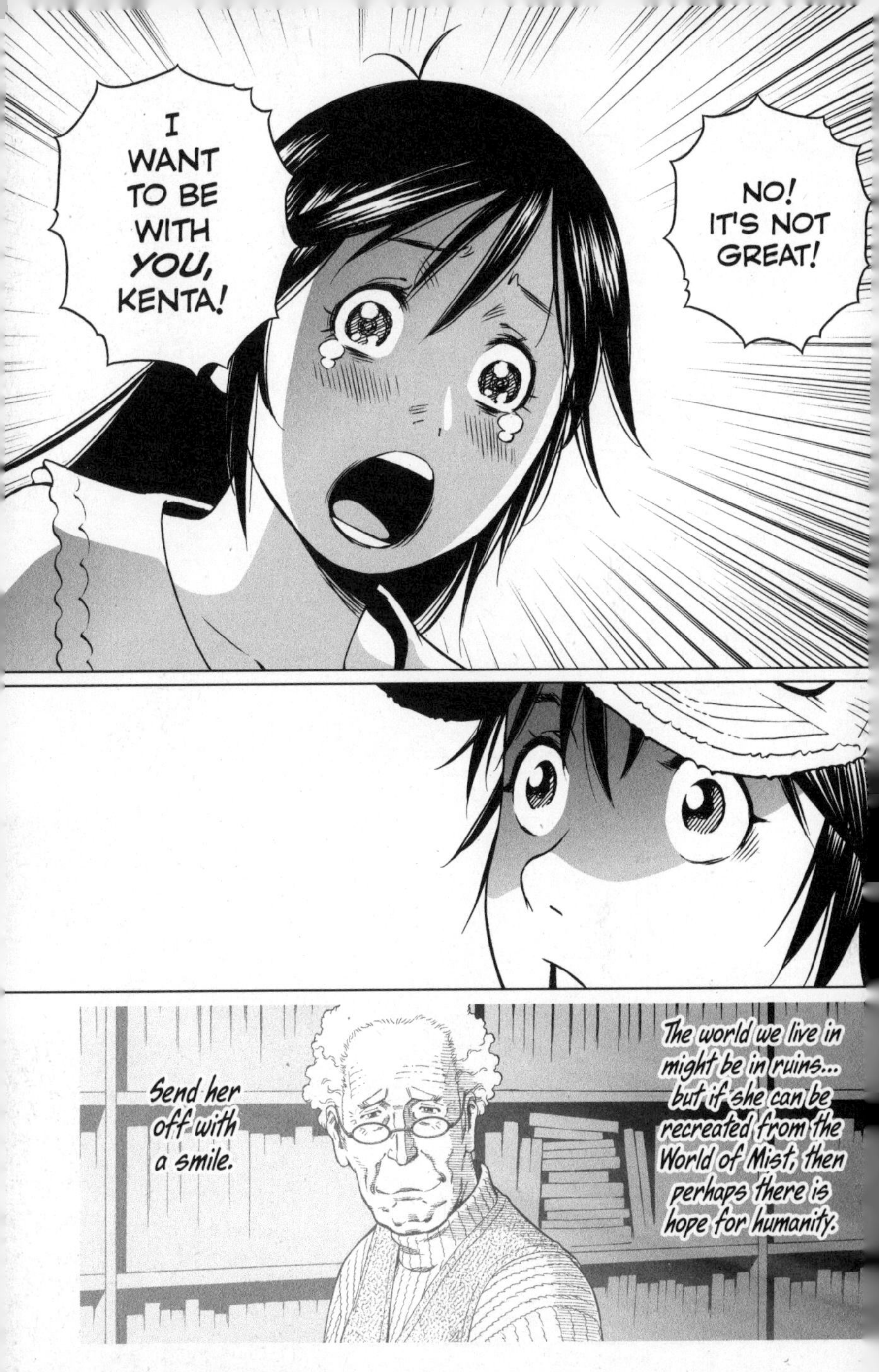
NO! IT'S NOT GREAT!
I WANT TO BE WITH YOU, KENTA!
The world we live in might be in ruins... but if she can be recreated from the World of Mist, then perhaps there is hope for humanity.
Send her off with a smile.

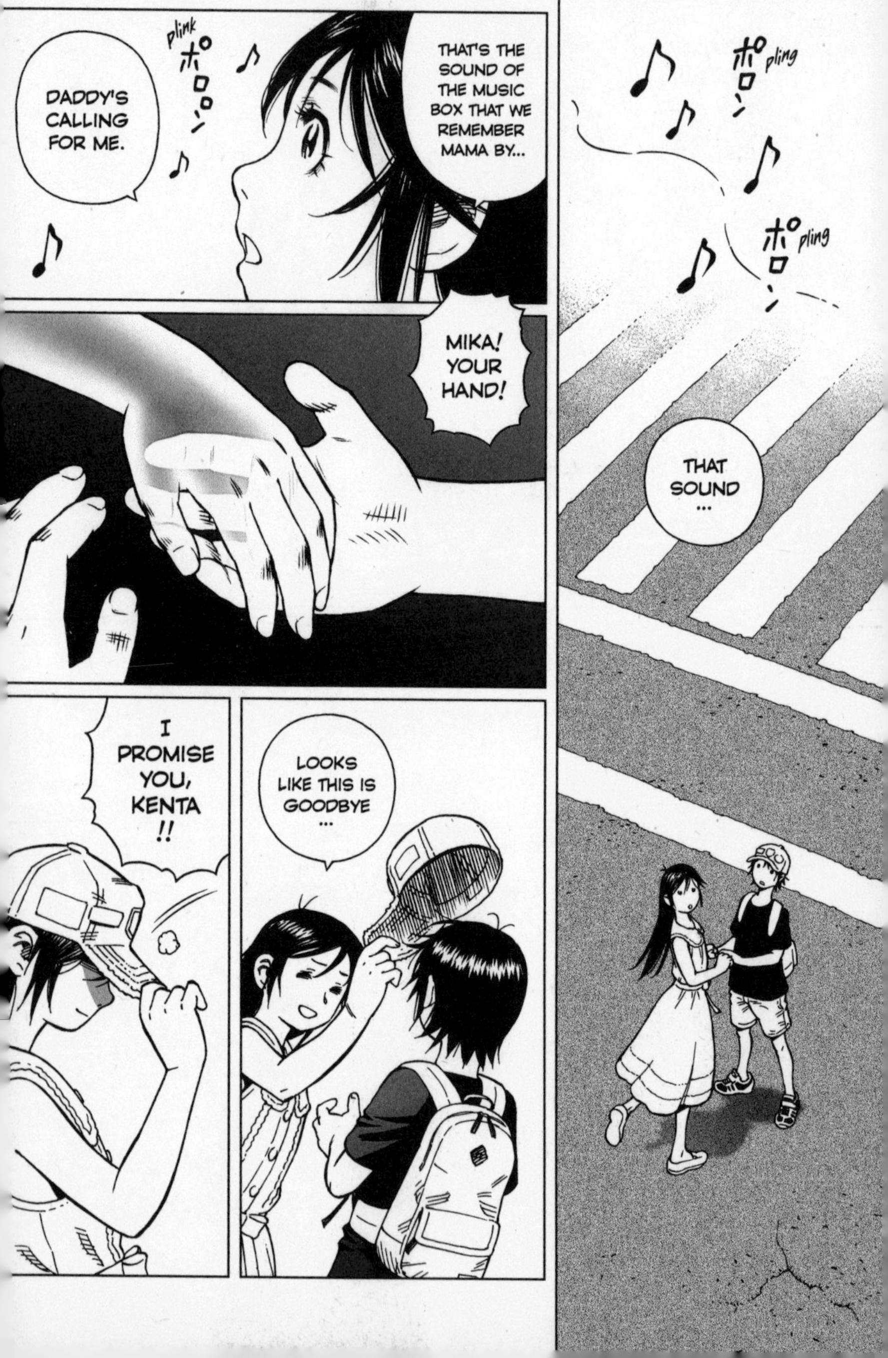

ポロン pling
ポロン pling
THAT SOUND ...
THAT'S THE SOUND OF THE MUSIC BOX THAT WE REMEMBER MAMA BY...
ポロロン plink
DADDY'S CALLING FOR ME.
MIKA! YOUR HAND!
LOOKS LIKE THIS IS GOODBYE ...
I PROMISE YOU, KENTA !!

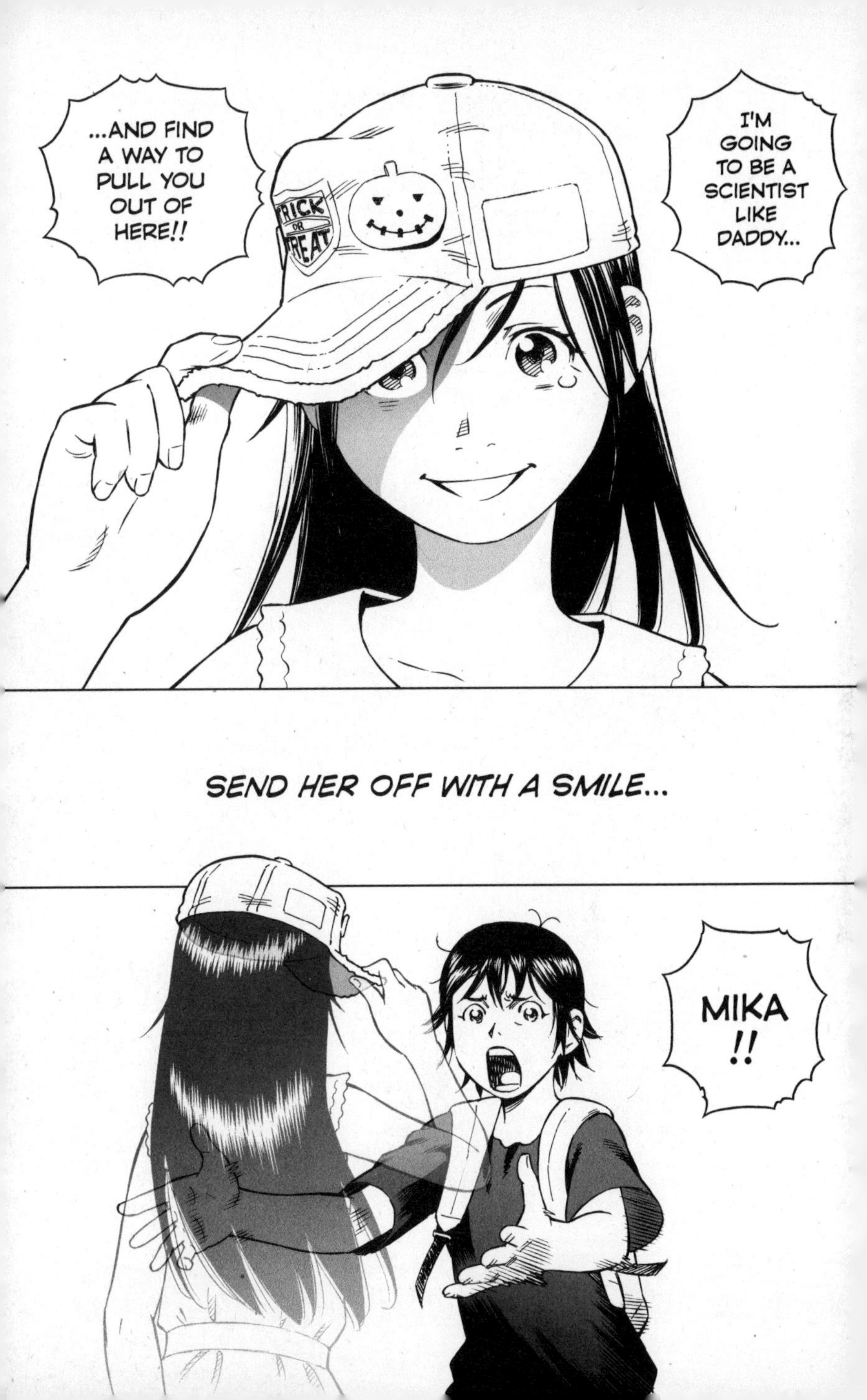
I'M GOING TO BE A SCIENTIST LIKE DADDY...
...AND FIND A WAY TO PULL YOU OUT OF HERE!!
TRICK OR TREAT
SEND HER OFF WITH A SMILE...
MIKA !!

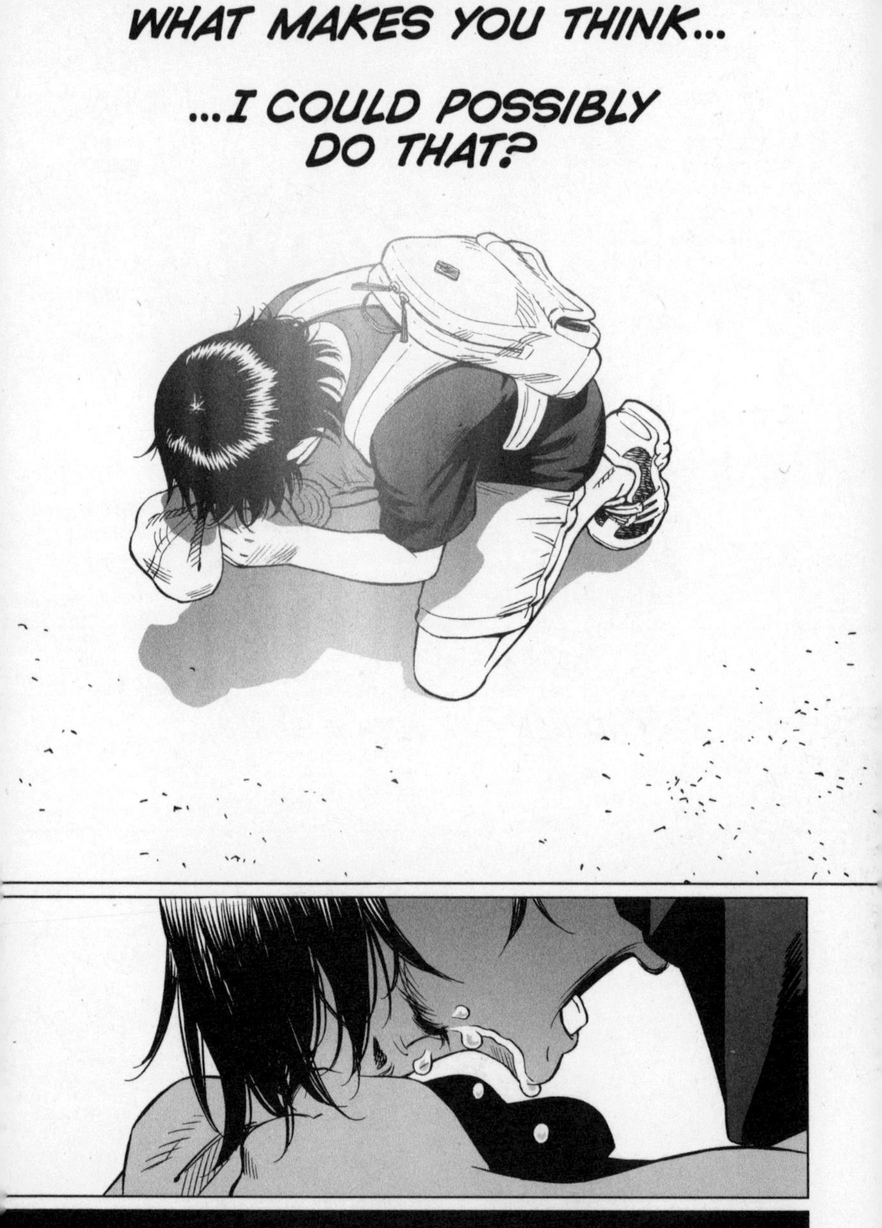
WHAT MAKES YOU THINK...
...I COULD POSSIBLY DO THAT?

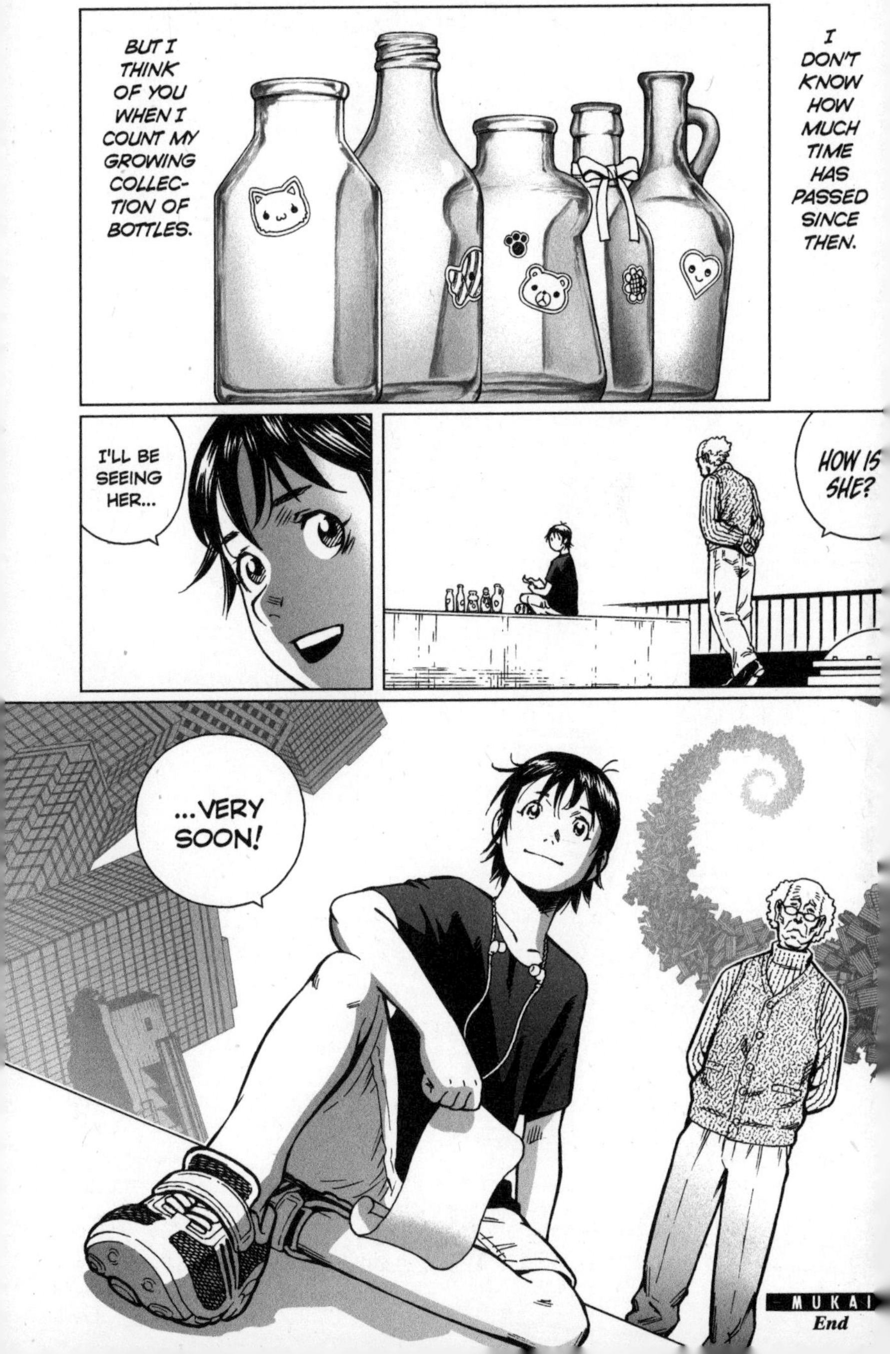
I DON'T KNOW HOW MUCH TIME HAS PASSED SINCE THEN.
BUT I THINK OF YOU WHEN I COUNT MY GROWING COLLECTION OF BOTTLES.
HOW IS SHE?
I'LL BE SEEING HER...
...VERY SOON!
MUKAI
End

BATTLE ANGEL ALITA

MARS CHRONICLE

PRESENTED by YUKITO KISHIRO

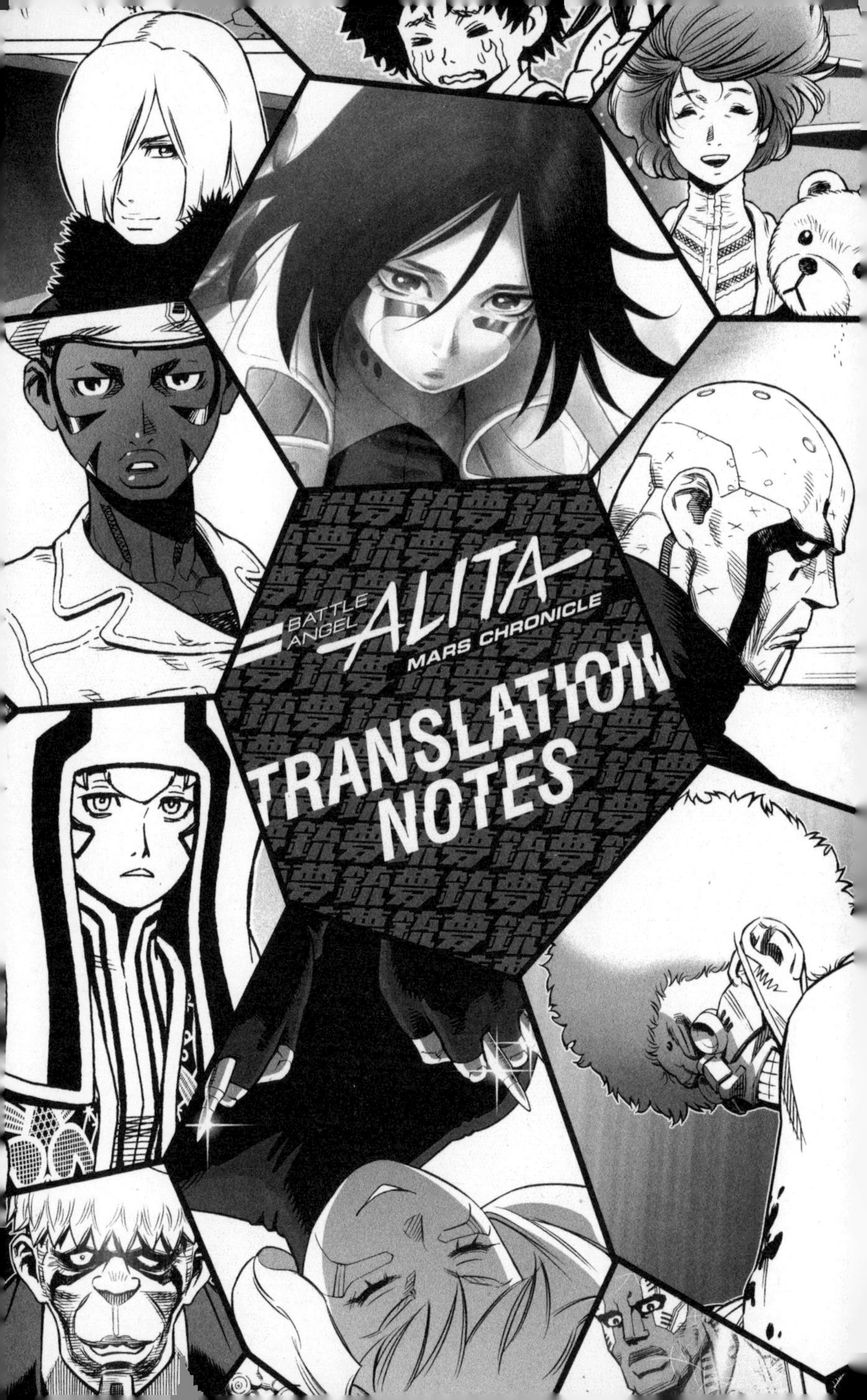
BATTLE ANGEL
ALITA
MARS CHRONICLE
TRANSLATION NOTES

...BUT HAVE YOU FORGOTTEN PANZER-KUNST, TOO?
OR HAVE YOU BATTLED TOO MANY MUSCLEHEADED KARATE-KA...
...AND CAUGHT THEIR STUPIDITY?

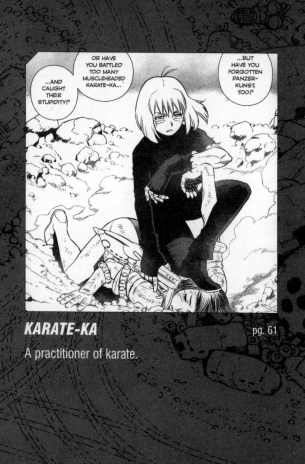

## ***KARATE-KA*** pg. 61

A practitioner of karate.

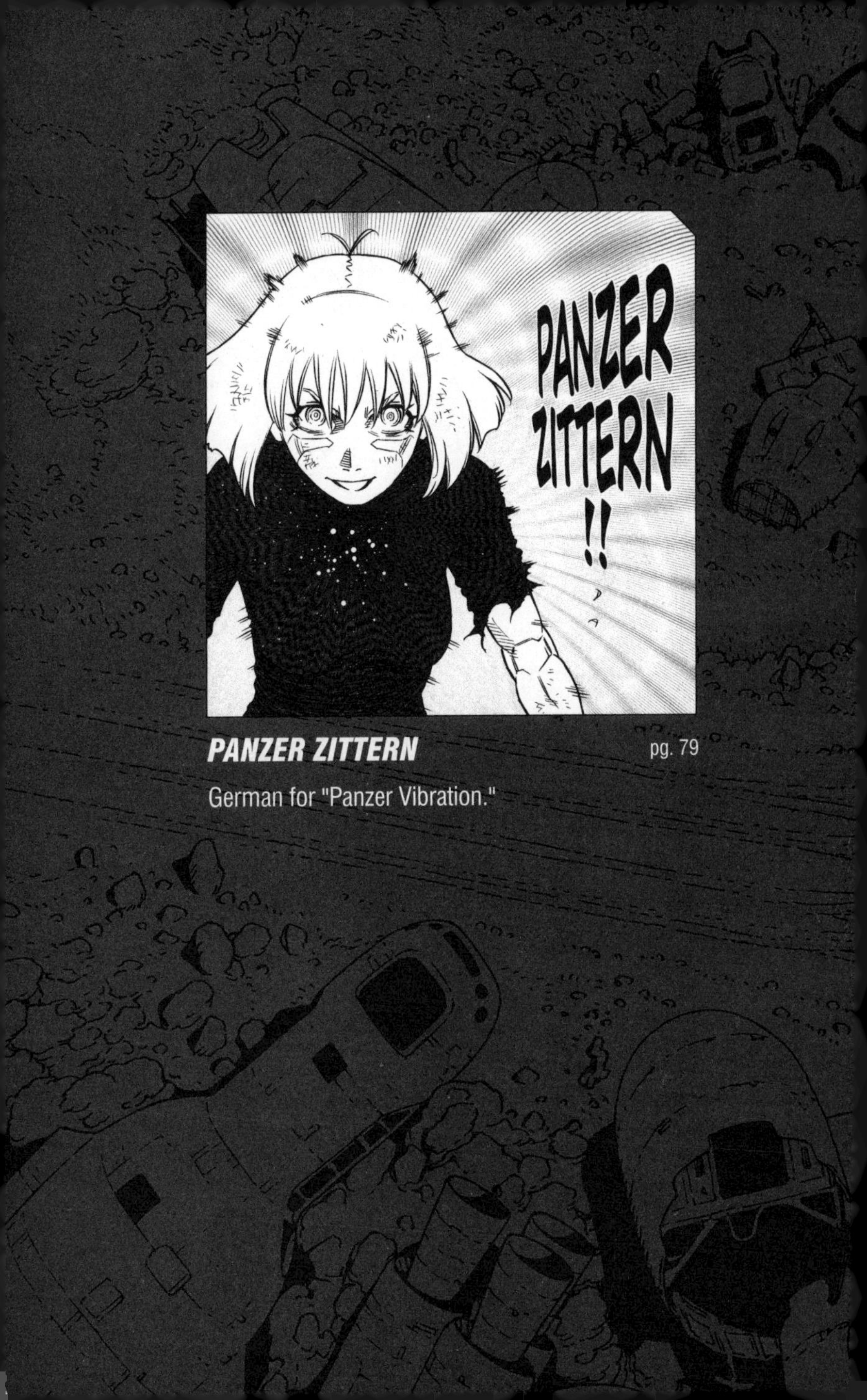
PANZER ZITTERN!!

***PANZER ZITTERN*** pg. 79

German for "Panzer Vibration."

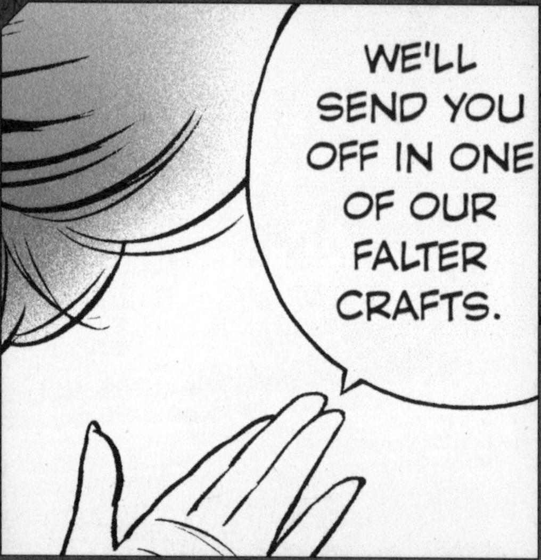
WE'LL SEND YOU OFF IN ONE OF OUR FALTER CRAFTS.

***FALTER*** pg. 125

German for "butterfly."

FOR NO GOOD REASON.

NO BULLIES WHO HIDE OUR SHOES AT SCHOOL.

## SCHOOL SHOES

pg. 174

Special indoor slippers, called *uwabaki*, that are often part of the Japanese school uniform. The front entrance of a school is the locker room, where students stash their own shoes and put on the indoor slippers that are cleaner and softer on the floor, as well as unified like all other aspects of a uniform. Because of this, hiding a student's school shoes or placing tacks inside of them are pretty stereotypical forms of bullying or teasing activities.

# BATTLE ANGEL ALITA

After more than a decade out of print, the original cyberpunk action classic returns in glorious 400-page hardcover deluxe editions, featuring an all-new translation, color pages, and new cover designs!

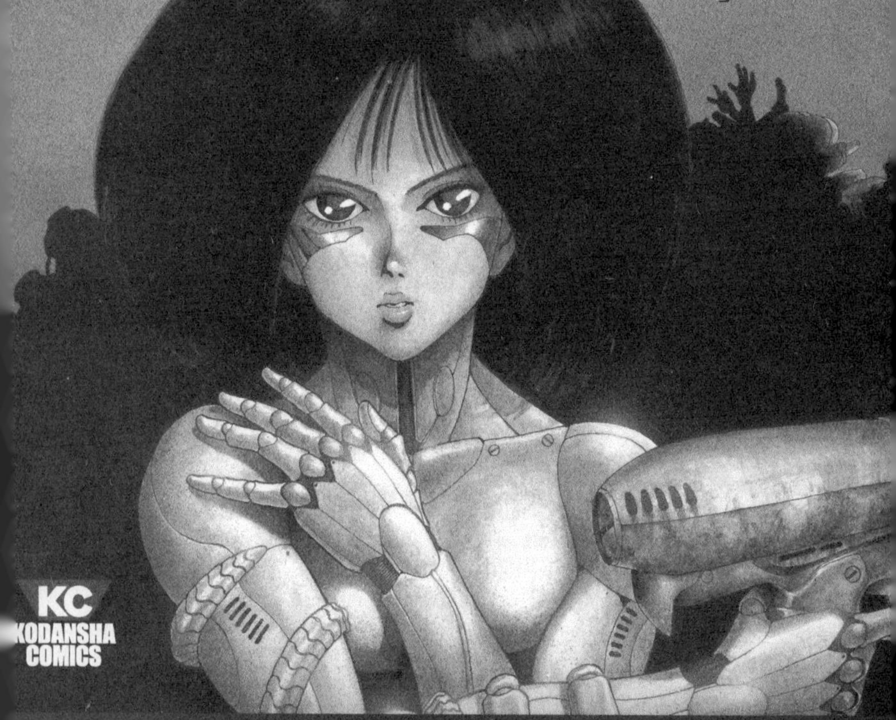

**KC**
**KODANSHA COMICS**

Far beneath the shimmering space-city of Zalem lie the trash-heaps of The Scrapyard... Here, cyber-doctor and bounty hunter Daisuke Ido finds the head and torso of an amnesiac cyborg girl. He names her Alita and vows to fill her life with beauty, but in a moment of desperation, a fragment of Alita's mysterious past awakens in her. She discovers that she possesses uncanny prowess in the legendary martial art known as panzerkunst. With her newfound skills, Alita decides to become a hunter-warrior - tracking down and taking out those who prey on the weak. But can she hold onto her humanity in the dark and gritty world of The Scrapyard?

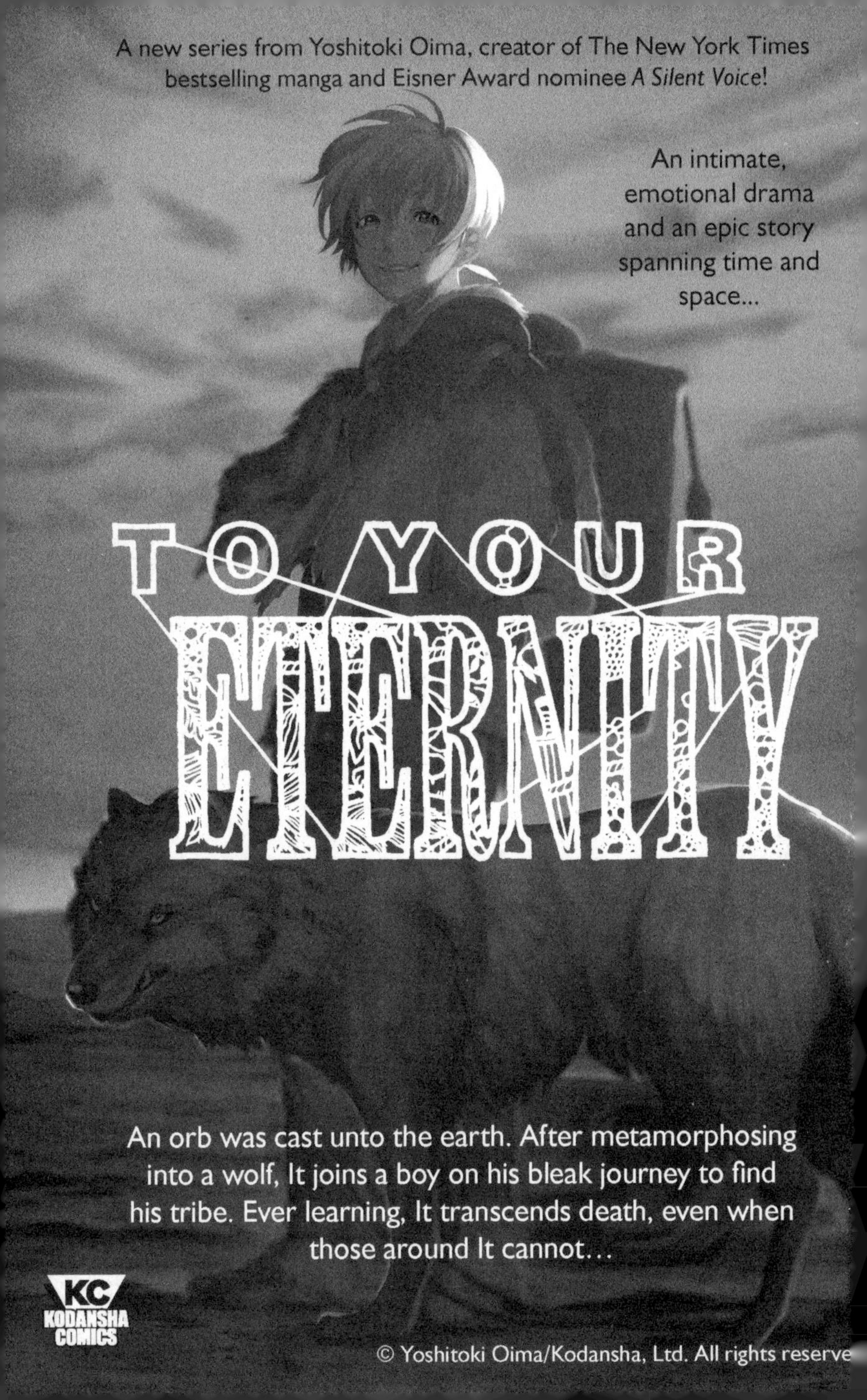
A new series from Yoshitoki Oima, creator of The New York Times bestselling manga and Eisner Award nominee *A Silent Voice*!
An intimate, emotional drama and an epic story spanning time and space...
TO YOUR ETERNITY
An orb was cast unto the earth. After metamorphosing into a wolf, It joins a boy on his bleak journey to find his tribe. Ever learning, It transcends death, even when those around It cannot...
KC KODANSHA COMICS
© Yoshitoki Oima/Kodansha, Ltd. All rights reserve

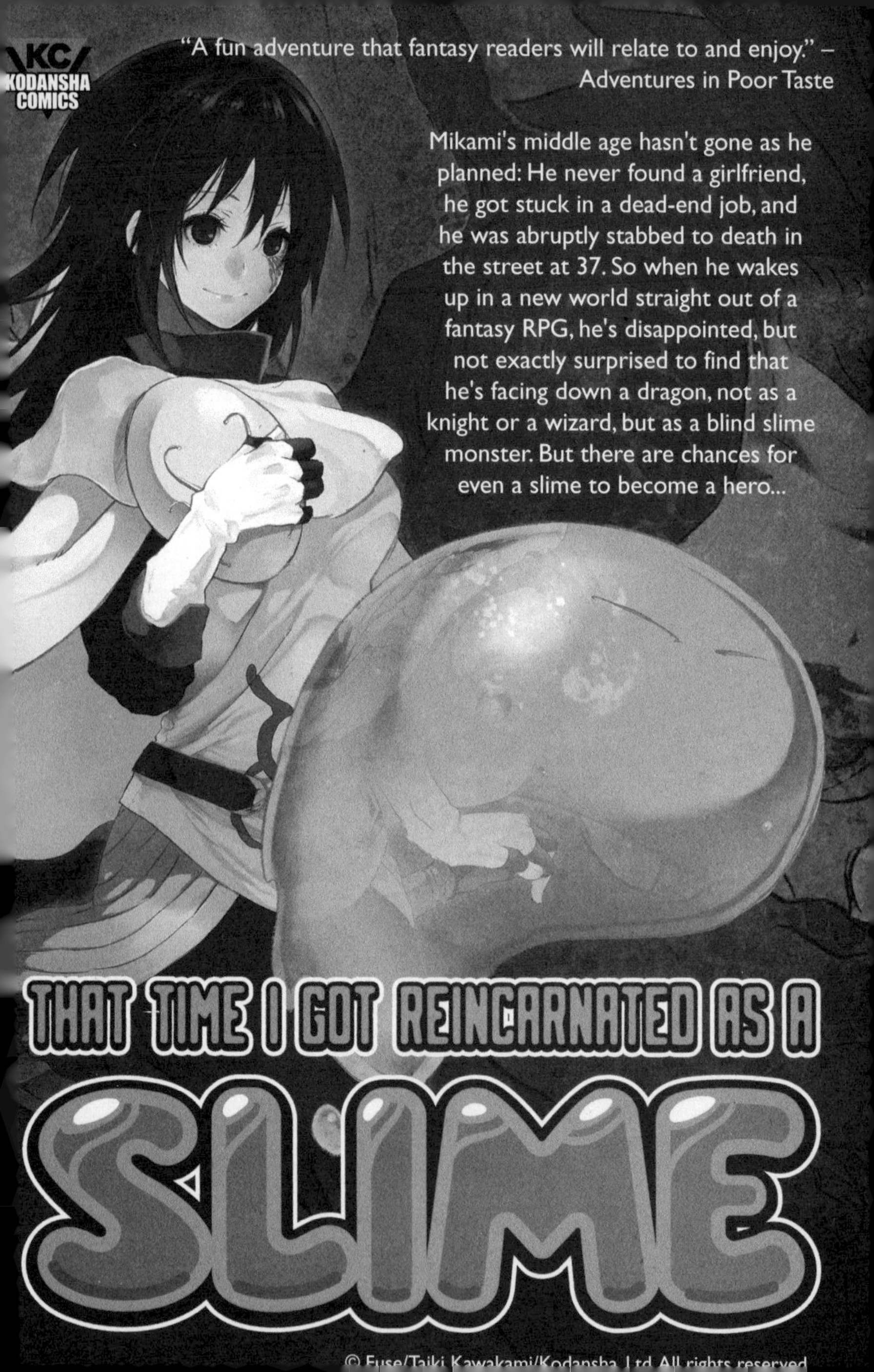
KC KODANSHA COMICS
"A fun adventure that fantasy readers will relate to and enjoy." – Adventures in Poor Taste
Mikami's middle age hasn't gone as he planned: He never found a girlfriend, he got stuck in a dead-end job, and he was abruptly stabbed to death in the street at 37. So when he wakes up in a new world straight out of a fantasy RPG, he's disappointed, but not exactly surprised to find that he's facing down a dragon, not as a knight or a wizard, but as a blind slime monster. But there are chances for even a slime to become a hero...
THAT TIME I GOT REINCARNATED AS A
SLIME
© Fuse/Taiki Kawakami/Kodansha Ltd. All rights reserved.

# The Black Museum: The Ghost and the Lady

### By Kazuhiro Fujita

Deep in Scotland Yard in London sits an evidence room dedicated to the greatest mysteries of British history. In this "Black Museum" sits a misshapen hunk of lead—two bullets fused together—the key to a wartime encounter between Florence Nightingale, the mother of modern nursing, and a supernatural Man in Grey. This story is unknown to most scholars of history, but a special guest of the museum will tell the tale of *The Ghost and the Lady*...

#### Praise for Kazuhiro Fujita's *Ushio and Tora*

"A charming revival that combines a classic look with modern depth and pacing... **Essential viewing both for curmudgeons and new fans alike.**" — Anime News Network

"**GREAT!** The first episode of *Ushio and Tora* captures the essence of '90s anime." — IGN

Japan's most powerful spirit medium delves into the ghost world's greatest mysteries!

Story by Kyo Shirodaira, famed author of mystery fiction and creator of *Spiral*, *Blast of Tempest*, and *The Record of a Fallen Vampire*.

Both touched by spirits called yôkai, Kotoko and Kurô have gained unique superhuman powers. But to gain her powers Kotoko has given up an eye and a leg, and Kurô's personal life is in shambles. So when Kotoko suggests they team up to deal with renegades from the spirit world, Kurô doesn't have many other choices, but Kotoko might just have a few ulterior motives...

# IN/SPECTRE

## STORY BY KYO SHIRODAIRA
## ART BY CHASHIBA KATASE

**KC KODANSHA COMICS**

New action series from Hiroyuki Takei, creator of the classic shonen franchise Shaman King!

In medieval Japan, a bell hanging on the collar is a sign that a cat has a master. Norachiyo's bell hangs from his katana sheath, but he is nonetheless a stray — a ronin. This one-eyed cat samurai travels across a dishonest world, cutting through pretense and deception with his blade.

# Nekogahara

## STRAY CAT SAMURAI

By
Hiroyuki Takei

# HAPPINESS

ハピネス

**By Shuzo Oshimi**

**From the creator of *The Flowers of Evil***

Nothing interesting is happening in Makoto Ozaki's first year of high school. HIs life is a series of quiet humiliations: low-grade bullies, unreliable friends, and the constant frustration of his adolescent lust. But one night, a pale, thin girl knocks him to the ground in an alley and offers him a choice.

Now everything is different. Daylight is searingly bright. Food tastes awful. And worse than anything is the terrible, consuming thirst...

**Praise for Shuzo Oshimi's *The Flowers of Evil***

"A shockingly readable story that vividly—one might even say queasily—evokes the fear and confusion of discovering one's own sexuality. Recommended." —The Manga Critic

"A page-turning tale of sordid middle school blackmail." —Otaku USA Magazine

"A stunning new horror manga." —Third Eye Comics

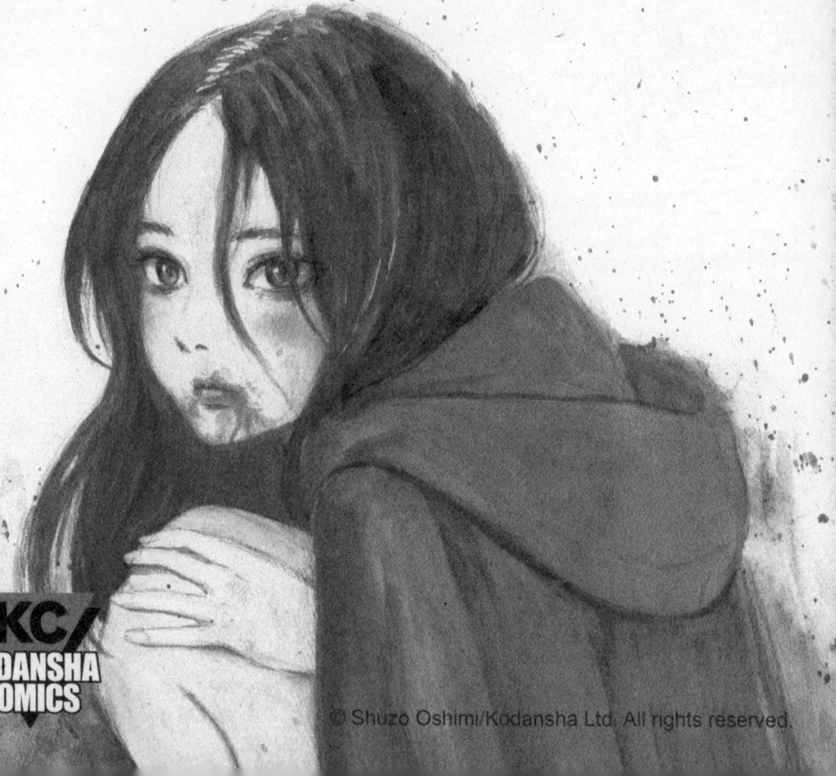

KC KODANSHA COMICS

"I'm pleasantly surprised to find modern shojo using cross-dressing as a dramatic device to deliver social commentary... Recommended."

-Otaku USA Magazine

# The prince in his dark days

By **Hico Yamanaka**

A drunkard for a father, a household of poverty... For 17-year-old Atsuko misfortune is all she knows and believes in. Until one day, a chance encounter with Itaru-the wealthy heir of a huge corporation-change everything. The two look identical, uncannily so. When Itaru curiously goes missing, Atsuko is roped into being his stand-in. There, in his shoes Atsuko must parade like a prince in a palace. She encounters many new experiences, but at what cost...?

*attle Angel Alita: Mars Chronicle* volume 2 ,
haracters, places, and incidents are the products of the author's
magination or are used fictitiously. Any resemblance to actual events,
ocales, or persons, living or dead, is entirely coincidental.

Kodansha Comics Trade Paperback Original.



ublished in the United States by Kodansha Comics, an imprint of
odansha USA Publishing, LLC, New York.

ublication rights for this English edition arranged through Kodansha
td., Tokyo.

irst published in Japan in 2015 by Kodansha Ltd., Tokyo, as *Gunnm:
ars Chronicle* 2.

SBN 978-1-63236-616-0

rinted in the United States of America.

www.kodanshacomics.com

8 7 6 5 4 3 2 1

ranslator: Stephen Paul
ettering: Evan Hayden
diting: Ajani Oloye
odansha Comics edition cover design: Phil Balsman